Presented to

_____

From

_____

Date

_____

IN THE PRESENCE OF GOD

THE LORD HIMSELF WILL BE WITH YOU;
HE WILL NEVER LEAVE YOU NOR FORSAKE YOU. DEUT. 31:8

CHRISTIAN ART
PUBLISHERS

Originally published by Christelike Uitgewersmaatskappy
under the title *In die Teenwoordigheid van God*

© 2004 Izak de Villiers

English edition © 2006 Christian Art Publishers,
PO Box 1599, Vereeniging, 1930, RSA

First edition 2006

English edition © 2006 Izak de Villiers

© 2010 C. J. de Villiers

Translated by Louise Emerton

Cover designed by Christian Art Publishers

Artwork on cover: Supper at Emmaus by Rembrandt (Louvre, Paris)

Set in 11 on 13 pt Palatino Linotype by Christian Art Publishers

Printed in China

ISBN 978-1-86920-659-8

12 13 14 15 16 17 18 19 20 21 – 14 13 12 11 10 9 8 7 6 5

Dedicated to

the memory of Prof. J. C. G. (Kolie) Kotzé
Professor of Homiletics
University of Stellenbosch

PREFACE

This is not a book with beautiful thoughts tied together with a fancy bow. It is an effort to cover biblical highlights and to find a message for every day of the year. Because the Old and New Testament dovetail so perfectly, I devoted the first part of every month to the Old Testament and the second part to the New Testament. I only deviated from this method in the month of December, because Advent determines its own rules.

It is also quite clear that the Bible determines its own rules and makes you pause at different passages with every reading. Right from the start this book seemed to follow its own direction and gradually developed its own theme from the Holy Scriptures: the mystic Presence of God that is everywhere at every moment. While writing this book, I was constantly aware of a strangely familiar but intense Presence and of divine help. That is why the word Presence is spelled mostly with a capital P.

Unfortunately, I did not touch on all the books in the Bible: the dam is simply too big to be emptied with a small bucket and, depending on one's frame of reference, the possibilities are endless. I am no exegete or dogmatist, but rather a newsman who has learnt to evaluate the news and the main points.

Old friends from the world of literature sometimes assisted me in this task: T. S. Eliot, Milton, Gerard Manley Hopkins, Robert Browning, Tennyson, Shakespeare, Sheila Cussons, Van Wyk Louw, Totius and others.

In the Presence of God can also be read in themes and not only as a devotional. For instance, if you feel like doing a quick read of all the devotions of a specific month and then return to the daily readings at a later stage, it will also make sense. Due to space limitations, some poems or quotes from poems were treated like prose with a / to separate the poetic lines.

When I was about halfway through the manuscript, I suddenly started wondering whether anyone would want to read it. Then I received an e-mail from a woman from one of my early congregations. She wrote that she still remembered me as a young pastor and that I had contributed largely to establishing her spiritual foundation when she was a teenager. After many years she wanted to thank me for it. She testified that she had grown spiritually strong, but wished that I would write a devotional that one could read every day. Suddenly it was as if an angel had smiled at me just when I felt like Elijah who wanted to sit and sulk under a broom tree.

It is said that when Thomas Aquinas had finished writing his major work, *Summa Theologiae*, he felt as though everything he had written was worthless. This is no *Summa* and I am no Aquinas, but I understand how he felt.

Nevertheless, it was a privilege to write this book. It has brought me closer to the Word and to God. I pray the same for you.

~ Izak de Villiers

JANUARY

Eternal God

Once again it is time for a new beginning.
Everything that was "closed" during December –
often with cheerful parties and decorations, and some prize-giving –
is now ceremoniously "opened" again,
mostly with moralizing sermonettes and clichés of encouragement.

Old folks said that the first twelve days set the tone for the rest of
the year.
Should it rain during this time, it will rain throughout the year.
Should it be dry during the first twelve days,
then it will be a dry year.
Should these days be joyful, it will be a year of gladness,
a good year, such as Your prophets announced ages ago
with the advent of Jesus Christ.

However, You determine the year, although a year is nothing to You.
It is a mere second in Your awesome Creation.
Not even a second.
I ask for Your help and Presence during times of difficulty.
I thank You for normal, everyday times with a normal
fluctuating graph.
I pray that You will hold my hand at all times and help me
to see the good that could spring from everything.
And, should I experience joy, teach me to handle it
with grace and gratitude.

My beginning is in the name of the Lord
who created heaven and earth.

Amen.

BEFORE THE BEGINNING

In the beginning God created the heavens and the earth (Gen. 1:1).

A university professor, known for his intellect and wit, once gave a very complicated assignment to his postgraduate students. They were dumbfounded.

One eventually dared to ask, "Professor, where does one start with such an assignment?"

The professor calmly replied, "Ladies and gentlemen, this is the easiest question of them all: you simply start at the beginning!"

Therefore, I start with Genesis 1:1 at the beginning of a new year, like most devotionals do.

Everyone knows that God created the heavens and the earth "in the beginning". Those who don't know this or who don't want to know it, would not have taken the trouble to read this. And those who have indeed taken that trouble and do not believe that God created the heavens and the earth "in the beginning", would not read much further in any case.

There was a beginning with God as Planner and Architect, when He gave a sign and spoke the word. But it is important to remember that God was there even before the beginning. He is the Beginningless Beginning. The Unmovable Mover. He has no beginning and no end. He has no need to look at a calendar or watch. He does not think in terms of days or months or centuries. He exists outside space and time, in a totally different dimension from all that He created.

God creates us from His eternal thoughts and sends us to His Creation to experience the big adventure in time and space that we call life. Life has a beginning and an end: we learn some things, enjoy some things; are hurt by some and are healed by some. And God, the Timeless One, is also present in all these temporary things.

He was not and will not be. He is. Today. At the beginning. Every day. With you. Eternally.

Lord, You are with me at the beginning of the year and every day. Preserve me and help me to remember this.

FIRST LIGHT

"Let there be light!" (Gen. 1:3).

L ight is one of the ancient elements. God "let it be" long before
the earth's "lamps", the sun and the moon, were in place. Light
is not dependent on the sun and moon. God is light.

If the primitive universe was created in the beginning, one that
would at the command of God, and according to His master plan,
develop through the days or ages (which could stretch over millions
of years and still only be a moment to God) destined by Him, then
the second step was light.

In answer to God's word, it came from somewhere. The allusion
is that God looked at the foundations of everything and that He did
not like the dark void. No foundation of any structure is ever beautiful. "Let there be light!" He said. Everything looks better in the light.
In the light He could further develop His ideas for Creation and allow them to follow a logical process. In general, developmental processes need the light. Plants will grow higher and will even push
through cracks in order to reach the light.

We also want to live in the light, and a night without stars is in-
conceivable. When the electricity is cut off, we frantically search for
candles and flashlights.

And yet, darkness does come; darkness that is sometimes needed
so that we can sleep and rest. Darkness that is needed to develop the
most beautiful color photos.

It is the same with our faith and emotional growth. Sometimes
we feel like Creation before light: desolate and empty with "darkness over the surface of the deep" (Gen. 1:2). In such times, even a
candle of hope will help us to see.

And then, in a single moment, suddenly, God says, "Let there be
light!" Like in the beginning, it is a sign that He is continuing with
your Creation and formation, and that you must contribute too.

He can light a candle or can allow the sun to shine for you. Somewhere there will always be light for you.

Thank You, Lord, that there will always be light for me.

GOD FOUND IT TO BE GOOD

God saw that it was good (Gen. 1:10).

A Dutch politician was once taken on a tour of a town he was visiting. They stopped at a vantage point close to the granite rocks to look down at the valley. It was one of those special winter days that sparkled like diamonds after the rain. The sun shone softly on the landscape: the river and the green vineyards, the distant blue mountains and their snow-capped peaks, the haziness of the large dams in the valley, the tranquility.

The politician said, "Now I am beginning to understand something of how God looked at His Creation and saw that it was good."

There is a subdued, contented, eternal excitement in these words. God saw that His plan worked and He was pleased. Of course, the plan had to work because God is infallible, but the components of that plan which had to function in space and time … those components are fallible. Man, which He would later create, would also be fallible.

At this early stage God was still busy with the foundation. The details were still to follow. However, as everything developed under His hand – dry ground, plants, reptiles, birds, animals, man – God saw with excitement that this was good.

We experience a glimpse of that divine excitement when we do something and when, upon finishing, we see that it is beautiful and that it works. We simply feel good about it. Struggling through a demanding task, facing a challenge, planting a small seedling or taking the hand of our fellow man – anything from making tea to closing a major deal, to helping a child with a math problem – all form part of God's continuing Creation.

We accept that God regards us with interest, love, empathy and care. Why else did He create us than to take pleasure in us?

Lord, You created me and I should acknowledge with gratitude … that it was good.

THUS WAS IT

This is the account of the heavens and the earth when they were created (Gen. 2:4).

One after the other wonderfully created objects came into being at God's word and from His mind. The Bible summarizes this awesome process in little more than one chapter and emphasizes only one major fact: God did it. Exactly how it happened is for scientists to research and philosophers to ponder on. However, nothing changes the fact that God created it.

Two academics once took part in a debate. The one, a paleontologist, was asked how old humankind was. He answered that it was still being argued by scientists, but that it was millions of years old. There was a lively discussion on his answer, because even science works on suppositions in some cases. When God was mentioned in the debate, the next question was presented to a second professor, a medical practitioner, "If God is somewhere in the picture, why are there so many weak links in the universe? If man is so wonderful, why does he suffer from incurable diseases?"

The second professor replied, "Man, a mere molecule in Creation, consists of legions of cells and, in turn, every cell is a miraculous microcosm of moving particles. Should something go wrong in only one of the multitude of cells, the process of disease starts. The tragedy, therefore, is not that people become terminally ill. The miracle is that so many people do not become ill. A further miracle is that, considering the billions of disasters that could happen, percentagewise few disasters occur and everything is kept on track by God."

God keeps everything on track and regenerates everything until He makes everything completely new again. The Bible could have started with scientific formulae that few people, if any, would have understood. God prefers a simple narrative, just like Jesus preferred parables to emphasize a major truth.

This truth is: This is how it was, this is how it is, this is how it will be. God is in control of our lives, whether we are sick or healthy.

Thank You, Lord, for all that is and above all, that You are what You are.

LABOR AND JOY

So the LORD God banished him from the Garden of Eden to work the ground (Gen. 3:23).

Sometimes one wonders what it would have been like if we had still been living in paradise. This thought could take your imagination on a thousand paths. The fact is that the people were banished from the Garden of Eden after they had committed an act that disturbed the balance of Creation. Almost like amateurs who fiddled with the distribution box of a building's electricity: the wires caught fire and they themselves got burnt as well.

God was displeased, but He was also merciful. He did not destroy them. He pointed out the consequences of their actions, and then He gave man a command, "Go and work the ground." In other words, help to restore what you have spoiled. God always provides an opportunity to repair at least some of the damage man has caused.

Adam and Eve had to learn to make a contribution by doing the best they could through their labor. Calvin remarked, "Show me what people have built and I will know how far they have progressed in God."

Much of what we accomplish here on earth will of course perish. Nevertheless, one of the greatest joys is to be doing something, devising something, giving something, helping something to grow, trying to understand and explain something. People who work hard sometimes long for a more comfortable existence, for "paradise". However, many people who have retired often yearn for something to do – and find it too!

During the inauguration of a modern church building, two elderly men proudly told the large number of visitors, "The two of us laid the vestry floor." The joy of labor does indeed lie in giving something of yourself. This holds true for everything, from loving to working in the garden. Therefore, God's "punishment" of labor was, in fact, a favor to His people. (This also whispers the liberating promise that we will not have to sit and play the harp for all eternity!)

Lord, let my labor be my privilege and my joy.

FIRST WORSHIP

At that time men began to call on the name of the LORD (Gen. 4:26).

After the first people had left the garden, there was a distance between God and man – the people that He had created in His "image". But in the third generation, man's need for God – something with which they had been created, the seed of religion as it was called by Calvin, an intrinsic longing for the Eternal and the Unseen – began to stir in them. They started calling on God. Moreover, they called on Him in the first kind of prayer.

The less God intervened in their lives, the greater their need for Him became. They had already sinned and made sacrifices, great separations already existed between man and man, and the distance between man and God increased. But they sensed this and started calling on God as the Lord.

The psychologist, C. G. Jung said people want to worship, even if that meant worshiping themselves or their possessions or their own inventions. Of course they will deny that this is a form of "worship", but it is a basic instinct. People may also deny that they hide their desire for God behind other things.

However, the calling on the name of the Lord that a handful of people started to do at an early stage – regardless of how they did it – was the right thing to do. It is a powerful Name and with the remnant of a divine spark in man, God could once again make contact. Years later, it would result in the greatest contact between God and man ever: the coming of Jesus Christ.

He is in contact with you today. And you are in contact with Him – if you call on His name, regardless of where you find yourself.

Lord, I call on Your powerful name. I call on You like the first people of Genesis did. You heard them. You also hear me, and You help me.

WITH GOD

Enoch walked with God (Gen. 5:24).

Someone once reminded me of a very close friend of mine during my student days, who died early in life. "When I see you," he said, "I think of John. Wherever you walked, John walked, and wherever John walked, you went along. Always together."

It was true, we were interested in the same things, we discussed the same issues, studied the same subjects, enjoyed the same activities, and laughed at the same jokes. When we were not together, one of us would sense when something was wrong with the other one. We had our disagreements at times, but we always ended them with immediate understanding and humor.

Enoch, who "walked with God" was actually God's close friend for the duration of his long life on earth. Wherever Enoch found himself in thought, emotion, spirit or physical presence, there God was. And, from a human perspective, wherever God, the major Presence was, Enoch was.

It was a sublime, mystical togetherness of a loving Creator and a well-loved human being. Perhaps, in some remarkable way, Enoch retained something of the awareness of God that he had experienced before birth, somewhere in the eternal thoughts of the Almighty. We are all born with this awareness, but sometimes it fades very fast. Wordsworth sighs about it, "But yet I know, where'er I go, / that there hath passed away a glory from the earth" (from *Ode to Intimations of Immortality*).

Very little is said about Enoch's history, except that he "walked with God". What a history!

God was constantly in Enoch's company. If we wish for it and ask for it, God is constantly in our company. He listens, He hears, He helps, and we hope that He enjoys our presence (sometimes), just as we enjoy His presence.

Lord, make me constantly aware of the fact that You walk with me.

Go In

"Go into the ark, you and your whole family" (Gen. 7:1).

It is strange that in spite of people like Enoch, and in spite of the fact that men began to call on the name of the Lord since early times, the separation between God and His people, His earth, the work of His hands, became unbridgeable. From the "it was good," which delighted God during Creation, very little eventually remained. The processes of Creation and the relationship between man, nature and God was totally off balance.

The major destruction of the Flood was inevitable. God's image within man had faded. However, there were still people, like Noah, who wanted to worship Him. And the Lord offered them special protection, "Go into the ark!"

Whether the ark looked like the pictures in children's Bibles (with a little chimney and all), or whether it was a special state of preservation (a reference to an ark can be found in accounts of almost all civilizations), the entire narration merely explains that God's people must live in God's protection.

One does not know whether the modern world, with its technology and wonders, is "better" or "worse" than the one from which Noah's story dates. Every day we face a flood of possible threats and dangers. Almost every day we experience bigger or smaller storms in our lives, wherever we are. Sometimes we think the sun will never shine again, the waters will continue to rise and in the turbulent flood that we call modern life, the large tree trunks that drift by will hit us.

With this in mind, God says to us as well, "Go into the ark!" When you close your eyes, or look up to God to pray, you go into the ark. When you ask the Lord's help in traffic, you go into the ark while keeping your eyes on the road. When your child goes to school and you cannot be there all the time with advice and guidance, and you believe that God will protect you, you both go into the ark.

And, should your ark be hit by enormous waves, it will not capsize. People who trust in God are safe in His shelter.

Lord, for this day and night, I enter the shelter of Your ark and I thank You for Your presence.

LEAVE

The LORD had said to Abram, "Leave your country" (Gen. 12:1).

It is a major disruption to move house. It is an adjustment to leave your place of birth and, even worse, to say farewell to your country, your familiar environment, your work, friends and community. When Robert Burns had to leave his beloved Scottish Highlands behind, he sobbed, "Farewell to the Highlands, farewell to the North / The birthplace of valor, the country of worth (from *My Heart's in the Highlands*).

Abram had to do all of this. He could have argued that he could serve the Lord just as well from where he was and that the Lord could very well just bless him there. But he had to go and stake out the claim for the people, especially the chosen people who would be born from him.

Perhaps things went too well for Abram in his place of birth. As an important leader in the Middle East, he had to pack up his possessions and spread his tents in the direction of Hebron. All of that formed part of a Plan of which Abram was only given an outline. The Lord would gradually provide the detail.

Sometimes we feel that we are forced to make changes because of our circumstances or by conviction. It is as though Someone says to us, "Leave!" Drop the things that are wasting your time. Stop unpleasant habits. Stop the complaining that has become part of your life. Give up an undermining friendship. Look for new opportunities and spread your tents during the new year. Enlarge your territory under the wings of the Lord. Leave your nest.

Or simply decide to carry out a good intention, even though it may be to call upon the Lord more often and to really leave the street of unbelief and uncertainty behind. God will be with you. God will help you find the way.

Lord, even if I only go to work with new intentions, or to my loved ones, take me under Your wing when I leave and return again.

DRIVE THEM AWAY!

Then the birds of prey came down on the carcasses, but Abram drove them away (Gen. 15:11).

When two parties made a covenant in Abram's time, they had to cut a sacrificial animal in two (in Hebrew it is literally "to cut a covenant"). Then both parties had to step between the two halves and offer the animal. In this way, the agreement was legally settled.

In God's covenant with Abram, He made major promises. Abram prepared a number of sacrificial animals, cut them in two and waited for God to pass between them. Everything was ready, Abram was ready, the offering was ready, but God did not come.

However, the birds of prey came down on the carcasses. Abram sat there almost the entire day, driving the birds of prey away. "Where is God?" he could have asked. By sunset, when the birds of prey had fled, he became anxious and fell asleep. Then the Lord spoke to him and promised him descendants and a country. Just after sunset, a fire and a blazing torch suddenly appeared and passed between the offerings. The covenant was made. God came in a way that was mysterious, strange, divine.

God always comes, even though you have to wait. The birds of prey also come. They swoop down on our prayers, on our faith, on our efforts to do something for God and our fellow man, on our expectation of a touch and a covenant.

Doubt is a major bird of prey. Uncertainty is a bird of prey. Undue haste is a bird of prey. Trying to understand God's ways and failing to do so, can become a bird of prey. Guilt is a bird of prey. Excessive worry is a bird of prey. Anxiety is a bird of prey.

Drive them all away! God will come, either with a blazing torch and a fiery furnace or in the whispering of a gentle silence.

Lord, help me to drive away all birds of prey until You come, because You will come.

DOUBT TURNS INTO JOY

Abraham fell face down; he laughed and said to himself, "Will a son be born to a man a hundred years old?" (Gen. 17:17).

One is often inclined to forget that Abraham laughed with Sarah at the promise of a child. Often it is believed that only Sarah laughed at God's promise about Isaac. But here was Abraham, on his knees, respectfully worshiping God, and he laughed!

He probably thought to himself, *Well, the Lord means well in making all these promises, and I do not want to be disrespectful or ungrateful, but in the case of Sarah and me, the Lord is somewhat like a politician promising higher subsidies and lower taxes.* He would serve and revere the Lord, he would worship Him and thank Him for everything. But this did not stop him from laughing ruefully, feeling grateful but also thinking that God was not very realistic.

There was once an eccentric man who lived in a small town; he was virtually a legend. One day a man reminded him that he had promised him a basketful of potatoes, and that he would like to have it. "Well," the old man said, "one cannot promise *and* give!"

God promises and He gives. Abraham made a mistake that we often make ourselves – he underestimated God. A child was born to Abraham. He was called Isaac, which means "laughter". It is the laughter of disbelief and the laughter of joy. The impossible was indeed possible.

Like Abraham, we also laugh ruefully at times, thinking things are impossible. Then we discover that God mercifully transforms this laughter into a grateful, silent chuckle, or an exuberant burst of joy over multiple blessings.

Forgive me if I laugh like Abraham, but teach me to kneel like Abraham nevertheless, because You will bless me with jubilant laughter.

GOD HEARS US WHEN WE CRY

God heard the boy crying, and the angel of God called to Hagar from heaven (Gen. 21:17).

It is true that people who laugh at others do not like to be ridiculed themselves. Sarah laughed about herself bearing a son, but was sensitive to being mocked for apparently being "too old" for motherhood. Abraham's son, Ishmael, from the maidservant Hagar, also laughed. Sarah then ordered Abraham to get rid of the slave woman and the child.

Probably to keep peace in the marital bed, Abraham did this after getting a promise from God that He would watch over them. God kept His promise and when the boy Ishmael lay crying and dying in the desert, the Angel of God took care of both of them. Ishmael also received a promise. He and his descendants adapted well in the desert and they became skillful archers.

Questions abound about this part of history. Why did God allow such a seemingly heartless transgression? Why did He not give Abraham different advice for his marital problems? Why were Sarah's outrageous demands met? What about justice and humanity? These are the same kind of questions that we often ask when we find ourselves in a desert. Why does God allow this glaring injustice?

There is no explanation to be found in this history. That is the great mystery of God's plans: eventually He transforms the injustice into a blessing. This is one of the major themes in the Bible: out of adversity comes solace. Out of disaster good things are born. The crying in the desert is heard in heaven and acted upon.

God knows human attitudes, failings and whims. He also knew Sarah and Abraham's. He did not tamper with them, and allowed their actions to take their course. But God intervened when a child cried. He blessed and helped both mother and child. Because He is God, He knew the consequences: that this human injustice would result in animosity stretching over generations, even to this day. But God's way is to allow people and events to develop until He intervenes and bestows His blessing.

Lord, You hear me when I laugh and cry. You know when I become a victim of injustice. But You transform everything into a blessing, even though I may not understand it.

TO GOD'S MOUNTAIN

"On the mountain of the LORD it will be provided" (Gen. 22:14).

An annual memorial service is held on top of Cape Town's famous Table Mountain for the casualties of the World Wars and Korea. It takes place at a spot where the late South African Statesman and General, Jan Smuts, often sat down to rest after climbing the mountain. He continued doing so even when he was in his late seventies. I once officiated at this service and I referred to Smuts's famous speech, *The Religion of the Mountain*. Smuts said that major encounters between the Creator and His chosen followers often took place on top of a mountain or in a desert. God spoke to Moses on the mountain, Abraham had to make a sacrifice there, Elijah was there, Christ was glorified on the mountain. All of us are sometimes called by God to high and lonely places to become aware of God's greatness, because we are people and not saints.

Abraham was no saint either. Amidst all his goodness, he laughed at God and lied to the king of Egypt. Then God instructed him to go and sacrifice his son, Isaac, on Mount Moriah. He obeyed and God intervened by providing another offering, and honored Abraham's obedience.

Here, God does indeed (once again) act strangely towards Abraham. In essence it is a hard and heartless request and even a crueler "test". The method is inexplicable, but the lesson to Abraham is clear: God provides on His mountain in His good time.

Sometimes we feel that we are making little progress up the slope of life's mountain. The direction of God's plan with us often seems unclear, extremely unreasonable or simply in conflict with what we think He should do for us. We can be sure of one thing: God will provide on the way ahead. He will see to the offering and He will provide the blessing.

Lord, we are on our way to You, to Your mountain every moment of the day. The miracle is that You are keeping us company on the way. You will provide in Your time and way.

GOD IS WITH YOU!

"We saw clearly that the LORD was with you" (Gen. 26:28).

Isaac was not exactly a hero. He was actually very ordinary when compared to the patriarchs. He dug open old wells, he was a successful farmer, his crop yielded a hundredfold and his herds increased. Like his father he told lies out of fear, he had a beautiful wife and his two sons probably did not regard him as an outstanding father. His wife raised the one son, Jacob, and the wild raised the other son, Esau.

Therefore, he was an average man with ordinary weaknesses. And yet he was one of the patriarchs.

However ordinary as he was, and with children who were "a source of grief" to him and Rebekah (Gen. 26:35), he received people with grace and he was actually a man of peace. Abimelech, the king, gave him an exceptional testimonial, "We saw clearly that the Lord was with you."

There was something about Isaac which caused people to look at him twice; a certain quality, glamor, entitlement, a presence. This held great advantages for him: God blessed him, in spite of all his disappointments and mistakes, and his enemies preferred to live in peace with him because they could sense that this man was not fighting his battle alone.

And nowhere is it written that Isaac was aware of the Presence. It was a natural thing to him: God is there, God is worshiped, God is revered, although not with the pious words or grandiose statements of faith used by his father.

Sometimes one gets the impression from the Bible that God actually likes ordinary people, people with weaknesses, with a common touch and sometimes also moments of exceptional greatness. We need not perform great deeds of faith. We may be ordinary, because it is remarkable how God uses ordinary people and guides them.

Lord, I am an ordinary person, an ordinary sinner and an ordinary pursuer of what is good. I pray that people will be able to see something of You in me.

TO WRESTLE AND WIN

So Jacob was left alone, and a man wrestled with him till daybreak (Gen. 32:24).

Jacob's wrestling on the banks of the Jabbok before meeting his brother Esau, and before serving God at Bethel again, has touched thinkers, artists, poets and singers through the ages. It is understandable because it is one of the most mystical events in the Bible: a human being, greatly burdened by his conscience and his past, "wrestling" with an unknown being. It ends in victory for Jacob, but a victory at a price – he is blessed, but he is left with a limp by his Opponent, an angel of God, an appearance by God Himself.

Why such a violent, physical wrestling? Why during the night, as a matter of fact right through the night? Why is so little being said? Jacob's Opponent refuses to give His name. He remains unknown and yet familiar. He also gives Jacob a new name, Israel, and explains it briefly, "You have struggled with God and with men and have overcome" (v. 28).

"Struggled with God and with men" is a mystical indication that the Divine Being and mankind were interwoven in the Opponent, physically and spiritually, terrestrial and supernatural. It is one of the most cryptic parts of the Bible, but also one of the most enlightening and comforting incidents.

It contains prophetic elements of a man, a son of Jacob, a son of David, a king and a servant. Someone in whom the divine and the human would be closely interwoven. Someone who would come to wrestle on behalf of all people and on behalf of God with forces and authorities until death, death on the cross – only to be resurrected to a new dawn for the whole of Creation.

Those elements are all present. Jacob's wrestling "with God and with men" also signifies our struggles. But God, who wrestled with death in Christ, gives us victory. Sometimes we are left with a limp. Sometimes our hearts are broken. Sometimes we are bruised and crushed. But we are also blessed, and we are blessed increasingly every day.

Lord, we thank You for allowing us to win when wrestling with You, and receive Your blessing, even though we might still be limping when the sun rises.

THE TRUE LIGHT IS COMING!

The true light that gives light to every man was coming into the world (John 1:9).

Genesis begins with God saying, "Let there be light!" John also starts his account of the coming of Jesus Christ with "the beginning" and the sublime announcement that the "True Light" was coming into the world. However, before this Light would shine and appear in its full glory, there had to be an announcer, John the Baptist, a "man sent from God". This John would some day at the river point to Jesus, saying, "Look, the Lamb of God!"

The Light was coming.

What an enormous expectation this creates! God's Son was on His way from another dimension to show us a photo of the Father. The turbulent world of 2,000 years ago was waiting for Someone. The candle would be lit in a small country among an oppressed nation. It would become a huge fire quickly spreading its light far across the then familiar Western and Middle Eastern world. From there it would light up the entire world.

God sent prophets to His people. He appeared in burning bushes and in smoke and fire at Mount Sinai. He sent His angels. And now His Son was coming, Jesus Christ, the true light.

We need this Light more than we need the everyday light. It is this Light that puts everything in perspective, including God's cryptography in His Creation that is mostly too difficult for us to read. It is this Light that is at the center of the Plan of God, as well as at the center of our lives, even though our faith may be like a flickering match. It is the certainty of knowing, sometimes faintly, sometimes clearly, that Christ is here! Christ is coming!

Lord, You were going to come, You came, You are with us and You will come again. That is our comfort.

THE WORD BECAME FLESH

The Word became flesh (John 1:14).

Major debates have been waged and bulky theological books written about this verse. The best known ones are by Thomas Aquinas, Calvin, Karl Barth and other great theologians. The Word, the Logos, the Divine Principle, the Concept, the Creator, the Eternal became flesh. He came to live among us, "pitching His tent" so to speak.

The Swiss philosopher Karl Jaspers said that the concept that God could become man or man could be God was absurd. Such an event transgresses all the laws of the intellect. The English hymn-writer John Marriott sensed it and circumvented it, "Thou, whose eternal Word / Chaos and darkness heard / and took their flight …".

The human mind is in any case far too limited to understand God. And many things that we take for granted at first glance seem a bit absurd. Look at the dry, barren plains – it is surely absurd that anything could grow there. But look again after the rain – the flowers are in full bloom. Many divine things are absurd and even contradictory: the physical love between man and woman is, on close inspection, absurd, but in essence divine. Trust between people is risky and often disappointing and, yes, also absurd. Yet we build civilizations on it. Some of the greatest truths contradict and simultaneously complement each other inexplicably, like the Word that became flesh.

The poet, D. J. Opperman, spoke of us as little straw huts of flesh and bone. In such a little straw hut or tent, the Son of God came and touched our bodies with a new sanctity. As a God who understands, He had to come and experience His Creation. He had to come and feel what we feel.

An old Scottish preacher constantly repeated this in his sermons, "There's a Man on the throne up there!" One who bled. One who sweated. One who knows pain. One who understands. One who forgives.

Lord, thank You that the Word came. Let the Word speak to us in our hearts and whisper God's solace to us.

IT FLOWS FROM GOD

We have seen His glory, the glory of the One and Only, who came from the Father, full of grace and truth (John 1:14).

Grace and truth. Two full and divine words that touch on so many aspects and are firmly anchored in God; and yet are also probably two of the most misused words.

Grace is something that you can never go and find somewhere, or uncover, invent or work for. You can only receive it without condition. Grace comes in to play when you are guilty. If you are genuinely innocent you stand on your rights by law. When you know that you are guilty, you ask for grace. And we are all guilty, because all of us have an agenda, and we all have a weakness.

When Jesus Christ, the Word, came, it spelled out two major concepts about Him: I am Grace. I am Truth.

To enjoy a good meal is grace. To be able to sleep is grace. To love is grace. To receive love is grace. To work is grace. To be accepted is grace. To experience terrible things and in one way or another overcome, is grace. God is in there. God is grace.

And Jesus is truth. When Pilate asked Christ, "What is truth?" (John 18:38), he was neither cynical nor mocking. It is the big question asked by the confused individual and by philosophers of all ages; the big question about the meaning of life.

Then the Truth stood in front of Pilate. "I am the Truth," says Jesus. The truth means all the facts, and all the facts in the right relation, as God intended it. It is the intuition of the divine. It is complete understanding.

All of this, grace and truth, came in Jesus in a remarkable, visible expression of God's Being. "It flows from God and returns to God," as the old hymn goes. It is still flowing to us like a gentle stream; always taking us back to God.

Sustain us today, heavenly Father, with the grace and truth of the Word, wherever we may go and whatever we may do.

STRIKING GOLD!

We have found the Messiah (John 1:41).

Many stories are told about the discovery of gold in South Africa. For ages, people lived on this reef of gold, allowed their cattle to graze there, farmed there and moved away again. Here and there they might have caught a glimpse of the enormous underground treasure, but they just left it. They told amazing stories about the wealth of Prester John, a very wealthy king somewhere in Africa. They went in search of Prester John but didn't find him or his treasures.

The legend was true, though: there was a treasure, hidden underground. One day, a man called Harrison saw a piece of limelike rock sticking up in the veld, analyzed it and discovered the richest gold field in the world.

For ages the Jews heard that the Messiah was coming, the great King who would herald a new dispensation – the Savior, the Redeemer. John the Baptist, the one who had to bear testimony to the Light, pointed Jesus out to two people. One of them, Andrew, Simon Peter's brother, followed Him and said to his brother, "We have found the Messiah!"

That was striking gold in faith. It was actually a minor process: one pointed it out, two followed it up, they believed what they saw, and one "brought his brother to Jesus" for the big encounter between the Messiah and the impulsive weakling, Peter, who would later become the rock on which God built His church.

Often we pass through this world like nomadic people. We do not see God in anything and even less do we see Christ. We start to despair and doubt. Then, one day, it is as though our blindness disappears and we see Jesus, the Messiah, God's gold.

Just look around you and inside yourself. He is there. You can tell other people, "I have found the Messiah!" This is sometimes a very ordinary experience and can happen every day. Sometimes it is rare and very special. But Christ will reveal Himself to you if you acknowledge Him. Anywhere and everywhere.

Lord Jesus, You are my Messiah, my gold, my God, my hope, my life.

THE CHOICE WINE

"Everyone brings out the choice wine first and then the cheaper wine after the guests have had too much to drink; but you have saved the best till now" (John 2:10).

I experienced this truth while serving as a pastor in a wine producing region. The wine farmers and cooperatives held a congress and invited me to join them for a meal.

After the meal I went to the kitchen of the function hall to thank everyone. There I noticed the waiters hard at work, changing labels on wine bottles. When I asked what they were doing, the head waiter (one of my dear elders) said laconically, "Reverend, the people are still asking for expensive wine, but it's finished. Now we stick the expensive wine's labels on our ordinary local wine and they suspect nothing!"

This custom, dating from the time of Jesus, to serve the best wine first during festivities, and gradually the wine of inferior quality as the people become more jolly, continues. People remain people, customs remain customs, savings methods remain savings methods.

It was only Jesus who overturned the accepted economic rule (serving the choice wine first ...) as He overturned numerous human values and customs. He is unfamiliar with inferior quality. His first miracle already emphasized the quality of His work. He did it so well that the host's choice wine was regarded as cheaper wine.

Jesus is not out to spoil our fun. He is also not stingy. He knows how to make people happy at a feast. And when we cry He knows how to bring solace.

Eventually, like the master of ceremonies, we discover that regardless of what Jesus gives us, in the end it is the best. His best.

Lord Jesus, turn this ordinary day into a day of celebration for me by blessing me with the joy of Your presence.

WHERE TO DRAW THE LINE?

"Zeal for your house will consume me" (John 2:17).

After the miracle of the wine, Jesus only stayed in Capernaum for a short while before He went to Jerusalem to celebrate the Passover like all Jewish believers. The temple teemed with traders and people who exchanged money. The surroundings of the sacred place had become a busy and greedy market-place.

The traders could have argued that they were offering an essential service: people came from afar to sacrifice to God and they merely made it easy for them to buy sacrificial animals and exchange money to carry out their transactions. To their utter amazement this young rabbi drove them out of there with a whip – a clear message that nothing can be justified which in essence, is unjustifiable.

And it is that very love or zeal for the house of God that "consumed" Jesus. Only holy operations should be practiced on a holy site. Only God had to be worshiped, not Mammon.

With this deed a different Jesus from the genial man at the wedding came to the fore. Jesus is not merely, as the old song goes, "so glorious and so good". His eyes could flash fire. And He could handle a whip.

This did not make him very popular. It also did not put an end to the trading, but Jesus had drawn His line.

He was not a man who lacked understanding. He was not lacking in humor either. He was definitely also not lacking in forgiveness. But He said: I draw the line.

Perhaps we should ask Him every day, "Lord, for the sake of the zeal for Your house, where do I draw the line?" He will answer you.

Yes Lord, You always answer. Show us the limits for our behavior and guide us by our zeal for You and Your house.

He knows what is in a man

Now while He was in Jerusalem at the Passover Feast, many people saw the miraculous signs He was doing and trusted in His name. But Jesus would not entrust Himself to them, for He knew all men. He did not need man's testimony about man, for He knew what was in a man (John 2:23-25).

These verses contain a harsh reality: Jesus performed miracles, people saw this, people believed in Him. But Jesus did not bother about this type of faith, incited by miracles and sensation, "for He knew what was in a man".

People are like the waves of the ocean. Seething with excitement, foaming on the beach, and then ... nothing more, just another surging wave and a roar. That is not the kind of faith that Jesus is looking for. He is, after all, no magician or charlatan. He performed His miracles very sparingly, most probably because He knew that people through the ages kept looking for exactly the same thing: sensation and more sensation. A one-day faith that, without new miracles and new amusement, will wilt by evening.

However, those who really seek Him – not for the sake of sensation, nor for the sake of what He can do for them – those He comes to love with an eternal love. They are the ones who realize that sensation does not lie in wonders, but in cherishing a divine Presence.

Jesus knows what is inside us. It makes one uncomfortable, while bringing comfort at the same time. If we do not seek Him for the sake of more money in the bank or a life devoid of problems, but to be with Him, come what may ... then He knows what is in our hearts, then He recognizes our needs, then He understands our weaknesses and then He will perform a miracle for us. Sometimes He will take us by the hand. Sometimes He will lift us onto His shoulders. And the angels will constantly watch over us. Because He knows that we are like sheep. We need a shepherd.

Lord, You know everything about us, please forgive us and help us.

BORN AGAIN

"No one can see the kingdom of God unless he is born again" (John 3:3).

To be born again is to become aware of your own mortality *and* of eternity; of your own humanity and of your Creator; of your own guilt and forgiveness; of another wavelength of life; of God who is everything and wants to be everything for you in Jesus Christ. Every new birth is a process. It all depends on our frame of reference.

I do not know anything about my own birth. My mother and my uncle, the doctor, told me that it was a rather difficult birth. I was unaware of it. Other births could be easy, while some could go totally wrong. This is also the case with being born again. We become aware of God in us and with us perhaps suddenly, perhaps in a process, difficult for some, easy for others. We become aware of guilt. We become aware of forgiveness. We become aware of the fact that we are accepted. The theologian Paul Tillich said this was the major discovery of being a Christian "You have been accepted!" God's Spirit is working with our spirit. W. B. Yeats writes about being "reborn as an idea, something intended, complete" (from *Essays and Introductions*).

Nicodemus, who visited Jesus at night, wanted to know everything about Him. He was a learned and respected man, "Israel's teacher". He knew everything about the law and about the right behavior. But he knew nothing about the essence of faith, God residing in you and the awareness of something new growing in you.

He was a man with specific insights and sincere aspirations. He had questions about a worldly birth and the impossibility of a second birth. Jesus does not even argue this point. He merely says that God requires a new beginning, a beginning from inside, a beginning that grows and continues to grow every day, a new awareness or repentance, even though it may be merely the knowledge that "God is great and God is my Father."

Lord, somewhere in time we were born in You and You in us. That is our solace. Instill this in us.

MYSTERY

"The wind blows wherever it pleases. You hear its sound, but you cannot tell where it comes from or where it is going. So it is with everyone born of the Spirit" (John 3:8).

The wind is a mystery. Yes, we explain it by atmospheric pressure systems and natural laws. But do we really explain it? However, the more you seek the truth, the deeper the mystery becomes, and the more you stand amazed at the mystery.

Sometimes I sit in my study listening to the winds of winter howling around the corners of the house. Sometimes I see the leaves rustling in the wind. Sometimes I can feel the roof shudder from the gusts of wind. Sometimes I only feel it faintly through my shirt. This reminds me that there are forces and powers outside of me that I cannot control, let alone understand. Jesus says that the same kind of things take place within me. God is busy in me and with me.

Sometimes He shakes me around and I feel as if I am in a storm, before the big rains come. Sometimes voices from eternity cry over me and over what I've done. Sometimes the Spirit of God rustles through me, making me aware of a truth that I have not grasped before. Sometimes God's wind sears through me like the Sirocco, the savage wind of the desert. Sometimes the wind of God talks to me in gentle silences and cool breezes. That is God's way of teaching me the full tonality of life, from the bass notes of sorrow to the fine notes of the hymns of angels.

It is one of the most beautiful images of God's work in the Bible. The wind that sears, howls, cools, refreshes, consoles and blows clean. Jesus says this happens to everyone born of the Spirit.

This is the balm when we feel that we are perishing in the heat and dust. This is the balm when the tonality changes and God blesses us with the rustle of His Presence and power. It is His touch, His breath.

You who control the wind, control me as well. You who are a mystery, You understand me.

SO GREAT A LOVE

"For God so loved the world that He gave His one and only Son, that whoever believes in Him shall not perish but have eternal life" (John 3:16).

This is a well-known verse in the Bible. It is a simple text. It is a complicated text. It is an exhaustive text. And it is personal.

Well-known, because virtually everybody has learnt it off by heart at some time or another. Simple, because it summarizes the great truth of the New Testament in a single sentence. Complicated, because it states that God has a Son whom He "gave" to die so that "eternal life" could come of it. Exhaustive, because it covers God's plan of recreation. Personal, because it requires faith from everyone to make this promise his or her own.

It is written that God "loved the world" – but the "world" can be a deserted and oppressive place, a desert wider than the Sahara, a snowed-in mountain pass, a terrible, yawning abyss without meaning, sense and light. But God said, "Let there be light." The light of His love. And love is always an action. Sometimes love is pain, as the poet Sheila Cussons wrote long after she had sustained terrible burns from an accident with a gas stove. "Oh my cosmic Christ: / thirty-three years disguised in the small dark flesh / which you slashed open in one night to free yourself for me / ... yet you wait / for me to say, say in full: seize my hands then ... (from *Christ of the Burnt Men*). Love is meant to give (and also to receive gracefully), love is always meant to save and to help, love is always meant to lead out of the desert to the safe dwelling of the loved one.

Sometimes it feels as though the desert and the abyss and the wind storm are threatening us from all sides. We sometimes feel the way I once felt when I was waiting for a plane in Moscow and could not understand the language or read the signs, and I didn't know where my hotel was. A stranger eventually helped me. In life situations like this God proved His love: Jesus came. And everyone who takes His hand, no matter how weak or guilt-ridden, He will bring safely to His eternal destination with the Father.

Lord, make it clearer to me every day that You love me, as well as the world. We know it, but I sometimes forget it.

PLAYING SECOND FIDDLE

You yourselves can testify that I said, "I am not the Christ but am sent ahead of Him" (John 3:28).

John the Baptist was an exceptional man: a type of ascetic, a Nazarene, a seer, a man with an unappetizing diet, a fearless man, a phenomenon, a man who preached fire and of trees that would be cut down. But he was also a man who knew his place, who could retreat and play second fiddle.

His disciples saw the numbers around the Baptist dwindling. They heard about the miracles Jesus performed and how the crowds went to see Him. Arguments started between John's disciples and some bystanders. John was aware of this and, when his disciples complained to him, he had an answer ready, "I am not the Christ. I am the messenger who announces Him. That is all." Because the messenger's role is fulfilled once the message has been conveyed. And John makes it clear: he himself could not save anyone; it was and remains the work of the Christ of God. Like Jesus, he would be executed. In his case as a result of the whimsical wish of a revengeful woman. In Jesus' case as a result of a bigoted Sanhedrin and an inflamed crowd.

There was something formidable about John. A man who could clearly point to a direction away from himself. How rare such people are. Someone who knew no jealousy, only joy and the expectation of the coming of the One he announced.

How glad I am to say with John that I am not the Christ! How glad I am that He has to judge and decide in my place. How glad I am that He had to die in my place. How glad I am that I may live to tell the tale.

Lord, let me hear the voice of the Bridegroom again today and rejoice in it like John did.

TO REJOICE IN OTHERS

That joy is mine, and it is now complete (John 3:29).

It is easy to rejoice in your own success or happiness. It is easy to rejoice when your child brings home a good report card, or succeeds in his plans. It is natural to rejoice when things work out exactly the way you intended them. Then you want to light candles and play joyous music. And when people congratulate you, you are inclined to say, "Oh, it's not a big deal," while in fact you are bursting with satisfaction. The majority of ordinary people are like this, although there are exceptions.

John the Baptist was such an exception. He rejoiced in the coming of Jesus, the Christ, and was very excited about it. This was not merely because he does not envy Jesus His magnificent deeds and learning. It was a source of great joy to him, actually complete joy.

On the one hand, it was probably easy for John to step back because he could sense the divinity of Jesus and see it as a privilege. However, it takes more to rejoice in the success of another person, especially when you see that your own path is going downhill.

A young man failed his difficult final exam and still attended the graduation ceremony to cheer his friends who had passed. This said a lot about him. He passed the supplementary examination and later, as a professional, he surpassed his friends. Perhaps success also has something to do with the realization that you have to accept certain things, and that you must rejoice completely in the success of others, as a recipe for your own success.

This was not granted to John. His career was over. But he experienced joy: the joy of seeing Jesus, of hearing what He said, of sensing the kingdom of God.

May God grant us this joy in Jesus today.

Lord, You are as busy today as You were during the time of John and Jesus. Make us aware of Jesus, and help us to rejoice.

STARTING A CONVERSATION

Jesus said to her, "Will you give Me a drink?" (John 4:7).

One day Jesus and His disciples passed through Samaria, which is known today as Nablus. He sat down at a well and asked a woman who came to draw water for a drink.

This was unusual, because there was no love lost between the Jews and the Samaritans. Jewish men of those times did not speak to women they did not know. Even less so when the person had a major moral problem of which He, as a prophet, was aware. But He asked for a drink of water in order to start a conversation.

This surprised the woman. She was used to being ignored, also by her fellow townsmen, who were aware of her many loves. But Jesus wanted to talk to her. Why? He did not even speak first in the presence of Pilate. But here He starts a conversation with an outcast and, in addition, the woman had a ready tongue. She felt strongly about the faith of her fathers. She also did not easily give in during an argument. In fact, she performed better in this argument than the learned Nicodemus did!

Jesus probably sensed a hunger in her; a hunger for acceptance and company, and also a certain degree of openness to persuasion, even though she offered strong counter-arguments.

It always works like this. It is always God who starts a conversation with us, either through an incident that we cannot understand or deal with, or through a moment or period of pain and rejection, or through a sudden realization of emptiness and guilt, or through the strange feeling that you have suddenly been left alone with nobody who understands, or through happiness. There are countless possibilities for God to ask something and then wait for our answer.

And our answer can only be, "Lord, let us start the conversation anew – if needs be, from the beginning."

Lord, You sense what is in me, my longings. Talk to me in words and silences. Words of silence. And teach me.

FAITH OF THE FATHERS

"Are you greater than our father Jacob, who gave us the well?" (John 4:12).

It is interesting how often people, when they are slightly cornered by a question regarding their faith, fall back on their religious background, or their pious grandfather, or on a good upbringing. The Samaritan woman was no exception.

Years ago when we were walking from door to door in order to help establish a congregation in a nearby town, we came upon a man who was enjoying a sundowner. We asked him if he would not like to join our congregation, as his name was "on the books". He rather condescendingly told us, "My grandfather was a pillar of the church." To which I – perhaps too presumptuously – replied, "Sir, God has no grandchildren. Only children." However, he simply ignored this and bade us a "fond farewell".

The Samaritan woman also played the trump card of "the fathers". Our father Jacob did this and that. We have tradition on our side. You Jews say it should be like this, but our tradition is different.

However, far above tradition, far above history, far above our own (sometimes even unpleasant) history, far above our achievements and far above our failures, is God. He shaped and knew the fathers, warts and all. Jesus Christ built His congregation from a history of human error, digression and confusion – also from women such as the Samaritan woman, and the one who washed His feet with her tears.

We all have so many "forefathers", so many traditions, so many narratives, so many ties with the past. This is good because our spiritual forefather Jacob helped to establish a faith that was eventually revealed in Jesus. However, it is not enough. Jesus requires a personal conversation with Him, a personal trust in the Father, a personal realization of dependence on God and a personal acknowledgement that God has always been good to us and that He will guide and comfort us always.

Lord, You are a personal God, the One who frees us from bondage. You took care of our forefathers. I believe that You also take care of me today.

The mysterious revelation

"God is spirit, and His worshipers must worship in spirit and in truth" (John 4:24).

The woman from Samaria thought she could ruin Jesus' argument with a trick question. Where must we worship God? On this mountain or in Jerusalem?

Like her fathers, she wanted to tie God to a place. But God is not tied to a place. He is everywhere. Even though we talk about God in human terms, God is not human and human terms are merely images we use to understand something about His character. God is also not bound to time and He never has to look where the sun sits in the sky. He controls the sun. God is everything and everywhere. God is a Presence, a mystery, but He's also familiar. An enigma but also an experience, free but also committed to us, omnipresent but always personally close, far beyond the stars, yet in us, totally inaccessible through our intellect, yet a child can sense His presence, the Eternal One who also finds a place in the secular world, the great Concept and the Mystery beyond description … *Spirit*. God is Spirit.

It is one of Jesus' greatest pronouncements to the sons of man. God must be worshiped "in spirit", because it is actually God Himself who prays through us when we pray. "The Spirit Himself intercedes for us with groans that words cannot express" (Rom. 8:26). In ourselves we are inadequate to do anything. The Spirit is God's wavelength, and the Spirit must tune us in to that wavelength.

Only then can we begin worshiping "in truth". This means that God's words speak through us, and God utters no falsehood. Even our lamentations are carried by this truth.

We understand very little of it, nothing actually, but in worshiping we know that something overwhelming is at work, something filled with strength, Someone filled with strength who will carry us through every crisis. The Spirit in us and through us. God Himself.

Spirit of God, come to my aid! What I want to pray is locked deep in my heart, where only Your Spirit can heal me.

THE SPECIAL REVELATION

"I who speak to you am He" (John 4:26).

An old man was on his deathbed, delirious and confused. "Where is Jake?" he kept on mumbling. His son was holding his hand and kept on saying, "I am here, Father. I am holding your hand, Father. It is me, Father. I am Jake. I arrived earlier this morning. There is no need for concern, Father." The old man never indicated that he recognized his son. He only held his son's hand with both his farmer's hands that were once so powerful.

The woman at the well played her final trump card, "You may teach all these wonderful things, but we are waiting for the Messiah. He will teach us everything."

To which Jesus, like the son to his dying father, replied, "I am the Messiah. I who speak to you am He. I came a while ago. I am here with you now." For the woman it had to be the kind of experience that Herman Melville calls "one shock of recognition".

To this special revelation, the woman could offer no further argument. She went back to the town with the news, "Come, see ... Could this be the Christ?" And that day she and many of the Samaritans came to believe in Him (cf. v. 39).

Like the woman of Samaria, we can sometimes say that we have faith. We can say that we know things, that we wait, that we feel, that we experience pain, that we experience resistance, that we have strength, but too little, that we find ourselves in disgrace or filled with joy, while we anxiously look for a hand, asking, "Where is God? Where is the Christ?"

We need not look too far. He is already holding our hand. He already knows our need. He is already offering salvation. He is already coming with us. He, the Messiah, the One who speaks to you.

Lord, speak to me and stay with me. Soothe me. Offer me Your hand. Thank You.

FEBRUARY

Lord, My God

I want to worship You in Spirit and in truth.
I call with hesitation, but also with trust,
in faith, but also with questions,
with gratitude, but also with grief,
with love, but also with fear.
It is already the second month of the year,
deep into the height of summer in the southern hemisphere
with the heat quivering over the plains.
And in the northern hemisphere the long cold nights
seem never ending while the days touch everything with frosty fingers:
You are indeed a God of variety and paradox.

The seasons pass under Your hands on our small planet.
Your season of growth and maturity;
Your season of nature's rest and hibernation –
all are Your generous gifts from Your generous heart,
every season, dark and light, is Your time of blessing.

I pray for those I love,
for the people in my neighborhood,
for peace and kind hearts on my daily path
and, above all, that I will never forget You,
but that I will always remember
that the God of January is also the God of February,
up to December and on again,
because You never change,
and year after year, from eternity to eternity,
You are our gracious God.

Amen.

GOD THINKS OF US

God heard their groaning and He remembered His covenant with Abraham, with Isaac and with Jacob. So God looked on the Israelites and was concerned about them (Exod. 2:24-25).

Jacob experienced tragedy after his return to his promised land. No promised land is ever without drought and sorrow. In the end, Jacob and his family ended up in Egypt where his son, Joseph, had become viceroy, and he could die in peace.

But his descendants were soon oppressed by other rulers. They experienced the great constitutional truth that still applies today: a minority in a region is more exposed than its people care to admit. A minority must become strong by honoring the traditions of their fathers, by sticking to their morals and by trusting God.

The descendants of Jacob became a threat to the rulers. Their persecution began. How near they were to God during this time is not very clear. Only when they were subjected to the most cruel laws and forced labor "their cry for help ... went up to God" (cf. v. 23).

God heard them. In fact, when they started to pray earnestly, God's plan was already in action. Moses was kept safe on the Nile and, ironically enough, he was taught to lead a nation by the Egyptians themselves. He was already there where he would meet God – in the desert tending the sheep.

The Lord "remembered" His people; it is clear that He thought about them constantly. His plan did not comprise a sudden intervention to turn His slave people into shining angels. They probably felt at times that God was sleeping, but His plans stretch over years, because He is eternal and He takes the finest detail into consideration.

People expect instant miracles. God sees the bigger picture, bears everything in mind, and offers hope across all generations. And the children of Israel had to start praying earnestly first!

Lord, we sometimes feel that Your ways are too tedious at times, but we know that You know us personally and that You already have Your plan in place. I want to think of You sincerely every day.

AT YOUR SERVICE

"Moses! Moses!" And Moses said, "Here I am" (Exod. 3:4).

Some time ago, a man died in the Australian desert because he waited in vain for weeks on end next to his broken-down car for someone to pass by. No one came. A desert is not a popular meeting place.

However, God chose the desert to reveal Himself in the burning bush that kept burning. He came and called Moses by name, the way He knows and calls us all by name, and announces Himself as the "God of your fathers", the God of the covenant with Abraham.

It must have been an awe-inspiring encounter for the lonely shepherd. Initially, you sense some uncertainty in Moses – like somebody who has been invited to a state banquet but does not know where to sit or stand or what to say.

It was only Moses, his sheep, the desert wind, the burning bush and the voice of Someone who knew him, Someone who knew his fathers, the Eternal One. Almost all the great prophets had a desert or a high-mountain experience, even Jesus. Ordinary people who earnestly seek God experience times of shifting sand dunes and cold, lonely mountain peaks. Of isolation and estrangement. Of disappointment and spiritual drought while they wait for God.

It is in these times that God appears in all His glory: the barren times are almost always a prelude to remarkable things to come, to an overwhelming encounter, to the sublime solution, or to new hope and direction. It is not an easy place to find yourself. It requires endurance and tears. And very often you see only later how the roads in the desert converged at a specific point to form a meaningful pattern.

In times like these you should merely echo Moses, "Here I am, Lord." And then God speaks – sometimes in strange ways, sometimes in everyday expressions. Just listen; you will hear Him.

Lord, sometimes even when I'm among people, I feel as lonely as in a desert. Speak to me. Teach me to listen.

BY YOUR SIDE

Moses said to God, "Who am I, that I should go to Pharaoh and bring the Israelites out of Egypt?" And God said, "I will be with you" (Exod. 3:11-12).

By this stage of the great encounter, Moses, the stutterer, had managed to say a few words and learn a bit of divine etiquette. He had taken off his shoes because he found himself in the presence of the Presence. Perhaps we should remember this more often – God is our beloved Father and Savior, He is not our neighbor with whom we are making casual conversation. Take off your shoes. Show respect, especially in a place of worship, which is actually everywhere.

Strangely enough, Moses finds himself in the presence of the Supreme Ruler, but he is afraid to venture into the court of a worldly king. He does, after all, know the pharaohs and their ways of doing things and he does, after all, have a murder to answer for. He feels safe in the desert.

God instructs him to leave the safety of the desert – his comfort zone, his rut, his shelter – and go to the focal point of world politics in his day. He had to venture into the center of a powerful establishment, to the court of the great Pharaoh with his intrigues, his dangers, his backstabbing and his quick and formidable revenge.

The barren desert of hardship sometimes becomes a place where people withdraw to from life. It is the easiest way out. Follow the path of least resistance. Rather stay out of the way of people and princes.

God says to Moses he must face life, go to the Pharaoh and to the center of life, to his work and often to difficult people, to where he could make a difference.

And then the great promise follows, "I will be with you." With Me by your side, God says, you can face kings. You can take on wrong and evil. You will triumph. Because I never lose.

Our Father, we experience desert times, and then You send us back into the fray. We are scared of the turmoil, but You say, "I will be with you."

THE NAME

God said to Moses, "I AM WHO I AM" (Exod. 3:14).

Moses was looking for the credentials of the One who sent him. He asks God's name. And he got a simple, but infinitely complicated reply, "I am who I am." In the ancient manuscripts, no vowels were used. All that we have is JHWH, which sounds something like Yahweh in Hebrew. A Name that devout Jews never spoke out loud and which indicates something of the existence of all existences.

As a young pastor, I once tried to explain this reply from God and this Name during a service and, for presumptuous effect, I repeated the "am" over and over again: I am, am, am, am, am, am, am, am, am, am, am, am, am. An elderly lady in one of the front pews shuddered and I knew immediately that I had gone too far and never repeated this gimmick again. After all, God does not keep Himself busy with gimmicks.

It is a mystical Name, filled with meaning and mystery that is inexplicable and more perplexing than trillions of relativity theories.

Mysticism starts when "strange" revelations are made. Like Moses experienced with his sheep in Midian. Like Jesus who fought against the devil in the desert. The poet Robert Frost said that a poem begins as a lump in the throat. Perhaps all mystical experiences start like this: a moment of seeing or hearing something, or a glimpse of the true, great Reality. A feeling, a sudden insight, shifting boundaries, a realization … a Name?

Then the adoration and amazement come. As Milton said, "Such sober certainty of waking bliss / I never heard till now." Amen to that, although few of us can be a Milton. And even fewer of us can be a Moses who found himself barefoot standing at a burning bush that did not burn out.

However, most of us, even all of us if we are observant, will experience something in a moment of joy or pain, at a sudden turn in the road or in green pastures, and see something of eternity that "is" forever. The presence of "I am who I am". God.

If it pleases You, grant me a glimpse of Your Name today, Lord.

A BIG QUESTION

Who is the LORD? (Exod. 5:2).

The great encounter in the desert was something of the past. The mighty conversation as well, stormy as it was. Aaron now stood with Moses in front of Pharaoh and requested Israel's freedom.

Pharaoh responded with exactly the same answer so often heard in history, coming from big and small, the powerful and powerless, and which will still be heard as long as this order continues, "The Lord, who might He be?"

Big words. Challenging words. Filled with pride and arrogance. Merciless and even scornfully callous. Pharaoh played a game that he would lose terribly. His question would eventually be answered by his destruction. In the mean time, he angrily made the Israelites' lot infinitely worse.

"Who is the Lord …?"

It is just as well that God is God and able to answer a question like this in His own way. The fact that He did not strike Pharaoh with lightning at that moment was probably sheer mercy. God always works through a process, and often the process is the truth plus a spokesperson.

I have heard great philosophers ask who God is, as well as ignorant people who pretend to be clever. But I have also heard it said by children of God, in moments of utter despair, "Where is God? Why is He not doing anything? What kind of a God is He?"

God sees the heart and the motive behind the question, and judges accordingly, always with understanding, always with compassion, and peace of mind.

"Who is the Lord?" As a believer I have the right to say that He is my Father who protects me. In the same way that He protected Moses in the presence of Pharaoh.

Thank You that we may call You our Father.

YET ANOTHER BIG QUESTION

Moses returned to the LORD and said, "O LORD, why have You brought trouble upon this people?" (Exod. 5:22).

Moses asks a fair question, "O Lord, why have You brought trouble upon this people?" What are Your reasons? What do You want to prove? Do You perhaps want to prove how cruel You can be?

It is a question that is often asked: why does the Lord do this or that? Why is He so cruel? Why is He so inconsistent? What about all His promises?

Moses made a crucial mistake. It was not the Lord who made the Israelites build pyramids and make bricks, and beat them with whips and killed their children. It was humans who did this, other people, people belonging to a powerful nation under the rule of a powerful king. People do terrible things to people. Like the Romans of old used to say: *homo homini lupus* – man is a wolf to man. People wage wars. People attack one another with atomic bombs and suicide planes. God gave man enormous power to do good, but also the power to destroy themselves and other people. This is the tragic part of Creation. The recreation only started later on in Christ, with a great intervention of which delivering Israel from Egypt was a mighty prelude. It will be completed with the second coming of Christ.

God listened patiently to Moses' complaints and He answered, "Now you will see what I would do to Pharaoh" (Exod. 6:1). God confirmed that they are His own people (cf. 6:7) and that He will dramatically deliver them (cf. 6:8). Pharaoh would receive one last warning and then the plagues would strike.

Pharaoh and all the people were going to learn something: God may linger, God may be working too slow for our liking, God may appear not interested, but He is always in control. And eventually He unveils a master plan for those who are His people, those who believe.

Father, when we ask questions like Moses, make us realize that there are many forces at work, but that You are more powerful than everything and everyone.

HOLY DAY

This is a day you are to commemorate (Exod. 12:14).

The terrible plagues with which the Lord struck the Egyptians were reaching a climax. God was powerfully demonstrating His intervention in the lives of His people, like He has done so often in the past.

The water of the Nile became undrinkable. Frogs, gnats, flies, the plague on livestock, boils, hail, locusts, darkness. It was as if God brought nature in its entirety into play against the Egyptians. And every time the Lord "hardened Pharaoh's heart" (cf. 10:20) not to take heed of it. Pharaoh disdainfully challenged God and it was as if God wanted to administer to him a good dose of His power. No one plays with God.

Before the final plague, the people were instructed to slaughter a year-old lamb, to eat it with hyssop and unleavened bread, and to put the blood of the lamb on the door frames of every house, so that death would pass by that house. That was the holy day, the birth of the nation of Israel, the day of deliverance celebrated with a strange but meaningful ritual.

Then God struck again with the death of the firstborn son among the Egyptians. After that a lamentation rose to the heavens. The Israelites were spared. That was the prophecy of Jesus Christ, the Passover Lamb. From this strange Passover ceremony, it became evident that the Plan of God in Christ had been in place for a very long time, many centuries before it actually happened.

Christ would come "to be slaughtered". The mystery of the cross remains an unfathomable sign, a "celebration" of a God who cares. Higher laws than those of the human mind are at play here: the love of a Lord who goes to extremes to save us. That includes today.

Lord, I know that when You truly intervene, it is often overwhelming and inexplicable, but so very clear ... Teach me to wait on You, O Lord.

Up and leave!

Up! Leave my people! Go, worship the LORD as you have requested (Exod. 12:31).

Pharaoh got the message loud and clear: he had challenged forces residing in the Lord God and he had paid a terrible price. The Israelites had to leave immediately to go and "worship the LORD as you have requested".

The Israelites did not hesitate. They baked unleavened bread "because they did not have time to prepare food for themselves" (cf. v. 39).

It is rather ironic and true to the often totally inexplicable modus operandi of the Almighty God. At first it seemed as if He was on a go-slow strike, but when deliverance came, it was with a mighty bang, so that God's people did not even have time to prepare for the journey.

Like an old woman said to me shortly before her death, "I waited on the Lord for a long time during my illness. Everything was so dark. It has been two days now that I see everything; my entire life clearly. I thank God for this clarity. I do not have much time left to prepare for my last journey. But I am going to Him now. After my suffering, He still shows me more of the wonderful life. I go like the people of Israel, but not even with a small unleavened bread!" A day later she passed away peacefully. To go and worship God forever.

The Israelites moved away. Before them lay the outstretched desert and the sea. They would learn that bondage was hard, but that freedom also had its price. And the Pharaoh would learn to rather stick to his good intentions and to think of God in everything you do.

We all learn. Like Bunyan's pilgrim, we are on a journey to eternity. On this road, we are met by devils and angels. But the Lord is with us. He knows the direction. His presence remains, and, when His deliverance comes, it is often as quick as a flash of lightning.

We are moving, Lord. We have upped and left and are on our way to You. Keep us on track.

THE WONDERFUL ANGEL

Then the angel of God, who had been traveling in front of Israel's army, withdrew and went behind them. The pillar of cloud also moved from in front and stood behind them, coming between the armies of Egypt and Israel (Exod. 14:19-20).

God usually works with visible signs in our lives, like the pillar of cloud and the pillar of fire at night for the Israelites. If we do not see them, we can't blame God. A mere new day is a "pillar of cloud", a blessing, but often we shut the windows.

God also works continually in an invisible way in our lives and we can sometimes sense it, if we become really quiet and think about it. Here God worked with the wonderful Angel, the appearance of Jesus in the Old Testament. The Israelites could not see this Angel, but when danger closed in and the stubborn Pharaoh pursued them with his troops, a soul-stirring, magnificent thing happened: "The Angel of God, who had been traveling in front of them, now went behind them. The pillar of cloud also."

The Angel knows where the dangers lurk. The Angel knows human strategies. The Angel knows God's strategies with unsearchable attunement. If the danger lies ahead and the road is unknown, the Angel is in front. If the danger lies behind us, the Angel moves to the back to cover the rear. So it was with the people of God. So it is with us.

During the First World War, a small number of allied soldiers were trapped in a town called Mons. Suddenly, the soldiers saw angels in front of them and behind them. The enemy withdrew. It is not easy to establish how true this tale is, but I am naive enough to believe it. However, no one needs to be naive about the protection offered by the Angel of God, Jesus, our Lord. He is above us, in front of us, behind us and next to us. We live and move in the shadow of His protective wings.

Lord, make us aware, constantly aware, that Your Angel is moving with us, like an invisible source of strength, like a gentle wind that propels our small sailing vessels.

Respect

When the Israelites saw the great power of the Lord displayed against the Egyptians, the people feared the Lord (Exod. 14:31).

Someone once asked an acquaintance after the well-being of a mutual friend. The acquaintance replied, "I cannot say that we are friends. I do not know him that well. But, what I have seen of him, is enough to convince me that I need to respect him."

What a wonderful testimonial. The Israelites could probably have said the same after Moses had stretched out his hand over the sea so that all of them could safely pass through, while Pharaoh's army was mercilessly swept away by the water. What exactly happened there no one really knows, except the hint of a great divine miracle in which people, enemies, a cloud, water and an angel collaborated.

God often performs His miracles on a big stage. Sometimes He performs them in a small, intimate way, like an ache that suddenly disappears. Like the acquaintance said above, we do not always know God's ways. In fact, we can echo the words of a poet, "I dare scarcely speak of God, I know Him little." But we have sufficient knowledge to have respect for Him, like the Israelites when they reached the other side of the sea.

No, they did not understand Him. The great drama that they experienced probably gave them a lot to think about. After all, they accused God of doing nothing while they suffered. Now they stood in awe as people delivered from their enemies.

Awe, respect, is a cornerstone on which civilizations are built. Other stones such as law and order follow on it as well as leadership, survival and knowledge. Love is also closely linked to respect. I respect my child. She respects me. There is love between us, but also rules to be honored.

God does not demonstrate His power as a mere show. He calls for our respect, every day.

Lord, from Your love and power flow my love and respect.

BITTER WATER

And the water became sweet (Exod. 15:25).

It is only human to think that major events or great miracles should result in lasting bliss, peace, victory, prosperity and even perfection. In the 1960s, American President Lyndon B. Johnson declared that poverty would be eradicated within a decade to form a "great society". This was an excellent idea, but even a major power like the USA could not succeed in this. As a matter of fact, already during Johnson's time, one crisis after another struck the USA. There is almost something deterministic to it.

If this were a story, we would have expected the delivered people now to be entering the psalmist's "green pastures" with green grass and palm trees. However, the Bible is not fiction, and the Israelites found themselves in the Desert of Shur, a place where the water was undrinkably bitter. This they did not expect. The people grumbled against Moses (cf. v. 24). That is one thing that people through centuries have done very well: complain.

Secretly they were expecting instant paradise, especially after they had sung and danced on the shores of the Red Sea, with Miriam and her tambourine leading the way, rejoicing because the Egyptians had been hurled into the sea. At Shur with its bitter water Miriam put her tambourine away. She and all the people wanted water to drink.

Of course this was a fair request. But God did not intend to transform every stop into a place of convenience and comfort for them. They were, after all, in a training school to become a nation.

God will also not provide modern luxuries at every place we find ourselves, or make our paths straight at every turn. We must learn to handle everything with faith and obedience to Him. Then He brings us to a resting place like Elim, with fountains and palm trees.

If I have to drink bitter water today, Lord, think of me and bring me to Elim. If I find joy, let me rejoice in You like Miriam with her tambourine.

FOOD FOR ONE DAY

That evening quail came and covered the camp, and in the morning, thin flakes like frost on the ground appeared on the desert floor. Moses said to them, "It is the bread the LORD has given you to eat" (Exod. 16:13-15).

The logistics behind moving a big army is one of the great challenges of battle: Sufficient food, chefs, water, supplies, uniforms, emergency rations, medicine, doctors, field hospitals, engineers, guides, experienced officers ... even personal articles for everyday use. The migrating Israelites had none of these. They were a primitive lot of amateur migrants used to making bricks, not to endless dunes of sand and rocks.

But the cloud went ahead of them and they had to endure the inhospitable world. They complained more and more and true to human nature, they soon started to glorify their suffering in Egypt as a joyous life with "pots of meat" (cf. 16:3). Today's struggles can easily make yesterday's suffering seem like a bed of roses.

Then God provided for them: bread and meat, food from above. There were still some of them who expected the Lord to deliver the food to their tents. It is also clear that some of them were lazy, because some collected bread just for one day, while others collected enough for a few days. God taught them a lesson of just enough for every day.

Yes, they had to endure a lot. Yes, they had to sweat and often had to sleep on the open, dry ground. Yes, they did become tired. Yes, some did die. Yes, they had to give birth on a rug in the sand. The move was not easy. But life is not easy, in spite of all our modern facilities.

Sometimes we get tired and despondent. Sometimes we feel totally stressed out and shattered. Sometimes we feel alone, like the Israelites without food. And then, early in the morning, we see the glory of God, manna on the endless dunes, and quail flying low at sunset ... And we know: God will provide for every day. God will provide during the night. God always provides.

Lord, forgive me my rebelliousness and the fact that I tend to forget yesterday's blessings. Make me mindful of You today.

Hold your hands up

When Moses' hands grew tired Aaron and Hur held his hands up – one on one side, one on the other (Exod. 17:12).

With a big group of people on the move there was bound to be war. Among themselves and against the enemy. At Rephidim, near Horeb, the Amalekites attacked. Joshua was the commander-in-chief of Israel's military action.

God promised to help them, but they themselves had to fight. As a matter of fact, their leaders had to do more. As long as Moses held up his hands in prayer, the Israelites were winning. When his arms became tired and he lowered them, Israel fell back. Aaron and Hur had to hold his arms up until sunset to give Joshua enough time to finish the battle.

This is a meaningful image of supporting one another, of continuous prayer for victory, of help from the Lord, of the faith of people in battle and of leaders who, with the help of God, can devise a plan. "No man is an island," wrote the poet and priest John Donne. And neither was Moses, even though he lived in unprecedented communication with God. His arms became tired. He needed help and received it from his fellow leaders.

We are not super humans. We form part of a state, a place, a family, a group, a language, a church, a culture. There is an old saying that we are like crayfish in a bucket. One crayfish fights to get out of the bucket by pushing the other crayfish down. This is a bad testimonial and it is perhaps also true of many cultural groups. The Israelites also did it in the desert epic – it is human.

But when the hands are raised, the prayer starts and then the battle progresses. And then we must hold one another's hands up, to God.

Eternal Father, teach us to pray. Let us hold up one another's hands, precisely because it is in conflict with our human nature. And precisely because it is necessary for victory.

AT HOME WITH GOD — EVERYWHERE

F
E
B
R
U
A
R
Y

14

"I am with you and will watch over you wherever you go, and I will bring you back to this land" (Gen. 28:15).

L et us go back to Jacob for a moment. Unlike his father, Isaac, Jacob was no "ordinary" man. He was capable of great love, great sacrifice, great shame and great roguery. He schemed with his mother to get his father's blessing and then he had to flee before the wrath of his brother, Esau.

One would not vote for Jacob in an election or appoint him as the executor of your estate. He was also not always successful in his deception. But from him the nomadic nation would be born. The Lord chose him specifically as the "executor" of God's "inheritance" to His people.

In Genesis 28:15 God makes it clear to Jacob, the fugitive, that He would watch over him and be with him. When Jacob woke up, he called out: This is the house of God, this is Bethel. He continued his journey until he met with God again at Bethel, years later, as a man bearing the scars of a hard life, of humiliation, fraud, prosperity and of sin. And through all of this God watched over him. Indeed, everywhere Jacob went, he found himself in the house of God.

The Lord always brings us back to Him, as He promised Jacob. He chooses us as His children just the way we are, warts and all - often with more warts than healthy skin. And for reasons we don't understand, God continues to watch over us, even when we cry and disappoint Him. Even when we try to leave the house of God. Which is something that we will never be able to do because He will never let us go.

Lord, we know that where we are, there Your house is. Bethel.

INTRODUCTION

"I am the LORD your God, who brought you out of Egypt, out of the land of slavery. You shall have no other gods before Me" (Exod. 20:2-3).

By the time of the commandments the Lord had been accompanying His people through the desert for a long time. The time had come to lay down the rules of this lasting covenant. It was a terrifying encounter; smoke, trembling and fire. And the people were afraid. Moses had to go and speak on their behalf.

Before God gave His Law, He introduced Himself to the people. He could have said, "I am the God of the heavens." That is true. He could have said, "I am the God in everything." That is also true. He could have said, "I am the God from eternity to eternity." Also true. He could have introduced Himself in many ways.

But He chose to introduce Himself as a personal God, "I am the LORD your God, who brought you out of Egypt, out of the land of slavery."

In other words: I am your personal God, the One who intervened when you were in distress, the One who stopped a powerful king in his tracks for your sake, the One who parted the sea for you, the One who heard your cries and saw your misery, the One who had a plan and carried it out to deliver you. The One who brought you to where you are now.

The message is clear: I, your God, enter into a personal relationship with you, My people, and with you as individuals. I am more than the God of the open spaces and of detail, says God. For you, I am all heart. For you, I take action.

He also says it to me: I am *your* God. He says it when I am afraid. He says it when I am sad. He says it when I succeed. He says, "Think about everything that I have done for you. Because of that, you shall have no other gods before Me!"

———

*L*ord, You are my God. You and You alone.

THE WORK OF CHRIST

"My Father is always at His work to this very day, and I, too, am working" (John 5:17).

The Angel of the Lord was hard at work in the Old Testament. And here Jesus said that it is in His nature to work, after the Jews confronted Him because He had healed a man and told him to pick up his sleeping mat on the Sabbath. He made a remarkable statement that stretches back to the times before the beginning of Creation and which will continue to where time ends and eternity starts. "My Father is always at His work to this very day, and I, too, am working."

Willebrord, a missionary of old who went to Britain, pointed out the infinity of life and the temporary nature of a worldly existence to the king. He said, "You sit here with your counselors in this big hall. A swallow flies in through one of the big windows, flutters around and flies out again through another window, into open space – the open space of which you take no notice while you are sitting here consulting and eating. Majesty, think of this: in essence, you are nothing more than the swallow who comes flying in from eternity, lingers a while in this hall, and then flies out again, into eternal space."

With reference to the depth and timelessness of the work of the Father and the Son, how it functions, how the Father acts through the Son, for how long it has been going on and for how long it will still continue, Jesus says with startling simplicity, "My Father works, and I work." These words make Willebrord's image of the swallow something to think about. This life is merely a "big hall" into which we fly, only to fly out again. Where our beginning is, we do not know. Where our final destination is, we do not know either. All that we know is that it is with God, with the Father and the Son, who work on it, "who are always at work to this very day".

And to know that is enough. Everything concerning us, even our "coming" and our "going" (cf. Psalm 121), is in God's hands.

Lord, You work for me and You work through me. Let me be Your hands today.

LIKE THE FATHER

"The Son can do nothing by Himself; He can do only what He sees His Father doing, because whatever the Father does the Son also does" (John 5:19).

If the Son can do nothing "by Himself", why then are there a Father and a Son and, above all – together with the Holy Spirit – one God?

That is how God reveals Himself. I am also a three-in-one: a father, a husband and a pastor, but only one man. Yet this and every other human explanation of the mystery of God's existence and work fall far short and could even miss or distort the truth.

"He can do only what He sees His Father doing." An image true to modern times (taking into account all the limitations of imagery), could perhaps assist us with these words of Jesus. If I want a specific program on my computer, I first have to download it from another computer onto a computer disk. Then I can take the disk and download the entire program onto my computer again, up to the last dot and line. I cannot expect the program to do anything that was not downloaded onto the disk. Jesus Christ is God's disk. God's entire program was inside that Man. He could print out parts of that program as He chose: resurrect the dead, heal the sick, feed the crowds. But He could only remain faithful to the Program, namely the Father.

After Jesus' resurrection, a new order began where the Spirit of the Father and the Son, the Holy Spirit, was transplanted into the heart of every believer, after which we became miniature "disks" of the Father and the Son. However, we do not receive the complete "program". Only parts of it, simply because we would abuse it due to our sinful nature. God knows what He can give to whom.

Jesus used His divine "program" very "economically" on earth. He did not heal all the sick people and resurrected only a few – just enough to demonstrate the authenticity of His "program". He also gives us just enough to demonstrate God's program to us. And, in particular, enough to experience the power of God and to live in faith, trusting in Him.

Lord, expand the divine program in me so that I can sense more of You and so that I will be able to perform some of Your work.

From Moses to Jesus

"If you believed Moses, you would believe Me, for he wrote about Me" (John 5:46).

There is a direct line running from Moses to Jesus; from the Dispensation of the Law and the deliverance from human bondage to the Dispensation of Grace and Salvation from human despair and guilt. There are some scholars who claim that the Old Testament does not mention Christ, and that all the prophecies of the coming of the Messiah have nothing to do with Jesus. If people believe this, they should also reject the New Testament completely.

Jesus spelled it out to the Jewish priests. Calm, assured in the full knowledge of the Father's "program". In fact, Jesus challenged them to once again have a good look at what Moses had written in the Law and the prophecies, "Your accuser is Moses, on whom your hopes are set ... for he wrote about Me" (vv. 45-46). He who invokes the Law, Moses' Law, will be judged by the Law. He who invokes Jesus Christ, will be freed by grace.

Strange that sensible people could overlook such important things. People who form part of historical events are often not even aware of it. Would the ancient Greeks in the famous naval Battle of Salamis have known that their victory would form the foundation of Western civilization for thousands of years? The Jews were probably like that. They acted based on what they thought they knew. And what they thought they knew, they did not even know! Because God was making history in their midst.

We are often also none the wiser while God is making "history" in our lives. We often fail completely to see the truth and imminence of God within us. We sometimes think we are lost, but Christ is guiding us. We sometimes say that God is asleep, but it is in fact us who are too blind or foolish to see, like the Jews did with Jesus. Of course this is human nature. Of course God understands.

Lord, comfort me with the knowledge that You are close to me, and make me aware of Your Presence.

HE KNOWS WHAT TO DO!

He already had in mind what He was going to do (John 6:6).

Jesus was at the peak of His popularity. People everywhere had heard about Him and flocked to Him where He was teaching at the lakeside. The majority of them, thoughtlessly, or because they were needy, brought no food along.

Jesus realized immediately that He had a major problem. One can only imagine what could happen with a crowd of hungry people, and Jesus knew that. He noticed the most intimate detail of the ordinary needs of a group of people. And He asked His disciples what they could do about it. He knew that they would have no idea of what to do, because He knew what He was going to do.

People might be at a loss for answers and incapable of warding off or defusing a crisis. Jesus is never at a loss for anything but, in a typically divine manner, He first allows the drama to unfold although He already knows the Plan completely. Indeed, He expects some effort on the part of His pupils. And Andrew offered a somewhat absurd solution: five small barley loaves and two small fish from a little boy, a drop in the ocean.

That was enough for Jesus. His Grand Plan almost always has a tiny beginning. The long journey starts with the first step. The great idea starts with a minor principle, like Sir Alexander Fleming who saw that mould destroyed microbes, and penicillin and antibiotics were born.

The crowd had to sit down. Jesus would provide the food. Because He knew exactly what to do for them. And He knows exactly what to do for you.

Lord, more often than not, I am at my wit's end. Use my fish and bread. You have known for a long time what to do.

FOLLOWERS FOR FOOD

Jesus, knowing that they intended to come and make Him king by force, withdrew again to a mountain by Himself (John 6:15).

I once stood next to a well-known politician shortly after he was defeated by a small majority in his constituency. It was remarkable to see how bravely his supporters with their rosettes cheered him on at first, only to disappear shortly afterwards. He and his wife stood against a wall, embarrassed, waiting for their car while the supporters of the victor made all kinds of unpleasant remarks.

Jesus, the Son of man, and an expert on people, was only too aware of this human trait. He fed a large crowd and there were baskets full of food left over. A truly "miraculous sign" as it is stated in verse 14. Such a man, the people argued, someone who can provide us with more than enough food from almost nothing ... such a man must be our king so that He can provide food for us every day! He could be nothing less than a true Prophet. We will simply have to follow Him without ever having to work again. We vote: make Him king!

What an easy life the people sought once they got a little taste of it! It is so human – also for us who sometimes expect the Lord to remove every obstacle in our way and fill up every plate. What George Herbert wrote is true: God knows that man "would adore My gifts instead of Me ... and losers be" (from *The Pulley*).

Jesus does not like such an attitude. He is nobody's personal waiter or valet with merely the title of "king". He withdraws from such an attitude. He knows that today's honor is tomorrow's criticism. We still do that. And then we wonder at times why Jesus feels so far away, so high up on the mountain ...

Lord Jesus, help us to thoroughly question our motives as to why we call You King. Let us seek You for the sake of who You are and not for the sake of our comforts. Do not withdraw from us!

A SAVIOR IN STORMS

"It is I; don't be afraid" (John 6:20).

The disciples were in a boat on their way back to Capernaum, in the dark, caught in a storm. Jesus was still up on the mountain.

A few kilometers from the shore, they suddenly saw Someone walking on the stormy waters. And of course they were afraid. Then Jesus called above the force of the storm, "It is I; don't be afraid."

Could it be? Is it possible for a Man to feed thousands from a small portion of food, then withdraw to a mountain and after that walk on water to the boat of His disciples – in the dark and during a storm? It sounds like a story; a tale about phantoms or wandering spirits.

And yet, if He was indeed what He said He was; if God's entire "program" was inside Him; if He wanted to be the Savior to all, then one would expect that walking on water and multiplying food would be nothing out of the ordinary for Him. What we call a "miracle" is actually nothing out of the ordinary for God. Furthermore, the principle lies already locked in Creation, but we simply have not found and/or mastered it yet. Would Jan Van Riebeeck have believed that his arduous journey from Holland, taking over three months, to the Cape of Good Hope, with three small ships would now take an "iron ship" which flies through the air, less than ten hours?

Jesus' miracles show us what is possible. Often a miracle is concealed in the mundane: the love of a child, the care of a parent. Jesus did not walk on water to play the role of magician. He walked towards His people who were facing difficulties and who were afraid. He could calm them down, as well as calm down the waters.

He also comes to us in our own darkness, during our own storm. And listen, He says, "It is I; don't be afraid!"

Lord Jesus, please come to us in calm days, stay with us, walk by our side – but especially, yes especially, when darkness falls and the waters turn stormy.

BREAD

"I am the bread of life" (John 6:35).

After the huge meal and the storm, there was consternation in the vicinity of the lake. Everyone was looking for Jesus and set off for Capernaum. Everyone wanted to eat, or learn the secret of eating without having to work. They even had the audacity to ask for a sign, something along the line of Moses giving manna to their ancestors.

The fact that Jesus kept His cool and did not chase them away with a bolt of thunder was a further divine miracle of understanding human weaknesses. He spoke of the "bread of God" (cf. v. 33), and immediately these people wanted this "bread of God". Everyone wanted to fill their stomachs. "From now on give us this bread" (v. 34). Their attitudes are not all that inexplicable either, because even today some people think that the gospel is about distributing food parcels to the hungry.

"I am the bread of life," says Jesus. I am the life-giving divine principle; I still the innermost hunger and the longing that you cannot explain or do anything about.

On another occasion Jesus stated that man cannot live on bread alone. Obviously. But man cannot do without it for very long either. To eat is an acknowledgment of our dependence – on food and on each other. But it also reminds us of another kind of emptiness within us, a longing, a great need and a plea that the tastiest menu of man cannot satisfy. It is the emptiness and the search for God, for meaning, for understanding, for infinitely more than what is in the refrigerator.

Jesus says that He can satisfy that hunger: I am the "bread" for the longing and the emptiness beyond physical needs. I give you true life: he who believes in Me will never be hungry again. And if the internal hunger gnaws at us, we go on our knees in search of eternal Bread, Jesus Christ, because we are dependent …

Lord, we want Bread, You, eternal refreshment, that which satisfies our yearning for the eternal. You provide it. You embody it.

BREAD FROM HIS DEATH

"This bread is My flesh, which I will give." [Jesus] said this while teaching in the synagogue in Capernaum (John 6:51, 59).

B read has to be cut or broken into pieces. It has to be chewed. It has to be swallowed. It has to be digested. Therefore, the bread has to "die" in order to give life.

When Jesus uses this powerful metaphor to refer to Himself, it means exactly this: like the bread, He would be broken, cut, chewed and swallowed by the grave, to give life. With one big difference: death swallowed Him, but did not "consume" Him. In this respect heavenly bread differs from worldly bread: the life-giving principle is always preserved.

The heart can stop beating and the blood can congeal, but the divine cannot die. It is like eternal nuclear energy. It does not burn out, it continues to supply power, it is indestructible, it "nourishes" more than only this dispensation, it nourishes the eternal dispensation. It is the dispensation from where the Bread comes and where those of us who partake of this Bread are headed.

"Jesus said this while teaching in the synagogue in Capernaum." And what an awe-inspiring, profound teaching that was. It is like the poet who feels the words forming inside him and then looks for images. And images, as the poet knows so well, enlighten what he sees. But the words also conceal his experiences because human language is limited and words often fail us.

It seems as if the majority of people who heard Jesus that day did not have the faintest idea of what He was saying. Their needs were the needs of that day: bread falling like manna from heaven, putting the farmer and the miller out of business.

Jesus said that He came from heaven. He provides daily bread. But He is also willing to be broken and swallowed like bread to satisfy that "something" in us that yearns for more than bread alone. It is His assistance, His imminence, His comfort and His guidance until we reach His eternal city.

When I eat a piece of bread today, let me remember that You became bread and were broken so that I may live.

TURNING BACK

From this time many of His disciples turned back and no longer followed Him (John 6:66).

It is human to change your mind. It is human to turn back. It is human to desert a leader or give up on a dream. When things are going well you will find that you will have many friends with you along for the ride, but when things start going downhill and the ride requires some sacrifice, those friends will leave.

Jesus saw that many of His followers did not really accept or understand what He said. They descended on Him in Capernaum with great expectations but then they found His words "a hard teaching" (cf. v. 60). Besides, it offered no material benefit, or even a promise of material benefit. They also just went along "for the ride". They joined in the glory days of crowds flocking to Him and to baskets full of bread. But when His teachings no longer suited their expectations, they said, "Goodbye, Capernaum! Goodbye Jesus!" and went back to their homes.

This is still happening, even today. How often have I seen people all fired up with enthusiasm, joining the church. They want to do things. They have big plans. And after a few months they disappear as suddenly as they appeared. This could happen to a relationship, to a friendship, to a partnership, to any commitment. Probably because we are human and lack wisdom. We do not have enough perseverance, we have our own hidden agendas and in addition, we lack the faith or spiritual eyes to see the unseen.

Jesus saw it for what it was. He did not run after His former followers. He let them go. From then onwards the road would become steeper for Him. And when we find the road becoming steeper for us, He can help and He understands. After all, He experienced and witnessed it Himself.

Lord, we often disappoint You and turn away from You. Bring us back through the whispering of Your Spirit in our hearts, "My child, come back, I understand."

WHO ELSE?

Lord, to whom shall we go? You have the words of eternal life (John 6:68).

This is one of the most touching responses in the entire Bible – a small confession, "Lord, to whom (else) shall we go? We are dependent on You because You speak the language of eternal life." Therefore, You know the direction. You know what it is all about. Who else would know?

Simon Peter realized that you really only have one choice: either you choose Christ with all the accompanying problems of understanding and not understanding, with human faith and the lack of faith, the entire "risk" with God; or you choose the ghastly, yawning abyss of nothingness, the darkness of total chaos, the confusion of the full realization of the futility of it all, with no purpose, no plan and no meaning.

The followers who deserted Jesus went back to their homes and said that they had expectations, but that they would rather continue with their daily existence, going nowhere. The handful of disciples who stayed with Jesus probably knew that they opted for the "difficult" choice. Their leader did strange things and said even stranger things.

But Peter and the others also sensed that the option of nothingness meant choosing chaos. The option of Christ is no easy option, but essential for people who realize that there is more to life than the here and now.

With this realization our spiritual eyes open. This choice is the beginning of a new birth, as Jesus wanted Nicodemus to understand. And this choice inevitably results in this statement, "We know that You are the Holy One of God" (v. 69).

After this, the disciples would experience great things in the presence of Jesus, but also terrible things, because the traitor was one of them (cf. v. 71). But after this they belonged to Jesus. And Christ belonged to them. And in His light they could tackle chaos and problems. Just as we can.

You are the only One to whom we can go, whom we can approach, and with whom we can stay.

A LACK OF FAITH

For even His own brothers did not believe in Him (John 7:5).

In business and especially in the media industry, public relations officers must see to it that the organization which they represent gets the best publicity and the greatest public exposure possible.

Jesus' brothers should have been public relations officers. They wanted Him to go to Judea, because "no one who wants to become a public figure acts in secret" (v. 4). But these public relations officers did not really believe in their "product". In fact, they wanted to test Him to see whether He would dare to go to Judea where the Jews wanted to kill Him. In reality, they were cynical public relations officers of unbelief, exactly like the devil in the desert.

There is no consensus about Jesus' brothers. According to some narratives, He was an only child – supported by the fact that, at the cross, Jesus entrusted His mother to John. The word brother can also mean half-brothers or cousins and in some cultures, especially in the East, you refer to people close to you as "my brother" or "my sister".

Regardless of the specific kinship, people who were close to Him did not believe in Him. This is not unusual. A major organization decided to abolish the opening of meetings with prayer, "because it could offend someone". The proposal – with fitting words – came from a pastor.

Sometimes the biggest lack of faith or misguided belief originates from the "brotherhood" of the church. This is the reality of being human. But Jesus seeks His "brothers and sisters" in a different way: He seeks those who become one with Him in purpose and life: doing the will of the Father. He seeks those with faults, but who are willing to acknowledge that. He seeks those who fall, but who get up again with His help. He seeks those who do not want to face a single day without Him. *They* are His true public relations officers.

That is what we want to be, Lord, people of truth, people who reflect something of You, people who live through You and people through whom You live here on earth.

STREAMS OF BLESSINGS

"Whoever believes in Me, as the Scripture has said, streams of living water will flow from within him" (John 7:38).

Jesus taught in the temple, to the surprise of the high priests and the teachers of the law, who wanted to arrest Him. He previously taught about bread. Here, as with the Samaritan woman, He speaks about water. Streams of water, blessings, will flow from within the one who believes. "By this He meant the Spirit" (v. 39).

The Holy Spirit is the Spirit of the Father and the Son. Where Jesus is God *with* us, the Spirit is God *in* us. This results in abundant faith.

In the street next to ours, people drilled for water in their backyard. They hit such a strong underground watercourse that the water spontaneously gushed from the hole for days, running down the sidewalk. In our street, numerous neighbors drilled for water in vain. They either found very small quantities that only lasted for a few days, or nothing at all. There is no underground water here.

The Source of life becomes stronger and more intense in people who believe. It is like the water in the street next to mine. It flows spontaneously through them and from them, comforting others. A person with little faith or no faith is like our street: there is no underground watercourse and no water. Someone like that can communicate nothing of worth and is of no spiritual value to others, even though, like the chief priests in the temple, they might know everything about the law and the prophets.

Water gives life. I am sometimes amazed when I see the water after a good season of rain gushing in streams from the hills, as if it comes from deep within the earth. This explains what Jesus meant with, "Streams of living water will flow from within him." We must constantly pray that the Spirit of Jesus will stream through us. That is God's big source of water. This is how God "flows through us". Otherwise our boreholes will run dry, our courage will weaken, our hope will fade, and our work will be futile.

Lord, it is water that we seek. Living water, so that we may turn into a fountain for You and so that Your Spirit may flow through us and bless us.

THE MASTER

No one ever spoke the way this man does (John 7:46).

The clouds were gathering around Jesus' head. The chief priests and teachers of the law sent the temple guards to arrest Him. They came back empty-handed and said, "No one ever spoke the way this man does."

He could convey eternity to people in straightforward language and with divine conviction. But this was also the reason why they wanted to arrest Him: the chief priests were also teachers and they felt threatened. Threatened in terms of their own positions, and threatened in terms of what they themselves taught. Jesus had to go!

They pretended not to be impressed, but if they were not impressed, why then were they so agitated by what He said with authority about the Scriptures? Why were they so enraged when He healed a man on the Sabbath while they themselves performed sacrificial offerings on the Sabbath? They said that He was only followed by "this mob that knows nothing of the law" and that "there is a curse on them" (cf. v. 49). Or could they privately have sensed that their ruthless law, which did not tolerate healing on the Sabbath, was becoming obsolete?

Nicodemus cautiously asked why they were acting so cruelly towards the Teacher. They scolded him. Perhaps they clearly sensed that Jesus was in a totally different league to their own. Like George Herbert sings of Jesus, "I got me flowers to strew Thy way; I got me boughs of many a tree; / But Thou wast up by break of day ..." (from *Easter*).

In a manner of speaking Jesus "rose earlier" than the teachers of the people. He was and is *the* Master. He teaches like no one else. He sacrifices nothing but Himself. He has no other agenda but to save us. He seeks no other acknowledgment than a love for God. He does not spend His time on trivialities, but He teaches us, heals us and comforts us. Even though they seek His downfall – He remains the Master always!

Lord, You are our Teacher. Today we want to do what You teach.

CHARGE AND EXONERATION

"If any one of you is without sin, let him be the first to throw a stone at her" (John 8:7).

As a journalist and editor, I was always surprised to see how "moral" misdemeanors of well-known people made the headlines. It was most often reports written and tales told by people who would often not pass moral tests either – which in fact includes all of us.

Since the time of Jesus and even before, man has not changed a bit. In many respects we are all still pious Pharisees who pretend to be serious about the law. And yet we like a sensational and juicy(!) incident; probably because we recognize something of ourselves in it and we want to hang it on the handle of someone else's front door. Matthew Arnold said that the high morality of some people covered the entire city, but stopped short of their own front door.

The temple chiefs dragged a woman to Jesus. According to the law, she had to be stoned. They said they knew what the law stated, but they wanted to know what Jesus had to say. A clever trap set for the Master. And the Master wrote on the ground – words over which there has been much speculation, even of the words being accusations against the accusers themselves. When Jesus spoke His famous words about the first stone, they disappeared, "the older ones first" (cf. v. 9).

Everybody left except the woman and Jesus' famous exoneration followed. It is only divine wisdom that can read and understand a situation so completely; who knows people so well. There is pure majesty in the words, "Neither do I condemn you. Go now …" "You're dismissed." Stop sinning.

Jesus is the Teacher and the Judge, the Man of wisdom, insight and grace. If this behavior reflects God's "program", then I thank God for being my God; I thank Jesus that He came: I pray for streams of blessings and grace and wisdom to flow from within me through His Spirit.

Lord, we cannot but worship You. You are filled with mercy and majesty!

MARCH

Lord, My God

The past two months are only memories now.
Teach me to cherish and nurture mine.
Especially let me enjoy the richness of the good days
and learn the sometimes bitter lessons of the bad days.
When I page through Your Bible,
voices from the distant past speak to me;
voices of people who passed away,
but continue to counsel and console;
voices of Moses and Your people;
voices of Jesus and His disciples;
voices of belief and unbelief.

I am filled with awe and amazement
about the way things have changed, fashions and habits,
but how man remains essentially the same through the ages.

We all need a Savior.
We thirst for You every day,
because our every step becomes part of the past,
just like every breath we take.
We are not much more than a breath in eternity.
And yet we are so precious to You that You came to teach us
through Your people and through Your Son,
and especially now through Your Spirit.
You sanctify us so that we may sanctify others.
For that I thank You.

Amen.

GOD OF DARKNESS

The people remained at a distance, while Moses approached the thick darkness where God was (Exod. 20:21).

After God had spelled out the basic principles of the law to His people, He was ready to explain His Commandments in more detail. But the people had had enough and Moses had to speak on their behalf. Moses then approached the "thick darkness where God was".

This is the other side of God, who is light, and Jesus who calls Himself the light of the world. Here God concealed Himself in the darkness of a pitch-black cloud that hovered strangely and awe-inspiringly over the mountain. God had retreated. And with this retreat into darkness He prepared Himself to communicate with the leader of His people about how He was guiding them to the Promised Land.

Moses approached. He had already met God at the burning bush and a few other times. Here he entered the darkness *where God was*.

The Lord appears in many guises and He has many ways in which He reveals Himself. Here, for the sake of His people, He concealed Himself. There are many opposing truths about God that seem to contradict one another and yet complement one another as a unit: God is love and judgment; God is light and darkness; God is law and grace; God requires respect, but embraces us in love.

Many of the Lord's children sometimes find themselves, like Moses, facing a dark cloud in their lives. Or they are in the depth of darkness. But like Moses, we have to face it and go through it, because there God speaks to us. One is extra observant in the dark, and one listens carefully to the sounds of the night.

God's darkness is often a sign that you have to listen very attentively: He wants to speak to you and He wants to guide you. He wants to assure you of His closeness. He wants you to ask Him to take your hand, and to lead you step by step into the light.

When darkness surrounds me, Lord, make me aware of the fact that You have an appointment with me, and that You want to meet me and bestow Your blessings upon me as You did with Moses.

PRACTICAL ADVICE

"You are to be My holy people" (Exod. 22:31).

After Moses' encounter with God, he returned with practical instructions on how the people were to live as God's holy people. They had to strive to honor Him and to do what He commanded them to do.

Here, and also later in the Bible, we find a whole series of instructions, some primitive (the death penalty was immediately applied to a variety of offences; there were, after all, no jails in the desert). Some laws concerned cleanliness and the prevention of disease (there were no hospitals in the desert). Others were simply good principles that are just as valid today, "Do not spread false reports" (which is at times a problem for many of us). "Do not follow the crowd in doing wrong" (today known as giving in to "peer pressure"). "When you give testimony in a lawsuit, do not pervert justice by siding with the crowd" (a problem even for leaders) (cf. Exod. 23:1-3).

The Israelites consecrated themselves to God and so must we. That means that we have to examine everything carefully before our conscience and before God and not just go with the flow. We must remember that it is God's honor that is at stake in our lives (a problem for us because we often fail the test).

He requires holiness (something we only have a vague understanding of). He requires respect (which we taint with exaggerated piety). He requires adherence to His principles (He often says, "I am the Lord").

The laws were to His glory and for Israel's own salvation; good advice, like that of a caring father. And the full message is: "I want to be your God. I *am* your God. You must honor Me and I will honor you." That is the core principle that we can test under all circumstances. That is exactly how it works.

We often seek advice. Teach us to apply Your advice to our daily needs, especially to avoid the potholes and the stones.

ANGEL AHEAD OF ME

"See, I am sending an angel ahead of you to guard you along the way" (Exod. 23:20).

This is a wonderful promise and a great comfort. The angel will "bring you to the place I have prepared. Pay attention to him" (vv. 20-21). It is a guardian angel from God, a protecting angel, a guiding angel, a fighting angel.

One would expect the angel to bring them to places of peace. However, the opposite is true: God warned Moses about what was in store for them. "My angel will bring you into the land of the Amorites, Hittites, Perizzites, Canaanites, Hivites and Jebusites" – all of them enemies of God's people who would try and make life unbearable for them – "and I will wipe them out."

One major fact stands out time and again in the molding of God's people: they were not spared from conflict and storms; in fact, they were led into crises and were honed, like soldiers are honed in tough boot camps. But the angel was sent ahead of them, and God helped them in their struggle.

Hannah Pearsall Smith tells the story of someone who got hold of the pupa of an Emperor Moth. When the moth started its struggle to break free from its cocoon, the woman cut the cocoon open with a pair of scissors to free the moth. By doing this she "delivered" a moth that would never be able to fly, because its wings remained limp. The struggle to break free from the cocoon is necessary to allow the wings to open properly and the distinctive colors to develop fully.

That is how it is with God's children. We have to learn to "fly". We must spread our wings fully. We must learn to live and walk in the steps of the angel who is sent before us.

Lord, I know that You sent Your angel ahead of me. The thought comforts me when I struggle over rough terrain.

LITTLE BY LITTLE

"Little by little I will drive them out before you, until you have increased enough to take possession of the land" (Exod. 23:30).

This is one of the most-loved verses of the great nineteenth century London preacher, Charles H. Spurgeon, who led crowds of people to the Lord. People constantly wanted to know from him: Why is the life of a Christian so hard at times, the enemies so many, the resistance so fierce, and why does God work so slowly that at times one can almost not see it?

This verse was one of his most popular answers. God said He would drive His people's enemies out before them "little by little", in other words, gradually, until they were strong enough to take possession of the land. The Lord never rushes. God is eternal and He progresses step by step, day after day, "little by little".

The Roman poet Virgil said that Rome was built the day the first brick was laid. The principle was in place. The rest would follow. This is how God works with His Creation and His people.

To obtain something instantly is to go against the entire principle of Creation. To give your child the most expensive gifts straightaway is to deny him the adventure of chasing after a dream. The things that make memories are the difficult times that you share with your parents, partner or child.

The Israelites complained bitterly about everything that they had to give up. They would cry and meet with adversity, but "little by little" their enemies were driven away. We too will progress "little by little". "Little by little" we will come closer to God's purpose for us. "Little by little" we will start feeling … that we are winning.

We respect Your methods, Lord. But grant us a bit more light so that, at times, we can see something of our progress.

A CONSUMING FIRE

On the seventh day the LORD called to Moses from within the cloud.
To the Israelites the glory of the LORD looked like a consuming fire on
top of the mountain (Exod. 24:16-17).

When you read the Bible numerous contradictions strike you;
contradictions that seem strange but in the end form a powerful pattern of unity: God is a God of the eternal and immeasurable –
and to us sometimes irreconcilable – facets which create a mystical
impression of transparent perfection, that at the same time conceals
as much as it illuminates. How else, if we truly want to commune
with God in a profound way? He is after all God the LORD, "*Yahweh*",
"I am who I am".

First, the Lord was inside a dark cloud. Here He is in the light
again, in a cloud "like a consuming fire on top of the mountain".
Which is more awe-inspiring: the darkness or the consuming cloud
of fire?

But Moses had to enter into it once again. The Lord called him
closer. He went further up the mountain; a man in the full strength
of his wisdom, leadership and faith. One can see him ascending the
mountain of fire; small and alone on a rough path to another encounter with God, more intimate than at the burning bush long before.

He did not receive his instructions while sleeping soundly in his
tent. He did not sit like a prophet under a tree waiting for illumina-
tion. Nowhere do we read that Moses invented doctrines: he climbed
the mountain of fire with difficulty to listen to God's instructions,
specifically about the tabernacle service. Because this service would
later become the communication line between God and His people.

We sometimes think that God does not know that we are in the
darkness, or struggling up a mountain of fire. We even start doubting whether He cares, and whether He is who He says He is. That
is when we most often start experiencing God's presence, because
in the fire and in the dark He often calls us closer, sometimes to stay
particularly close to Him for a certain time.

Lord, Consuming Fire of darkness, we want to be with You.

OUR IDOLS

"Do not be angry, my lord," Aaron answered. "You know how prone these people are to evil" (Exod. 32:22).

If God's appearances represent a perpetual variety, then human behavior through the ages has followed a predictable pattern of highs and lows, of good and evil. The Israelites were delivered by God, addressed by God, agreed to everything in the law of God, and danced with tambourines before God. But the moment Moses turned his back and went up the mountain where he stayed with God for forty days, they became impatient and very quickly made themselves another god. And around this god, a calf that the high priest had made of gold, they danced in cultic song and celebrations (cf. v. 18).

God was enraged. Moses was furious and he threw the tablets of stone on the ground, breaking them. Aaron shrugged his shoulders, "You know how prone these people are to evil." Therefore they are to blame. He, who stood with Moses before the Pharaoh, apparently allowed himself to be led by "the people".

This is a hackneyed excuse used by leaders. When Hitler nearly destroyed his people, he wrote in one of his very last letters that the Germans were so useless that they did not deserve to exist. Aaron even told a foolish lie: that he threw the gold into the fire, "and out came this calf!" And interestingly enough, in modern politics one regularly comes across this kind of behavior and lies. It is also the fate of cultures and churches that make calves of gold and whose leaders do not tell the truth.

It is the fate of each one who so easily forgets about God and who is so quick to follow other gods or schools of thought, or fashionable theologies. We forget about God's miracles in our lives and look for other solutions when it seems as if God is far away. And in the meantime, He is in the cloud on the mountain. Did the Israelites ever look up? Is our problem that we fail to look up?

Lord, make me constantly aware of You. Help me to look up to You. Calm me down when I become doubtful. And protect me from disaster.

NOT WITH US; YET WITH US

"Go up to the land flowing with milk and honey. But I will not go with you, because ... I might destroy you on the way" (Exod. 33:3).

A well-known philosopher once made the following candid remark, "If I were God, I would have written off the entire earth as a failed experiment long ago and destroyed it in a collision with another planet." He said this to shock people. But people who knew the Bible were not surprised. They knew that in many cases in the Bible, God almost reached the end of His inexhaustible patience, only to soften and forgive again, but mostly not without a sound lesson.

A terrible punishment befell the Israelites and God spoke harshly to Moses, "I will not go with you because I might destroy you." The truth is that He sometimes draws back from people who ignore Him to follow their own thoughts, notions, activities or gods. And then one day they realize that God is no longer with them. A great man of God, Peter Marshall, once prayed, "What happened between You and me, God?"

Like me, you have probably also asked this question, because without God and with only our "idols", we become lonely and the world seems empty. The Israelites experienced this and, since leaving Horeb to move on, they "stripped off their ornaments" (cf. v. 6). It was a sign of remorse. And God saw it, just as He beholds our broken hearts when our tears turn into silver prayers from a heart overflowing with guilt and want.

Then the Lord softened toward Moses, "My Presence will go with you, and I will give you rest." Moses replied that they did not want to go anywhere without God's Presence. And God said that He would do what Moses asked.

The marvel of our Father is that we often disappoint Him terribly, but He is quick to forgive. And, of course, we cannot go anywhere without Him.

Lord, I disappoint You and sometimes I lose You. But You are always there. Thank You.

TO SEE GOD

Then Moses said, "Now show me Your glory" (Exod. 33:18).

The Lord spoke to Moses directly, as a man speaks with his friend (cf. v. 11). But Moses wanted more: he wanted to see God's glory, God Himself, because he had perceived God's presence in various forms before. To see God in His true glory is actually the yearning of every human heart.

It is as if everything within us calls out: Show me Your glory, only once, because I am tired of continuing in faith without seeing You. My faith is worn-out and the world is desolate. Voices call from all over and confuse me. Things happen that make no sense to me at all. Show me Your glory but once.

Should this happen, we will obviously keep asking, like people in love who assure one another repeatedly of their love, and never tire of it. God pointed out the danger to Moses: He lives in a dimension that is not accessible to man, not even to Moses. It would be like someone who walks into the heart of a nuclear power station without wearing protective clothing. If He had granted Moses' request, Moses would have died.

And yet God understood and He said that He would cause His "goodness" to pass in front of Moses. He would protect Moses with His own hands in a cleft in the rock so that Moses would "see His back". But God's face, the way He really looks, no man can see.

There is a great truth hidden in this – what really matters in life (like love) can open doors, but can also close doors. The Dutch poet, Marsman, said that those who are intent on finding explanations for everything tarnish reality. For example, when love becomes "commonplace", it fades away. The adventure lies in the mystery. To observe belongs to a higher, more profound, dimension.

We know that we cannot see You. Therefore, make us aware of Your presence and glory in our lives – in the eyes of someone we love; or when we look at something beautiful.

TO STAND WITH GOD

Then the LORD came down in the cloud and stood there with him and proclaimed His name, the LORD (Exod. 34:5).

When God appeared to Moses, it was a gesture of love. God came and "stood with" Moses. This is a gesture of comfort. Moses had to make a sacrifice for this wonderful experience and early in the morning he had to climb Mount Sinai because God said, "Present yourself to Me there on top of the mountain" (v. 2).

Soul-stirring. It is a prominent theme in the Word of God: Wait there for Me because I will certainly come and stand next to you.

The Lord came to Moses, and Moses climbed the mountain to the Lord. There was movement from both sides, like with conversion, like being born-again, like the mystery of great love. This was probably a once-in-a-lifetime experience for Moses, a sensing of the rustling of eternity, an awareness of strength that was inexplicably joyful. He had to be alone with God. No one else was allowed on the mountain.

Macharios, one of the Hesychastic fathers (*hesychia* means tranquility), writes, "The one who wants to approach the Lord while the Lord is approaching at the same time, must approach with undivided attention, focused on the Lord, with an effort of the heart and with austerity of thought." It is difficult but attainable – especially in times of retreat. Just you, your thoughts and your heart focused on God.

And then you have to wait, which is perhaps the biggest stumbling block. The Lord will come and reveal His will and His law to you. Perhaps we will then feel what the poet Gerard Manley Hopkins wrote, "The world is charged with the grandeur of God. It will flame out, like shining from shook foil" (from *God's Grandeur*).

O Lord, come and stand with me, next to me, and let me see You in the grandeur of Your world, like endless strips of shook foil that unfold and shimmer in the light of a million stars.

THE RADIANT FACE

When Moses came down from Mount Sinai with the two tablets of the Testimony in his hands, he was not aware that his face was radiant because he had spoken with the LORD. When Aaron and all the Israelites saw Moses, his face was radiant, and they were afraid to come near him (Exod. 34:29-30).

After forty days on the mountain, Moses returned to his people with two stone tablets with the law written on them. After such a long time in the presence of the Lord, his face was radiant. Something of the splendor of God had rubbed off on him.

To experience the splendor of God personally, to feel it radiating from your face like a warm glow, to physically reflect something of the glory of God to such an extent that others draw back from it, unable to look at it: what an immense mystery and sublime incident this must have been!

Michelangelo's famous statue of Moses in the San Pietro in Vincoli in Rome, reflects something of this mystery: with a mistake in it! Translators of old translated "radiance" as "horns" and Michelangelo portrayed Moses with two small, blunt horns. He sits there with his tablets of stone, his fiery eyes, prominent nose, strong arms, and shoulders and strong legs. Perhaps something of God also radiated from Michelangelo when he chiseled this magnificent work. It is as if a supernatural majesty, horns and all, radiates from it.

It is probably the desire of every heart that is focused on God to have something of His splendor radiating from our faces and our actions. Most often this does not happen, but sometimes it does, although not nearly in the way that Moses reflected the glory of God.

I was still young when I saw Michelangelo's statue of Moses for the first time. I have grown old and I don't know if I have ever experienced anything like that. But we continue to strive towards it and, perhaps one day God will radiantly break through in something that we do or say or experience, a part of Himself that will briefly light up the mundane with eternal grace and awe.

We seek Your splendor, Lord, especially in our sometimes dull lives. We seek Your splendor.

GOD OF BEAUTIFUL THINGS

All the Israelite men and women who were willing brought to the LORD freewill offerings for all the work the LORD through Moses had commanded them to do (Exod. 35:29).

Moses was instructed by God to build a place of worship, a tent, a tabernacle, "God's house". It had to be beautiful and no inferior work was allowed. God "lives" in a tent, but God remains God. Majesty.

Out of their own free will, the people brought some of their most cherished possessions, jewelry and gold (they must have taken quite a lot from Egypt!) to decorate the Tent of Meeting. Two artists were appointed, Bezalel and his assistant, Oholiab, "to make artistic designs for work in gold, silver and bronze, to cut and set stones, to work in wood" (vv. 32-33). They also had to embroider "blue, purple and scarlet yarn and fine linen" (v. 35). The true artist spares no trouble. In the tent the ark of the covenant, the table for the sacrificial bread, the lampstand, the altar of incense, the altar of burnt offering and the bronze basin for washing would be placed; everything made of precious materials, even the priestly garments. Therefore, no trouble was spared.

To read about these ancient objects and God's instructions to His people and the problems surrounding this (they would for example, have to work very carefully with the burnt offerings in a big tent) in the often harsh circumstances on the road, reminds us that God is a God of beautiful things. It is true that we can worship Him under a tree, or in a large, modern hall without any trimmings. But the Tent of Meeting does say something: that the Lord also seeks the hand of the artist, the combination of beautiful things in His place of meeting.

Sometimes one's taste for beauty can get a bit dull. And God is a God of style. All art comes from Him and flows to Him. Everything that we do with commitment and sacrifice for Him is accepted by Him with love. The gold and jewels of His Creation in the holy place were beautiful to Him. How beautiful He created the earth for us.

Lord, let me serve You, even though it may only be with a clean face, or with something good that I can do to glorify You.

MAGNIFICENCE!

Then the cloud covered the Tent of Meeting, and the glory of the LORD filled the tabernacle (Exod. 40:34).

The tabernacle had been completed. The Lord could "move in" and initially not even Moses was allowed to enter the Tent of Meeting. The Glorious Presence or the *shekinah* glory as the Jewish rabbis would refer to it, the "cloud" as a sign of God's Presence, filled it completely.

From then onwards, a remarkable "ritual" was established: "In all the travels of the Israelites, whenever the cloud lifted from above the tabernacle, they would set out; the cloud of the LORD was over the tabernacle by day, and fire was in the cloud by night, in the sight of all the house of Israel during all their travels" (vv. 36, 38).

What would we give for such a visible cloud! How often are we not confronted with questions about when to continue and where we need to go. How much easier would a cloud have made our decisions: about a relationship, a job, moving to another place, a change in attitude. When the cloud moves, we know we should go along. When the cloud remains stationary, we know it is time to pause.

And yet, one assumes that the Israelites, regardless of cloud and fire, still made mistakes during their journey. It is human. Regardless of the Word and the sacrament and modern miracles, we still make mistakes. In our modern world, we would have been quick to analyze the cloud and the fire and find a rational explanation for them.

But the faithful know, if we want to follow the Lord, He will lead us. Often along detours and strange routes. This miracle still happens, the angel is still sent ahead of us and the cloud still moves.

Lord, stay with me, even though I cannot see You. Let me do only Your will. I live in Your magnificence.

HEAD OR TAIL?

The LORD will make you the head, not the tail. If you pay attention to the commands of the LORD your God that I give you this day and carefully follow them, you will always be at the top, never at the bottom. Do not turn aside from any of the commands I give you today, to the right or to the left, following other gods and serving them (Deut. 28:13-14).

We usually feel as if we are the tail in life. We look at other people and think they have everything: they must be the Lord's "head". In my life I have met the greatest nobility, people who are the Lord's "head", in the simplest of dwellings. And sometimes, inside the high walls of palatial houses, I have seen the most dreadful spiritual and emotional misery – the "tail".

God's people received detailed commands, some harsh, some perhaps far too harsh, some beyond their understanding. But when one looks beyond the detail to the greater message of the law, it is simply that they had to refrain from worshiping other gods, and love God and one another. Then they would be the "head" and not the "tail". You can have nothing in your pocket, but still be filled with the assurance that God is with you. That is if you listen to what God is whispering. The nineteenth-century poet and priest John Bode prayed,

O let me hear Thee speaking
In accents clear and still,
Above the storms of passion,
The murmurs of self-will.
O speak to reassure me,
To hasten or control;
O speak, and make me listen,
Thou Guardian of my soul.

If we want to be at the top, the "head", we must stay close to the Head. Or rather go and sit at His feet to listen. If we want to be the "tail" we must simply pretend not to know or hear.

I will listen, Lord.

MAN OF GOD

This is the blessing that Moses the man of God pronounced on the Israelites before his death (Deut. 33:1).

Some people are honored with medals or degrees at the end of their career. Such as the old DES (Decoration for Excellent Service) or the LH (Legion d'Honneur), the famous French Legion of Honor. Moses received the greatest award ever in the Word of God.

Behind his name was written MOG: "Man of God." Higher than a noble knight, higher than an honorary doctorate, higher than a king and an emperor. In this capacity he blessed the people for the last time and pronounced one prophecy after the other, tribe after tribe.

He spoke with the voice of a poet, "The eternal God is your refuge, and underneath are the everlasting arms" (v. 27). Behind all his pronouncements lay a lifetime of experience, of falling and getting up again, of trials and triumph, of irritation and faith, of God and God once more.

To be blessed by such a man is a privilege. To experience the wisdom of such a person is a bonus. Not everyone is privileged enough to have a teacher who knows what he is talking about. Moses was their teacher.

Jesus is our Teacher. The line runs from Moses to Jesus, Jesus the true Man of God, the Son of God, God in the flesh.

The Israelites found it difficult to understand and obey Moses' instructions – God's Commandments – even though they were God's people, as we are God's people in Christ. We also find it difficult.

We believe, yes, but we stumble in our words and fall flat in our deeds. We try to be people of God. We cannot write Man or Woman of God behind our names. And yet we can, although in small letters, because Christ came to us and sacrificed Himself on our behalf.

———

Man of God, we also want to be men of God. That is what we can be through You. Thank You, Lord.

FINAL ACT

And Moses the servant of the LORD died there in Moab, as the LORD had said. His eyes were not weak nor his strength gone (Deut. 34:5, 7).

The poignant final chapter in the final act of one of the greatest people who ever lived, starts with the brief narrative, "Then Moses climbed Mount Nebo from the plains of Moab to the top of Pisgah, across from Jericho. There the LORD showed him the whole land" (v. 1).

And Moses looked and looked, as far as the sea to the west and the palms of Jericho near by. He could see all of it and see it clearly because at his advanced age, his strength remained. What else could be expected from a man who constantly had the presence of God shining upon him?

A middle-aged man who spent his last days paralyzed, sat looking at the sea day after day from his flat: the waves, the wind and the passing ships. "It is so good", he told visitors, "that I can sit here as if I have an appointment with the Lord, and that I may wonder what the world will be like for my children and grandchildren, and that I can revel in it and pray for them."

Moses could see the land of his grandchildren and could lay his hands upon his successor, Joshua. His affairs were in order. God would take over from then on, also regarding his last resting place. A final act to wish for. A life lived to the full.

But above all: a life lived for God and ending in God. He never saw a jet plane or a TV or surfed the Internet. But he saw God. And it is God whom we want to see. And God in whom we long to live.

Eternal God, God of Moses, Father of Jesus Christ, my Father: teach me something of Moses and everything of Christ.

THE MASTER SERVANT

After that, He poured water into a basin and began to wash His disciples' feet (John 13:5).

The life of Jesus was in its final act, just like that of Moses at the end of Deuteronomy. But, where Moses' end was the conclusion of a full life, Jesus' end was the true purpose for His coming to earth: He had to take the entire fate of all people – past, present and future – on His shoulders and had to place Himself on the altar in one glorious deed of redemption.

It was the last time that Jesus and His disciples would celebrate and share a meal. They were celebrating His death and the disciples were not even aware of it. They celebrated God's salvation. They knew something of that because they knew about the Passover, but they knew nothing of what would happen in the following few hours, or of the divine meaning of it all.

During such a large meal a servant normally washed the invited guests' feet – it was simply good manners in times of dusty roads and open sandals. However, Jesus the Lord, was doing it here. He washed everybody's feet, including those of Judas. And Peter's, who initially protested and who would later disown Him.

Jesus asked if they understood what He had done: a deed that they had to do for one another, a deed of redemption, the washing away of sin. Obviously they understood nothing. Jesus had been teaching them for a long time, but they grasped very little, if any, of what was going on.

Perhaps 2,000 years later we still do not grasp it. To be one another's servant, is one of the most neglected virtues of Christianity. This is because it is not easy. To understand the Cross is totally beyond our comprehension. Jesus has to teach us over and over, insight upon insight, touch upon touch, cleansing upon cleansing, washing upon washing … until something of the mysticism of His Being and conduct starts to dawn and gladden our hearts.

Lord Jesus, for this we pray: that You will continue teaching us through Your Spirit and through what You do, and that we may follow in Your footsteps, even though we might be like infants stumbling after their mother.

A LESSON IN BETRAYAL

"He who shares My bread has lifted up his heel against Me" (John 13:18).

Jesus was speaking about the traitor, Judas Iscariot, who sat at the table with Him. He referred to Psalm 41:9. One may well ask whether this terrible incident was necessary. The Jewish chief priests could have arrested Him at any time without Judas' help. If Nicodemus knew where He had been long before, why would the other officials not have known?

Yes, there was such a prophecy, but it was a rather dramatic warning of another kind – the traitor often sits with you at the table. The one who is going to talk to the outside world about what has been said in the inner circle, is *part* of the inner circle.

Working at the newspaper, we were always surprised to see how easily people leaked revealing news from the inner circle of a group or company or party. We cynically regarded it as a part of life, but the Bible also reveals harsh truths about life. After all, it portrays a cross and a cross is often accompanied by betrayal. I am convinced that if Judas, in his remorse, had gone to the cross and knelt there in the blood, the blood that he had helped to spill, Jesus would have forgiven him and reinstated him as a disciple. But, as a "child of the devil", he knew but one road after the betrayal – the abyss.

Judas teaches us vigilance in Christ, and that is a lesson that is hard to learn because the Evil One easily camouflages himself. Much has been written about Judas and his motives, but one fact remains: his type of behavior lives on and, at one time or another, we might even play the role of Judas. That drives us to the cross, calling, "Lord, help! Lord, preserve! Lord, forgive!"

And He does. Always.

Lord, we want to take shelter with You against the heels that are lifted up against us, as well as against the heels that we may want to lift. We want to take shelter beneath Your wings, like weak fledglings take shelter under the hen, like vulnerable plants find shelter against the frost underneath a large tree.

NERVES

"Do not let your hearts be troubled. Trust in God; trust also in Me" (John 14:1).

We often hear of people who "suffer from nerves". Or that such and such a person has had a nervous breakdown. This could mean anything from serious depression to getting a big fright, to rare anxiety attacks, to being upset about something that has happened or is going to happen. The possibilities of "nerves" are and have always been endless, as is the case with any emotional upheaval.

Jesus noticed that His disciples were "very nervous". After all, strange things were happening. Their meal was somber. Jesus said that He was going away and that they could not go with Him. A traitor was exposed in their midst. And Jesus said that Peter would disown Him that very night. Not an easy time for a serious disciple.

But Jesus comforted them. "Trust in God; trust also in Me." These words have comforted disciples of the Savior for ages. Add to it, "I will not leave you as orphans; I will come to you" (v. 18). This probably calmed the disciples down to a certain extent before they would scatter later that night.

There are times of great dismay in the life of any Christian, times when the "nerves" are raw and life is sad and somber. The cause could be congenital. Or the trigger for it could be an external stimulus: shock, loss, disappointment. Then we do not want to feel like "orphans" who have been abandoned by God, people who have lost Him forever (although we could sometimes feel this way). Then we seek assurance. Then we seek the cross. We seek the living Jesus. And He says that He is there. He is near. He will come again. We should be calm.

Of course, we do not calm down – at least not easily. But if we hold on to our faith, if we hold on to the eternal Word, our inner ears will open and hear. And the Spirit will come to our aid because Jesus meant what He said.

Lord, I am sometimes just as alarmed as the disciples. I am nervous. You calm me down. You accompany me into the darkest night. You bring back the light.

SHOW US!

"Lord, show us the Father and that will be enough for us" (John 14:8).

Moses asked to see God after he had already communicated with Him in the desert, on the road and on the mountain. It is a typical human request. One understands the almost muffled request from Philip, one of the quiet disciples: Show us the Father but once and we will be satisfied.

He is looking for reassurance because he does not understand the "complicated" events he is participating in. He does not realize that he is part of a process that will bring about an adjustment in God's entire Creation. I don't think any of us would have understood it: betrayal, suffering, the cross, leaving to come back again … It is too much for the human spirit.

Psychologists know that for a single action to originate from the brain – for example to get up out of your chair – a process of trillions of brain stimuli is required. Within nanoseconds the brain is capable of processing stimuli and planting a simple thought in your mind. How remarkable! However, it is not enough. Regardless of the trillions of stimuli, there are some things that our minds simply cannot handle. It is then that we ask for the easiest solution, "Show us!" However, more often than not, when we have seen, we still do not believe. I recently listened to a stage performer saying how easily he could "read people's minds". Impressive, but I did not believe him at all.

Should Jesus have given the disciples a mere glimpse of the Father – which is in any case impossible – would they actually have believed? Would they have thought that it was a trick? One does not know. Jesus says, "If you know Me, you know the Father." His entire 'program' is in Me. Philip, you were present at all My miracles, but it is not enough."

However, regardless of the slight reproach, Jesus understands human nature. He says: Simply accept My word. I will provide …

Lord, Your Spirit probably sighs at times during our prayers because we understand so little. But You understand that we are human. We accept Your comfort and Your care.

"You will do what I do"

"Anyone who has faith in Me will do what I have been doing. He will do even greater things than these" (John 14:12).

It is a great truth that Jesus pronounced here. One which, in all probability, nobody has yet fully fathomed. It could mean many things and actually Jesus says that we can improve on His work here on earth. In this chapter, He reveals that He is merely the start of the miracles of the New Testament.

He could heal the sick in remarkable ways. Today we can also do it with perplexing techniques and remedies. He could never travel further than 200 kilometers. In the space of one day, we can almost fly around the world. He sailed in a small boat and walked upon stormy waters. We have not yet figured out this secret, but people sail on luxury ships that weigh millions of tons, like the Queen Mary II that is several storeys high. We can also have great plans that fail catastrophically. In 1920, an American journalist visited the former Soviet Union and said, "I have seen the future and it works." However, the "future" disintegrated because Christ was not in it.

During his life in the early eighteenth century, John Wesley traveled 25,000 miles on horseback and founded many congregations and preached to more people than Jesus had seen in one place. Billy Graham preached on TV for millions all over the world. The Gospel is spread via books and CDs. Indeed techniques which would have been regarded as great miracles during the time of Jesus.

However, all these things are still of this world. Jesus probably meant that, with faith, we could open doors to the world. My Huguenot ancestors came from France to South Africa as people persecuted for God's name and they glorified His name here. When we pray, we sometimes stand in awe of God's help and intervention. When we work under God's blessing and in worship to Him, great things start to happen. If only we would be willing to risk it with Jesus.

Lord, I don't do many things that are great, but I can pray and work for all those I love, for my neighborhood, for Your world. I believe that in this way You are working greater things through me than when You were here Yourself.

THE SPIRIT WILL TEACH

"But the Counselor, the Holy Spirit, whom the Father will send in My name, will teach you all things" (John 14:26).

One of the disciples, the other Judas, asked Jesus quite reasonably why He only revealed Himself to such a small circle "and not to the world". Could Jesus not have chosen a way of revealing Himself that would have announced Him to the whole of mankind like a burst of thunder? Very early on, the Bible made it clear that God preferred to work with people through a process based on a step-by-step principle: a small beginning; a powerful end.

According to legend, Jesus was asked by the archangels after His ascension, why He did not stay on earth longer to continue His work. Jesus then answered, "It is not necessary, because My servant Peter is there. My servant John is there. All My true apostles are there and I am preparing my servant Paul. After them others will come to continue My work."

This tale teaches us, like the Scripture verse above, that the Lord continues His work on earth through His followers: you and I. The Teacher is the Holy Spirit who teaches us "all things", up to this day. The Spirit fathoms the depths of God and represents in us the lamentation and the expression of the most holy truths and the most profound love from the Father and the Son. It is through the Spirit that we are aware of God. It is through the Spirit that God guides us from within our innermost being.

Bernard of Clairvaux said in his teachings that we should not search for the experience of God, but for the God of experience. It is only the God of experience who can teach us what His Son had to learn as a man. This is worth a thought, because the only way to learn Jesus' way is to be quiet so that the Holy Spirit can blow through us like a fresh breeze, with all the "experience", with all the whisperings of the great imminence of God, regardless of where we find ourselves.

―――――

Spirit of God, teach me today. I am here. I am looking for holy guidance from the God of experience.

JOY

"So that My joy may be in you" (John 15:11).

It was the eve of Jesus' death and He talked about joy. How ironic! He wished His disciples His joy, the joy that is in Him. Such a joy under such circumstances was only possible because He had found an inner point of calm, of stillness, inside Himself. And more than peace and joy flowed from this point – a joy that could even become exuberant in the glory of redeeming grace and faith.

The poet T. S. Eliot captures it in *Burnt Norton*, "At the still point of the turning world. / Neither flesh nor fleshless; / Neither from nor towards; / at the still point, there the dance is ... "

The point of stillness in the storm, the calm inner being, the calmness of the Spirit in our hearts in the midst of the howling wind: that is the divine joy, it turns into a dance! "Except for the point, / the still point, / there would be no dance ..."

I once saw an elderly professor sitting in the park while unwarranted storms were breaking around his head in the press. He sat alone, drinking tea and reading from his pocket Bible. He looked peaceful, almost like he was smiling inside. In the midst of his crisis, he climbed up to God and looked in towards God, and he reached the "still point", because it looked as if he was inwardly dancing. The storms quickly subsided. He "danced on" in God, until God came to fetch him.

The great author Nikos Kazantzakis said, "God is fire, and you must walk upon it, not only walk, but – most difficult of all – you must dance on this fire. And the moment you are able to dance on it, the fire will become cool water; but until you reach that point, what a struggle, my Lord, what agony!"

The suffering. The still point. The fire. The dance. The living water. All of these constitute the joy of which Jesus is speaking. It is a mystical union. It is experiencing God.

Lord, teach us Your dance. Bring us to the still point, like Jesus. Fill us with fire. Refresh us with cool water.

HIS FRIENDS

"I have called you friends" (John 15:15).

Remarkable. Jesus called them "friends" and within a matter of hours, his "friends" would fall into a deep sleep while He struggled in Gethsemane with what awaited Him. Then they fled into the darkness of Jerusalem while Jesus was led away to be tried. And later by the fire, Peter would deny that He had ever known Him. At the cross there was only the man who penned these words, John, the disciple who loved Him, His mother and a few weeping women. His "friends" were not even good students – bridges made of sand, with the courage of jackals slinking away. A somewhat strange but realistically human "circle of friends".

Someone once said that if Jesus had a dog it would have followed Him loyally to the cross. A dog stays at the side of the person it loves, but many "friends" are quick to disappear when adversity strikes. And yet … the disciples sought each other's company again afterwards. They would marvel at all the events happening at the cross and at the grave of Jesus. After His resurrection they would regroup and He would once again reveal Himself to them. And from then onwards they would remain faithful and call out His name before the high priests and all who wanted to listen.

They would really be His friends because, through His Spirit, He walked with them. They would be His companions because a strange, wonderful strength drove them to go everywhere in His name. They would sense a "bond" with Him, regardless of where they were. They would gain courage from the mere thought, "I know the Lord. He calls me His friend." They would sense a love burning inside them like a cleansing fire.

We are also His students, His companions, His friends. At times, we also disappear when He needs us or when we need one another. But, He never goes away from us. He comes when we call, as one would expect from a true Friend.

It is good for us to know, Lord: although we sometimes forget You, You always understand and You always remain our Friend.

GOD LOVES US

"The Father Himself loves you because you have loved Me and have believed that I came from God" (John 16:27).

This is a major consolation, "The Father loves you." It couldn't be any different because Jesus loved His disciples, warts and all, and He and the Father are one. And it is asking a lot of God – to love people: unpredictable, volatile, emotional, striving, dear, unreliable people. But He does, because, in their weak, human way, they did love Jesus and therefore have seized God's "program", although they understood very little of it.

In the Jewish Midrash, there is an interesting story about Isaac, the Patriarch. Isaac is said to have asked the Eternal, "Every time You created something in the beginning, You said that it was good. Light. Plants and animals, the sun and the moon. Every time You said that it was good. Why, when You created man, did You not say that it was good?" Then God answered, "Because man is not yet perfect. He could only become so by obeying the Torah (the law). In this way, he would perfect himself and the world."

However, no man can fully obey the law and be perfected through the law. One Man had to come and do this. That Man, who was more than a man, has the complete love of the Father. And through Him, through the fact that the disciples accepted Him, His love flowed to them, as it flows to us.

Love is many things; among others, a major form of communication, a union of hearts. The Lord grants people the greatest dignity by loving us. The spark of God, the breath of God resides in the human spirit. And within us, resides the deep desire of God's heart, the Holy Spirit, who communicates love and turns our relationship with God into a living spirit-to-Spirit relationship.

Lord, our understanding of what love is, is so limited when it comes to Your love. We often think about romantic love, but the love of Jesus is a Presence, a union, a desire and a prayer for guidance.

THE KING

Jesus said, "My kingdom is not of this world. If it were, My servants would fight to prevent My arrest by the Jews" (John 18:36).

Jesus stood before Pilate and Pilate was clearly impressed by this prisoner, but he did not know what to do with this man whom the Jewish leaders had brought before him. Charles Péguy cynically remarked, "Religion eventually ends in politics." Pilate illustrated this: he thought about political sovereignty, but he did sound sympathetic, "Are you the king of the Jews?" Because, he implied, that his understanding of the Jews was limited.

Everyday modern politics proves that religion and politics could sometimes become horribly intertwined. Jesus was not interested in that. He told Pilate that he had no soldiers. He did not want any territory nor the crown of an emperor. He did not think of that at all. He thought about the kingdom of the freed spirit, of the redeemed person, of people saturated with God. A kingdom that transcended boundaries and time and that was a totally different concept to Pilate's Rome and the emperor's empire.

Yes, Jesus replied: I am a king, but a king of truth, a king of love, king of a kingdom that was there in the very beginning, before the world existed and which will still exist long after Rome and after this world has come to an end. I do not need the power of the sword, Jesus said. He conquers people with love.

One cannot blame Pilate for not understanding any of this. He tried to set Jesus free, but love seldom applies in politics. When love between Ruler and subject is the law, only then such a kingdom becomes divine.

Lord, Your Kingdom has already come in You and we are already citizens, Your subjects. But in You the kingdom will also finally come on the day when You will make everything new.

THE FOOL

The soldiers twisted together a crown of thorns and put it on His head (John 19:2).

It's no fun to be made a fool of. No one likes to be ridiculed. Humiliation and rejection are some of the most hurtful experiences, leaving emotional scars that are difficult to resolve or forget.

In order to sink to the deepest pit of human misery, Jesus also had to face extreme ridicule, otherwise the redemption He brought would not have been complete. He became the clown, the fool, the lunatic, the one with the crown of thorns and the cloak of scorn.

There is considerable evidence that the Romans had some sort of celebration called the Feast of Fools. They would elect a "king" for the day and mockingly bow before him and, sometimes, the king of ridicule was even killed. The soldiers' ridicule of Jesus might have had something to do with this. Perhaps they were only looking for some entertainment, for someone they could laugh at, a Jew who had said that He was the king, but who was brought to justice by the Jews.

The one element that is missing from this ridicule is compassion. In order to make such a horrible fool out of someone implied a total lack of sympathy. In such a situation there are very few who will protect the "fool". After all, everyone is participating in the "fun".

This is a tragic bit of universal truth. The soldiers were unknown, "nameless" people who wielded a little bit of power for a short while. They disappeared over time. But their deeds lived on. And of much greater consequence, the "Fool" also lives on and in His name people are touched and saved. He is still rejected by many, but He is also worshiped by millions. The One who braved the ridicule will handle the ridicule today. He can help us to overcome our own feelings of rejection. He embraces us, He reigns and even the mockers will acknowledge this one day.

Lord, we worship You in earnest as our King with the crown of thorns. Because a King who once wore a crown of thorns will understand us in our desolation and rejection.

Passover Lamb

It was the day of Preparation of Passover Week, about the sixth hour (John 19:14).

When the Israelites fled from Egypt, the Lord commanded them to celebrate Passover every year in commemoration of their deliverance from slavery. And this is indeed true of the Jews: during the time of Jesus they celebrated this major celebration conscientiously. They prepared for it thoroughly, slaughtered the Passover lamb and did everything to the glory of God.

But what they did not know on this morning of preparation was that, in the eyes of God, the last Jewish Passover was about to be celebrated. The dispensation of sacrificial offerings and smoke, of priests who offer redemption and animals being slaughtered, was about to end. The entire nature of worship was about to be changed within hours, because the God who was far away had come closer. The Son of God Himself would brave the sacrificial fire and became the last true Passover Lamb, because God determined the punishment for sin and decided to carry it Himself.

This is a mystery. The patriarch, Irenaeus, wrote that God never announces His work with the sound of trumpets. And He did not do so with the death of the Savior either. Neither with the transition to a new dispensation and a new kingdom that included all the faithful.

In future, the Passover would become a celebration of Christ, thanking God who performs major miracles. Irenaeus wrote that God performed His work via His two "hands": the incarnate Word as the Passover Lamb and the Holy Spirit. The Lord developed His work in the silence of millions of years while He unfolded the powers that were locked in the first seed of Creation. That is the reason for Jesus' silence before Pilate.

But the seed of the new dispensation had been sown early on the morning of the celebration. In future, the Passover would be different. In future, God would be with His people. In future, God would be with you, allowing you to live in the glory of the victory of the Lamb.

Lord, I seek Your imminence, Your festival. I share in the victory of Jesus. Make my day one of victory.

GOING HOME

"Here is your mother" (John 19:27).

This scene has touched people through the ages: a mother with her beloved Son dying on the cross. She stood there, with the other weeping women of Golgotha, to the very end. Tradition wants us to believe that, when they took the body of Jesus down from the cross, she took Him into her arms one last time and He lay on her lap, broken, wounded and covered in blood. In Michelangelo's first famous *Pietà*, the marble statue of Mary and Jesus, he portrayed her with downcast eyes, drenched in sorrow, but almost with a heavenly acceptance.

Woman of sorrows. A sword pierced her heart, as the old prophet Simeon predicted in the temple years ago. We as Protestants are inclined to push Mary to the background; but this woman played a major and mystical role in the life of Jesus. She took care of Him. She followed Him to Jerusalem. Joseph probably died early on and Jesus took care of Mary with His earnings as a carpenter. She was with Him in His forsakenness, witnessing His death.

Dying, Jesus saw her, desolate in her mourning, and He saw His beloved disciple, John, and said, "Here is your son." And to John, "Here is your mother." This was His worldly will, placing Mary in the care of a friend, because they took even His clothes. Strange scenes happened on Golgotha. Unusual roads of God crossed in the life of Mary.

And strange roads of God sometimes cross in our lives. We are part of a mystery, but we miss the acknowledgment of a mystery greater than us. Pain and grace are sometimes inexplicably interwoven. Death is close to life. Defeat is close to victory. Tears are close to comfort. When it turned dark on Golgotha, Mary went home with John. And when the final darkness descends on us here on earth, we will go home with Jesus where we belong, with the Father.

Your plan is a mystery! We know that it all comes from You and we belong with You.

Finished!

When He had received the drink, Jesus said, "It is finished" (John 19:30).

Jesus, the source of living water, was thirsty. Rather ironic, because He was also human and since the previous night He had been pushed around, slapped and ridiculed, while no one really took pity on Him. Someone put a sponge soaked in wine vinegar on a stalk of a hyssop plant and lifted it to His lips – a scant deed of compassion. Wine vinegar was offered as relief. The Son of God experienced all the octaves of sorrow during His suffering, from the low notes of searing pain to the fine, high notes of ridicule and the slight sympathy of wine vinegar.

But now it was finished. Humiliation ends at some point. The Jewish high priests got their way. The crowd who wanted His blood had slipped away, some perhaps with a feeling of emptiness, feeling that they had taken part in an injustice. But they could do nothing about that then. Jesus' body would soon be with His loved ones and they would wash it, anoint it and take care of it. He surrendered His Spirit to the Father.

The bitter part, the sacrificial part, was over and unusual things would happen at the tombs in Jerusalem, as well as in the temple. Jesus would rise early on the Sunday morning and reveal Himself in all His glory to His people.

The Cross bears testimony to the best and the worst that man is capable of. The best because a man (*more* than a man) carried out His divine duty until the end, and the worst because it went hand in hand with the most ghastly actions that man is capable of. Ironically, two traditionally noble institutions were involved in Jesus' death: Jewish devotion and Roman law. How easy it is to tarnish and abuse what is pure! It still happens today.

But where Jesus was concerned, the battle was over. A message of hope radiated from the Cross: the message that God really cares about you and me.

Lord, this I know, this I believe and this I gives me courage for today and for the remainder of my days and unto eternity.

MAJOR TESTIMONY

The man who saw it has given testimony, and his testimony is true. He knows that he tells the truth, and he testifies so that you also may believe (John 19:35).

These are significant words. When someone writes in all earnest, "I saw it. I saw everything. I wrote down what I saw. I know, because I have put everything to the test myself: I speak the truth. And I write it down so that you may also believe that which I saw."

When a reporter wrote such a news report on any noteworthy event, I did not hesitate to publish it straight away. After all, the truth is a scarce commodity in this world. But someone who says what John is saying here would cause me to think twice, a hundred times, should I doubt.

Something in these words shook me when I was a first-year student of Greek and we had to translate this passage in an examination. In the heat of writing the test I suddenly realized – these words carry the full weight of the truth from a man who was close to Jesus and who lived close to God. He put his name on the line for centuries to come, "so that you may believe". I cannot but believe it.

Reporters write about things as they see and experience them. Sometimes they leave something out and add something that might have escaped someone else. John is the faithful reporter, overcome by events, stirred by the overwhelming scenes, touched by the personal love, convinced of the injustice, but jubilant about the victory.

This verse is an anchor for our faith, a firm assurance: this is how it happened. This was how far God was willing to go. That was His love. That was His Great Deed. I may live in this knowledge. This truth gives me strength. He who was crucified is going ahead of me.

Lord, strengthen my faith so that I may "see" it all in my mind, reflect on it, experience it.

BEAUTIFUL GESTURE

At the place where Jesus was crucified, there was a garden, and in the garden a new tomb, in which no one had ever been laid ... they laid Jesus there (John 19:41-42).

A fairly common myth is that the composer Mozart was unceremoniously dumped in a pauper's grave after his death and that no one knows where he was buried. This is not true. According to his biographer, Robert W. Gutman, Mozart was buried after a proper funeral service, but in an ordinary communal grave, as was customary at that time. Only the very rich in Vienna could afford graves, and Mozart was not rich.

During the time of Jesus, owning a private grave was also the privilege of the rich. It was a status symbol. Joseph of Arimathea, a rich follower of Jesus, gave his grave to the Savior and he and Nicodemus, the one who visited Jesus at night, took care of the expensive tending of the body.

What they did was soul-stirring. They prevented the body of Jesus from being thrown on the rubbish dump with those of executed criminals. But today no one knows where the grave was.

In Jerusalem, they show you a church as the place of burial. Outside Jerusalem, they take you to a hill in the shape of a skull with graves in the vicinity, to one that is open to the public, chiseled out of a rock, which is what Jesus' grave probably looked like. One's sentiment says that the body of Jesus rested more or less in a grave like this, and that leaves one with a feeling of great humility and peace.

But what does it really matter that the place of Mozart's grave is not known; his music lives on. And what does it matter that the place of Jesus' grave is not really known? There is nothing to worship because His body was only there for a few days. Soon the grave was empty, because He waited for His disciples at the lake. Just like He waits for you and me. And like we sometimes wait for Him. He will come. He will wait. He will help.

I so want to do something good for You today, something in commemoration of You, something out of gratitude that You live, something for someone in Your name.

APRIL

Eternal God

In the times of the death and resurrection of our Lord,
Jesus Christ, who came to show us Your love,
and to make us part of Your renewal,
and of the recreation of all that You have made,
we search for the point of stillness in our lives,
we search for the wisdom of Your Spirit,
we search for You in everything we see and experience.
We want to stand beside our Savior with His crown of thorns
and move with Joshua into the new month,
and conquer cities and learn the laws of faith
and promise to serve You and join the battle in Your name.

Because victory lies in the cross
and death becomes a gateway to life.
Bless all our loved ones wherever they are.
Bless us where we are, where You have placed us,
even though, at times, we want to flee into the desert
like a dove, like David Your servant, once sighed in song.
Fill us with the courage of Christ
and the will and obedience of Joshua.
Make us strong in our everyday battles
and make us gentle, but inwardly joyful in Your victory.

Amen.

New Journey

"Moses My servant is dead. Now then ... get ready to cross the Jordan River" (Josh. 1:2).

Generations come and go. And often children refuse to accept the fact that their parents are growing old (or they pretend not to believe it!), but you can see it clearly in the mirror.

It is their time now and after theirs it will be their children's time, in the continuous cycle of centuries and millennia. Moses' time was over. It would never be the same again. But the time of Joshua, the son of Nun, had come. He had to lead now.

The Jordan that they had to cross was lying in front of Joshua, just like the grave that Jesus (whose name is also Joshua in Hebrew) had to go through awaited Him. Joshua led the people on a new journey across the wide river, the boundary between alien territory and the Promised Land. Jesus leads His people in a new, transfigured life and sanctifies everything that He touches as God's territory. Joshua led as a warrior. Jesus leads as a King. The old dispensation and the new dispensation ... How intimately they are interwoven and how miraculously the new flows from the old!

Moses served God like no man before him or after him. But God's plan is still continuing to develop as it will until the trumpets announce the grand finale – and a brand new beginning. From the mud of yesterday's rise and fall often grows the flower of today's promise and tomorrow's victory.

Joshua knew that the months and years ahead of him would not be easy. He knew that his people were fickle. But in Moses he had a teacher like no other. And we have Christ as our teacher, Christ who transforms the old to the new, Christ who never changes, but faithfully keeps vigil over His people. He will also guard you today.

Thank You, Lord, whether I come or go, You keep vigil.

BE STRONG!

"Be strong and courageous. Do not be terrified; do not be discouraged, for the LORD your God will be with you wherever you go" (Josh. 1:9).

The Roman orator and statesman Cato said that success was difficult to control but that he was determined to earn it! This is some boasting. Nowhere in the Bible does it say whether Moses, at the end of his life, thought that it had been successful. Neither does anyone know if Joshua, at the end of his life, could write "success" across his life. Only Jesus could claim success by saying, "It is finished!"

But Joshua was not Jesus. Joshua was clearly not brimming with self-confidence. The Lord had to repeat to him a few times, "Be strong and courageous," because the Lord would go with him. On this condition: Joshua had to "meditate on the law day and night" and "do everything written in it" (v 8). This was already a major challenge, because man is fallible, but Joshua rose to it many times in his life. And yet, how can you be "strong and courageous" when you don't feel like that at all? You can take a deep breath and say that the situation is not that bad – and then fail to believe it! You can think positively and tell yourself that you are a success and only need to come out of your shell. Negative thoughts about yourself do not help anyone, especially not yourself. Shakespeare said, "Nor stony tower, nor walls of beaten brass ... / Can be retentive to the strength of spirit ..." (from *Julius Caesar*).

And for an ordinary person to be "strong and courageous" is a matter of praying incessantly, and then going ahead with all your might, doing whatever you have to do or have to contend with. As a result, you are often going to sweat in the process. After all, Jesus sweated drops of blood before His major ordeal. Joshua's patience was tested to its utmost here.

Joshua progressed and Jesus triumphed. We can only be strong in God by praying that we may be able to sense the depth of the Lord's commands and be able to obey them.

Only in You can I be strong, Lord, only through Your strength.

SHAMEFUL SYMBOL OF SALVATION

Unless, when we enter the land, you have tied this scarlet cord in the window ... (Josh. 2:18).

As befits a leader, Joshua first sent a reconnaissance expedition to the city he wanted to invade. Two spies were sent in; they were discovered, hid in the house of Rahab, the prostitute and she secretly helped them to escape down the city wall, using a red rope. They promised her that she and her house would be spared when they attacked the city, if the red rope (the advertisement of her questionable profession) was tied in the same place, almost like the blood on the door frames of Israel during the Egyptian night of death.

A brothel was a convenient hiding place: public and yet with discrete access. But why did this woman of dubious morals not simply hand them over? She said that she had heard about the victorious reputation of the Israelites and that no one could hold out against their God. It had to be something more: could she, despite all her immoral practices, have sensed something about these scouts? Could she have noticed something of the Presence of God in them? It would seem so; almost like Mary Magdalene who sensed God in Christ and anointed His feet. She was also someone with a reputation.

How remarkable: it is as if the Lord sometimes reaches out especially to people with a reputation. Rahab became one of the ancestors of David and Jesus. Mary Magdalene became the first witness to the resurrection of Jesus. The red line of immorality became a symbol of salvation. The cross of death became a symbol of redemption. It is as if God turned values upside-down.

He does it in our lives as well. Each one of us has a reputation", good or not so good. Each of us has something to hide. Nobody, not one of us, is pure. But God hangs a red rope of protection from our windows.

Eternal Father, I know that I am a red rope person, filled with guilt, but also filled with forgiveness. Filled with what is wrong, but also filled with Your love. Filled with shame, but also filled with the joy of being Your child.

YESTERDAY, TODAY, TOMORROW

Joshua said to the priests, "Take up the ark of the covenant and pass on ahead of the people" (Josh. 3:6).

The ark of the covenant was Israel's holiest symbol, the great sign of God's Presence, containing the gold jar of manna, Aaron's staff and the stone tablets of the covenant (cf. Heb. 9:4). The mighty invasion across the Jordan started. Ahead of Israel went the remarkable symbols of God's great deeds of the past, of the entire holy tradition.

We often think this is the wrong way round. After all, tradition is something of the past, it is finalized, history. The clarion call is that yesterday belongs to the past and that it is the future that requires our attention. But God is yesterday, today and tomorrow, and His holy things, the religious cultural things, don't merely form the rearguard: they go in front. People who want to know where they are going have to know where they came from. Everyone has a history, one where God helped. This we must keep in mind for courage and direction. Because there is something holy and reassuring in it. W. B. Yeats says we "Chose for theme / Traditional sanctity and loveliness" (from *Coole Park and Ballylee*).

Our "modern" way of thinking would not have placed the priests at the front of the invasion. Nowadays it is the position for soldiers and tanks. But here the people of God position the objects of God in front. Have we changed our priorities around through the ages?

Most often matters concerning God are not given a prominent position in our lives. Are we aware of the ark, the Presence of God, the required respect for God and God's direction? Or do these things remain somewhere in the background? Irrelevant?

It is a matter of priorities: God, and everything received from Him, first. And then me, following in faith.

Lord, please go in front, especially in memory of all the great things that You have done for us human beings, to strengthen our faith and to keep us on track.

REMEMBER!

In the future, when your children ask you, "What do these stones mean?" tell them that the flow of the Jordan was cut off before the ark of the covenant of the LORD. These stones are to be a memorial to the people of Israel forever (Josh. 4:6-7).

The first Marquis of Halifax, George Savile, a seventeenth-century scholar and student of politics, wrote, "The best way to suppose what may come, is to remember what is past." Recollection is the best preparation for the future. Because, the same centripetal and centrifugal forces that were at work in people, nations, and events during Joshua's time, are still at work today and will still be at work tomorrow and the day after that, to unite or to pull asunder.

Hence, the Israelites had to set up a stone for each tribe as a memorial; a reminder for generations to come that God had performed miracles. The flow of the Jordan was cut off before the people so that they could cross it with the ark ahead of them.

When people grow older, many become overwhelmingly aware of things that happened in the past, especially things in which the hand of God could be seen clearly. It is as if these were "memorial stones", sometimes minor events that constituted a major turning point and which cannot be ascribed to anything other than God's divine intervention. And that happens time and again. T. S. Eliot wrote, "Time present and time past / Are both perhaps present in time future, / And time future contained in time past" (from *Burnt Norton*).

Times blend into one another, good and evil, past and future. It is a sobering thought, but also a consolation: that God, who in the past had caused the waters of my own Jordan to dry up inexplicably before me so that I could get through a crisis, will do so again. And that the Lord will help me not to get caught in the same traps that I was caught in yesterday. Therefore, I will set up "beacons". Thoughts and intentions that I honor and which allow me to take refuge near Christ.

Lord, my times also blend into one another in levels of good and evil. Deliver me from evil so that it may not be repeated, and bless me with the good. I will never forget Your kindness.

THE COMMANDER IS COMING!

Now when Joshua was near Jericho, he looked up and saw a man standing in front of him with a drawn sword in his hand. Joshua went up to him and asked, "Are you for us or for our enemies?" "Neither," he replied, "but as commander of the army of the LORD I have now come." (Josh. 5:13-14).

Israel fulfilled all the required promises and complied with all the customs. They were circumcised as a sign of the covenant and they celebrated the Passover on the plains of Jericho. They were ready for battle and God was now prepared to offer His assistance. God knows His time.

Joshua saw a foreigner near Jericho and wanted to know whether he was for or against Israel. The man had a sword in his hand. He introduced himself as the commander of the Lord's army. Therefore, God would be the Grand Tactician and General in the battle. Joshua also had to take off his sandals, like Moses once, because he was standing on holy ground.

Who was this "man"? Apparently it was God revealing Himself, a divine being or perhaps an angel, or it could even have been Jesus revealing Himself. It is difficult to explain this mystery. Joshua simply accepted the man's word and did not ask any probing questions. He recognized Authority when he saw and sensed it. He knew that he was in the company of a magnificent Presence.

But he was also receptive to this Presence. One wonders whether he, while scouting the territory, did not expect God to reveal a plan to him. And then he received the big assurance: The Commander has come! He returned to the camp with renewed strength.

God will also come in Christ, one day on the clouds, in all His glory. But He will also come today as the Commander in your and my battle. As the Way, the Truth and the Life. As the One who battles on our behalf, while simultaneously sheltering us from whatever may be threatening us.

This we believe, Lord, You are our Commander and Protector.

SHOUT FIRST!

When the trumpets sounded, the people shouted, and ... the wall collapsed; so every man charged straight in, and they took the city (Josh. 6:20).

This must have been an awe-inspiring drama. The procession of priests blowing the trumpets, the armed men, God's ark of the covenant, seven days around the barricaded, walled-in key city of Jericho. And the command was for everything that was seized to go into the treasure-chest of the Lord.

Once again, the Lord's plan of attack and method were completely different from what we would expect. We would think it to be strategically better for the ark, as a holy symbol, to be kept as far away as possible from the line of fighting. But no, the ark was in the frontline.

We would think that the priests could blow the trumpets to their heart's content, but rather in the camp, removed from the battle. Or we might think that, for the sake of the element of surprise, the enemy had to see as little of us as possible, and that we should definitely not expose ourselves by making a noise while marching around the walls. Last but not least, if it were to be a battle of faith with the Lord's commander and the ark at the front, we would expect the walls to collapse first before we sounded the battle-cry to charge.

Even today we still expect God to first perform the miracle in our lives and cause the walls to collapse before we shout in jubilation and take action. God expects us to shout for joy in faith and in expectation first ... and then He causes the walls to collapse before us.

One does not know exactly what God allowed to happen here. An earthquake? A tremor? When Jericho was excavated, it became clear that a catastrophe had caused the walls to collapse. But God made sure that He laid the foundation for victories to come. As He made sure that Jesus Himself laid the foundation for all future victory over death, as well as for our minor, everyday victories. We can trust Him with this: Whether we whisper to Him ... or whether we shout.

Lord, we call, we whisper, we ask, we shout for You. You will do the rest.

JOSHUA AND YET ANOTHER ONE

So the LORD was with Joshua, and his fame spread throughout the land (Josh. 6:27).

In the drama *Henry VIII* by William Shakespeare, Cardinal Wolsey, who had fallen into disfavor, says,

Had I but served my God with half the zeal
I served my king, he would not in mine age
Have left me naked to mine enemies (Act 3, Scene 2).

The archbishop was a competent politician, but as a man of the church he put the king's affairs first in his life. Thus, the reproach to himself. And this is a reproach that everyone should consider carefully:

Had I but served my God with half the zeal I served my own interests
> *my company*
> *my home*
> *my possessions*
> *my own wishes ...*

Joshua was not troubled by such a reproach. There was always Someone else with him: the Lord Himself. And Joshua cleared all his decisions in worship: an example for all people to keep in mind.

God's method is the truth, His Truth, plus someone serving Him. He always uses someone as His grand instrument. He always gets a spokesperson, but the spokesperson should not become entangled in things that seem more important to him. That is where the archbishop's problems started.

As with Joshua, there is Someone else with us who expects us to thank Him and serve Him, and always take Him into account.

It is always I and yet another One. I know this and I forget this. Remind me! And thank You, Lord!

SET-BACK AND RECOVERY

At this the hearts of the people melted and became like water (Josh. 7:5).

At one time or another, what happened to "the people", happens to everybody. They felt devastated. They suffered defeat against the seemingly insignificant little city, Ai. One of them transgressed and disregarded God's clear command that no one might take any of the booty of Jericho for themselves.

And after the major defeat a terrible punishment for the guilty party and his entire family followed. Those were primitive, harsh times of conflict and violence. Times that demanded total obedience, otherwise the entire plan could be jeopardized.

Sometimes we also feel despondent. Then it is good to discuss the issue with the Lord once again. However, we can mistakenly focus on issues we wrongly believe we are being "punished" for. But, we are living in the dispensation where Jesus Christ has taken our guilt upon Himself; He who triumphed over death and who obliges us and who helps us through His Spirit. "For God did not give us a spirit of timidity, but a spirit of power, of love and of self-discipline" (2 Tim. 1:7). It does not mean that the Lord does not bring us to our senses at times, but He always does this with the loving heart of Jesus Christ.

William Cowper, the inspired poet of the eighteenth century, urges us, "Ye fearful saints, fresh courage take / The clouds ye so much dread ... shall break / in blessings on your head" (from *Olney Hymns*).

And often, the salvation and victory soon follow. From this point on, "the people" conquered one territory after the other, and every tribe "came into its own" like Moses wanted it. The people had come home. And us? Actually, we are at home where God is ... and His Presence is everywhere ... we should feel free to speak before we become disheartened. Being there knows and helps.

Lord, like Israel, we sometimes find ourselves disheartened somewhere beyond Jericho. But You strengthen us every time.

WE WILL DO SO

"Now fear the LORD and serve Him with all faithfulness. Throw away the gods your forefathers worshiped." But the people said to Joshua, "No! We will serve the LORD" (Josh. 24:14,21).

It was not as if Israel did not know who they had to serve. Neither was it as if God concealed Himself from them. But Joshua knew his people: they tended to forget and started to stray quickly, just as we are inclined to do.

And usually one gets stuck precisely with those things from the past that are of no real importance, just as they were of little importance then. One realizes that after all the miracles that the people had experienced, they still did not part completely with the idols of their ancestors; these statuettes and customs were still around somewhere. That is true of us and of every generation. Every civilization and every person tries, besides serving God, to serve an idol as well. And every generation realizes that Baal or Mammon cannot help them.

Joshua bade farewell to his people after a brilliant career as a leader and told them to choose: the Lord or the gods of Egypt beyond the Euphrates. They solemnly promised to serve the Lord, like Joshua.

It does not sound as if this decision was a difficult one, because it was an emotional occasion and, in times of great emotion, people easily make promises "because everyone does it". Major movements in history made huge promises at major rallies to "fight to the end" and to be "faithful until death", only to forget about everything soon afterwards. People do this when emotion takes over.

It is human, and major promises are necessary. Provided one keeps one's word, especially what you have promised God. Even better: provided one holds onto God every day. Because one thing is true about promises: God always keeps His. And Christ sealed His with His life.

Lord, when I start to waver and doubt, remind me that You keep Your word, and that I should worship You, in turn, with reverence.

STRENGTH LIKE THE SUN

May they who love You be like the sun when it rises in its strength (Judg. 5:31).

The time of the judges who succeeded Joshua in the occupation of the Promised Land, was turbulent: triumph and disaster, obedience and disobedience followed one another as regularly as changing seasons. There were tides of God and tides of oppression, tides of God's help and tides of God's judgment. The judges came and went, sometimes after a single victory. Sometimes they sinned collectively, following another victory, and paid the price. When one reads the narratives of the judges, one gets to understand today's politics, society and the turbulence of nations. It is the here and now in an ancient idiom.

The verse above is also in an "ancient idiom", a paean by Deborah, the prophetess. Even today the sun remains the symbol of life and strength and light and joy. This is how "they who love you" are, she sang. And it is just as true today as it was when she sang it.

When we were children, we sang, "Jesus wants me for a sunbeam of sunshine / to shine for Him each day. / In every way try to please Him / at home, at school, at play ..." A bit sentimental but sung with good intentions, although one isn't sure if we actually realized what we were singing. That's okay. God also understands our childlike verse-mongering.

But what we do have to understand is what Deborah understood as a prophetess: that God's love is as full of vitality as the sun. And not a subdued sun, or one that is partially hidden by a cloud: a sun that "rises in its strength". This we should grasp: God is our everything – energy, light, love – if we open ourselves to His love by admitting our own weaknesses and by answering His love in grateful prayer.

Lord, let me be like a sun that is shining in all its strength: aware of the fact that the sun and the solar systems also receive their strength from You.

THE STRENGTH YOU HAVE

"Go in the strength you have and save Israel out of Midian's hand. Am I not sending you?" (Judg. 6:14).

During the time of Gideon, the Israelites were once again following Baal and Astarte, the gods of the land, in actual fact, fertility gods requiring sexual worshiping practices. In addition, the Midianites had them in a stranglehold.

The angel of the Lord appeared to Gideon with instructions to end the service of Baal and to defeat the Midianites. Understandably Gideon was not exactly a model of courage. He had many objections and asked for signs. But God's word came to him, "Go in the strength you have. Am I not sending you?"

"In the strength you have …" There is a story of an important athletic high school meeting in which the great American athlete, Jim Thorpe, took part. When the big teams passed by, they asked Jim's coach where his team was. The coach pointed to Jim and said, "He is our entire team." Everyone laughed, until the remarkable Jim Thorpe, with his phenomenal stamina, won more medals on his own in various numbers, than some of the bigger teams did.

The Lord usually uses what we have and He helps us overcome our lack of faith like He did with Gideon. He defeats the Midianites with 300 men and achieves the impossible, after his initial trepidation. But he was willing, and God can transform willingness and a sincere heart into a flaming sword.

Most of the time, Gideon led Israel well – although he also slipped at times – because he discovered where his true strength lay: not with the 300 men or necessarily within himself, but in the realization that he was dependent upon the Lord. This transformed the miserable farmer's son from Ofra, who was threshing wheat in secret, into a hero.

Eternal Father, sometimes I complain of a lack of strength, a lack of influence, a lack of meaning in my life, a lack of purpose in what I do. You be my strength.

STRONG IN GOD

Then Samson prayed to the LORD, "O Sovereign LORD, remember me. O God, please strengthen me just once more" (Judg. 16:28).

Judges came and went, well-known and obscure, good and not so good. Often the people did not even pay attention to the judges. One judge who stood out, was Samson, the human tank, the embodiment of physical strength (of which his hair was the symbol), who inflicted major defeats on the Philistines.

His mind and emotions were not on a par with his great physical strength, however. He thought in hot blood, as we often do, and chose to spend times among the Philistines where, unthinkingly, he got involved with a woman. One who betrayed him. He was captured, his eyes were gouged and he had to "entertain" the enemy in their thousands in the temple of their god, Dagon. Crude, but remember, betrayal is equally destructive today.

In the end, Samson stood alone with his blind eyes, a pathetic shadow of the man who was once mighty in battle. But he called on God – the first time in his life that it was recorded. And when he called out in anguish and humiliation, God was there. Next to him. Present.

Through God's strength he performed a heroic deed of which the Bible still sings today. He pulled down the pillars of the pagan temple and destroyed a great number of his enemies. That is why his name is still a favorite trademark for anyone who manufactures something that is exceptionally strong: from trucks to overalls and cement mixers.

In the end he was not strong in himself, but the Lord was his strength. In the name of the Lord we can endure, we can persevere, we can do the right thing at the right time, we can obtain insight into a problem when we grope about in the dark. Perhaps we have to wait a while. But strength will come. And remember Dostoevsky's warning, "Power is only vouchsafed to the man who dares to stoop and to pick it up" (from *Crime and Punishment*).

We know that You are coming with Your strength, Lord, even though we may feel blind. Let us extend our hands to You.

TEARS BEFORE GOD

I was pouring out my soul to the LORD (I Sam. 1:15).

The era of the judges was coming to an end and the flame of faith was burning low in Israel. Even the priest, Eli, was not a very understanding man of God. The majority of pastors who find a woman praying in their church (regardless of the circumstances), would probably be the first to approach her in sympathy.

Hannah, the woman who had no children and who was being questioned about drunkenness in the temple, prayed in tears and whispered promises to God, "I was pouring out my soul to the Lord." Sometimes we feel like Byron's *Childe Harold*:

None are so desolate but something dear,
Dearer than self, possesses or possessed
A thought, and claims the homage of a tear ...

Eli realized his mistake and said to Hannah, "May the God of Israel grant you what you have asked of him." The baby boy that was born was Samuel, the last judge of Israel.

There is a question: if God had already decided that Samuel was to be the last judge, why did Hannah have to struggle and cry so bitterly?

It is inexplicable, way beyond human logic, way beyond concepts such as "How?", "What?" and "Where?" It is like the majority of God's great truths. White and black are confused to the extent that they become an incomprehensible gray. But they flow imperceptibly, like strong sea currents that mingle in the depths of eternity and in a woman. And often tears accompany such great mingling truths. Tears that God dries. A mystery.

Lord, bless my tears in Your plan. Also bless my smile. That is also Your plan.

LORD, DRAW NEAR

In those days the word of the LORD was rare; there were not many visions (1 Sam. 3:1).

During the time of the judges, grim verdicts were pronounced regarding the people of God; such as "everyone did that which was right in his own eyes" and that "in those days the word of the LORD was rare". Today's believers sometimes feel as we are living in the time of the judges again. Appearances or manifestations of the Lord were/are hardly ever mentioned. God is/was scarce because He no longer lives/lived in the hearts of His people.

We make our own "appearances", the appearances of man. We hear, "The conclusion of any reasonable argument is that the Person of Christ is doubted. After all, we live in an age where the cloning of cells, and of man landing in outer space are discussed." Like some scientist said about cloning, "There is, after all, nothing mysterious about human existence. It is all about logical, chemical processes. We are close to the key of what we call Creation."

"Logical life" is strange. Today we are able to do things that would have been described as miracles in the time of Samuel. However, with all our knowledge, we have made life that much poorer: lacking the deepest stirrings of the soul, lacking the mystical experience of true worship, lacking a vision of the Unseen, lacking faith, hope and love. Lacking God.

But the "lamp of God" is still burning in places like Samuel's temple. God has not left us. Neither has God lost control. It is also not as if God is no longer interested or that He simply no longer "is". He is still what He is. He still speaks to us in many voices. Sometimes, like with Samuel, He speaks through a child; sometimes He speaks through something that happens; sometimes we simply become aware of the fact that we, "modern" people, need Him now more than ever – and that He is drawing nearer …

O Lord, draw near and give us Your blessing. You are our eternal Father and we are one with You.

Barren Womb, Empty Tomb

While it was still dark, Mary Magdalene went to the tomb and saw that the stone had been removed from the entrance (John 20:1).

During the days of the judges, Hannah cried over her barren womb. Here a woman was crying over an empty tomb, the tomb of Jesus, her Teacher. Very often God's great work runs through the tears of a religious woman. Saint Teresa of Avila told her students,

Listen, my young sisters, our generation is the generation of tears. Our hands are the hands that serve. Our feet those that stand at the cross till the end. Our weak thoughts and prayers are those that shine around the Lord's head like an arc of light.

Hannah received her little boy despite her barren womb and he became one of the great leaders of the people. And, from an empty tomb, which she at first thought was a disaster, Mary Magdalene got her Savior back, the firstborn from death and the Redeemer of all the faithful through the ages.

A light is radiating from the barren womb, as well as from the empty tomb, a wonderful light that banishes the darkness and fills people with joy. It is like a little candle in the night of the world, a small lantern against the dark wind, a small flashlight that helps us find the road.

In the neighborhood adjacent to where I live, there is a large Greek Orthodox cathedral. One night, the Saturday before the Greek Passover, I drove past it at half past eleven. The entire congregation was outside in the garden, each with a little candle. They were waiting for the doors of the cathedral to be opened at midnight by the priests with the greeting, "The Lord has risen!" It looked so blissful, filled with joy and God.

One wishes that Christians would shine in unison like little candles in the night. Often we look more like open, dark graves. More than once we lose our song. We must "sing" it to each other and to ourselves every day: The Lord has risen!

We mourn by the graves of the good that was, and over an empty heart. Lord, You fill that empty heart.

THE GRAND FACT

They still did not understand from Scripture that Jesus had to rise from the dead (John 20:9).

Peter and John saw the empty tomb. John even said that they "believed", but they returned home because they did not "understand" this unique event even though it was in the prophecies and even though Jesus once told them about it.

Who can blame them? They experienced strange events in the days prior to this. They experienced how the dream of Christ as king and of a new state of justice was shattered with the death of the One they regarded king. After all, John testified about His death, about the spear in His side, about the bodies that were not allowed to remain on the cross on the Sabbath. However, not one of us can regard ourselves as superior to them.

Yes, we have an idea about the truth of the Resurrection, but many still argue about it. Even theologians (some of them in name only) who examine the Scriptures. From time to time, prominent people come to the fore and say yes, they acknowledge Jesus as their teacher, but they cannot reconcile the issue of the Resurrection with their way of thinking.

But the Resurrection is an experience, an expectation like the Greeks with their little candles just before midnight. It is faith filled with joy; the acceptance that, for God, everything is possible. You open yourself up to a mystery that is a fact, enshrouded in holiness; an Amen – it is so! – to what God does and how He does it.

It is a song of redemption like the song of Deborah, that those who love God will shine like the sun when it rises in its strength. Without the fact of the redemption, the Gospel collapses like a house of cards. With this fact, it becomes the blessed message that nothing stands in Christ's way.

Lord, let every day be a day of Passover to me. Today, tomorrow, forever.

THE SECOND ENCOUNTER

Mary Magdalene went to the disciples with the news: "I have seen the Lord!" And she told them that He had said these things to her (John 20:18).

Many years ago, a famous film star, Tyrone Power, paid a visit to my hometown. Word quickly spread that he was staying in a well-known hotel. Teenagers in Capri pants with "Tyrone, we love you!"-banners, took up the entire road. My aunt was curious and went closer, holding me by the hand (The more things change, the more they stay the same).

Cameras flashed. The fans formed a scrum when the film star, apparently already going downhill, suddenly appeared and started giving his autograph. From the crowd a girl in a red top appeared, screaming ecstatically, "I saw him! I touched him! He asked my name!"

When Jesus appeared there was no crowd. Throughout the Bible it becomes clear that God is economical when it comes to big crowds. Big crowds are fickle, easy to influence and, most often, lacking in depth. Jesus spoke to Mary Magdalene, she recognized Him, He told her not to "hold on" to Him – His presence was already in an "exalted" dimension – and He let His "brothers", His disciples, know that He was returning to His Father.

Unlike Tyrone Power, who asked the name of the ecstatic girl, Jesus called Mary Magdalene by her name. And she called out His beloved title, "Teacher!" The grand recognition, the grand encounter, more so than a million Tyrone Powers of yesteryear.

Jesus was born from the womb of a woman and a female follower was the first to recognize Him when He returned from the womb of the earth. She went to search for Him, hoping to find something, even if it was only a tomb. The miracle of Jesus is that He did not keep her waiting for long. And what follows, is ecstasy.

We often go searching and we call out, Lord. Show us where to look, because we are quick to feel lost.

THROUGH LOCKED DOORS

On the evening of that first day of the week, when the disciples were together, with the doors locked for fear of the Jews, Jesus came and stood among them and said, "Peace be with you!" (John 20:19).

F or fear of the Jews." One cannot blame the disciples, because they were all marked men, at the forefront of the followers of a Man who was regarded by the skeptical Jews as a blasphemer, a violator of the law and a troublemaker. They probably had their spies everywhere. But the disciples regrouped and locked the door.

They felt that they belonged together, sheep waiting for their shepherd. There is, after all, often great strength in small, intimate groups who wait together on the Lord in prayer. Not only does it help to banish fear, but it also creates an expectation: there are other people here who feel the way I do, who are searching for what I am searching (This is one of the reasons why we go to church).

And suddenly, Jesus entered through the locked door and stood among them saying, "Peace be with you!" Interesting possibilities arose regarding His body. This body was in a different dimension and He was not to be stopped by locks and keys. It could not be held on to. He appeared and disappeared. He could travel through space and time. He was recognizable, even His wounds, but He was also ready to return to the Father.

Prominent thinkers have speculated about this: Christ made Himself recognizable and intelligible, but started withdrawing Himself physically because the time and dimension of the Spirit, Pentecost, was approaching. Thomas Aquinas wrote that this offers the key as to what we would look like after death. But Jesus was unique.

One thing is certain: our personality, the essence of who we are, our life principle, "signs" and all, will rise, even though we leave our earthly dwelling behind. We will receive a "new body" that is known to God. And today, while we are still in this body, Jesus comes and says, "Peace be with you!"

Lord, bestow Your peace upon me.

"MY LORD!"

Thomas said to Him, "My Lord and my God!" (John 20:28).

It is rather ironic, but characteristic of the way in which God works. The doubting Thomas, his entire attitude and his confession, became one of the cornerstones in the testimony of the resurrection of Jesus. Regarding the word of Mary Magdalene as well as that of the other women, one could perhaps have said that they were emotional and had seen something that they dearly would have liked to have seen, but was not really there. The same is true of the majority of the disciples. Peter, for example, was quick to believe and just as quick to doubt again. Quick to swear eternal allegiance and quick to deny it.

But a realist is speaking here, a man who was not with the others when Jesus entered through the locked door. He said that the stories of others did not impress him: he wanted to see and feel for himself. There has been many a sermon about just how skeptical he was and how he had no faith in the words of Jesus. But one is grateful that he was like that, even though he was lightly reprimanded by Jesus who said that those who did not see were blessed. However, Jesus understood that it is difficult for people to see more than what they can actually see with their eyes.

It was a good thing that he doubted and a good thing that he saw, because he did so on behalf of all of us; we with our many questions. Besides, God does not conceal Himself. He can be seen in everything, if only we would look. As the old English song states, "Teach me, my God and King, / in all things Thee to see / and what I do in anything, / to do it as for Thee."

Legend has it that Thomas went on and preached the truth about Jesus as far as India and the coast of Malabar. But of greater importance is what he proclaims through the ages to all of us through the Bible as knowledge based on experience: "My Lord and my God!"

Lord, we also want to see You. Show Your hand in our lives. Thank You.

FAREWELL AT THE LAKE

Simon Peter, Thomas (called Didymus), Nathanael from Cana in Galilee, the sons of Zebedee, and two other disciples were together [at Tiberias]. "I'm going out to fish," Simon Peter told them (John 21:2-3).

It is clear that the disciples were at a loose end during the days between the resurrection of Jesus and the descent of the Spirit. Who could blame them? They did not have many assignments. For three years they had roamed about and learned and experienced miracles. What else did they know but their former profession: to launch the boats and go fishing?

In the mean time, however, the "ordinary" had changed unnoticed but dramatically. It was almost as if they had lost their touch when it came to fishing, as they did not catch a thing. And for the last time Jesus taught them a fishing lesson. He stood on the shore telling them to cast their net on the right side and, like before, they netted a large catch of fish. When John recognized Jesus, Peter became so overwhelmed that he jumped into the water to go to Jesus. And on the shore a meal was waiting. Jesus had prepared breakfast.

It was on this same shore that Jesus had called them. Therefore it could not be any different now: on the shore, at the boats and the nets, He had to make one of His last appearances. This small reunion is remarkable, because it signifies the end of an era. Shortly afterwards, all of them would go into the then familiar world in the service of the Lord.

If I were Rembrandt, I would have painted it: the Savior who radiates glory, the disciples, the lake, the boats, the fish, the small fire and the meal. If I could paint myself in the ideal circumstances, I would paint my home, my people, my work, my familiar environment and especially the Savior, somewhere nearby, glowing with divine strength. I hope that this holds true for you and me. And should the rest disappear from the picture over time, that the Savior will remain with you and me, radiant with eternal strength and love.

Lord, please remain in the picture – remain in my picture forever.

LOVE ALONG UNFAMILIAR ROADS

"When you were younger you dressed yourself and went where you wanted; but when you are old you will stretch out your hands, and someone else will dress you and lead you where you do not want to go" (John 21:18).

During breakfast at the lake, Jesus asked Peter three times whether he loved Him. Peter felt heavy-hearted, because he must have sensed that their time with Jesus was running out. In addition, Jesus' question had a great impact on him. Peter was forgiven and, as it were, reappointed; he was reprimanded and embraced, but like before, when he bravely said that he would always stand by Jesus, he was once again warned.

This time it had nothing to do with unfaithfulness and a crowing cock. Now Jesus told him that the love that he was professing would take him along unfamiliar roads. He would indeed dress hurriedly and do great things in the name of the Lord. But there would also be times when he would be weak and would be led "where he did not want to go".

Sometimes, the love of God leads us where we do not want to go. It is not always a stroll through a rose garden. It is not only visions of snow-covered peaks and green valleys. The love of God sometimes leads us through deep streams and around dark corners, over steep roads and through arid deserts, exactly like God's people entered the Promised Land.

In love, after all, we must learn. You learn from the one whom you love, especially from Christ, what it means to live and love. Peter's life would end as an old man crucified in Rome. It is said that he regarded it as an honor and asked to be hanged upside-down on the cross. But Jesus would also walk this road with him, especially in his weakness, and keep him strengthened with His love, like when He gave them bread on that misty morning on the shores of the lake.

Lord, when I am led to places where I do not really want to go, I will stretch out my hands to You.

FOLLOW ME!

Then He said to him, "Follow Me!" (John 21:19).

Rembrandt did in fact paint the risen Christ in one of his greatest masterpieces, *Christ at Emmaus*, which hangs in the Louvre in Paris. Jesus is sitting with His two traveling companions at an old-fashioned table in a bleak room. He has joined them inconspicuously on the road.

For them this is the moment of recognition. His hands are lifted slightly above the cream-colored tablecloth, as if He is deep in thought. His face is shining brightly and there is a light haze surrounding Him. His head is slightly tilted and His eyes stare into space as though He is seeing beyond time and walls. Typically Rembrandt, with a focal point of light in a dark scene.

Christ remains the focal point in every scene, also with the last miraculous appearance of Jesus at the lake. And on the shore He reinstated Peter in the office of apostle (almost like a reformed sacrament with three questions on the same topic!) and gave him instructions. Peter, whether we want to acknowledge it or not, played a major role in the church and was in fact the leader of the early Christian church, the rock.

Whether or not he is the foundation of the church, he is given the pertinent instruction, "Follow Me!" He is not the new king of the church on earth. He is the leader, but the leader also has to learn to follow. It is what Jesus said previously about picking up the cross which, in Peter's case, came true.

In order to build any building, the actual builders, from the cement mixers to the bricklayers to the plasterers, have to do some hard labor. We are, after all, not the architect who walks around with the plans. Christ is the Architect and our "cross" is to do what we have to do because we are His students, the people who follow Him. But, He consoles us, His burden is light. It is true. It is actually sheer joy.

Teach us today to follow You. And, if You so ordain, make our burden light.

To Follow is not to Imitate

"You must follow Me" (John 21:22).

In all his errant ways, his humiliations and acceptances, Peter remained the same impulsive person who interfered everywhere and who wanted to anticipate everything. After all, the Lord does not change our personality; He gradually sanctifies it. Peter wanted to know what was going to become of John, and Jesus explained to him that it did not concern him in the least, "You must follow Me."

As time went by, a thought developed in the Christian church that, with these words, Jesus meant that we should imitate Him. Everything that He did, we must repeat like a parrot. But He did not even expect Peter and John to try and imitate Him. Everyone is allocated his place according to his abilities. It is also dangerous to say, "I must be *like* Jesus." The intention is good, but if we truly want to be like Jesus, we must die on a cross with the sins of the world upon our shoulders, rise again in glory after three days and accomplish everything that followed.

Beautiful, touching sentiment is not always the reality of being a Christian. Neither are good intentions, formulated in finely modulated language. To go and live in isolation might be commendable, but Jesus interacts with life, life as a whole, with people.

To follow Jesus, as Peter was ordered to do, is to accompany Jesus. To follow means that Someone is going ahead of me, I have a Guide. And when one has a guide in a strange big city – which is what life is like – you make sure that you stay as close as possible to the Guide in order to hear everything He says and to follow His every move. Otherwise you will be lost. Peter would be the leader of the congregation, but Jesus walks ahead, up to the very end.

Enlighten us through Your teaching; we find it in Your Word. We follow You through repentance – those of us who belong to You. You are our friend and king, and we kneel in worship. And when we enter Your abode, we will revere You forever.

WAIT FOR THE GIFT

After His suffering, He showed Himself to these men and gave many convincing proofs that He was alive. He appeared to them over a period of forty days and spoke about the kingdom of God. On one occasion, while He was eating with them, He gave them this command: "Do not leave Jerusalem, but wait for the gift My Father promised, which you have heard Me speak about" (Acts 1:3-4).

The apostle John left the disciples at the lake for the time being. He would later write letters to the churches about the grand encounter with the transfigured Savior in Revelation. But here Luke takes up the course of events.

The disciples probably returned to Jerusalem shortly after the appearance at the lake to go to the scene of Jesus' death and resurrection. During these forty days Jesus often appeared to them and spoke about the "kingdom", an idea of which they understood very little at the time. This is not so difficult to explain, because it often happens that we do not grasp much of what Christ does and plans in our lives. And the harder we try, the more confused we become.

When I was in high school, I tried to memorize math formulae in a somewhat mechanical fashion, while the basic principle never really dawned on me. I started to lose interest. Then, one day, I was forced to solve a few algebra problems and suddenly I grasped the underlying principle. After that I did not excel in math, but it no longer presented a problem to me.

In our faith, we often have to wait for the gift of spiritual insight. Sometimes it comes gradually. But it can also happen instantly, like in the case of the waiting disciples. When you lack insight into a situation, you must pray for wisdom and continue to pray. It will come. Slowly or instantly. It will come.

---

*A*men, Lord, it will come. You will come. Because You are life and wisdom.

THE KINGDOM

"Lord, are You at this time going to restore the kingdom to Israel?"
(Acts 1:6).

One could have been in the company of Jesus for any length
of time and yet, for some reason or another, not understand
anything of what He taught. We are still doing it every day. We
see a few trees of truth, which is good, but do not comprehend the
infinite forest of divine planning. We think as far as we are capable
of thinking – and sometimes not even that far! – but we don't see a
thing in terms of the great *mystery* that is God. Perhaps we think like
John Keats, "Much have I travell'd in the realms of gold, And many
goodly states and kingdoms seen" (from *Chapman's Homer*).

The concept "kingdom of God" was too vast for the disciples.
They still thought that the Lord would restore Israel, with Himself
as David. They wanted to know if it was about to happen "in those
days". Jesus did not deny that He was in the process of establishing
a kingdom. Neither did He deny that a "new Israel" would come
into existence, one without boundaries, encompassing the entire
earth, a "kingdom" of the faithful, of which they themselves would
extend the boundaries.

It is strange that the disciples, Jesus' daily students, struggled so
much to understand the concept of the kingdom, while the criminal
on the cross grasped something of it, saying, "remember me when
You come into Your kingdom" (Luke 23:42). Could it be that when
people who believe in God are dying they can see and understand
more clearly than they normally would? An old friend of mine believed that to be the case. Perhaps our thoughts are too busy with
many other things.

The kingdom of God has already come in Jesus with the visit of
the King Himself. Where the testimony of the King has already been
proclaimed, there it already exists. And it will also be coming when
the final dispensation dawns in full force. In the mean time, it is sufficient to understand that I am a subject of Christ the King and that
He, the King of kings, is taking care of His subjects.

You are King. I am a grateful subject.

HEAVENLY DYNAMITE!

"You will receive power when the Holy Spirit comes on you; and you will be My witnesses in Jerusalem, and in all Judea and Samaria, and to the ends of the earth" (Acts 1:8).

It is quite tragic: where Samaria used to be in the time of the disciples, these days there is not much more than neglect and misery and ruins. But for the Gospel it constituted a landmark after Jerusalem – Jerusalem that became a city of conflict not long after Jesus' earthly visit, and remains one today.

But the Gospel indeed reached the "ends of the earth" as Jesus predicted. For the places of origin, the grand message and Royal Visit that took place there could perhaps be irrelevant, but it is being preached and experienced in San Francisco, Johannesburg, Buenos Aires, Sydney, Montreal – still uncharted waters and unborn cities in Jesus' time. Even the East is not unaware of Jesus Christ, although it is still unclear how those millions fit into God's plan.

But the spreading of the Gospel is a miracle of God. It can only be attributed to devoted people, driven by the Spirit of God and filled with strength (the Greek word is *dunamis*, where the word, dynamics, comes from). Jesus said they would be His *martures* (martyrs, "blood witnesses"). That was indeed the case for many. Christianity, the kingdom, moves in tides like the sea: it has its high tides and low tides, times of powerful deeds by the faithful and times of decline.

Our lives are like that: times of great progress in faith, times of stagnation and even regression, times of consolidation, and times of returning to God. But we are progressing towards God. We are "compelled" towards Him, as a poet once said. We are restless until we find Him again. We are weak, but at the right time, now, He gives us *dunamis*, dynamics (dynamite!), strength. For this life it will suffice.

I am praying for strength now, Lord. Strength for today. Strength so that my life might be testimony to something of You.

HE WILL COME BACK!

"Men of Galilee, why do you stand here looking into the sky? This same Jesus, who has been taken from you into heaven, will come back the same way" (Acts 1:11).

Jesus' earthly sojourn was over – after a relatively short time. "Jesus, the hasty," as the poet Sheila Cussons described the Lord in a poignant poem about His Second Coming.

Thus, the final coming of the Perfect One. But now the disciples see how, in front of their very eyes, He disappears into another dimension, as though behind a cloud. In the language and idiom of that time Luke wrote that they saw Him being "taken up" and that "a cloud hid Him" from their sight. He merely, in the language of our time, switched over to another frequency, like we will all one day switch over to.

They probably stood there looking up, with a lump in their throats until the two heavenly men consoled them by telling them that He would come again in the desired final pattern, as Sheila Cussons wrote. A time of miracles had passed. But a time of miracles also started. And may the Lord perform a miracle in your and my life today, even though it may merely be to see something beautiful that touches our hearts.

And, of course: He will come again! Everything that is happening is pointing to it. That which is imperfect and unfinished, He will "synthesize and save". Yes, men and women of Galilee, men and women of today, Jesus will come again!

Yes, come, Lord Jesus!

CHOICE AND PLAN

Then they cast lots, and the lot fell to Matthias; so he was added to the eleven apostles (Acts 1:26).

Peter made a speech to point out the void left by Judas, following his betrayal and suicide. He quoted from the psalms and the prophesies. But, regardless of prophesies, should Judas have lived and joined them somewhere along the line, showing sincere remorse, the Savior would certainly have opened His heart to him and reinstated him like He reinstated Peter. But Judas' remorse drove him deeper into darkness. Deeds have consequences and consequences can only be mitigated and revoked by answering Jesus' question anew: "Do you love Me?" A "Yes, Lord", more often than not ends in tears, but lightens the burden of shame.

But the disciples felt that his place had to be filled. They set requirements for the "witness": "Therefore it is necessary to choose one of the men who have been with us the whole time" (v. 21), although not one of Jesus' inner circle of twelve.

Proposals were called for and two candidates were named; two who had the necessary qualifications. After fervent and sincere prayer, they cast lots. And the lot fell to Matthias. He was worthy to be with the remaining Eleven, but is never heard of again. Perhaps, who knows, he might have done good work like other apostles of whom one does not hear of either.

One cannot help but wonder whether the Eleven acted correctly by appointing another so hastily. The Lord was already in the process of preparing another apostle, one who did not really meet their requirements of "having been with us". God was already preparing His man, the truly formidable apostle: Saul of Tarsus, a scholar from none other than the Pharisees!

Ironic. How often God reverses decisions made by man. How strangely, but shrewdly does He work His plan. And how well it works out!

Lord, what we do often constitutes a problem for us. But we know that You know what You are doing.

FILLED WITH THE SPIRIT

Suddenly a sound like the blowing of a violent wind came from heaven and filled the whole house where they were sitting. All of them were filled with the Holy Spirit (Acts 2:2, 4).

The wonder of Pentecost and the descending of the Holy Spirit upon the followers of Jesus is reminiscent of Psalm 148:7-8 and 12 "Praise the LORD from the earth, you great sea creatures and all ocean depths, lightning and hail, snow and clouds, stormy winds that do His bidding ... young men and maidens, old men and children." It is as though all the mighty elements of nature must reverberate in the human heart of young and old, "His splendor is above the earth and the heavens" (v. 13).

Here, all those who were gathered at Pentecost were struck by powerful signs. It is reminiscent of Jesus' explanation to Nicodemus when He compared being born again with the wind, as well as of His statement that He would baptize His followers by fire. Fire is one of the signs of the Holy Spirit: a sign of love and sacrifice and cleansing, of an encounter like the one at the burning bush, of clarity and power and light and life.

During the feast of the firstfruits of the harvest, this great miracle happened. A wave of testimony of the great works of God flowed over their lips in all the languages of the people in Jerusalem. God no longer communicated only with the Jews, but with all the people on His earth. And so typical of the Bible, so beautifully realistic, neither the doubt of the infidels nor the mockery is concealed, "They have had too much wine" (cf. Acts 2:13).

God, through His Spirit, would be with all who believe in Him from then onwards. This Presence comforts us, guides us, delivers us from Evil, makes us aware of the Lord's guidance. It casts a glow in and around us. It is as if electricity was turned on in eternity. It not only dries our tears but prepares us for battle every day. Use it!

Grant us clear spiritual sight, serving the Father and the Son in truth. O Spirit, emanating from both, You came to comfort us, to stand by us.

MAY

Eternal God

Your world is a world of contrasts – just like faith –
because You, as Creator, are the essence of diversity.
In the northern hemisphere, May is the month of spring.
In the southern hemisphere, winter is setting in.
We often experience this in our lives:
a succession of the beautiful with the less beautiful,
experiencing Your vitality and divine strength
and then a slower pace in wintry spiritual circumstances –
You always maintain the balance.
I pray for the world:
    hallowed be Thy name.
I pray for my country:
    hallowed be Thy name.
I pray for the church:
    hallowed be Thy name.
I pray for my home:
    hallowed be Thy name.
I pray for the safety of my loved ones:
    hallowed be Thy name.
I pray for protection and for Your love:
    hallowed be Thy name.
I pray that You will provide warmth when it is cold,
and a cool breath of air – like for Elijah –
when life gets uncomfortable:
    hallowed be Thy name.

Amen.

WHEN SOMEONE CALLS YOU

Then Eli realized that the Lord was calling the boy. So Eli told Samuel, "Go and lie down, and if He calls you, say, 'Speak, Lord, for Your servant is listening'" (I Sam. 3:8-9).

With the Holy Spirit powerfully descending on the praying believers in Jerusalem, one sometimes forgets that the Spirit of God had already been operating in the Old Testament. However, it was only in individual cases, like with the calling of a prophet or a king. It was a narrow road of revelation that would lead to the great "descent", but God's plan often follows narrow roads. In the Book of Samuel, reference is made a few times to the Spirit of God who "came upon" someone "in power" (1 Sam. 10:10).

In 1 Samuel 3 the Lord calls, and one accepts that it is the Spirit of the Lord, but Samuel "did not yet know the Lord" because, although he helped in the temple, "the word of the Lord had not yet been revealed to him" (v. 7). Samuel was not a prophet yet, but the Lord decided that the time was right. He did not speak to the priest of His time. He spoke to the boy.

Sometimes strange things happen in the development of God's kingdom. Sometimes strange things happen in the development of us, His children, of His church and of His people. Judgment was proclaimed on the house of Eli and his sons, because Eli allowed corruption in the temple. Eventually Samuel had to tell this to Eli and one feels sorry for the old man.

If God cannot work through His seasoned church people, He works through a boy. The Lord watches over His people and He watches over His plan in particular; His plan that will continue until the second coming of Christ and beyond.

We are part of His plan. We must pray every day, "Speak to me Lord. We, who want to serve You, are listening."

Yes, we want to listen, Lord.

GREAT IN THE LORD

The LORD was with Samuel as he grew up, and He let none of His words fall to the ground. And all Israel from Dan to Beersheba recognized that Samuel was attested as a prophet of the LORD (I Sam. 3:19-20).

The Spirit of God, the Spirit of Pentecost's mighty wind, was truly with Samuel, like a burning glass concentrates light on one spot. "The Lord was with Samuel." What an overwhelming testimonial! With God as his source, this young man would speak with authority over Israel and anoint kings. The Lord was once again present in a man in Shiloh where the tabernacle stood; the holy place where the name of the Lord was worshiped.

Samuel's cradle stood in the light, because his mother "gave him up" to the Lord. He would also make errors of judgment and sometimes act too harshly, but he was a man of God and everyone, "from Dan to Beersheba recognized that Samuel was attested as a prophet of the LORD".

Today still, under the dispensation of the Holy Spirit, God chooses people to carry out specific tasks on His behalf. Often these people are weak and sometimes they have serious shortcomings, but they have to carry out a specific service for Him. They receive certain talents: of prayer, insight, understanding, prophecy and the ability to preach the Word of God.

We are in fact all God's prophets through our behavior and actions, our attitudes, our smiles, our zeal, our principles, our salutation, and especially that divine "something" that radiates from us. We can all become "great" in the Lord in our small circles. Yes, we sometimes wish that we could hear the Lord calling out to us like He did with Samuel. But He "calls" us in many ways. And, best of all, we can always call on Him in the name of the Lord Jesus Christ and through the whispering of the Holy Spirit.

I pray that I may become great through and in Your Spirit.

CAREFUL WITH HOLY OBJECTS

She said, "The glory has departed from Israel, for the ark of God has been captured" (1 Sam. 4:22).

These are the words of the daughter-in-law of Eli, the wife of Phinehas, after disaster had struck the people when they went into battle against the Philistines and lost.

In desperation, the Israelites, with Eli's unruly sons, Hophni and Phinehas in the front, went to fetch the ark of the covenant from the holy place to put it in Israel's battle zone. They thought that the holy symbol of God's Presence would help them defeat the Philistines. That is why the troops "raised such a great shout that the ground shook" (v. 5).

However, they had broken the cardinal rule of respect for God's holy symbol. The ark of the covenant had to remain in the holy place unless God ordered differently. It had to be handled with the greatest of care, because holy objects and symbols could become a double-edged sword.

The enemy heard about the ark being there and that spurred them on to fight twice as hard against the Israelites and defeat them, ark and all. To make matters worse, they captured the ark and Eli died upon hearing the news. His daughter-in-law named his grandson Ichabod, because "the glory has departed from Israel."

In this way, Samuel's prophecy was fulfilled. Respect for the Lord and His service, and everything accompanying it, is a prerequisite of a holy God. He is our father, but a father also requires respect for what he says and for what he asks in love.

Throughout history, holy objects have often been handled in a dangerous way. In the name of the Word of God wars were declared and heresy was preached. Stakes were built under crosses. That is to the discredit of the Christendom.

We must be careful in our judgment. We must be filled with respect for the One we serve, but also filled with respect in our worship. And filled with respect for fellow sinners who seek our help.

Lord, You show us the respect worthy of Your children. Let us, as children, serve You with renewed respect.

Memorial

Then Samuel took a stone and set it up between Mizpah and Shen. He named it Ebenezer, saying, "Thus far has the LORD helped us" (I Sam. 7:12).

The Philistines sent the ark back after they had been struck by one disaster after another. But the oppression did not stop. Samuel called Israel together at Mizpah where he (once again) had to teach them right from wrong (v. 6). They (once again) undertook to serve the Lord. They had to rid themselves of foreign gods, and (once again) of the sex goddess, Ashtoreth. They (once again) cried out to the Lord (v. 8). And the Lord (once again) saved them through a natural wonder, a thunderstorm, which confused the Philistines and enabled the Israelites to defeat them.

It seems as though the people of Israel were almost passive "victims" of wrong-doing. And it is not only the people of Israel: it is the flaw of civilizations. They come and go and make the same mistakes time and again.

We are also like that. We learn and think that we will never do this or that again; we have learnt our lesson. Like Samuel, we erect "memorials" to God's help. But we soon forget and get caught in the same trap over and over. This is one of the reasons why it is essential to read these histories so that we can recognize ourselves in those people of bygone times. We make a promise to the Lord who has helped us that "we will not forget".

The Lord understands this and listens and helps us every time we "cry out to Him". Henry Francis Lyte, the eighteenth-century clergyman from Brixham, Devon, clearly understood this when he, weak and ill, wrote, "When other helpers fail, and comforts flee / Help of the helpless, O abide with me!" These words have brought comfort to thousands of helpless people; people filled with guilt like Israel, like you and me. Thus far has the Lord helped us. He will help us again. Ebenezer.

O You who are constant, stay with us who are so inconstant.

AT THE ALTAR

But he always went back to Ramah, where his home was, and there he also judged Israel. And he built an altar there to the LORD (1 Sam. 7:17).

One could almost guess that where someone like Samuel stayed, he would build an altar to the Lord. For him, everything started with God and service to God and everything ended with God and service to God. He grew up at the altar in the temple where the "lamp of the Lord burnt at night". In his bed, in the sanctum, the Lord spoke to him and appointed him as judge and prophet of His people. It was at the altar where he would live.

Samuel traveled around to administer justice in Israel at Bethel, Gilgal and Mizpah. People came to him to hear their cases. And Samuel served the Lord. He had a rare nobility of spirit, the spirit of a sincere man. The Irish philosopher Edmund Burke spoke of "that sensibility of principle, that chastity of honor … which ennobled whatever it touched." That spirit was in Samuel, the man who walked with the Lord.

The species has not became extinct. I have met a few such men in my life, among others a farmer, a man of the earth, but an honorable person, a refined "altar" spirit. Such people are not without flaws, definitely not, but it is as if they build "altars" wherever they go. The lives that they touch become aware of that inherent "sensibility of principle" of which Burke spoke and for which he mourned, because it had been so corrupted in most of us.

This principle is something to pursue: where we live, where we go, where we work. To be people who carry the "altar" of God in our hearts. It will probably not make us important – whatever "important" might mean (!) – but, in the slightly adapted words of Burke, it will enable His Spirit in us "to ennoble whatever we touch".

───────

Let us live close to Your altar and let us build altars everywhere to Your glory.

GIVE US A KING!

They said to Samuel, "Give us a king to lead us" (1 Sam. 8:5-6).

How tragic, but how true! The people saw that Samuel was growing old and they had no faith in his sons, "Your sons do not walk in your ways; now appoint a king to lead us" (v. 5). Strange that the sons of Samuel, the man of God, acted the same way as the sons of Eli. It had to be an unpleasant reality to Samuel, although, unlike Eli, he certainly admonished them and set them an excellent example.

Could it be true that nothing grows in the shade of a big tree? Those were the words of my old mentor and editor, who warned me never to judge or criticize parents by looking at their children. But how children develop, even when they have an example of noble humanity, is a mystery: sometimes they build on the excellence, sometimes they are ordinary, and sometimes they stray.

The people rejected Samuel's sons. They wanted a new king. Like Napoleon remarked somewhat cynically, "Do you think that I won my battles for a so-called 'revolution'? No, the people want a monarch!"

How wonderful it would have been if a "revolution" or a "monarch" was not necessary, if everyone would heed their own conduct under the eyes of the Lord! Great philosophers like Calvin and Sir Thomas More (and Samuel) thought that this was already possible on earth. But it is the ideal state of Christ and, despite the crooked and warped paths of men and governments, God is working towards something eternal and lasting.

In the mean time, God shines in Zion as our King and with the angels we sing His praises every day. The mere thought gives enough courage for today.

Lord, sometimes things seem to be terribly strange and we feel desolate, but You reign and will reign for ever and ever.

LET THEM HAVE THEIR WAY!

The LORD answered, "Listen to them and give them a king" (1 Sam. 8:22).

There is an old warning that makes one think: "Be careful what you pray for, because you might just get it!" In the end, you might find that you misjudged the situation.

In this case the Lord granted the people's wishes – against Samuel's clear warning. Great things would come of this, but repeated evil as well. It is once again the mystery of God, the mystery of His decision and the twists in His paths. Through Samuel He said, "You chose, you will get what you have chosen." Samuel conveyed the message and sent the elders of the tribes home.

We once hired a young man to work in our garden. For a long time he was at his post without a break in service. On the day after Nelson Mandela had been freed from prison, he glowed with expectation. Perhaps he thought that his days of working in the garden were over. Then he stayed away for a very long time. One day friends brought him to us, pitifully crippled for life after a gang attack. No new statesman could save him.

Like the Irish poet W. B. Yeats told a laborer who asked whether Ireland would ever be free, "Yes, Ireland will be free, but you will still be toiling on the roads." Because "freedom" is the same for the road worker, the gardener and the professor – a free spirit, liberated in the Lord.

Samuel wanted the people to be free to be obedient to God only. But God knows our innermost thoughts, as Jesus said. He loved them and His constant friction with His people, like His constant friction with you and me, is a "lover's quarrel", the natural expression of a lasting relationship. He is not unaware of the fact that we are emotionally crippled. He will help us along. And heal us.

Lord, You are my King. You are aware of me and You know me. You heal me.

STAMPED

The Spirit of the LORD will come upon you (Saul) in power, and you will prophesy with them; and you will be changed into a different person (1 Sam. 10:6).

The Lord chose a king for Israel – Saul, the son of Kish, from the tribe of Benjamin. Through a strange coincidence of ordinary events, (he went in search of his father's donkeys) he met up with Samuel who was instructed by God to anoint him as king. God often uses "ordinary" events to bring about major changes; in the same way that a chance meeting can change our lives. God was also present in the search for the donkeys. The poet Milton was amazed by this, "As he who, seeking asses, found a kingdom" (from *Paradise Regained*). The mundane and even the absurd result in the crowning of a king.

Samuel sent Saul to a group of prophets and promised that the Spirit of the Lord would come upon him and that he would also become a prophet and "be changed into a different person". When all these signs came upon him, he would have to do what was expected of him, in the full realization that God was by his side. As Saul left Samuel, "God changed Saul's heart" (v. 9). He joined the prophets, and the people asked, "What is this that has happened to the son of Kish?"

God marked him as His special instrument, although Saul even kept it from his family that he had been anointed as king. The people still had to appoint him as king officially.

The Spirit of God, like everywhere in the Old Testament, acts in people for a specific task. For reasons known only to God, this is one of His major methods to send His love and care into the entire world.

After Pentecost we now live in the love and care of the Spirit of God. This means that if we believe, regardless of how humanly flawed it is, God has stamped us as His. Something of this is always recognizable in us, even though it might only be a strange yearning to worship and pray.

Hear my prayer, Lord; I know that I have been marked by You as Your own.

To keep quiet

But some troublemakers said, "How can this fellow save us?" They despised him and brought him no gifts. But Saul kept silent (I Sam. 10:27).

The process of the people's approval of the Lord's choice as king was rather impressive. The tribes came past and the tribe of Benjamin was selected first. Then came Saul's family and, in the end, Samuel had to send for Saul where he was hiding "among the baggage" (v. 22).

The young man might have wanted to shy away from it all, aware of the responsibility. It could also have been due to the modesty of a farm boy used to looking for donkeys.

Samuel presented Saul as the Lord's choice to the people and they shouted, "Long live the king!" After that Samuel presented the meeting with a "constitution" for kingdom and kingship, which was written down on a scroll. And then Samuel went home, his task completed for the time being, probably with (justifiably) serious misgivings. The Lord let Israel have their way, but …

In the meantime, Saul had already faced the harsh reality of leadership and kingship. "Troublemakers" (almost always present in any situation) made cutting remarks and "despised" Saul. He was not presented with the customary gifts by these people, but "Saul kept silent". Because the true "valiant men" (v. 26) accompanied him.

This type of mindset is worth pursuing: the constant realization that people are not necessarily sympathetic towards you and that, like Saul, you could brush it off gracefully. He did not even react to their insolence.

I wish that I could manage this, in the assurance that I only need to answer to the Lord. This is only possible by appealing to the powerful Presence of the Lord through His Spirit; the same Spirit that came upon Saul.

Lord, teach me to see the malice of people for what it is and to take refuge with You.

OFFICIAL FAREWELL

Be sure to fear the LORD and serve Him faithfully with all your heart; consider what great things He has done for you. Yet if you persist in doing evil, both you and your king will be swept away (1 Sam. 12:24-25).

Here Samuel resigned as practical ruler of the people. Like a successful chief executive officer under whose leadership a company has performed well, Samuel also realized that the time had come to stand down for somebody else. From his speech it becomes clear that he was concerned – after all, he knew his "company" – and he cautioned them to "fear the Lord" and to serve Him "faithfully".

Then the ominous warning followed: "Yet if you persist in doing evil, both you and your king will be swept away." After all, God continues to be a God of justice. If they were well aware of the fact that what they were doing could impugn the Lord's honor, and nevertheless persisted in doing it, without any remorse, then there would be a price to pay.

Samuel would still be there to give advice and execute a few major tasks for the Lord, but only as an "elderly statesman" or elder, a sage and prophet of his people. For a moment the people listened to the gray old man who had been in the service of God from his childhood, one who had vision. And things would go well at first, before the cracks started to appear.

However, Samuel also speaks to you and me. Not that we should introduce ourselves as being righteous, bluffing ourselves that we serve God, but that we should ask the Lord sincerely for His constant Presence. That He would grant us insight, and that we may risk it with Him, step by step.

It is our prayer, Lord, as sinners, that we will take risks with You, day after day in this dangerous world.

WHAT HAVE YOU DONE?

Just as he finished making the offering, Samuel arrived, and Saul went out to greet him. "What have you done?" asked Samuel (1 Sam. 13:10-11).

Saul was not a bad or a completely disobedient king. He was not a bad ruler or a bad commander of his troops. He was also not without God. But there was a streak of self-righteousness in him that developed like a wild sprig from a fine rose, and that sprig gradually started to take over.

His kingship started with a battle against the Philistines and the Philistines would lead to his demise. But in reality, the wild shoots of his personality were his downfall. Saul, fearful of the enemy, simply took it upon himself to act as priest and make the offerings. One can almost call it superstition, that God will help when the smoke of the offering – any offering regardless – rises upwards. When Samuel arrived, he rebuked Saul. A sincere prayer from Saul would have meant more than his offering. He also got his first warning regarding his kingship.

Why does this happen? Had God not chosen Saul? He should have known that Saul would fail. To theorize about God's ways – as about predestination – is like fitting in all of the Himalayas on one printed page. Any member of the press knows what that means. It is simply not possible; it is two-dimensional, while the Lord's work is multi-dimensional. But the fact that you love and know someone and therefore know what he is going to do even before he does it, does not mean that that person cannot still do what he chooses to.

The Lord knows us, but leaves us a choice. The choice is a simple, heartfelt prayer, "Lord, what do You want me to do?" And should I then misunderstand or falter … as a Father, the Lord will understand and forgive, and will help us out.

Lord, teach me that a simple prayer for help is better than pious acts and insincere offerings.

VALIANT SAUL

After Saul had assumed rule over Israel, he fought against their enemies on every side. He fought valiantly, delivering Israel from the hands of those who had plundered them (1 Sam. 14:47-48).

On a one-dimensional level, one can understand why God had Saul anointed as king and even equipped him with His Spirit. In spite of his mistakes, no one could simply challenge his authority, and he fought valiantly against the enemies of his people.

Israel was still attacked on a regular basis; the tragic consequence of his ancestors who failed to get the land under their full control. There was no relief for Saul as a warrior and "whenever he saw a mighty or brave man, he took him into his service" (v. 52).

It is said that Abraham Lincoln was in reality a "war president". Initially he struggled in battle because his advisors and generals were not the best there was. However, when he acquired capable generals, the tide turned in his favor. A wise leader is not scared to follow wise advice and he surrounds himself with the bravest of men.

Saul was like that (in the beginning). But too often, with a Samuel close by and surrounded by brave men, he followed his own head. Apparently, he became so sure of himself that the Lord indicated that He was "grieved" that He had made Saul king, "because he has turned away from Me" (1 Sam. 15:11).

I once heard an old man praying, "Lord Jesus, I hope that You never regret dying for me." This simple, sincere prayer touches me to this day. God rejoices in our successes, like in Saul's valor. But, like any good parent, He expects a simple and sincere token of love, even if it is simply a quiet, whispered, "Thank You, Lord, for Your hand in this."

Lord, when I, like Saul, turn away from You, remind me of Your Presence and the fact that, like a good parent, You rejoice in my love.

THE GOLD OF OBEDIENCE

Arrogance is like the evil of idolatry (1 Sam. 15:23).

John Monsell, a nineteenth-century English clergyman, wrote a beautiful hymn on worshiping God:

O worship the Lord in the beauty of holiness,
Bow down before Him, His glory proclaim;
With gold of obedience and incense of lowliness,
Kneel and adore Him; the Lord is His name.

It is beautiful, so poignant and so ... unattainable. But the mere thought of the "gold of obedience" and the "beauty of holiness" inspires one to "kneel down and adore Him". To touch His robe in love and experience a feeling of renewal and cleansing.

If we could make a wish for Saul, if we could make a wish for ourselves, it would probably be to be constantly aware of this "gold of obedience" to understand it and to keep searching for it. Saul did not listen and always made excuses. Very often he wanted to make an "offering". Samuel rejected his excuses with a scathing: "To obey is better than sacrifice" and, "arrogance is like the evil of idolatry" (vv. 22-23).

It boils down to the fact that arrogance is, in fact, worshiping yourself. You are the idol and your worship is "evil". God does not ask for "offerings". He can do without them. He asks that we, as people in whom His Spirit resides, will call upon Him because He is more than willing to help, to forgive and to bestow His grace on us. That is His "gold".

Lord, we want to worship You in the beauty of holiness. We want to bow down before You and adore You.

FROM THE SONS OF JESSE ... A KING!

The LORD said to Samuel, "How long will you mourn for Saul, since I have rejected him as king over Israel? Fill your horn with oil and be on your way; I am sending you to Jesse of Bethlehem. I have chosen one of his sons to be king" (I Sam. 16:1).

These were violent times in the history of Israel, harsh times, brutal times, times of the sword and of destruction. It is said that Martin Luther, upon translating this section into German, called his wife, Käthe, saying, "Herr Käthe! (his good-natured nickname for her as the boss in the house), bring bread and wine, because although I am being threatened from all sides, I want to celebrate the fact that I did not live in those harsh times!"

(The question is whether the times of Luther, which were characterized by burning at the stake, were not equally brutal, to say nothing of our times of atomic bombs and wars.)

But in the midst of Samuel's bloody times of war and judgment, Saul was failing. Samuel "mourned" for his people and the king whom he had anointed. However, the Lord moved on. Saul had had his chance and the time came to anoint a new king. That king, still a boy, had already been selected by God. A man who, though a sinner, would serve the Lord to the end; a man "after God's own heart". He would not only bring splendor to the people of Israel, he would be the ancestor of Jesus, the Christ, who would be born in Bethlehem where, at that moment, David was tending his sheep.

God always holds a fine thread in His hand (even in times of chaos). And then He starts to weave. And weave and weave. He is constantly working on the plan. Always with a single aim in mind: the regeneration of His Creation and the salvation of man. Always, somewhere in our own lives, the Lord picks up a fine golden thread ... which, one day, will make us happy and grateful.

Weave, Lord, weave Your plan for me.

NEWLY ANOINTED

Then the LORD said, "Rise and anoint him; he is the one" (I Sam. 16:12).

On a warm summer's morning, many years ago, I used this text in my induction sermon (which I delivered in formal black clerical garb). The sermon, painfully and nervously prepared, fell rather flat (except for my dear old mother who, being extremely loyal, called it a "soul-enriching" message). But this wonderful verse stayed with me: God took a king from the veld in order for Samuel to anoint him.

It is as if the Lord, as He has done many times on various occasions in the Bible, played a bit of a guessing game with Samuel. He only provided Samuel with an address: the house of Jesse in Bethlehem. He provided no name. It was as if He said to His servant, Samuel, "See if you can see what I see. Let the sons walk past." And every time Samuel's guess was totally wrong. Something of the Lord's fine sense of humor manifests itself here in all the earnestness.

Poor Samuel went to Bethlehem, fearing Saul, but the Lord gave him a valid excuse to hide behind – he had to go in order to hold a sacrificial meal. And then the puzzle was completed because the youngest, the shepherd with the ruddy complexion and handsome features ... he was God's man! How strange, dramatic, and even humorously the Lord acted! The great Saul would be replaced by a youngster. "Samuel anointed him in the presence of his brothers" and "from that day on the Spirit of the LORD came upon David in power" (v. 13).

The Lord works in countless ways, and somewhere He pulls the threads together. He uses people of all ages. His method is always divinely fascinating and often surprising. It sometimes requires great sacrifice and the courage to overcome your fear. But, as the Afrikaans writer and poet, Langenhoven, said, "My Father above has His hand on the wheel, with His eyes on the twist in the road."

Lord, to follow You is sometimes a strange, painful and difficult experience, but it is always an adventure.

Saved!

Everyone who calls on the name of the Lord will be saved (Acts 2:21).

From the day that David was anointed as king, the Spirit of the Lord came upon him in power. And from the day that the believers were anointed by the Spirit with tongues of fire, the kingdom of God – of which David had been a forerunner – started to become mainstream. God was on His way and His plan involved His entire world.

At Pentecost, Peter stood up and, guided by the Holy Spirit, he outlined God's plan to the people. And the message was: "Everyone who calls on the name of the Lord will be saved."

Through the ages, people have added extra "qualifications" to becoming a Christian, or have taken some away. During the sixteenth century, the Pope sold letters of indulgence to ostensibly help souls on their way to heaven. During the eighteenth century of enlightenment (*Aufklärung*), salvation was not deemed necessary, and Christ was seen as merely a prophet, as is the case today in some circles.

There are people who think that a Christian who has been "saved" is one who does good deeds, adheres to every commandment, or is a pleasant, happy-go-lucky sort of person. Peter does not mention any of these things. He says Jesus is the Lord and everyone who calls on Him (in truth) will be saved, or become God's child.

Therefore: *a Christian is someone who constantly calls on Someone.* A Christian is someone who is on his way, and who has something in his heart indicating the direction (determined every day by the One called upon). A Christian feels uneasy outside this Presence, he knows a Name and constantly asks for direction. He knows that, one day – or rather in a moment of eternity – all will result in a face-to-face encounter with his Traveling Companion.

It is important to remember that Christians are not necessarily "better" than others. They are simply better informed, they know a Name; a Name that they use in love, distress and in worship.

Lord Jesus Christ, Son of God, have mercy on me, a sinner!

JOY

You will fill me with joy in Your presence (Acts 2:28).

Ask people what "happiness" is, and they paint pictures of comfortable homes, contented families, festivals, winning the lottery and – if they are poor and in rags living on the street – a hot meal. Like Eliza Doolittle sings, "Lots of choc'late for me to eat / Lots of coal making lots of heat / warm hands, warm face, warm feet / O, wouldn't it be luverly!" Understandable and even touching. Those who have, want more. And those who don't have, want what others already have. This is vaguely, among other things, described as happiness. But "happiness" is more than this.

And joy has other qualities – qualities that David, poet of the Psalms, and filled with the Holy Spirit, experienced more than once. That is what Peter quoted here in his speech. When Jesus wished His disciples His "happiness", He had something in mind that David had in mind: the joy of the Presence of Someone who you love, and who you know loves you, warts and all. God Himself, through His Spirit.

When Jesus conveyed His happiness and joy, He broke bread, in the knowledge that severe beatings, a crown of thorns and nails through His hands were awaiting Him. And He spoke about happiness! Joy! His joy! Even Eliza Doolittle would not have wanted this as she sat in poverty in the cold, selling flowers.

This suffering is, after all, something else than warm feet and chocolate. The joy of Christ is often as incomprehensible to the Christian as to the disciples during the Last Supper. But Peter realized that David poetically grasped something of this, "You will fill me with joy in Your *presence.*"

When I was a boy, my beloved Aunt Tita was a teacher and every Friday night she came home by train. What joy it was to wait for her at the station with my parents! And what a delight to embrace her. Her presence was joy and love. Being near a loved one taught me something of God's infinite love.

I want to rejoice in Your Presence every day.

"FAR OFF"

The promise is for all who are far off – for all whom the Lord our God will call (Acts 2:39).

Here God's long-standing covenant with His people, dating far back from Sinai in the desert, is extended to include everyone. Those who experienced the Spirit spoke in foreign tongues. One wonders whether Peter realized exactly what he was saying, because God would only explain to him later in a vision that He included the "Gentiles" or the non-Jews as well. This was a revolutionary thought – God is not only the God of one specific nation or tribe or culture, He calls all.

Peter's message so inspired the audience that three thousand people, enough to fill three relatively large church buildings, accepted Christ immediately and were baptized.

Approximately half-a-century ago, almost every child in Sunday school received a little "text book" with a Scripture verse and a verse from a hymn for every Sunday, which had to be memorized. Those verses that were drummed into their heads remained with many people. And this verse was a favorite in almost every textbook, year after year. Teachers had difficulty explaining it, but they did manage to bring across that "far off" meant unto all generations and that God was also the God of children and their children's children, and that He continues to call throughout all generations.

There is a beautiful story of Mary, as the "eternal mother of the Savior", seeking her Son through generations in every heart of every person. Let us rather apply this to the Father: He seeks His image, His Son, through the Spirit in our hearts, and if He finds even a mere desire in a heart to serve Him, then He comes in Christ through the Spirit, through all generations, to reside in each one of us. This is His covenant. This is His imminence.

You call me and I call on You. It is the call of love.

Ecstasy

All the believers were together and had everything in common (Acts 2:44).

Those were the first ecstatic days of idealism, "fellowship, the breaking of the bread and prayer" (v. 42). There was the rush of fresh excitement about the acts of God toward His people. Unity and sacrifice reached dizzy heights. Believers shared their possessions with one another, they sold and distributed their land and "every day they met in the temple" and worshiped (v. 46). Wonderful times of intense emotion. And the Lord granted them their ecstasy, as He does for all of us, although He knows that we cannot keep dancing on the mountain top forever.

To be realistic, quarrels would soon follow. The joint ownership of property was a well intended but failed experiment; it presented a trap for people quite early on. Ananias and Sapphira alleged that they gave "everything" to the church; a lie costing them their lives. Peter said "the money was at Ananias' disposal" (cf. 5:4). Later on, Paul even sent a slave, the property of fellow believer Philemon, back to him. Being a Christian does not abolish right of ownership.

Through the ages shared ownership has caused problems; even though Karl Marx, unbelieving as he was, quoted this first Christian zeal as the norm. However, what he and his Communist followers failed to acknowledge was that to idealistically "share everything" often resulted in someone (a clique, government or *nomenklatura*) holding the purse for others, mostly taking care of themselves first.

The first Christians truly wanted to help each other. All credit to them, even though they failed. But later on, Paul clearly explained the rule to the members of the church in Thessalonica, namely "to mind their own business and to work with their hands" (1 Thess. 4:11). He himself provided his own food with his own hands, not asking anything of anyone, but accepting a gift graciously. For Christians, the rule rather applies as follows: work as hard as you can, save as much as you can and share wherever you can. And God will bless you.

Lord, everything that I have flows from Your kindness. Let me remember this always.

WHAT I HAVE ...

"Silver or gold I do not have, but what I have I give you. In the name of Jesus Christ of Nazareth, walk" (Acts 3:6).

The lives of the first Christians were special times, times of revelation, of miracles and of benevolence. Peter and John were going up to the temple when a crippled man begged money from them. Peter emphatically said that he had no money, but that he could give him something far better: recovery in the name of Jesus Christ. "Taking him by the right hand, he helped him up, and instantly the man's feet and ankles became strong" (v. 7). The cured man was overcome with joy and the people who witnessed it and recognized him were "filled with wonder".

Even though the "shared ownership" of the first church failed after just a short period, the thought of openhandedness and giving, of testimony and love in Christ, of sympathy and compassion – the things that Jesus emphasized – was radical but lasting, up to this day.

An incident in the life of the nineteenth-century English poet, Samuel T. Coleridge, brings this point home. Coleridge was speaking in London on great British writers, and told the story of the famous Dr. Samuel Johnson who had carried an ill prostitute home on his back one night and took care of her. The "respectable" audience giggled surreptitiously and even shook their heads in disapproval. Coleridge quickly called them to order, saying, "May I remind you of the good Samaritan and 'Silver or gold I do not have, but ...'" No further argument was needed.

Like you, I have often wished that I could, like Peter, say to someone, "In the name of Jesus, walk." I do not have the gift of healing. Few people have. But unlike Peter, I do have something in my purse to give and, like Peter, I can pray in the name of Jesus for strength for the sick and wounded. And pray for myself to have open eyes and an open heart.

I ask especially for an open heart. I ask, Lord, to give, as well as to receive from You.

THE LINEAGE OF JESUS

The God of Abraham, Isaac and Jacob, the God of our fathers, has glorified His servant Jesus. You handed Him over to be killed, and you disowned Him before Pilate, though He had decided to let Him go. You disowned the Holy and Righteous One (Acts 3:13-14).

These are momentous words spoken with great conviction by an ordinary fisherman in the holiest place of the Jews. Peter draws the line right through from Abraham, Isaac and Jacob, from the ancestors, to Jesus, God's "glorified Servant". Could it be clearer? Since Abraham was called centuries ago, the line goes right through to Jesus the Christ. Peter also makes the damning pronouncement that the Jews had "disowned him before Pilate" when Pilate wanted to let Jesus go. About this there is no doubt.

Which makes one wonder: could Peter have been hiding at the back of the crowd early that morning when Jesus appeared before Pilate? Would he shamefacedly have sneaked along behind Jesus' pathetic "procession" of the cross, after he had heard the cock crow? Most likely.

He was convinced of his case, of guilt and innocence, of right and wrong. He was suddenly an orator before the people, a scholar, someone who could persuade people to listen. After all, for three years he had attended Jesus' "university", Jesus, the greatest Professor of all times. And where he had lacked the courage, the Holy Spirit enabled him to act from the strength of his conviction. He was a man saturated by Christ, the promise to the fathers Abraham, Isaac and Jacob.

Because, if Jesus had not come, the history of Abraham and the others, of Moses and David, would have been irrelevant to our worship, and merely interesting stories of people who lived in interesting times. But Jesus is God's focal point in the history of His Creation, as well as the focal point in your and my history. He must teach us. He must help us. In Him we meet our God. Every day.

We want to remain at Your feet and learn, our heavenly Professor.

COURAGE

Judge for yourselves whether it is right in God's sight to obey you rather than God. For we cannot help speaking about what we have seen and heard (Acts 4:19-20).

The Sanhedrin faced a dilemma. They knew that they had Jesus killed by manipulating Pilate. They were also able to sense trouble approaching. A mixture of guilt and a feeling of self-righteousness created an extremely dangerous hostility in the ones being confronted. This holds true even today.

The members of the Sanhedrin knew that an explosive situation was developing. They were also aware of the fact that these "unschooled, ordinary men" (v. 13) were undermining their authority. Peter and the others made it clear, "Judge for yourselves whether it is right in God's sight. For we cannot help speaking about it." The Sanhedrin (wisely) decided to let them go, as well as the beggar who had been healed. To touch them would have meant playing with fire before the crowd who was praising God.

God always has a witness. In major as well as minor cases. Centuries later, the same kind of event occurred before the Imperial Diet of Worms, when a 34-year-old monk, Martin Luther, was called before the young Emperor Charles V, about his "incitement" against the Pope. On the first day it seemed as though he, overwhelmed by the Emperor and the princes, was starting to waver. On the second day he respectfully stated, "Here I stand. I cannot do otherwise. God help me." The flames of the Reformation were lit.

At one time or another in our lives, we all stand alone. If our priorities are in place, the Spirit of God will be with us. In a crisis you pray for calm. God will give guidance – when we face major illness, death or a modern "Sanhedrin".

Lord, let us remain calm for the sake of the truth, but stand calmly on Your principles. Sustain us with Your wisdom.

Blessings in abundance

Crowds gathered also from the towns around Jerusalem, bringing their sick and those tormented by evil spirits, and all of them were healed (Acts 5:16).

It had to be something special for Luke, who reported on these events, to hear about the healings or to witness them himself. After all, he was a doctor and the majority of doctors through the ages did not readily accept miracle cures. Remarkable things also took place – testimonies confirming that the Spirit of God indeed shook Jerusalem and the surrounding areas. Because from here the message would be spread, as Jesus had promised.

I have heard about miracle cures as an answer to prayer more than once. I have witnessed a miracle cure, and possibly another. But here, after Pentecost, God really performed miracles to show people what the kingdom of God is all about: to heal, to help the broken, to reach out to the helpless. Physically and emotionally.

There are times in God's "economy" when He bestows blessings in abundance, like after Pentecost. Also remember the time when Jesus fed the people at the lake. He demonstrates His power generously. But there are also times in God's "economy" when He gives just enough for each day, and teaches us to make do with what we receive from Him. No one can understand God's "budget", like children do not understand the business affairs of their loving father and the reason for withholding some things from them. On the other hand, as a wonderful Father, the Lord often surprises us with unexpected blessings and emotional assurance because He truly knows what we need.

The Spirit-filled people of Jerusalem and surrounding areas lived in spiritual abundance at that time. However, soon the times came when they had to face difficulties. It is the same with us. But in times of abundance and "need" – God reigns and the "economy" from His hand is impeccable because He loves you.

Lord, I also ask for healing, for those whom I love and for myself; even if You would only heal my often impetuous heart.

JAIL MYSTERY

They arrested the apostles and put them in the public jail. But during the night an angel of the Lord opened the doors of the jail (Acts 5:18-19).

Trouble soon materialized for the apostles. The Sanhedrin had had enough. Desperate people take desperate measures – they had the apostles arrested and thrown in jail. During the night, an angel opened the doors of the jail and the next day the disciples taught in the temple again, to the great dismay of the Sanhedrin. The Sanhedrin would experience dismay many more times.

Peter and the others would not be silenced and the Lord would not remain idle. The apostles became acquainted with jail, corporal punishment, as well as with an angel and a remarkable deliverance. The road was not strewn with roses for Christ's witnesses. It was hard work. They were part of God's method. And God's method is often a mystery.

Of course, there are some mysteries that you can quite easily solve, like those in a detective story. But there are other more extensive mysteries of greater magnitude where the truth forms part of the mystery. For example, you know who you are, but do you understand the mystery of yourself every day? The more you try to fathom the mystery of God's work, the more complicated it becomes. It is the same with you: the more you try to understand yourself, the more the whole truth about yourself eludes you, and the more you discover things in yourself that leave you with more question marks. You do not live by solving your own mystery. You live by *living* your own "mystery" and leaving the rest to God.

To say that God and His ways are a mystery is to try and nail Him down. Even in the case of Christ this was in vain. Peter and the others were in jail. They were freed by an angel. They continued, and the mystery of God was at work to the benefit of all, yours too. Now. At this moment.

Lord, sometimes we are a mystery to our ourselves and You are also a mystery to us. But thank You that we understand what we need to know.

Wise words

I advise you: Leave these men alone! Let them go! For if their purpose or activity is of human origin, it will fail. But if it is from God, you will not be able to stop these men (Acts 5:38-39).

These are the words of Gamaliel to the Sanhedrin; words of wisdom, such wise words that you wish you had known Gamaliel. Because wisdom is often rare, as it also was among the learned Pharisees.

We are told that we are living in an era of "knowledge explosion" and of mind-boggling "information technology". Remarkable. But do we have wisdom, like Gamaliel? Wisdom differs from knowledge and from the information contained in a thousand libraries. T. S. Eliot said that, with all our knowledge, we have actually lost wisdom and life somewhere along the line:

Where is the Life we have lost in living?
Where is the wisdom we have lost in knowledge?
Where is the knowledge we have lost in information?

– from *The Rock*

Gamaliel speaks from experience, insight and intelligence. He has seen people come and go. Leave these people alone, he says, because if their work has been inspired by humans, it will blow over. But if it is from God, nobody will be able to stop them.

And yet, after centuries, people are still trying to appose the wisdom of God and play it off against the "knowledge explosion". But God's wisdom is everywhere and always at work. May He grant us the wisdom of Gamaliel today to not run away with an idea and not let anything get the better of us, but to allow the truth to run its course: the truth of His Presence, the Life in this life.

We know that everything that comes from You will not be stopped by anyone. Show us the difference.

LAYING ON OF HANDS

M
A
Y

26

They presented these men (the seven deacons) to the apostles, who prayed and laid their hands on them (Acts 6:6).

The apostles were (for a while) finished with the Jewish scholars. Everywhere they went, in the temple courts and at their houses, they "proclaimed the good news that Jesus is the Christ" (5:42). Jesus is the Christ, the Savior. That is the fundamental truth of the Gospel. Remember the irony – Jesus' persecutors were Jews; Peter and the others and the first thousand believers, were also Jews.

And yet another irony – the "church" is in the "world" and the "world" is in the "church". Quite soon disputes arose because some members of the church were treated "unfairly". Apparently, the widows of the Grecian Jews were being neglected. To solve this problem, a committee of seven deacons was elected to take proper care of the people, while the apostles paid attention to ministering the Word. The seven deacons were brought to the apostles who laid their hands on them and prayed for them.

It is a lovely gesture to lay hands on someone in the name of the Lord and to pray for him. Or simply to take someone's hand in prayer. There is something benedictory in this gesture, something of God, something of the Spirit, something of Christ who laid His hands on the sick and healingly touched the lepers. This gesture says the Lord is with you and I am thinking of you in what you are going through, or whatever your assignment may be. But more, the Lord Himself will shelter you with His hands. You are in the Lord's care.

Let us touch one another when we pray together. Because, in so doing, we state that we are dependent on one another – and on the Lord. Let us use our imagination in a positive way and, in our hearts and minds, let us lay our hands on all our loved ones in the name of Jesus. Because the apostles had now received help the kingdom was expanding. And in all of that, as in your life and mine, we can see the hand of the Lord.

Lord, in my heart and mind, I now lay hands on everyone, on everyone whom I know, on everyone whom I love, on everyone close to me.

PERSECUTED WITNESSES

Was there ever a prophet your fathers did not persecute? (Acts 7:52).

Stephen was one of the first people on whom the disciples laid hands, and he was the next to come before the high priest and the Sanhedrin.

At first they were listening with interest to what Stephen had to say. Like Peter, he supported his statements with evidence from the early history of Israel. Abraham, Isaac, Jacob, Moses. He referred to the disobedience of the people when Moses turned his back (cf. v. 39). He referred to the fathers' initial unwillingness to follow Moses (cf. v. 35). He referred to David who wanted to build a dwelling place for the Lord, because he "enjoyed God's favor" (cf. v. 46). And he referred to the prophets, one after the other, whom God sent to admonish them. And then came the damning question to the scholars who invoked and took pride in the law and the prophets: was there ever a prophet your fathers did not persecute?

One cannot really imagine such a person. All the people of God had to contend with unruliness and disbelief. At the beginning it was resistance against the law. Then they started to deify the law because they feared another exile. Through the generations it has been like this: the people echo the "in" politics and religion of the day. Woe betide the one with God in his heart, who starts to question ordinary things that are wrong.

Perhaps Stephen was too harsh with his words. The hearers were furious and gnashed their teeth at him (cf. v. 54). But the truth is always hard-hitting, especially when it concerns you. The golden rule always applies: judge yourself before you judge others. The prophets did this. So did Stephen. In the end, the Lord triumphed.

Lord, teach us how to conduct ourselves in a worthy manner. But when we stand up for Your name, You will stand up with us.

AN OPENING

> But Stephen, full of the Holy Spirit, looked up to heaven and saw the glory of God, and Jesus standing at the right hand of God. "Look," he said, "I see heaven open" (Acts 7:55-56).

The Sanhedrin was furious, so much so that they gnashed their teeth. They covered their ears to everything that Stephen had to say, they charged at him and dragged him out of the city, and stoned him. Up to this day guides point out the place where Stephen, the first martyr for Christ, was stoned. Learned and respected people can sometimes become rather barbaric when hysterical.

Billy Graham tells the story of his wife who wanted to establish a Christian club at her liberal university. According to the professors she had to abandon the idea because "it would give offence". Sometimes people stand on the freedom of opinion to such an extent that, in fact, only their own opinion enjoys freedom!

Stephen was stoned to death for his opinion. But he saw something that few mortals are privileged to see. He saw the heavens open. In his last moments he did not feel the fury of his persecutors, nor the rocks of those stoning him, because he was busy with something else; something infinitely greater, something overwhelming, something outside space and time. Heaven opened before his eyes and he saw his destination. For a moment God broke through space and time to help and comfort his witness with a heavenly vision of Himself. Stephen died, his soul ecstatic, with words of forgiveness on his lips.

It reminds me of the last words of a beloved uncle, "I see the gates of heaven being opened and I am walking in." That is a privilege. And for those of us who are still alive, it is an assurance: I have an address in eternity. I have a destination. I have a God who cares. I have a life that knows no end.

I would also wish for that ... "to see heaven open". But please, Lord, always be present.

MEET SAUL

Meanwhile, the witnesses laid their clothes at the feet of a young man named Saul (Acts 7:58).

And Saul was there, giving approval to his death (Acts 8:1).

Asked about the behavior of some priests, Anselmus of Canterbury said, "Priests are just like people, and people are like people, some only more so." Saul was such a young and educated Pharisee: when he persecuted people, he was an avid and bloodthirsty persecutor. When he was strong, he was stronger than others. When he was humble, he was more humble than others. When he bowed, he bowed deeper than others.

He, who witnessed Stephen's death, would become the key witness to Jesus' resurrection, the one who would "interpret" the Gospel, its depth and meaning. God's man. He heard Stephen's words, which must have shook him. The patriarch Origen said, "If Stephen had not cried out, the church would not have had Paul."

"But Saul began to destroy the church. Going from house to house, he dragged off men and women and put them in prison" (v. 8:3). A passionate man, on his way to greatness as a scholar, and a zealot where law and tradition were concerned. And on the road to self-destruction. God would choose this man.

Centuries later, Calvin would flee via Geneva to Italy. In Geneva, God stopped his carriage. There, Farel spoke to him saying, "The Lord wants to use you here." Calvin stayed and God gained control over him: temper, over-zealousness and all!

It is a continuous thread in the Bible – how the Lord put the right person in the right place at the right time. And then He often works in strange ways. He draws a straight line with a very crooked stick. He saw what He was looking for in Saul. He sees enough in you and me to honor us with His Presence.

Lord, I am a crooked stick, but willing in Your hand.

SORCERY?

Peter answered: "May your money perish with you, because you thought you could buy the gift of God with money!" (Acts 8:20).

When the persecution of the church in Jerusalem began in full force, the people took off, as though God wanted to force them out of their safe hiding places. They testified wherever they went. Philip went to preach in Samaria, they performed all kinds of miracles, and the people believed. The apostles then sent Peter and John to Samaria as reinforcement.

But there was another man in Samaria who saw an opportunity to boost his reputation: Simon, who had also become religious, and who earlier "practiced sorcery in the city and amazed all the people of Samaria" (v. 9). He offered Peter money to teach him the secret of the laying on of hands to bestow the Holy Spirit on people. What a wonderful bit of "sorcery" that would have been in his armory!

Peter turned him down with contempt. It was the time of God's revelation and the Spirit of God was not for sale, not even to placate Simon's "bitterness" (v. 23). Yes, he was more or less a believer, but he saw Peter and the others as a threat, people who did "tricks" that he could not do. Peter told him frankly to repent and Simon got such a fright that he asked for intercession so that "nothing may happen to him" (v. 24).

Serving God is no sorcery. As a young man, I attended a large rally one evening where the prayer leader shouted at the top of his voice over a microphone to the worshipers "to receive the Spirit". He told the audience how people's physical disabilities and cancers were being healed through his hands at that moment. I got up and left and never went back. The Spirit of the Lord comes in His own way to those who call upon Him. God is always silent in His Presence, but He announces Himself profoundly to us.

Lord, sometimes I am also looking for signs. But teach me to be attuned to You.

WHO?

Tell me, please, who is the prophet talking about, himself or someone else? (Acts 8:34).

Philip was sent by God on a "desert road" from Jerusalem to Gaza, the same Gaza that is a bubbling cauldron of unrest today. On this road there was an important financial official of the queen of Ethiopia; a eunuch (customary in those days for such officials). He was a so-called "proselyte of the portal", someone who was in the process of being instructed in the Jewish faith. He was in Jerusalem for Pentecost.

He studied the Scriptures but did not understand them. When Philip arrived at his side, he wanted to know what the prophet Isaiah meant when he said, "He was led like a sheep to the slaughter" (v. 32). This is a profound and relevant question, because no one who did not know of Jesus would have been able to answer it. Even the prophet could only provide an outline of what would happen. But here, in hindsight, Philip could explain it to him in one session; to such an extent that the official insisted on being baptized.

With this man the Gospel moved deep into Africa. However, without Christ the greatest prophesies would only be the history of civilization. And the opposite is also true: the appearance of Christ would have been difficult to explain at a later stage, without the Old Testament. Old and new run side by side, and the one flows into the other.

It is like a person who looks back on his life and realizes: if it were not for the help of the Lord here, there and everywhere, I would have perished. Because each one of us has a history and when we page through our own book with the enlightened eyes of the Spirit, we see the great works of God. And it continues, because every day we continue writing our own history, under the guidance of God.

Lord, I see Your hand in my own history. I see it now as well. Thank You.

JUNE

Eternal God

I have read in the newspaper of an accused who stood in court
with nothing to say but "Mercy, your honor".
That is how I stand before You, guilty as charged,
with nothing to offer, nothing but a prayer for mercy.
Sometimes, like Saul, I sin in self-righteousness,
and like the important Ethiopian I understand little of what I read.
I wish I could have the insight of Samuel, the judge
and Stephen, who saw You through the door
of an open heaven.
I pray that You anoint me to be Your special child,
like You did with David
and that You will make me joyful, celebrating You as Lord God,
like the first church in Jerusalem.
I pray to be constantly filled with Your Spirit
and to be attuned to the wavelength of the now of eternity.

I ask for the wisdom of Gamaliel, if that is possible,
not to act in my usual rash and hot-headed way
but to consider everything first, whether it emanates from You.
I celebrate the festival of Your coming in body and Spirit
and, like David, I want to sing to the God of my life.
Because, even though I sometimes feel as bare as the Syrian desert,
You constantly clothe me in new robes and give me renewed
strength.

In this month I want to be victorious with David
and travel with Saul who became Paul –
both were Your servants, which is what I want to be:
Your servant, in the company of the holy angels,
in the company of those who already reside in the eternal light,
in the name of Jesus Christ, the Lord.

Amen.

MUSIC RESEMBLES PRAYER

Whenever the spirit from God came upon Saul, David would take his harp and play. Then relief would come to Saul (1 Sam. 16:23).

Service to God and soul-stirring music go hand in hand. David, probably one of the most heaven-favored statesman who ever lived was, in addition to all his talents, also a poet and musician. According to tradition, he sang Psalm 8 while tending the sheep as a young teenager.

Ambrose established the major role that music played in the Early Church: the prayers that were sung, the songs of praise, and the *Kyrie Eleison*, that is to say "Lord, have mercy on us!" Luther, also a musician and composer, spread the message through wonderful hymns. Through the ages, music and prayer have gone hand in hand. All the truly great masters, the Bachs and Beethovens, were searching for some or other connection with the act of worshiping.

Music was God's plan to get David to Saul's court. Saul, who (sadly) most probably suffered from unipolar depression and which the people of that time described as an "evil spirit" (coming "from God" at that!). Those people understood little of complicated, emotional disturbances. But remarkably, God wove Saul's illness into His method to display David's music, and later on his courage, at the court.

One can believe that the beautiful sounds of the harp and the voice of a young man singing God's praises, calmed Saul or drove out "the evil spirit". My parents always started their day by singing a hymn together. One finds that worshipful piano concertos in the background, or choirs that sing God's praises, or an organ that greets you in jubilation at the church, attune you to God.

Or even to hum a song to His glory that drives morbid thoughts from your mind. Start the day with a hymn to God, even though it may only be in your heart, repeat it and see how it makes you aware of the Presence of God.

Lord, drive out the "evil spirits" of morbid thoughts with a song from my heart.

DO NOT LOSE HEART

David said to Saul, "Let no one lose heart on account of this Philistine; your servant will go and fight him" (1 Sam. 17:32).

It is only human and completely normal to lose heart, to become despondent, especially when confronted with a situation to which you have no solution. Here, the Philistines produced an "invincible" weapon: an armor-clad warrior, an enormously big man who challenged the soldiers of Israel every day to come and fight him. They preferred to take cover.

However, David who arrived at the battlefield with supplies for his brothers, told Saul that it was possible to defeat Goliath, as long as one did not become despondent. He was used to protecting his flock of sheep against a multitude of dangers.

David's secret was that he sang to the glory of his God while tending his sheep, and he had learnt since a very young age that nothing can hold its own against the power of God. And God even honored his youthful presumptuousness.

Years ago, when I was still very young, I struggled with a problem and I could not see any light. There was simply no solution. I walked past a church in the city and wanted to go and pray there. While walking up the steps, I said out loud, "Lord, I think the time has come for me to leave this problem that I cannot possibly solve in Your hands. You will help me." I turned around on the spot. And the Lord did help me; not by solving the problem immediately, but by teaching me how to handle it.

David knew that with God, he could handle anything. There were times when he, like all of us, became despondent and distressed. But God was always at his side. That gives us courage, even though our steps may be faltering. The Lord keeps us standing.

Lord, a great number of Goliaths come to meet us and make us despondent. But You also come to meet us. Teach us exactly how to handle the Goliaths in our lives.

IN GOD'S SPLENDOR

Saul was afraid of David, because the LORD was with David (1 Sam. 18:12).

David defeated Goliath with his sling and small stones. The women sang his praises, more than that of Saul. Saul became jealous of David's popularity, and jealousy is far more dangerous than a thousand Goliaths. It is an emotion that destroys others and – worst of all – destroys you and makes you afraid and distrustful, as it did Saul.

It was very clear to the king that David was someone exceptional; someone Mark Anthony describes in Shakespeare's *Julius Caesar*:

His life was gentle; and the elements
So mix'd in him that Nature might stand up;
And say to all the world: This was a man!

This was (ironically) said of Brutus, one of the assassins. Brutus did not fit the bill. David did, right through his life of triumph and sin, of adventure and love of God.

Such a man draws positive, as well as negative attention. His praises are sung, but he lives dangerously, exposed to the jealous spears of kings and colleagues, acquaintances and strangers.

Saul became "demented" about David and tried to pin him to the wall (v. 18:11). But David was accompanied by an Awesome Dimension: God in all His strength.

The Lord's splendor hung over this servant of His. And then the enemy became fearful, as well as dangerous. As my mother always prayed, "Let no one snatch me from the hollow of Your hand!"

Lord, we seek that dimension which David had; the feeling of being safely sheltered under Your hand, yes, that our name has been written in Your hand.

LOVE THAT IS CALLED FRIENDSHIP

Jonathan said to David, "Go in peace, for we have sworn friendship with each other in the name of the LORD" (I Sam. 20:42).

Saul's court was almost like the one Count Metternich described the Congress of Vienna in 1815: "Back-stabbing, furtiveness, disloyalty, attacks during the day and attacks in the dark, with princes and generals on the forefront, all the sharks of Europe together." David was in constant danger and had to be warned against Saul, and he had to flee time and again (and return again), and even became King Saul's son-in-law as a trap that the monarch had conceived (v. 18:21).

However, God once again provided a lifeline, one of friendship with the king's son, Jonathan. This friendship has become legendary. That is how it is with people who serve the Lord: in every major drama or disappointment, in every cul-de-sac and emotional darkness, most often someone will come to the fore somewhere, guided by the Lord to help, even though it may be with only a word of encouragement. "In every mess I find a friend," the saying goes. It could be a child or a simple word from a "down-to-earth" person. Like the man who had struggled with major problems and whose little girl crept into bed him with one night, saying, "I love you, Daddy."

David and Jonathan "have sworn friendship with each other in the name of the Lord". Someone like David had many fair-weather friends, but one friendship was genuine, the one with the son of the king, whom he called his "brother". When they parted, they embraced each other and cried on each other's shoulders and David fled from Saul's wrath.

Jesus is like Jonathan. The difference is that it is not the Father who creates our problems. We often create our own problems. But He helps us through "every mess". And unlike Jonathan, He and the Father accompany us everywhere through the Spirit, keeping us safe and protected.

Lord, it is a dangerous world, a world in which the Evil One sets traps for us. Protect us as You did David, in true friendship and tangible love.

THE OUTCASTS

All those who were in distress or in debt or discontented gathered round David, and he became their leader. About four hundred men were with him (I Sam. 22:2).

If the Bible were a storybook, one probably would have read that all the good men, the brave ones, the intelligent ones joined David because they were ostensibly "so sincere" because of their noble character. Almost like the legends of the knights of old, like Lohengrin and Sir Galahad.

In this Bible story the opposite happened. The outcasts of society gathered under his banner. David transformed them into a formidable fighting unit, that eventually would culminate in him triumphantly riding into Jerusalem.

David attracted the outcasts and the sinners, people of questionable character and often with even more questionable motives. In this he is a forerunner of Jesus who became the assembly point for the poor, the sinners, the outcasts, the sick and the hungry.

It is strange (but in many respects the rule in God's plan) that He sets different tests from the tests we would set for one another. The motley and dubious band of men who gathered around David would, in all probability, not have passed a single psychological personality test. It is as if God wants to demonstrate, time and again, that He is capable of turning any human material into an instrument for His glory. That He actually starts with chaos to create something new and miraculous.

One often looks back on one's own life and stands amazed that the Lord extended a hand to help at all. And should He extend His hand, it surely could not be for any other reason than giving you a slap. That is how we often perceive it, if we are really honest.

But God turned a band of anguished and discontented men into a victorious unit. He turns the church, with all its sinners, the wretched, the corrupt and the rejected through the ages, into those who prepare His kingdom. He transforms you, and others like you into His children and witnesses. That should set everyone thinking.

Lord, I am also one of the debtors, but under Your banner.

AUTHORITY

"The LORD forbid that I should do such a thing to my master, the LORD's anointed, or lift my hand against him" (I Sam. 24:6).

It is a difficult situation for David. In a fierce civil war, Saul had the priests of Nob murdered because they had given David bread. But then David had the perfect opportunity to kill Saul – in a cave, where Saul was in a vulnerable position. David did not do it, and he merely cut off a corner of Saul's robe. Because he would not lift his hand against his king, "the Lord's anointed", he later told Saul. But Saul wanted to destroy him. David had no illusions about that, because after Saul's emotional expression of gratitude, David returned to his stronghold (cf. v. 22).

On 6 May 1689, the three De Villiers brothers arrived at the Southern tip of Africa as French Huguenots in the ship the *Zion*. Legend has it that they toasted their safe arrival, drinking from shells on the beach, and took an oath that they and their descendants would never be unfaithful to the Lord and the reformed faith. Protestants to the quick. But they apparently also prayed for their king, Louis XIV, and drank a toast to him – the self-same king who had driven them from their fatherland because of their faith. It is like David, and one cannot quite understand it.

Jesus would have understood, though, because He is One who forgive. But for David there was more at stake (as there also was for the three brothers): the major issue of respecting authority. One can question authority and even flee from it, but one must be careful not to challenge authority. This could cause a heated debate, but we live in an era where respect for authority is diminishing more and more: parental authority, educational authority, the authority of God and of His Word.

At the entrance to the cave, David bowed down low before Saul. It would be fitting for us to bow deeply before our God every day, even though we may not always understand His "strange" actions.

Lord, You are authority. You are the law. You are also our Father and we bow down at Your feet.

Man of God

Now Samuel died, and all Israel assembled and mourned for him; and they buried him at his home in Ramah (1 Sam. 25:1).

They have remained a rare species through the ages: true men and women of God, people with only one objective, and that is to attune themselves to the Lord and to listen to His voice. That special disposition, that "anointing", that insight and walk with God and the mystical connection with the Most Holy of the Holy – such a man was Samuel. And the people acknowledged this and mourned for him at his funeral. He was not rich. He did not seek honor. He kneeled before God and listened to His voice and then anointed kings. What a special person!

I recently read something in the testimony of a priest that sets one thinking: some people on earth touch you like the angels. The priest said that his father – who died the previous year – was such a man. But the Lord has blessed this priest with such a living memory of his father that he feels as if his devout father is still with him every day. "When I say my prayers at the altar in church, there are tears for him at times, but I thank God that he died in the Lord and that he is with the angels now; but I still sense his wisdom and love surrounding me."

Such a father is a man of God, a Samuel. And as "all Israel" mourned for him, they probably realized that his wisdom and love would remain alive amongst them; yes, even for us today.

That is something to pursue – to focus more on the Lord in our own small circle, regardless of where we find ourselves, than on trivialities. Something of it could perhaps be conveyed to someone else: a child, a colleague, an acquaintance, a chance meeting. We are by no means flawless, but neither was Samuel. And yet God worked through him. Why not through you and me?

We want to serve You, Lord. Keep us focused on You in all circumstances.

SEEKING STRENGTH

But David found strength in the LORD his God (I Sam. 30:6).

During the civil war, and with Saul's battle against the Philistines, David and his men temporarily sought refuge with their families in Ziklag. Upon returning from fighting the Philistines, they found Ziklag plundered and burnt by a band of Amalekites who had captured their families.

Typically human, David's men were "bitter in spirit" and (also typically) they blamed their commander, David, to such an extent that they wanted to stone him. He could bitterly and ruefully have echoed T. S. Eliot, "Hell is alone … / There is nothing to escape from / and nothing to escape to. / One is always alone" (from *The Cocktail Party*). A leader is indeed alone and David was greatly distressed , but he did not find himself in Eliot's "hell".

Even though David's men were no longer loyal to him, David's God did not desert him. David "found strength in the LORD his God". And when he turned to God for advice, God gave him advice. He had to advance against the band.

He did that and found the Amalekites in a field. David and the others freed their wives and children. They recovered everything the Amalekites had looted. His insight as a leader once again became apparent. The men who went into battle did not want to share the plunder with those who did not want to advance against the Amalekites (cf. v. 22). David simply said: All will share alike.

This man displayed a generosity of spirit, but he also knew that in future, he would be able to count on a great number of the "useless". Good leadership looks beyond today's victory.

Sometimes we also find ourselves in predicaments that we are not to be blamed for. All of us find ourselves in dire straits at some time or another. The self-same God of David is still "on duty" where we are concerned. Ask Him for advice. Recognize and honor Him. He will help.

Yes, Lord, You always help. Grant us peace of mind while we wait.

LAMENT

"Jonathan lies slain on your heights. I grieve for you, Jonathan my brother; you were very dear to me" (2 Sam. 1:25-26).

S aul was overtaken by the Philistines and he and his three sons, including Jonathan, died on Mount Gilboa. A life that had started off well ended in tragedy, with Saul falling on his own sword. In a poignant lament, David mourns for him, but especially for Jonathan, his eternal friend who "lies slain on your heights".

It is tremendous grief that speaks here in poetic language with beautiful rhythm and soul-stirring metaphors. Death always has a terrible impact on the lives of the loved ones who remain behind. In this case, the bodies of Saul and his sons were treated with contempt by the Philistines and nailed to the city wall, from where the kind-hearted people of Jabesh took them down. David mourned in his song, which is good. When you bravely try to contain your tears, it is not good for your emotional health. Yes, we honor and celebrate a life and a friendship that has passed, but tears are more than accept-able, precisely because the person is no longer with us.

The poet Swinburne observed how the deeply religious Christian poet Christina Rosetti died in extreme distress but with the greatest dignity. He wrote a poignant lament on her death. The handwriting on the manuscript is wobbly and stained with tears and alcohol. It is remarkable that he, who was not much of a believer and who at times abused alcohol, could grieve so intensely for one of the best Christian poets of the time.

And yet, to grieve is healing, cleansing, filled with deeply felt loss but also filled with pure love. David had a friend and this prince would live on for centuries after his death, in the tears of mourning and in the music of the harp in the Word of God.

When we think of loved ones long gone, they "live" anew with us for a moment, to our solace and gratitude.

Lord, thank You for all those whom I loved. Even though they are gone, they live on.

THE CITY OF DAVID

David then took up residence in the fortress and called it the City of David. And he became more and more powerful, because the LORD God Almighty was with him (2 Sam. 5:9-10).

D avid was crowned at Hebron and after battles with the remainder of Saul's army, he reclaimed the city of Jerusalem, the city of peace, from the Jebusites, who had once ridiculed him. David was now the undisputed monarch, the commander in battle, the one who commanded respect from his people and from other sovereigns, such as Hiram of Tyre, who helped him to build his palace with its terraces.

The city of David, Zion, is a wonderful city with its walls and gates, with its stonework and its holy places where David and Jesus walked. I saw this city for the first time after the Yom Kippur War of 1973, when a spirit of hostility ruled, as it still does now. When I woke up one morning and looked out of the hotel window, Jerusalem was covered in pure white snow almost as if God still chooses this place, over which so many disputes are raging, for special beauty. Just imagine what it must have looked like in David's time!

And the Almighty was with David. It is as if there was a special closeness between David and God, an extraordinary intimacy. Why was he in particular blessed in this way: from shepherd to king to ancestor of the Savior? God, in His eternal wisdom, delights in His Creation, also in the Creation of special people, just as He delights in the Creation of "ordinary" people who serve Him in simple prayer.

Recently I walked past the supervisor of a building who was sitting in his cubicle, reading his Bible. God delights in that man because in that act of Bible reading, I could observe a Presence as I was passing.

Abide with me, Lord, and give me strength.

POWERFUL LESSON

David was afraid of the LORD that day and said, "How can the ark of
the LORD ever come to me?" (2 Sam. 6:9).

David was God's chosen servant, but one day he came to an
overwhelming realization that God also draws clear boundaries
for His loved ones. God never allows His name, His honor or His
Person to be impugned, neither the symbol over which His name
has been proclaimed.

After David had conquered Jerusalem, he wanted the symbol of
God's Presence, the ark of the covenant, with him and he sent for the
ark. The ark had to be carried by the Levites, but they loaded it onto
a cart and when the oxen stumbled and the ark threatened to topple,
Uzzah, one of the drivers, wanted to prop it up. A good intention but
a deed of self-destruction – like someone who wants to restore the
power in his house while a storm is raging, by trying to connect the
wires on the roof with his bare hands. God is infinite creative power
and that power and glory are not to be tampered with. We are dealing with a holy, untouchable God.

When Uzzah, the co-driver of the ark, touched the ark with un-
consecrated hands, he died. And the sacred festivities came to an
abrupt end. David was "angry" (v. 8) and wanted to know how the
ark of the Lord could ever come to him. All he and the Levites had
to do was to go and read the instructions on how the ark had to be
transported.

The ark was temporarily taken to the house of Obed-Edom, where
it was respectfully kept. The self-same power that destroyed brought
a blessing upon that house. It is like electricity that not only provides
light and power, but also destroys. It requires caution.

We love God and God loves us, but every now and then God, as
He did with David, makes it clear to us that we are out of bounds.
Then we must kneel before God in forgiveness and, like the house of
Obed-Edom, the power of God's Presence will bless us.

*Lord, sometimes we make serious mistakes, sometimes with good
intentions. Preserve us and forgive us.*

FEAST FOLLOWING FRIGHT

David, wearing a linen ephod, danced before the LORD with all his might (2 Sam. 6:14).

The Reverend H. A. Visser from the historic Westerkerk in Amsterdam (where Rembrandt was buried), said a moving prayer on the antique pulpit one morning, "O Lord, I am flawed! Hear me, Lord, I have sinned! Lord, forgive!" The congregation was moved when the elderly man of God prayed in this fashion. No one asked why, but everybody understood that he was calling for the love of God about which he preached with so much conviction and tangible veneration. Everyone called out with him, because all of us are sometimes out of bounds.

David received the message of the blessings that the ark had brought for Obed-Edom and "his entire household" (cf. v. 11). Sometimes God blesses us with material wealth, but He uses it sparingly according to the principle of "give me only my daily bread" (Prov. 30:8). But He indeed made David rich and famous, as He did with Solomon after him, and Abraham long before both of them.

Obtaining riches and blessings was not David's motive: he suddenly came to realize that if there were blessings, the breach with God about the ark had been restored and therefore, he wanted the symbol of God's presence with him. The Levites fetched the ark and carried it, and in front of the ark there were exuberant celebrations with sacrificial offerings every six steps. Suddenly they knew what exuberant joy, as well as respect, meant.

The elderly Reverend Visser from Amsterdam also knew, because following his moving prayer that morning in church, he led the congregation in a song of praise, his voice filled with joy. He knew God and knew that sometimes He gives you a quick rap, but that He is also quick to bless you. David also realized this and danced in front of the ark, wearing only an ephod. The king leading the symbol of God … What a day it must have been! And what a day today could be for us!

Lord, if it is Your will, let me dance before You this day with the joy of David.

TO ENJOY GOD

It was before the LORD, who chose me rather than your father or anyone from his house when he appointed me ruler over the LORD's people
Israel – I will celebrate before the LORD (2 Sam. 6:21).

The Reverend Visser from the Westerkerk in Amsterdam often
said in his books and sermons, "God loves exuberance." The
Lord enjoys cheerfulness and even exuberant gaiety in His name.
And one assumes that the celebrations in Jerusalem during the holy
and grand procession, and David's dance (that symbolized joy and
also humility before God to His glory) were pleasing to Him. After
the ark had been put in its rightful place, David blessed his people
in the name of the Lord.

However, David's wife Michal, the daughter of Saul, did not
share his joy. She seriously reprimanded him for making a spectacle
of himself in front the whole nation and all the slaves both male and
female. From her position as a princess and the wife of the monarch,
she had a right to her opinion. But she "despised" him (cf. v. 16)
for his behavior and she did not address him in the right way. And
David turned away from her for good. After all, those were difficult
times and he had just replaced her father.

David did not offer any apologies or explanations, "I will celebrate before the LORD", he told her. He who had sung while tending
the sheep, and played the harp for her father, would dance for joy,
also in the presence of all the slaves.

Exuberant joy is wonderful in any person's life. Even a child's
enjoyment of a present is something wonderful to a parent. But the
celebrations did not continue. The challenges of ruling and managing
the affairs of the country as well as enemies were awaiting David.

It is the same for us, but while working and coping with problems every day, an intention of joy in God in our hearts as well as in
His "ark", always results in blessings.

Let us enjoy You today, Lord!

ETERNAL KING

Your house and your kingdom will endure forever before Me; your throne will be established forever (2 Sam. 7:16).

These are the words of the prophet, Nathan, to David, after David had found it in his heart to build a temple to the glory of the Lord. The Lord did not allow him to do so. After all, the people still had to be stabilized and consolidated so that David's successor could rule in peace. He could then build the temple.

Through the prophet, however, the Lord made a profound promise to David that still impacts us today: that his kingdom will endure "forever" and that his throne will be "established forever". Yes, the royal house would crumble and experience testing times, but a descendant of David would ascend to the eternal throne as Savior of all nations, Jesus Christ, our Lord and King. And centuries later in the Acts of the apostles, His Kingdom would be spread throughout the earth and would be proclaimed today and unto all eternity.

That is all that Nathan could have meant with these words, because otherwise the prophet was telling lies. And it is the same prophet who would reprimand David at a later stage. Therefore, it was not in his nature to make idle talk in order to flatter someone's ego. He spoke those words on behalf of God, and the throne of Jesus Christ will endure forever and ever as the house of David.

I would like to have been there the day David entered Jerusalem, dancing. I would have served with pride at his royal court. But I wonder whether I would ever have been able to sense exactly whose ancestor David would be. Would David himself have realized what Nathan had actually said? That Christ would come: the first time to stake His claim to the throne with His blood, and the second time with a heavenly host to finally establish His Kingdom over everything and for ever. Would David have been able to understand and sing the praises of this kingdom? Do we realize it every day? That the Son of David reigns where the sun never sets ...

Lord, You are King eternal in my heart.

FOR THE SAKE OF ...

"Don't be afraid ... for I will surely show you kindness for the sake of your father Jonathan" (2 Sam. 9:7).

Mephibosheth was the crippled son of Jonathan, David's loyal friend who had perished with Saul. David sent for Mephibosheth, a man of misery, and gave him gifts and the right to become part of his household. Naturally, Mephibosheth was scared when he was summoned, but David immediately put his mind at ease by saying that he was being honored "for the sake of your father Jonathan".

David honored his old friend through Jonathan's descendants. It was a matter of principle to him. Someone from the house of Saul had to be treated well for the sake of Jonathan's memory. As it was a matter of principle for Jesus to forgive His persecutors and killers. It was, in fact, more than just a matter of principle, because too often principles can be manipulated to suit the circumstances or events, or to curry favor.

David was not looking for any favors; he wanted to do someone a favor. It was more than mere principle to him – he had loved his friend Jonathan and this love lived on.

Jesus forgave His persecutors and executioners on principle because it was in accordance with the will of His Father. However, His forgiveness goes far deeper than principles: He loved His persecutors in an inexplicable way. They could harm Him. He did not want to do them harm. This is the essence of Christian love, and it is not easy.

Mephibosheth became part of David's royal household, but when Absalom rebelled against David he did not accompany David. He had good reasons, but he nevertheless chose to stay. That is often the nature of human behavior. David would forgive him for that.

After all, notwithstanding all the times that he stumbled, David was the predecessor of Christ the Savior. And Christ's life is love.

Lord, teach us to do good. Out of more than mere principle; out of love. To be in line with David and, especially with the King, Jesus Christ.

Encounter

"I am Jesus, whom you are persecuting," He replied. "Now get up and go into the city" (Acts 9:5-6).

Almost all people who know something about the Gospel, or think that they know something, know about Saul's Damascus experience, his right about-turn, his complete transformation, his zeal to persecute, followed by his zeal to convert people and his own constant castigation by persecution. When the light from heaven enveloped him, he asked, "Who are You, Lord?" He obviously knew full well with whom he was dealing. His zeal to persecute, following the death of Stephen, was his last agonizing attempt to withstand believing in Jesus Christ.

God had chosen well. Like David, Saul was a complex person with many talents as well as weaknesses, but with a fervent love for God and a fervor for the Lord's house. Just as David had to organize and establish the people of Israel, Saul, who became Paul, had to explain to the Christian communities with awe-inspiring logic the significance of Jesus' divine appearance. Jesus hit the world like a flash of lightning. Paul had to consider everything carefully, after these cosmic events, and then complete the puzzle of how everything fitted together. Peter and the others gloried in the Father and the wonderful events of Jesus' life on earth. Through Paul, the Lord would explain to the faithful what would happen from then onwards.

Major questions awaited him: What was to be done with the Gospel? Why? Which way and, especially, how? And until when? With the thorn in his flesh, this man would start walking and traveling and preaching and performing miracles and writing letters; letters from someone who had been struck by people; letters from someone who had been struck by God; letters drenched in Christ and the love of Christ.

Oh yes, he knew full well who had appeared to him. And from his letters one can deduce that he worshipfully marveled at this for the rest of his life. When we really start to think and feel and reflect on it, we also know who appears time and again to help us.

Yes, Lord, it is You.

THE PROOF

Yet Saul grew more and more powerful and baffled the Jews living in Damascus by proving that Jesus is the Christ (Acts 9:22).

It is an age-old trick: when someone is trying to convince you and you do not want to be convinced, or when you know the truth but you do not want to admit it, you belittle the one who is trying to convince you, or you drive him away. In the time of Saul you would have killed him.

Something like scales fell from Saul's eyes, literally and figuratively speaking; his conversion caused a stir in the church in Damascus, as well as among the other Jews. The Spirit of God started to radiate through Saul's thoughts and actions. He "grew more and more powerful … by proving Jesus is the Christ".

And in his case it was difficult to question him because he was trained in Jewish thinking and piety and he had already made major discoveries regarding the way that Jesus fitted into all this. He could see that He was indeed the Christ, the One who would come as promised by the church fathers and the prophets.

The Jews did not want to hear this and Saul had to flee during the night. He went back to Jerusalem, but was then sent to Tarsus via Caesarea by the faithful in order to take a break and escape from his persecutors.

Later on he would say that he "takes pride" in his weakness, but he was a powerful preacher of God's plan, like David was a powerful conqueror in the name of the Lord.

God did not spare any of them setbacks, because He does not promise a smooth path. But the Lord was not sparing with His presence towards either one of them, neither is He towards you and me.

Lord, thank You that we may struggle through all our daily problems with You by our side.

GOD ACCEPTS MEN FROM ALL NATIONS

"I now realize how true it is that God does not show favoritism but accepts men from every nation who fear Him and do what is right" (Acts 10:34-35).

S aul went to Tarsus for the time being but in the meantime, Peter was not resting on his laurels either. His and Paul's methods of ministering and spreading the Gospel differed, and later on they even found themselves at loggerheads, but both ended up in Rome, the Roman capital, both as martyrs for Jesus Christ.

Peter had a vision in which the Lord finally made it clear to him that the boundaries between Jews and Gentiles were abolished and that the Gospel was also intended for the Gentiles. Meanwhile, the Roman centurion Cornelius from Caesarea ("devout and God-fearing"; who in all probability was also a student of Jewish law or a "proselyte of the portal") was looking for him to hear the Word of Christ.

Peter accompanied the messengers to the home of Cornelius and there he heard that a few days before, Cornelius had also had a vision in which he was commanded to go and see Peter and to fetch him from the home of Simon, the tanner. Upon his arrival at Cornelius's house, he found a keen family, in essence the start of an eager home church, that wanted to hear everything about Jesus Christ.

Notwithstanding the vision, Peter was overwhelmed and he admitted something that a devout Jew would find very difficult: that God does not distinguish between men and nations where salvation is concerned, "but accepts men from every nation who fear Him and do what is right". Afterwards Peter proclaimed Christ to them and the power that God bestowed on Christ.

Today I once again proclaim Christ to you, as well as to myself. Christ, the One who would come. The One who would shed sweat and blood. The One who understands. And because it so easily slips our minds, we need to hear this every day for the sake of His name and for the sake of our peace.

Holy Jesus, Lord of lords, You have been elevated to the heavenly throne. We bring You glory, Christ the Lord! You are crowned with glory!

THE CHURCH

While Peter was still speaking these words, the Holy Spirit came on all who heard the message (Acts 10:44).

Some people refer to these events as the Second Pentecost or the Pentecost of the Gentiles. At the first Pentecostal meeting, all those present were Jews. Here, Peter was in all probability the only Jew. But the same miraculous signs – testimony and praise in all languages – took place here. God blew His breath, like a powerful wind into the body that He created via His covenant of old. Just as He created man in the beginning, this "body" of people became His church, believers from all nations.

From here onwards there were no boundaries. The church of Christ would take shape and the Spirit would preserve it through the ages and constantly reform it. God decided that His church would be drawn together from all who believe in Christ and this family of God has been shaped and reshaped throughout the entire history by His Spirit that also came upon the Gentiles on that day.

But does it make you and me – "church people" to a greater or lesser extent, probably drawn from all forms of Christian worship – "holy"? In the Spirit, yes. In the flesh, no. The mystic, Bernard of Clairvaux, summarized it in a formidable way, "O humility! O sublimity! Both tabernacle of cedar and sanctuary of God; earthly dwelling and celestial place; house of clay and royal hall; body of death and temple of light; and at last both object of scorn to the proud and bride of Christ! She is black but beautiful, O daughters of Jerusalem, for even if the labor and pain of her long exile may have discolored her, yet heaven's beauty has adorned her." Our long and earthly exile darkens us. But the heavenly splendor is also there somewhere.

Amen to this. We, the church, the faithful, the people called from all nations, the people of the Spirit are once again like God's people of old on our journey through the desert of the Promised Land. Sometimes we worship our own idols and complain about shortages of meat and bread. But God always comes to meet us somewhere and makes us aware of Him once again – at a Sinai, or a Horeb, or a burning bush.

Lord, I pray for myself. I pray for my church. I pray for Your church. I pray for all who believe.

CHRISTIANS

Barnabas went to Tarsus to look for Saul, and when he found him, he brought him to Antioch. So for a whole year Barnabas and Saul met with the church. The disciples were called Christians first at Antioch (Acts 11:25-26).

C hristian." It is a profound title, one that is constantly under scrutiny, especially when people start to construct character tests. The eighteenth-century philosopher, Hume, said that a Christian was someone who believed in miracles that enabled him "to believe what is most contrary to custom and experience". Hume said it in a negative way, but it contains an element of truth. A Christian indeed believes in miracles, especially the miracle of Jesus Christ who lives.

From their way of life, the people of Antioch probably appeared to be somewhat "different", followers of Christ, people who applied the rule of love under the guidance of Barnabas and Paul. This title remained, deserved and undeserved.

Voltaire said it was a disgrace that America was not named after its founder, Columbus, but that it was an even bigger disgrace that the Christendom was named after Christ, its founder. This is food for thought, because our conduct is often in direct conflict with what Jesus taught and our service to our neighbors is also sadly lacking, not to mention our service to God.

It is easy to be a Christian because under the guidance of the Spirit, you believe in Christ as the Life. But to *live* as a Christian … well, often when we put down the Bible or walk out of the church gate, we have already forgotten what we have just learnt.

The co-ministers of Antioch, Paul, would have understood this. Later on, he complained that there were two of him: the one who wanted to do what was good and the other one who did what was bad. But with our good intentions, as well as our feet of clay, the Lord helps us along. And He is the only One who will do it, regardless of what Hume said.

Help me along, Lord, so that I can learn how to live like a Christian!

ONCE AGAIN AN ANGEL IS NEAR

He (the angel) struck Peter on the side and woke him up. "Quick, get up!" he said (Acts 12:7).

It had to happen again. At some time or another, Peter would end up in jail. James had already been killed by Herod, who soon discovered that the Jews agreed with his persecution of the church. It is clear that after Passover, he wanted to make a spectacle of Peter "before the people". He kept Peter under strict guard in jail.

It is noteworthy that it was a time of appearances by angels and the descending of the Holy Spirit, of miracles and heavenly teaching; but it was also a time of danger, persecution, suspicion, tension, political intrigue and ghastly violence against the cause of the Lord. Sometimes it would appear as if these paradoxes are always present in one way or another, especially in the lives of the faithful. That is one of the mysteries of God's plan.

However, angels appear in our lives when we are in deep distress, like they appeared to Peter during that night while he was asleep in jail. The angel touched him and led him to freedom, to the (initial) consternation of the household of the faithful who were praying for him, and also of the soldiers, who were blamed by Herod.

Some people allege that in times of major change and danger, angels are very active, as though God is keeping His celestial servants near His people. If this is so, then those times were a good example, because angels appear constantly to intervene and to help. One accepts that they are doing this again now, in these turbulent times, and we sometimes wish they would visibly show themselves now and again!

However, God is in control and angels do come to assist, and the jail doors do open. Problems that seem insoluble today will perhaps dissolve in remarkable solutions tomorrow. Light suddenly transforms a night that seemed never ending. And somewhere we regain direction, guided by an angel. As an old English hymn confidently states, "The angel of the Lord came down / And glory shone around."

*L*ord, surround me with Your angels and free me from my shackles.

IT SIMPLY CONTINUES!

Herod died. But the word of God continued to increase and spread (Acts 12:23-24).

When one thinks of King Herod, the words of the poet, Thomas Gray (creator of the famous *Elegy written in a Country Church-yard)*, come to mind: "Ruin seize thee, ruthless King! / Confusion on thy banners wait ..." (from *The Bard*).

Herod was merciless and murderous, even where his own family was concerned. He was a vassal of Rome with limited power, not an incompetent ruler, but a shrewd political maneuverer who knew how to exploit events and public opinion to benefit his cause. But his days of greatness were numbered: "Confusion on thy banners wait." He died "of worms", says Luke, probably from some severe infection. A great enemy of Christ was no longer, like all the enemies of Christ will eventually cease to exist.

"But the word of God continued to increase ..." That is a great consolation. Every sovereign on earth, every ruler, every great nation, every establishment will come to an end ... but the word of God continues. Sometimes painfully slowly, sometimes quickly, sometimes spectacularly, sometimes virtually unnoticed.

In my lifetime I have witnessed the disintegration of the British Empire, the rise and fall of Hitler's infamous Third Reich, as well as the fall of the dreaded Soviet Union. All three appeared to be un-stoppable at one stage, like Rome in the time of Herod. Like Herod before his handful of extolling subjects.

Many "prophets" have already predicted the "fall" of God and "Christianity", the end of the Empire of the Pale Galilean. But Christ triumphs time and again. Christ will always have His witnesses, just as He will have His persecutors. His banner is the cross. His consti-tution is love. His strength lies in the hearts of people. And when all has passed, only His Gospel will remain and only He will be there as Savior to help, to guide, to console. Because there is no other. There is no one else.

Lord, let us hold Your banners high and live out Your name to the full in front of all. In You alone we want to live in a kingdom without end.

INSTRUMENT

"Set apart for Me Barnabas and Saul for the work to which I have called them" (Acts 13:2).

The time of major events and powerful tempests of God's appearance, the time of ecstasy and excitement of mass conversion, was slowly passing, as it happens in the normal progression of time. No one can continue to live in ecstasy and excitement as it causes an addiction to even more excitement and ecstasy. The congregation had to continue their "normal" life with its ups and downs once again. And more importantly, God's work had to be executed daily with diligent labor and planning.

The church at Antioch worshiped together and received clear instruction to set Saul and Barnabas "apart" to do "the work to which I have called them". Especially Saul, whose name was quietly changed to Paul in this chapter, and whose major work was starting only then. The Lord considered his training to be completed. He was highly skilled in the law. He knew the Greek literature and philosophy and was a Roman citizen "by birth", a respected man – as well as a marked man. The ideal man for God's mission across the known world of that time.

God chooses simple people, uses them powerfully, and teaches them. God also makes use of people who have studied, and teaches them and adds to their knowledge.

A woman once sent a letter with numerous spelling mistakes and incorrect grammar to John Wesley, ending it with, "Mr. Wesley, God does not need your erudition." Wesley replied with a short letter, "Thank you for the admonition, I realize it, but neither does God need your illiteracy."

God needed Paul for His further plans, like He needed a Wesley later on. He always prepares His Moses. And regardless of how "ordinary" you and I may be, He also works on us to do something for Him, to touch someone else, to teach a child, to set an example and, above all, to be aware of Him.

Use me, Lord, use me.

THE BEAUTY OF DIVERSITY

He testified concerning him: "I have found David son of Jesse a man after My own heart" (Acts 13:22).

Paul and Barnabas departed on their first mission to the island of Cyprus where they were warmly welcomed and where they proceeded to preach. From there they traveled to Pisidian Antioch in Asia Minor. Like Peter, Paul traced the development of the Gospel very far back in his message. He addressed the Jews in the synagogue and pointed out the deliverance from Egypt, as well as the key role that David had played in the history of redemption.

It is remarkable to note just how widely the Jews had been dispersed by this time: Asia Minor, Greece, Italy, Egypt, as far as Spain. This Dispersion also formed part of God's scheme to proclaim the Gospel worldwide. Paul and the others always started preaching at Jewish synagogues and many Jews became believers in Christ. Other Jews clung to their old ways.

Paul's emphasis was on the kingship of the house of David, the oath that the Lord had "sworn by My holiness ... that his (David) line will continue forever" (Ps. 89:35-36), the "man after God's own heart". In the mystery of God's exciting actions involving mankind, it is as though He, as a God who prefers infinite diversity, often makes use of people and things that constitute major risks: brilliant and riddled with faults, beautiful and not so beautiful, like with David and Paul. It is almost as if God plans infinitely thoroughly, but also experiments.

One wonders whether the splendor of what we refer to as "the next world" would not be an experience of an awareness of a billion facets of glory and magnificence which, like in countless kaleidoscopes, are constantly changing, and yet will be permanently anchored in the tranquility and strength of the Presence.

Like David, all of us are God's kaleidoscopes with beautiful as well as less attractive colors. He turns us to face the light, the sun. He created us to please Him, regardless of the contrasts and diversity of our personalities. May we bring Him joy today.

Yes, we want to be people after Your own heart, Lord.

SHAKING THE DUST FROM YOUR FEET

So they shook the dust from their feet in protest against them (the people of the city of Antioch) and went to Iconium (Acts 13:51).

Shaking the dust from their feet should people refuse to receive them, is a "gesture" that refers to the words of Jesus when He sent out His first disciples to spread the Gospel. Jesus, the Great Realist, knew that some would receive His people, while others would refuse them. For those who received them there were blessings in store, but judgment awaited those who drove them away.

In Antioch, Asia Minor, the reception was initially positive and crowds gathered to listen to the Word. Jews as well as Gentiles were converted. The "Gentiles", especially, "honored the Word of the Lord" (v. 48) and the leading Jews became so disgruntled about this that they even incited the "God-fearing women" against Paul and the others, and Paul had to flee. They shook the dust from their feet, but there were still numerous disciples in Antioch who were "filled with joy". Paul would return to the city at a later stage.

We do not read about Paul ever shaking the dust from his feet again. Perhaps he was dismayed about what had happened, perhaps he, serious man that he was, really meant it at that moment. But these are clearly also the words of Jesus and, let us be honest, there are times in the lives of Christians when we (even though it might only be a symbolic act and even though no retribution or defiance is intended) "have to shake the dust from our feet".

It could be anything from a form of worship, like Luther and the others, to the termination of a friendship from which no blessing is forthcoming. There are times in our lives when we have to close a door, especially when we feel that it is starting to "hamper" our prayers. However, to "shake the dust from our feet" requires the wisdom of the Spirit of God in prayer. May the Lord guide us in all our decisions.

Lord, sometimes we need to make harsh decisions. Please, remain Present at all times.

FAITH RATHER THAN MIRACLES

Even with these words, they had difficulty keeping the crowd from
sacrificing to them (Acts 14:18).

In Lystra Paul looked directly at a man who had been paralyzed
since birth and said, "Stand up on your feet!" The man could walk
again and the crowd was ecstatic. "The gods have come down to
us in human form," they said. It was a miracle, even to people who
lived in the old-world culture of Roman polytheism. Paul raised serious objections against this and pointed out to them that they were
merely proclaiming Jesus Christ. But the people still wanted to sacrifice to them "as gods".

It is significant that from here onwards, signs and miracles became
increasingly rare in Acts. God would still intervene in a powerful
way every now and again, resulting in major testimony to His Gospel, but He was in the process of weaning His people from miraculous signs. The apostles had to learn to proceed in faith and prayer in
the Presence, as Moses had to do many a day in the desert.

What happened in Lystra partially explains why such visible miracles had to make space for faith alone. It is simply human to run
after miracles and signs, to live in the excitement of supernatural
events. However, it is also human for people to start idolizing those
through whom miracles take place. And it need not even be miracles. Think of how modern man "worships" the public presence of,
for example, a soccer or movie star. Even Paul and the others could
not escape this.

Miracles would not cease to happen, not then and not now. But
service to God is the simple acceptance of the fact of salvation in
Christ. Yes, sometimes we do sincerely desire miracles and some of
us do indeed experience miracles. In the Roman Catholic Church it
even forms part of the cult of the saints. And to extend our hand in
faith is perhaps not as dramatic and spectacular, but it is an adventure because we know that Someone is there to take our hand.

*Lord, I extend my hand to You in faith. Please take my hand and
lead me today and every day. I worship You alone.*

A SYNOD MEETING WITH OURSELVES

It seemed good to the Holy Spirit and to us not to burden you with anything beyond the following requirements ... (Acts 15:28).

Paul and the others returned from the first missionary journey and the congregations were glad to hear how many people, especially Gentiles, had seen the light. In the mean time the Pharisees had also joined the community of believers in Jerusalem and started to influence the Gospel by enforcing Jewish customs like circumcision.

The first "synod" was held in Jerusalem about this issue, and judgment was given in these beautiful words, "It seemed good to the Holy Spirit and to us ..." Inter alia, that the old legalistic customs, such as circumcision, were no longer required, but that they had to abstain from food sacrificed to idols (products were usually sold at a discount after the ceremony).

These people debated wisely, and they sought the will of God. Unfortunately I also attended synod meetings where decisions were made that would barely have stood the test of "the Holy Spirit and us". The more human customs and "proper behavior" are raised, the less the voice of the Spirit is heard.

The author Evelyn Waugh, whose work has already been described as "anarchy in defense of order", harshly remarked that anarchy was often closer to the solution than a good idea gone awry. An idea that has gone awry cannot be rectified, but good often comes from disenchantment with anarchy.

During synod meetings, good ideas sometimes went awry to such an extent that nothing could salvage them. Within ourselves ideas can also go awry to the extent that we are often left feeling disenchanted. We must constantly test ourselves in prayer to see whether what we believe and do are "the Holy Spirit and us".

And when doubt about issues is mounting, it is time to pause and hold a "synod meeting" with ourselves and the Spirit. And the Spirit will clarify the direction to take.

Lord, help us to live as "the Holy Spirit and us".

CALL

During the night in Troas Paul had a vision of a man of Macedonia standing and begging him, "Come over to Macedonia and help us" (Acts 16:9).

To the Lord the time had come for the Gospel to move out of the Middle East and Asia Minor to Europe, the center of the known world of that time. In a vision Paul saw a Greek man asking for help, almost as if the Lord was making a brief call to Paul with a concise instruction. Once again no specific address; merely a region and a direction. But Paul left for Macedonia as soon as possible. Silas went along, as well as a young man named Timothy. Somewhere along the line Luke also joined them.

On the Sabbath Paul and the others went in search of Jews at a place of prayer near the river, and came across a group of women. One of them, Lydia, a dealer in purple cloth, was converted and baptized. She became the first proselyte in Europe and therefore the spiritual mother to all of us who received the faith via the history of Europe. The entire development of the West would be determined by this, right into the New World, the undiscovered regions of the time, and today's major powers.

It is significant that the first European proselyte was a woman; apparently a serious woman and a good business person. She would play a major role in the early church – a role that women were gradually deprived of, but these days the wheel is turning.

The majority of us learnt our first prayers from our mothers. All credit to them, the Lydias of yesterday and today. It is quite possible that the Lord is once again preparing a Lydia or a Deborah. The world needs them, because social rehabilitation would in all probability start with mothers and families. Goethe wrote, *Das Ewig-Weibliche zieht uns hinan*. The eternal feminine draws us upwards.

In Paul's vision a man was calling, but the Lord "opened the heart" of a woman to Christ (cf. v. 14). May He call all of us today and make us willing to accept His call.

Help us Lord! Pull us upwards!

SHAKE IT OFF!

Paul shook the snake off into the fire and suffered no ill effects (Acts 28:5).

Paul and company once again experienced major adventures, successes and failures and blessings with the Gospel in Europe. Paul was jailed in Philippi and the Lord delivered him; his reasoning with the scholars in Athens was not successful; he established a church in Corinth; survived rioting in Ephesus; and in Jerusalem he once again clashed with the Jews. This resulted in his final arrest.

He defended himself excellently before King Agrippa and as a Roman citizen, he requested a hearing by the emperor. On his way to Rome he survived being shipwrecked, while encouraging everyone. And on Malta he simply shook off a snake that had bitten him, into the fire. In the meantime the Word of God became unstoppable through him and his companions.

What an exceptional career, and what a great man of God! One concludes from the account of the snake on Malta that he regarded the incident as an ordinary, everyday irritation, although the inhabitants of the island initially regarded him as a great criminal and then as a god. Typical. A few years ago a man let loose a few poisonous snakes in the headquarters of a major bank after a small difference of opinion with the bank. For days on end it was front-page news and one of the security guards even ended up in hospital. The man who released the snakes became something of a hero to many!

Paul would not have regarded his experience as front-page news. The Lord told him to go and preach the Gospel in Rome, and the Lord would ensure that no storm or snake would stop him. What is important is that the Lord did not spare him either the storm or the snake. He did not give him a smooth road, but He constantly created opportunities out of setbacks.

Often we fret about some "snake" that has bitten us on the hand, something that gets in our way or troubles us. Shake it off. God will ensure that you are able to continue your journey.

―――――

Lord, help us not to be unnecessarily troubled by setbacks. Help us to shake them off.

THE KINGDOM CONTINUES

He preached the kingdom of God and taught about the Lord Jesus Christ (Acts 28:31).

The Book of Acts ends on a triumphant note. It is as if Luke wanted to end it just there, with Paul who was a prisoner, but who in fact had great freedom to pursue his great "conquest" for the kingdom. There he took care of himself and received visitors. Apparently Timothy and numerous others saw him quite often. On one occasion Luke also stayed with him. There is even the possibility that Paul traveled from Rome to as far as Spain.

Luke does not, however, mention anything about Paul's death, or of Peter's. After all, his entire account was not the history of Paul and the apostles' adventures. These adventures were merely the backdrop against which the preaching of the Gospel took place. The Acts were of the Holy Spirit with a miracle or two in-between, and everything aimed at allowing the Gospel to continue.

Luke summarized what Paul had to say in one sentence, "He preached the kingdom of God and taught about the Lord Jesus Christ." This Paul would also do in his famous letters. It is so simple, although scholars sometimes allege that he "unnecessarily complicated and made the elementary words and doctrine of Jesus incomprehensible". But just in case people think that "you must love your neighbor as yourself" or, "you must love your enemies" or, "if your hand causes you to stumble, cut if off" could be regarded as an "elementary" or "easy" doctrine, they should think again.

Paul grasped the broad message of Christ, the Son of David, the Savior of all: the kingdom that will be in full bloom in the eternal high summer when Jesus comes again. Enthusiasm about this was Paul's life, because it is the future, also yours and mine. And that is the victory, as well as your and my strength for every day. Christ reigns forever! Amen.

Lord, like Paul, I am also a citizen of Your Kingdom. I honor You and live through You.

JULY

Lord Jesus Christ

I was caught in heavy traffic yesterday, inching forward
and standing still, listening to Brahms' violin concerto
and all the noises outside my car. I watched the other drivers:
bored, agitated, furious, all in a hurry to get somewhere.
In spite of Brahms I also became restless. I thought:
I cannot spend days listening to music with all the chaos outside.
I wondered what You would do, Lord Jesus, in a world of cars,
TV, traffic jams and rush hours.
I wished that You would join me, sit next to me and bless me
and listen to Brahms' soothing themes with me.
But You *were* there, like You were with the disciples
caught in a storm, and with the travelers to Emmaus
who could not understand the strange happenings in Jerusalem.
Even a traffic jam can't escape Your presence.

If You were not there I would have burst out in anger,
or done something stupid, in spite of the violin in the background.
But let me confess: I only realized that when the traffic moved again;
You are in the ebb and flow of our bustling days.

I keep on yearning for more of You
for Your imminence, Your Presence,
in the knowledge that You are to me what You were to Peter and
Paul – You are Lord at all times: a glowing fire in the night
and a melody that resounds like a lone violin under starry skies,
reassuring that You think of us all, and guard us and weep for us
and, in addition, anoint us as children of the Father.

Amen.

TABLE OF SINNERS

"You are the man!" (2 Sam. 12:7).

In the children's Bible of my childhood, there was a striking black-and-white picture that horrified me – Nathan, pointing an accusing finger at King David, saying, "You are the man who has sinned grievously!" After all, David had a man murdered and took that man's wife for himself.

The account of David and Bathsheba constitutes one of the Lord's greatest contrasts in the Bible. On one hand, extreme transgressions, especially from David and, on the other hand apparent love. On the one hand punishment, disappointment and mourning, but on the other hand forgiveness, and an act of love and comfort. Amidst all the happenings and intrigue, a little child died, but another was born, Solomon, whom the Lord loved (cf. v. 24), the future heir to the throne.

One actually needs Paul to explain just how these awful and yet wonderful events fit together. It is once again the mystery of God, the unfathomable love that chastises and admonishes, but also comforts and bestows blessings. David's personality alone – someone in whom virtue and vice were closely interwoven – tells us something of the complexity of God's work. It is as if God exerts Himself in wrath to turn the sinner into someone special. It is as if – with due respect – the situation holds an eternal challenge for Him.

This is a major consolation. Saint Therese of Lisieux (a young woman of impeccable character with a life of extreme sacrifice, despite severe nervous attacks) said that, in the fullness of time, she wanted to share a table with sinners, "because that is where I belong". I understand that, because that is where I belong too. Paul understood it very well. So did David, but he nevertheless sang that eventually he will be God's guest of honor (cf. Ps. 23). Correct, because Christ especially liked to accept invitations from sinners.

God could constantly point a finger at us saying, "You are the one!" Instead, He shows us a Cross, His own sacrifice of forgiveness. Unfathomable. Miraculous!

God of forgiveness, keep us in the circle of the light of Your love.

THE MOUNT OF OLIVES

But David continued up the Mount of Olives, weeping as he went (2 Sam. 15:30).

One day an old peasant woman knocked on our kitchen door and called out to my mother. When my mother opened the top door, the old woman almost doubled up over the lower door, crying. Her large body shook with tears. Her "difficult" son, who had caused her so many gray hairs, had died in unnatural circumstances. Such a sorrowful picture stays etched in a child's mind.

Such a sorrowful picture was King David, walking up the Mount of Olives, weeping as he went while his people evacuated Jerusalem before the troops of his rebellious favorite son, Absalom. Absalom was the essence of a parent's unrequited love. He challenged David in every possible way and won the favor of the people of Israel in a tawdry but effective way. David had to flee from his own son. The Levites even wanted to take the ark with David, but David sent the ark back with these poignant words, "If He (the Lord) says, 'I am not pleased with you,' then I am ready" (v. 26). That is true resignation to God, acceptance with resignation.

Then he walked up the Mount of Olives, weeping as he went, because to accept something does not stop the tears immediately. The Lord took care of him. Old comrades left him. Others remained faithful. Old enemies, like Shimei cursed him. An old advisor offered his services and a neat plan was devised to give Absalom the wrong advice that, in the end, would lead to his downfall. How touching were these events, how typically human! The ark was not with David, but the Presence, his God, was with him.

The day would come when Jesus Christ would also weep on the slopes of the Mount of Olives struggling with betrayal, love for His Father and pain. Those age-old olive trees in the garden of Gethsemane were witness to many things. Sorrow and disappointment formed part of David's life, as well as of Jesus' life. It is also part of our lives. Tears or victory: God is present. He will provide.

Thank You so much, Lord, that You will provide.

MY SON!

"Is the young man Absalom safe?" (2 Sam. 18:29).

No, Absalom was not safe. His rebellion had failed after a fierce battle in the forest of Ephraim, and Joab killed him while he was hanging helplessly from the branches of a tree. When David heard the news of the great victory, he first wanted to know if the "young man Absalom" was safe. They told him what had happened and he cried his heart out – for his son, for himself, for the rebellion, for all the intrigue, and because Joab had totally disregarded his royal command to protect Absalom. Joab also had to reprimand David at a later stage over his weeping and mourning for Absalom.

Afterwards he resumed his reign over Israel. Perhaps Joab was right; someone like Absalom had had many chances and would probably have become a threat to the king and his successor once again. David's sons were not exactly shining examples of what Rudyard Kipling later described as "you'll be a man, my son". After all, for that they had to meet some requirements: "If you can trust yourself when all men doubt you, / But make allowance for their doubting too …" (from Kipling's *If*). Well, Absalom was not that wise, like many other things he was not so.

This had to be a bitter pill for David to swallow, as it was for Samuel before him. But, in David's case, love had no end. "My son! My son!"

God understood. God understands everything. Sometimes, God allows disasters to happen for our own good. God had to experience this with Jesus. But there is always victory. Sometimes God keeps our eyes clear through the salt of our tears so that we can see the flowers on the side of the road again. There are many colors, and the Lord's blessings are abundant. So abundant that at times, we are rendered speechless and like David, can carry on again, strengthened.

Guide us companion Light, through terrestrial darkness …

"IMPOSSIBLE LOYALTY"

Rizpah daughter of Aiah took sackcloth and spread it out for herself on a rock. From the beginning of the harvest till the rain poured down from the heavens on the bodies, she did not let the birds of the air touch them by day or the wild animals by night. When David was told what Rizpah, Saul's concubine had done, he went and took the bones (2 Sam. 21:10-12).

This is a tragic but beautiful incident of motherly and wifely loyalty, even after death. Because of a mixture of honor, disaster, revenge, faith and superstition, the Gibeonites asked David for seven of Saul's descendants to be executed because Saul had prosecuted them. David had no choice but to accede on the principle of an eye for an eye (which applied at the time). Seven descendants of Saul were handed over and killed on a hill, and their bodies were left exposed to the elements of nature.

Rizpah, the mother of two of the men, kept watch at the bodies, day and night, for an entire season, until David heard of this remarkable woman and sent for the bodies, as well as for the bodies of Saul and Jonathan, to be buried in the tomb of their ancestor, Kish. The Gibeonites were satisfied and the disgrace was restored in accordance with the customs of "decency" of that time.

Customs and ghastly revenge in the name of justice may change, but loyalty and honor do not change. Matthew Arnold described the university city of Oxford as "a home of lost causes, and impossible loyalties". Perhaps he would have regarded Rizpah's nightly and daily vigils at the remains of her loved ones as an "impossible loyalty". But it was not. Even today it touches people's hearts, because a person's loyalty is an anchor for one's personality. Loyalty to your loved ones, loyalty to your people, loyalty to the customs of your ancestors (even though many people regard these as "dead men's bones"), loyalty to your word, loyalty to your God.

God remains loyal to us, day and night, winter and summer, in times of rejection and in victory. How else can we live, or be worthy of anything? How else than with a faithful God by our side?

Lord, thank You for Rizpah's example. It touches us. Thank You for Your loyalty. It strengthens us.

WATER AND BLOOD

But he refused to drink it; instead, he poured the water out before the LORD. "Far be it from me, O LORD, to do this!" he said. "Is it not the blood of men who went at the risk of their lives?" (2 Sam. 23:16-17).

In a short summary of the great deeds of David's very brave men, a particular snippet of great significance is mentioned, although it was prompted by a royal whim. The Philistines had occupied Bethlehem, and David became thirsty in the cave of Adullam. He longed for his place of birth and to drink water from the well near the gate of Bethlehem.

The three "heroes", or field officers heard David's wish and sneaked past the Philistine lines to get David water from Bethlehem. This touched the king deeply. He poured out the water as a sacrifice to the Lord saying that he could not drink it because the men who brought it had risked their lives. David acknowledged valor and courage, as well as his devotion to his God. The water become a sacrifice and David the poet uses the water in a sublime image that portrays the blood of life. Because the men had put their lives and blood at risk for it.

It reminds one of Communion where we drink a small amount of wine as a major toast to King Jesus who died, rose from the dead, and will come again. We refer to the wine as His blood in the same way David referred to the water from the well of Bethlehem as blood. Much was risked for it. Nobody died, but David blessed it and did not touch it. Jesus says we must drink His blood. He died. He conquered death on our behalf.

Perhaps we do not always grasp the immense significance of this completely. Our Savior is a Hero, endlessly more powerful than David's officers. Glory to Jesus who quenches our thirst today.

Yes, glory be to You, Lord, Hero, Victor, King.

THE PRICE OF A SACRIFICIAL OFFERING

No, I insist on paying you for it. I will not sacrifice to the LORD my God burnt offerings that cost me nothing (2 Sam. 24:24).

It is a peculiar account of events wherein this beautiful verse is hidden. David ordered the people of Israel to be counted because the "anger" of the Lord burnt against Israel, and the census was probably regarded as arrogant. At David's request to "rather fall into the hands of the Lord", a plague was sent upon Israel. On the surface the entire incident seems to be a very basic effort on the part of the narrator to find a contemporary explanation for a disastrous plague that hit the people of Israel.

David was instructed to make a sacrifice on the threshing floor of Araunah, and he tried to buy the threshing floor. Araunah, however, wanted to give it to David free of charge. David refused the generous offer and said that he could not sacrifice burnt offerings to the Lord that had cost him nothing. He then bought the threshing floor at great expense and made a sacrificial offering that brought an end to the plague.

This is reminiscent of the cartoon character Andy Capp who walked out of church after putting something into the collection plate. At the door the pastor said to him, "Brother Capp, I do not mind you dropping a button into the collection plate, but use one of your own buttons rather than one you got from the church's cushions!"

Sometimes we try to get past God in the cheapest way possible. We make empty promises in our hour of distress, but when the danger has passed we forget about them. When I was young, we had to drive through many farm gates to get to our house. There were always peasant children standing ready to open the gates in exchange for money. God is nobody's gate opener, eager to receive our small change. He loves us and expects love and respect from us, especially when we help others in His name.

David paid and did his best with his sacrifice. We have come a long way since his time, but his example remains in the service to God and help to others, without any ulterior motives.

Lord, I want to revere You in all I do. Let me do it well.

THE ANOINTING

Zadok the priest took the horn of oil from the sacred tent and anointed Solomon (I Kings 1:39).

After yet another chapter of court intrigue (like present day politics!) where Nathan the prophet and Bathsheba had acted on behalf of Solomon, David gave the order for Solomon to be anointed as king. Another one of David's sons, Adonijah, was quietly busy with a coup d'état (with the priest, Abiathar and Joab, the commander on his side this time) and had to be stopped. When someone had been anointed as king with oil from the tabernacle, it could not be undone. "Not all the water in the rough rude sea / Can wash the balm off from an anointed king" (Shakespeare, *King Richard II*).

Even after David's death, Adonijah tried yet more tricks, which caused Solomon to decide to have him executed, as well as to dispose of his major supporters. Too many people yearned for the glory of David.

But Solomon was the man and he ruled with great wisdom (wisdom he had asked from God and, in addition, he was also rewarded with riches). In the end his fame and fortune would become his downfall and cause his empire to split. Still, he was exceptional and renowned as a prince of peace and true patron of the arts. On David's instruction, he built the temple for the Lord from the best material, and with great and holy deference. A remarkable, magnificent king.

The Lord also anoints us with His Spirit to be a generation of kings, family of Jesus Christ. Once He has started to work in your heart and something of Him has stirred inside you, you have been anointed. Even though a thousand Adonijahs may try to trick you, even though you might have drifted away for years on end.

In the New Testament, the Spirit never completely deserted man. The direct line to God may not be in use and the number might even be forgotten, but it is never out of order. All we have to do is call on God's name; He will answer.

Lord, we are Your anointed. Teach us to live accordingly.

INTENTION

The LORD said to my father David, "Because it was in your heart to build a temple for My Name, you did well to have this in your heart" (1 Kings 8:18).

With the inauguration of the wonderful temple built to God's glory, Solomon "blessed the whole assembly of Israel" and referred to his father's wish.

David, a man after God's own heart, would never see the magnificent temple on Mount Zion or set foot in the great edifice of the sanctum. But in his heart he had the desire to build it for the Lord; to see it arise, stone by stone, cedar by cedar, golden ornament by golden ornament, pillar by pillar. The Lord regarded this as if David had already done it. But in His wisdom, the Lord also knew that there were still other tasks to be accomplished in order for the kingdom to be perpetuated.

One wonders whether the artistic David cherished a vision of a complete architectural model in his heart, sparkling in the sun on the temple hill, as the sons of Korah would later sing, "Great is the LORD, and most worthy of praise, in the city of our God, His holy mountain. It is beautiful in its loftiness, the joy of the whole earth" (Ps. 48:1-2). Perhaps David also reveled in such a picture while planning the temple.

And God saw into his heart and God noticed his sincere intentions and God rejoiced in it. And God praised David for it. It is wonderful for a father and a mother to take note of the good intentions of their children, however inept.

It is especially wonderful for our heavenly Father to look into our hearts and see our intentions, regardless of how weak they may be. And He says: Whatever your intention for My sake might have been, although not realized – I regard it as though you have carried it out already.

Lord, bless my intentions today.

PRIMEVAL PROPHET

Now Elijah the Tishbite, from Tishbe in Gilead ... (I Kings 17:1).

After the split of Solomon's Empire, an unstable period dawned during which a powerful prophet came forward, a man who even today is regarded as the archetype of all the prophets. He came from Gilead, someone who had never owned his own piece of land. Someone who had nothing, but who in fact had everything: he had God. And with God he could stand before kings and dispose of the Baal priests.

He was an outspoken man who followed God's road and radiated God's glory, regardless of his occasional grumpiness and depression. Teilhard de Chardin wrote that Jesus Christ, "shines transparently through some people as though He had once again risen in them with His transfigured body, to strengthen the faith of others and to make this dark world lighter." This kind of person hits mankind like a powerful wave splashing over a harbor wall.

They are rare in today's world of concrete and technology, but they are nevertheless there. God has people in many places, people with a special calling. They are most often not as spectacular as Elijah. In C. S. Lewis's *Screwtape Letters*, the old devil warns the young little devil to be on his guard against a little old woman praying in a back street of the city, because her prayers devastatingly counteracted the Evil One.

However, Elijah's God is also your God and my God. In His own special way He performs the miracles for us that Elijah performed. In His own way He provides for us like He provided for Elijah during the drought at the brook. In His own way He talks to us in the rustle of a soft silence. And in His own way He helps us to our feet again, as He helped Elijah. Because He is Present for us, just as He was Present for Elijah.

Bless this day for me, Lord, and let Christ radiate through me.

THE MIRACLE JAR

For the jar of flour was not used up and the jug of oil did not run dry, in keeping with the word of the LORD spoken by Elijah (I Kings 17:16).

A while ago a man spoke about the value of money, the vulnerability of savings and his fear that he may not be provided for in his old age. His fears are not unfounded, because people can be struck by any kind of disaster. The famous composer Claude Debussy died during World War One when the German artillery bombarded Paris. Debussy, old and successful, had to spend an entire day in the snow in a queue for his rations, where he became very sick and died.

Disasters spare no man, but perhaps the concerned man relies more on his savings than on God. This could result in a miserable life of constant worry over everything that could happen when the skies fall. On the other hand, God promised Elijah that He would be with him during the terrible times of decline in Israel, of the godless King Ahab and his wife, of the killing of God's prophets, and of the drought that destroyed everything.

God sent Elijah to a widow who had nothing, and during his stay with her the little bit of flour in the "miracle jar" was never used up, and neither did the oil in the "miracle jug" run dry. Too often we measure ourselves against what others have, and then we grumble that we have "nothing". And that while the flour does not get used up and the oil does not run dry.

God did not let His prophet survive in an expensive restaurant, but with just enough for a simple meal every day. He provides for us in the same way.

As a young pastor, I would sometimes become anxious about where Sunday's sermon would come from. But that flour did not get used up and the oil of the Spirit ensured that I could always go to the pulpit with something to say. And in lean times God provided miraculously. Thank the Lord for that, regardless of where I may die one day. As long as He is there.

Lord, our life is a miracle jar. Make us grateful.

Enough, lord!

Elijah went a day's journey into the desert. He came to a broom tree, sat down under it and prayed that he might die. "I have had enough, Lord," he said (1 Kings 19:4).

Have you ever felt this way? I have. Often.

Elijah had been wonderfully provided for. He gained a major victory over the priests of Baal in the presence of many people – and then he had to flee from the wrath of Queen Jezebel. Once again, the strange up-and-down curve of the graph of a child of God's life is striking. The Bible makes it clear, time and again, that a life in God is not a life in a convenient elevator to the top. It is, at times, a rocky road through green pastures, and often through the desert.

There in the desert Elijah felt that nothing was worthwhile. The darkness of the soul; bouts of depression and disappointment descending upon him like thick fog on a mountain road made it impossible for Elijah to see the way ahead. He wanted to die, and he meant it.

Some pastors say that you should not become like that because Jesus' joy must always fill you. They tend to forget that Jesus also became distressed and that He sweated blood under the olive trees. The Lord strengthened Elijah through the presence of an angel. However, the Lord did not get His angels to transport Elijah to a safe place on heavenly wings. He had to walk through the desert, for 40 days and 40 nights, to Horeb, the mountain of God where he sought refuge in a cave.

Many of us would recognize ourselves in this picture at one time or another: stooped, tired, alone, misunderstood, sick and tired of everything. After listening to an inanely cheerful sermon, the famous Samuel Johnson, known for his bouts of depression, said, "I find the merriment of parsons mighty offensive!" But on the road we are served by angels, by an encouraging word, the smile of a child, a job well done, and a sudden realization that the Lord is somewhere ahead or somewhere near. He watched Elijah closely all the way, just like He keeps an eye on you and me, knowing exactly when the time has come for Him to intervene on our behalf.

Thank You, Lord, that You understand and help.

GOD'S WHISPER

But the LORD was not in the fire. And after the fire came a gentle whisper (1 Kings 19:12).

God called Elijah from the cave to go out and stand on the mountain so that He, as in the days of Moses, could "pass by". God granted Elijah the immense privilege of a direct encounter in glory. At first (understandably), Elijah thought that the Lord was in the powerful wind. Then he thought (understandably) that the Lord was in the earthquake. Following that, God was not in the fire either. In a gentle whisper … that's where God was found. This reminds one of the night when Jesus taught Nicodemus about the ways of the wind being like birth in Christ.

Elijah knew that in the "gentle whisper" he was in the Presence of God. He pulled his cloak over his face and once again complained to God, but the Lord gave him fresh instructions to go and anoint a new king, as well as his own successor.

At times it seems as though the so-called post-modern man thinks that there is great value in noise and storms and fire. Politics is run like this. The media operates like this – with banner headlines screaming, many of which I myself wrote as a journalist. Entertainment is run like this, with the volume fully turned up. Sometimes religion is also run like this: major testimonies, microphones, miracles … Everything has its place. But is God always present in all this noise? Or is He most often found in a gentle whisper?

I suspect that He is often found in a glorious whisper. The English priest and poet, Hopkins, sings, "Elected Silence, sing to me / And beat upon my whorlèd ear, / Pipe me to pastures still and be / The music that I care to hear" (from *The Habit of Perfection*). God speaks in the major mass choir singing "Hallelujah!", God speaks in the fire of the crumbled World Trade Center. But most of us want to sense Him in the silence, simply to know that He is near, and that He sits with us and cradles us like a child, without saying a word because He loves us.

The mere knowledge is sufficient, my Lord, that You cradle me.

HEART AND WILL

As long as he (Uzziah) sought the LORD, God gave him success (2 Chron. 26:5).

The kings ruling the divided tribes of Israel came and went; some were good and some were bad. Great prophets came and issued warnings, many from God, but also false prophets who played up to the kings.

Uzziah was a good king, taught by the prophet Zechariah, who served the Lord. He organized his government well and strengthened himself on the military front. He "sought the Lord". This earned him a good report, as long as he kept it up.

It was not as if God expected him not to use his own discretion or think for himself. Some people think that is what the "will of God" means – you have no say and God has to pull all the necessary strings. However, people are individuals, not keys of a piano that someone else has to play. God respects our personality because He is Personality and we are created in His image. But He expects us to remain in contact with Him.

I do not tie my child to me because she has to learn to grow and make decisions on her own. However, I do expect her to phone me regularly and not charge ahead without consulting me in any way. At least we have to be aware of one another. God wants this as well.

Later on Uzziah no longer did this. He thought that he was great and no longer a child. He had become a powerful man and pushed the Lord to the background. This cost him dearly, because he died as a leper. God sees, as Karl Barth has said, even under a royal robe when a heart is no longer with Him. But He blesses the heart who constantly seeks Him, even though it may be under a dirty robe, as David stood before God many times.

Let my heart always remain with You, Lord, and please remind me constantly of Your kindness.

VISION

In the year that King Uzziah died, I saw the Lord seated on a throne, high and exalted, and the train of his robe filled the temple (Isa. 6:1).

The prophet Isaiah describes an awe-inspiring vision of God. In the year that King Uzziah died, Isaiah was called as a prophet and was granted what few people are granted: to experience the greatness of God in a vision, in such a way that he felt small and unclean. Almost as unclean as King Uzziah who had died of leprosy and therefore was not buried with the other kings. An angel touched Isaiah's lips with a live coal, a symbol of cleansing.

Isaiah describes God's holiness, splendor, grandeur, untouchability, greatness and sovereignty. Beautiful images are evoked by the vision of God: the train of His robe filled the temple. He was seated on a throne, high and exalted, He was surrounded by seraphs and they called out, "Holy, holy, holy is the Lord Almighty!"

How could Isaiah see the Lord and live, while Moses and Elijah were refused the experience? What Isaiah saw was a "filtered" image in human terms, a vision that was focused in such a way that it made the Lord known without exposing the onlooker.

John Donne says it beautifully, "My God, my God, Thou art a direct God ... a literal God ... But Thou art also a figurative ... a metaphorical God ..." (from *Devotions upon Emergent Occasions*). God is real, literal and sacred, invisible to man. But He reveals Himself in visions and metaphors, in human forms and terms and, above all, in Jesus Christ.

Still, we wish that we could see Him but once, like Isaiah did. But He comes to us in many forms and more specifically, He sends us numerous messages. Let us be on the lookout for Him today, and we might just receive a special message, like Isaiah did.

I would like to see You today, Lord, and hear You.

TEXT MESSAGE TO GOD

The LORD, the God of their fathers, sent word to them through His messengers again and again, because He had pity on His people and on His dwelling place. But they mocked God's messengers, despised His words and scoffed at His prophets (2 Chron. 36:15-16).

It is very annoying when you send messages to somebody and they never reply, or call and the person promises to call back but never does, or show interest that goes unnoticed. I once phoned a businessman I used to know. His secretary went and asked if he could speak to me. I heard how he told her loud and clear, "Tell the old man that I am busy!" She told me that he was in a meeting.

It is difficult to ascribe human emotions randomly to God. He is, after all, God. But does it not explain something of how the Lord must have felt when He sent messenger after messenger to His people "because He had pity on His people and on His dwelling place". They definitely could not say they didn't know what He was expecting of them, because He "sent word to them … again and again".

Rulers came and went. Some, like Hezekiah, took the Lord seriously, but towards the end the author of Chronicles wrote an outrageous indictment, "But they mocked God's messengers." And then, after centuries of indulgence from God, "there was no remedy" (cf. v. 16). They would be taken into exile. And yet, God would have mercy on them again as He sent His Son with the all-embracing, greatest message of all.

Sometimes one cannot help but wonder how God feels about our reaction to His love. And I presume that giving Him a mere thought, a mere prayer of "I am thinking about You and need You", would be enough to start with. As a daily text message or call from my child gives me great joy, so the Father rejoices daily in the fact that we acknowledge Him. Because He is a true Father.

My message to You: I love You.

THE TENANTS AND THE SON

"Then the owner of the vineyard said, 'What shall I do? I will send my son, whom I love; perhaps they will respect him'" (Luke 20:13).

Jesus summarized the unseemly behavior of Israel in the parable of the tenants who rented the vineyard. Every time the owner of the vineyard sent someone to collect his rent, the tenants beat the servant, scorned him and threw him out of the vineyard.

They gradually started to think that the vineyard belonged to them and that they did not owe anything to anyone. In their view, they managed it and they prepared the land according to their own insight. In the time of the prophets, the teachers of the law of Israel believed this and, especially during the time of Jesus, the Pharisees and the high priests were convinced of it: their religion and their customs were their vineyards. Others would do well to stay away. And this Man from Nazareth had to go.

According to Jesus, the owner of the vineyard thought that "perhaps they would respect" his son. They did not and killed him. But God knew that they would not respect His Son and that they would kill Him. The Chief priests knew this as well, because they realized that Jesus had referred to them in His parable (cf. v. 19). They wanted to arrest Him then and there, but they were cowards in front of the people. They would devise other sly plans.

The vineyard rented from God is also our own lives. The Lord wants recognition of His tenure, even if it is only a prayer of thanks, or a feeling of deep dependence on Him. Often we ignore the messages that He sends us ("Acknowledge Me, speak to Me") – until one day we face difficulties with our farming methods and look to God for help.

In Dostoevsky's major work, *The Brothers Karamazov*, Ivan cynically states, "If Christ were to appear today, we would crucify Him again." However, He comes in love and all that He asks is love. He is satisfied with our feeble human efforts, in the way that I appreciate the bookmark that my child drew for me in first grade.

Lord, accept our human and poor "yield" – and bless us abundantly nevertheless.

NEW CLOTH

He told them this parable: "No one tears a patch from a new garment and sews it on an old one" (Luke 5:36).

A major part of Jesus' teachings comprises remarkable narratives and parables. He goes about it like a poet, the image that He uses explains a truth that cause the listeners to think. At the same time, as it is with a good poetic image, it also veils the truth, in order to emphasize the enormous mystery of any truth. Because the Mystery of God always enjoys top priority and should be respected. We may think and debate about God, but there comes a moment when human thinking stops and divine "thinking" begins!

Years ago I wrote a poem:

Would I ever be able to think-know You? Touch-know? Feel-know? / or compare You over and over again / with something that is different, / which is more or less like You, / which I can comprehend? ...
(from *Gelykenisse en ander verse*)

The answer is a resounding no, of course not. Nothing earthly is like God, although the parables are small paintings of God's plan. However, the moment we think we understand the "inexhaustible wealth" of God, it escapes us, because God does not allow Himself to be molded into any human form of thought. We can only understand partially and continue to wonder and admire.

No one cuts fabric from new clothes to mend old clothes. After all, you destroy the new and it does not really match the old, says Jesus (cf. v. 36). Jesus does not merely paste a new patch onto the Old Covenant. Neither does He give us patched-up clothes. He gives us new clothes (cf. Eph. 4:24). And He does not merely patch our spirit, He makes it new. He provides for us every new day by making the day new for us. And He is always standing by to clothe us anew, every day. Also because He knows that somewhere during the day, we are going to pick up a dirty spot or two or three!

Clothe me today with Yourself, Lord, in a fashion that suits You.

NEW WINE

"And no one pours new wine into old wineskins. If he does, the new wine will burst the skins" (Luke 5:37).

My father was a winemaker and, during the grape-harvesting and afterwards, during the fermentation period when the must turns to wine, he often slept in the cellars. Anything can go wrong as far as fermenting wine is concerned. Great care has to be taken to keep the temperature constant and to guard against contamination. And with young wine one had to be extra careful to ensure that the maturing process runs smoothly.

Wine that is in the fermentation stage undergoes a chemical transformation that causes pressure to build up. Should you use the old method of wineskins today, the wineskins would have to be new, so as to "grow" with the young wine. Jesus carefully observed what the winemakers were doing. He also knew wine and the preference for matured wine.

The wine of which Jesus spoke was the wine of the Gospel. He still used the old grapevines of Moses, Elijah and the prophets, but He grafted new vine shoots onto them. The grapes He harvested were blended according to an entirely new method and recipe. This process holds great excitement – a totally new product. I remember my father coming home one evening with a small bottle of a red wine that is still famous today. They developed it as a new product then and he was very proud.

Jesus knew that the new message He brought would not fit into the wineskins of the Pharisees. You think of this parable when you see how the church wants to "renew" itself by making use of all kinds of gimmicks. The church should actually renew itself from the heart by finding itself in Christ once again, and, perhaps, by taking a careful look at the old root-stocks of our confession of faith. Major truths remain new in Christ, like the infallibility of His Word.

Perhaps the problem is even worse today because we offer new wineskins, without wine. May God make us excited about our faith. May we live in the renewal of Christ.

Lord, turn me into sparkling wine that grows into a new "me".

PLAY!

"We played the flute for you, and you did not dance; we sang a dirge, and you did not cry" (Luke 7:32).

One wonders if children still stage mock weddings and mock funerals. Jesus saw children playing joyous games as well as melancholic ones. And those who played wanted the others to play along, otherwise the game became one-sided and boring.

With this verse, Jesus made it clear that the Pharisees did not know which game they wanted to play. When John the Baptist came, they said he was an ascetic, too serious, "He has a demon." But when Jesus came, living with the people and even attending feasts, His song was too gay. According to them, He was too licentious, "a glutton and a drunkard" (cf. v. 34). Therefore, Jesus says, what do you want, apart from criticizing from the sideline?

This is often true of our society because there is much criticism (too serious, too joyous), but few are prepared to get involved and, at the very least, give a poor child a piece of bread or join in the singing of an exuberant song of joy because we are alive. Paul is an example of someone who played along with God in all circumstances. When the flutes of God played joyously, he danced in the love of Christ. And when the flutes of sorrow and suffering played, he accepted the fact that he had to share in the suffering of Christ. He mourned, but always hopefully.

Sometimes it seems as if the music has died down, but God never ceases to play! Sometimes He plays a joyous song of service and the joy of every day. Sometimes He brings us to our senses with dirges, like those of Gustav Mahler, and we blink away the tears. Life involves interchanging periods of joy and sorrow. Sometimes we are at the wedding with Jesus. Sometimes in jail with John. But always, God's flute is playing, stirring with emotion, bubbling with joy. Listen to His song: He lives!

Lord, play on Your flute the interchanging tunes that constitute life. We want to laugh and we want to cry. We want to live!

LOVE AND FORGIVENESS

"Two men owed money to a certain moneylender" (Luke 7:41).

The mystic, Julian of Norwich, asked whether people understood Jesus' meaning. "What do you wish to know: your Lord's meaning in this thing? Know it well, love was His meaning. Who reveals it to you? Love. What did He reveal to you? Love. Why does He reveal it to you? For love. So I was taught that love is our Lord's meaning."

During a meal at the house of the Pharisee Simon it seemed as if Jesus was not received with the customary cordiality: no welcoming kiss and no washing of the guest's feet. Perhaps Simon wanted to prove that, as a Pharisee, he did not identify with the Teacher, but he was nevertheless curious.

A woman with a bad reputation went and stood behind Jesus and her tears of shame and reverence fell on His feet; His feet on which she had poured perfume and then wiped with her hair. When Simon showed his dismay, Jesus told him the parable of the two debtors: the one who owed 500 denarii and the other 50. The banker canceled the debts of both and Simon conceded that the one who had owed more should love the moneylender more.

Most often, gratitude is a big motivation for love. Gratitude is also often the result of forgiveness. And gratitude is also blessed by the Lord. The woman left with a blessing of forgiveness and peace. Simon received no blessing. In fact, in the eyes of Jesus, he was the one who, in his pride, owed 500 denarii. But that love is the meaning of God and so too the remission of sins, he did not understand at all. Julian of Norwich understood. And a woman from the street understood. We should also understand.

Yes, Lord, we understand and we are grateful, for our tears as well, but especially for Your love and forgiveness.

PATHS AND ROCKY PLACES

"As he was scattering the seed, some fell along the path ... Some fell on rock" (Luke 8:5-6).

When Jesus told the parable of the sower, the crowds were large, but He knew the heart of each person. And He compared them to the different types of soil that a sower comes across. Obviously, Jesus is the Sower and the Word of God is the seed, but the type of soil, the listener, will finally determine what becomes of the seed.

Among the crowds, as is the case among us today, there were people whose hearts were like a denuded path running through a cultivated field. Even the seed of weeds could not penetrate it. They already knew all the answers. People with preconceived biases can seldom be convinced to change their mind. The Greeks had an expression, "Even the gods fight in vain against impudence." Often we are like that ourselves – we know our denuded paths. But do we retain the ability to receive when Jesus sows something in our hearts? Sensing God's Presence?

The seed that fell on the rock reminds me how I initially battled with my garden. Some of the older residents said that there was a rock formation just beneath the surface. You actually had to have it chiseled away or removed with a pickaxe before you could sow or plant anything.

Plants initially grew on this reef – and then withered. A man I know cried emotional tears while in hospital, and promised that he would serve the Lord if only he would recover from his illness. However, once he had recovered, he forgot everything on the rock of the world. Deep emotion is not always a barometer of deep faith. However, there are other listeners who are so intellectual or so in-clined to reason things out that they never learn that emotion is as important as intellect. No tear penetrates the rock, neither does any growth.

Sometimes we feel emotionally like a hard or rocky path. God understands times like that. He chisels the rock away and clears the paths. And the seed of hope and faith grows once again.

Yes, Lord, always prepare our hearts for what You want to sow.

THORNY WEEDS

"Other seed fell among thorns ... Still other seed fell on good soil"
(Luke 8:7-8).

Some of the sower's seed fell among thorns. It sprouted but was choked. Thorns are quick to take over an entire piece of soil, also the soil of a man's heart.

During the 1980s, we had a problem at the newspaper I worked for – we used an Atex system, which was not a bad IT system, but functioned on only one line. The technology was fast becoming obsolete and sometimes, when the newspaper office was at its busiest, a warning appeared on every computer screen: *Log off immediately!* If you failed to do so straightaway, you lost all your information. The system was overloaded with too much information, too many reports and advertisements. We were all instructed to empty our files as soon as possible.

Sometimes the human heart is overloaded with unnecessary things; thorns, which threaten to distort and push aside our priorities. We forget that we must first search for the kingdom of God by being still and by listening. Our daily troubles gain the upper hand and God's Word disappears. When a poet was asked in his old age whether he would publish yet another volume of poetry, he solemnly replied, "Yes, I have to. I have the poems, but I have such a confusion of papers!" I have empathy with him, especially when I think of my own desk.

Our lives are like that. Crowded by so many papers and issues and so much interference – "thorns" – that the essence of everything disappears.

The good soil is to be found in the heart that listens. People who listen to the voice of God also listen to other people. And God bestows His blessings on them, sometimes a hundredfold. An old pastor once said during a sermon, "Make it a rule to become still for only five minutes during the day's hustle and think of God, regardless of the nature of your thoughts and even though, like Job, you are discontented." It works! God allows something of Himself to come through when we tune in to Him – the seed grows.

Lord, there are many superfluous thorns in my life. Help me to remove them and to attune myself to You.

SPONTANEOUS LOVE

"Look after him" (Luke 10:35).

The Samaritans had as little time for the Jews as the Jews had for the Samaritans. Both had their own customs. Jesus knew this when, in answer to a question ("And who is my neighbor?"), He told the parable of the Good Samaritan.

The priest and the Levite, men of the church, walked past the injured man, because they adhered to certain religious regulations and they also had urgent religious duties to attend to. You will always find good excuses to not perform your real duty. But a Samaritan "took pity on him" (cf. v. 33), bandaged his wounds and took him to an inn to be taken care of, at his own expense.

With this, Jesus explained that God's love is not subject to all kinds of rules. His love is spontaneous, immediate, and direct. The Samaritan did not hesitate or ask himself whether he should offer help. He did what was right for the injured man. Circumstances played along.

But what are we to do when we are bombarded by hordes of beggars on every street corner? One is not even sure about the motives of some and stories of lazy people are legion. The child of God must learn to listen to the spontaneous whisper of God in his heart and help when and where he senses it. It is a fallible method because often we do not hear correctly and we are not always able to discern real distress. However, in the majority of cases, we can see the distress clearly, and then we should act like Jesus' Samaritan. If we expect God to see our distress then we should see the distress of others.

We are here, not so much to carry out religious actions, but to bandage wounds. And in our wounded world they abound. Let us learn this lesson: gratitude in such cases is sometimes rare. Jesus does not mention whether the Samaritan was ever thanked. But God is satisfied. And that gives us a wonderful feeling of being loved.

Lord, I ask for the necessary wisdom and spontaneity in living Your love to the full.

SUCCESS, PUNISHMENT AND BLESSING

"You fool!" (Luke 12:20).

The billionaire and philanthropist of the late nineteenth century, Andrew Carnegie, said before his death, "It is no sin to earn great riches, but it is obscene to try and hold on to it after death." His Carnegie foundations, which offer assistance to others, still exist today. But here, in Luke 12, a man complained to Jesus about his father's estate. And somewhat annoyed, Jesus replied that his greed could become a trap, as it did for the rich fool.

This man had good crops, he stored them and reasoned that he could take life easy, live without a care in the world, just for himself ... and then he died, and his goods ... yes, what became of his goods? There are people who manage their possessions well and who are generous when it comes to helping others. There are other rich fools who live only for themselves. Wealth is no disqualification and poverty is no recommendation. There are also covetous poor people who will steal the bread from the mouths of others, like the women beside the dying aunt in *Zorba the Greek*. But the man who thinks only of his own needs is a fool, says Jesus.

To be successful is often God's reward. To be successful and selfish is often God's judgment. It is His world in which we live. It is His land on which the rich fool farms. It is His favor that brings the rain for the crops. It is His breath that was blown into man. We are dependent on Him for everything. If we fail to realize that, we are foolish.

There are greater riches than a good harvest. It is the richness of the spirit, of true nobility, of civilized behavior and sincerity. That is something to pursue. But there is so much more – the blessed and glorious mystery, which Paul points out as being "Christ in you, the hope of glory" (Col. 1:27).

There is a very old story of a man who, when he was dying, asked the angel whether he could at least take something with him. The angel answered, "If you have to, everything that you have given away, you can take with you." There is a lesson to be learnt from this. Because God is the Great Giver.

Lord, I want to be rich in You, rich in love, rich in the Spirit.

A SECOND CHANCE

"Sir," the man replied, "leave it alone for one more year, and I'll dig around it and fertilize it. If it bears fruit next year, fine!" (Luke 13:8-9).

This parable is about the people of Israel, about the church, but also about each one of us individually. It is very clear that God is the owner of the fig tree. And the fig tree disappointed Him. The people of Israel and their leaders disappointed Him. And we have often disappointed Him.

Instead of fruit, He found only leaves; a sign that the season for figs was over before it had even begun. We are like that: often just leaves of pious display, but very little fruit. Israel was like that. The church is sometimes like that.

The gardener is evidently Jesus, who pleads for the tree to be preserved for "a second chance". We can, so to speak, listen to a conversation between Him and His Father, "Let me cultivate this tree until next year. Then we can think again about cutting it down." The miracle is that God is never quick to cut down. He always allows yet another chance to cultivate.

There have been incidents in your life, and in mine, which probably justified a cutting down. But the worst that happens is that God prunes us, and often severely prunes us, but regardless of the harsh warning, He patiently waits for us to bear fruit again. In my garden there is a rose bush that irritated me for a number of years. At first, I wanted to take it out, but then I pruned it right down instead. The following spring it boasted a lovely display of flowers. And now, it is in full bloom more than once every year.

Each of us desire to grow and flower and bear fruit in God. As long as we are aware of the fact that we are lacking and should ask the Lord to help us grow. God remains the God of second chances, of pruning and of cultivating and of even more chances. He loves us and we are His trees. We belong to Him.

Lord, I wish I could be like the rose – in full bloom during spring, and the fig tree, laden with figs in summer.

TINY SEED, BIG TREE

J
U
L
Y

26

"The kingdom is like a mustard seed, which a man took and planted in his garden" (Luke 13:18-19).

Sometimes it seems as if God is working in an invisible way, as if there is nothing much happening. Where are the major signs of the kingdom? Why does He not reveal His power, in no uncertain terms, to all people? Why does He work with a testimony here and a testimony there, a small church here and a congregation there? What about one single major deed to show all Who reigns?

God does not work like that. He works with small beginnings, things like little tiny seeds, mustard seeds, the tiniest of them all. Therefore, His great revelation of His Son began in small towns alongside a small lake, in a small community of fishermen and farmers. And it became a movement that is still rolling across the world today.

Sometimes we perceive the development of the kingdom with sadness, like Charlotte Brontë's famous verse, "We sowed in youth a mustard seed, / We cut an almond rod; / We are now grown up to riper age – / Are they withered in the sod?"

We do feel like that sometimes, as though no seed has budded, as though nothing ever sprouts, as though God is no longer interested. When Jesus told this parable, the disciples were unaware of the fact that, at that moment, they formed part of the mystical sowing of God. Each one of them was a seed; a seed of the kingdom. God was at work, slowly but surely, small but filled with vitality.

There are times in every person's life when you feel like throwing in the towel, that everything is a failure, and that you can see nothing of God's growth or fruit upon your work. But what we do for God forms part of the kingdom, says Jesus. It grows and, unnoticed, it becomes a big tree. Let us just work and believe: God will ensure growth.

Lord, You work unnoticed, but Your vitality is in everything. Grant vitality to me and to the world around me.

INVITED GUESTS

"Come, for everything is now ready" (Luke 14:17).

Parables are short stories with many nuances of meaning, but with one major point to illustrate. It is rather interesting that many of Jesus' parables are so realistic that they sparkle with a divine humor, which threatens to break through the serious content. This humor is easily recognized (like the man who built a house but could not pay for it) and it can sadden us slightly. One almost wants to smile, but like Jesus, you also want to get upset about human folly and, at times, wipe away a tear in spite of a smile.

The parable of the banquet is like that. You almost want to laugh at the excuses of the VIPs, or the elite of the community who had been invited, but who all made excuses – they offered everyday business transactions as sufficient reason; one even said that he had just got married and wanted, for now, to stay with his wife!

You can imagine the host's irritation at so many excuses, so many absurd excuses. In the end, He sent His servant to go and invite the poor, the crippled, the blind and the lame. They came and, what they knew of good table manners, or of social etiquette, one can only guess. But they came! And then there was still room because some were probably shy and nervous, and the host said, "Make them come!" The original invited guests, the social leaders, would not be invited again.

It is a short story about God and His people and, eventually, about the Gentiles, but it is more – it is your history and mine. We are God's invited guests and we don't always know how to behave as invited guests, but we know that we need Him. The Lord invites us to His festival of life, here and now, even though our "life manners" are sometimes like those of people from the streets. But He invites us to the celebratory banquet at the fullness of time, the victory of Jesus Christ, to the eternal Presence of God.

Lord, I am spiritually crippled, poor, blind and lame. But I am coming to Your banquet!

THE COST

"Suppose one of you wants to build a tower. Will he not first sit down and estimate the cost to see if he has enough money to complete it? For if he is not able to finish it, everyone who sees it will ridicule him" (Luke 14:28-29).

A huge, unfinished house stood high against a hill for more than five years. Everyone who drove past it came to know the story of the man who became rich overnight, had the house designed and started to build, and eventually had to give it up. Someone bought it years later and finished it, but the whole world wanted to know the history of the "modern ruin". And, naturally, everyone loudly ridiculed it. Jesus was right.

Many a story was told about the house, and about the owner. How many bathrooms had been planned, how many bedrooms, how long the passages were the size of the two kitchens, and some three guest apartments. Perhaps Jesus had seen evidence of someone who had built so extravagantly and without money in Capernaum. Who knows, perhaps as a carpenter, Jesus might even have worked on such a house Himself. Nonetheless, He had probably heard many such rumors.

He puts it in the context of discipleship – it requires some sacrifice from you to follow Him. He even makes use of Eastern hyperbole or exaggeration to bring home the seriousness of being a follower. Your father, mother and family, you yourself, take second place to Him. This may sound harsh but, after all, too many followed Jesus for the sake of miracles and free bread. Too many were followers just for a short while. The Lord does not need temporary followers. He asks a steely determination from you: I want to go with Jesus, come what may.

It is often the unconvinced followers who "bring shame" upon Christianity, the church, the Word and upon Jesus Christ. Those who follow Him in simplicity and in the knowledge that they can only live by His grace, have already calculated the costs. They know that they are nothing and have nothing without Him.

Lord, I realize that it requires the utmost grace to understand me, as well as to forgive me.

GOD'S ECONOMY

"Suppose one of you has a hundred sheep and loses one of them. Does he not ... go after the lost sheep until he finds it?" (Luke 15:4).

Anyone who knows something about economics would know that a loss of one percent is a limited risk. One can deal with it and recoup. A loss of five percent sets the alarm bells ringing. But in this parable only one sheep out of a hundred is lost, not five or ten. And yet, the shepherd goes out of his way to look for the one lost sheep.

God's economy works differently: a one percent loss is too much for Him, because each one of His flock – and that is us – is precious to Him. When I was a child, I wandered away from my father at a show once and, caught up in the large crowd, I did not know where I was. My father moved heaven and earth to find me because I was his only child. The officials at the show could have argued: Oh well, one child out of a thousand who gets lost in this crowd is a mere 0,01%. No loss. But the officials did all they could to help my father.

God is our Father, His Son is the Shepherd. No sheep is abandoned, not one out of a billion, and neither those whom the Pharisees had given up as sinners.

There are many ways to lose your way. You could lose your intimate relationship with God. You could lose your longing for God. You could lose your direction in life and start doubting the meaning of your existence. You could experience the feeling that God no longer cares about you. You could think that you had failed Him and that it was over and done with as far as He was concerned. And you could run the major risk of a child who wanders away, without even realizing that he is lost.

This parable says that God does not leave it there. He comes to fetch and help you. That's His nature. It is His economy. It is His love. For each one of us personally.

Thank You Lord, that You come to fetch me time and again, and that You will still fetch me a final time so that I will be with You for all eternity.

FEAST FOR A SON

"I will set out and go back to my father and say to him: Father, I have sinned against heaven and against you" (Luke 15:18).

In the renowned Hermitage Museum in St. Petersburg, Rembrandt's famous painting of the lost son is displayed. The son is in a wretched state. Ragged and tormented he kneels next to his father. He is pathetic in his shame, but his father is magnanimous in his warm welcome after all the grief he has been through.

The son's fall was tremendous: from heir to tendering pigs. A disgrace for a Hebrew man. As his money and friends gradually disappeared, he lowered his standards. In his loneliness, he came to realize that he was actually worse off than one of his father's laborers.

The father applied the golden rule that we all know to be true: If you truly love someone or something, let him go. If he returns to you, then he truly belongs to you. Otherwise, he has never really belonged to you. The Lord often applies this rule to us as well – He lets us have our way and allows us to follow (and bump) our own heads. But, like the Good Shepherd, He comes looking for us and, like the father, He runs to us, kisses us and organizes a feast for us.

In Rembrandt's painting, it is the torn and tattered sandals that strike you. An image of one who had walked a long way in order to return home. His father got him new sandals and a new robe and a ring … If Jesus were to show us a "photo" of the Father, this one would be the most touching: the Father who loves, the Father who understands and forgives all.

Thank You that You are a Father, full of understanding and love.

Accept!

"My son ... you are always with me, and everything I have is yours" (Luke 15:31).

The eldest son was in the field when his lost brother returned. He became angry about the feast prepared for his prodigal brother. Some of us have great sympathy for the elder brother, although some pastors allege that he was actually the lost son, even though he stayed with his father. Augustine even goes so far as to say, "A darkened heart is the 'far-off land', because it is not with our feet, but in our love that we forsake You or return to You."

This is right and true, but the elder brother had a good case. He did stay at home and he worked; worked very hard. In all probability, his father also thought that he had a case, that is why he went out "and pleaded with him" (cf. v. 28). He loved his sons, the elder one and the younger one; the one who stayed and the one who left. And he added to what he was saying to the elder son, "everything I have is yours" (cf. v. 31). It had indeed always been like that. But the broken family was united again. "Come on in," says the father, "we have to celebrate and be glad".

This is how the heavenly Father is, says Jesus: loyal and understanding towards the "exemplary" son, loving and receptive towards the disgraced son who came to beg for forgiveness.

There is something of both brothers to be found in the majority of us. As older Christians we sometimes think that we have every right to God and we complain with Saint Teresa of Avila, "It is no wonder that You have so few true children, because so often You treat us unfairly." The Father owes us nothing. And yet, He says everything is ours.

We are also the younger, lost son, the spendthrift and the scandal-maker. For this type of record each of us could compile a rather long list, if we were to be honest. And the father accepted both sons anew. That is how it is. That is how God is. Faith is to accept that we are being accepted, more, that we have been accepted!

Thank You, Lord, for this small picture of You which we see through Jesus.

AUGUST

Lord, My God

I wish to sing You a psalm of flowers and birds and trees
and passing clouds and the fresh smell of the morning.
I wish to sing of the wood pigeon I saw strolling past my window,
at peace with the world.
I wish to sing You a psalm of life and love,
of the days of my youth and my hope of my days to come.
Sometimes my heart is filled with wintry nostalgia,
and expected and unexpected times of sadness-in-joy hit me,
and a hankering after people and voices of long ago.

Outside in the streets, garbage removers are noisily picking up garbage,
the waste of my household and every house in the street.
Momentarily I feel like an eunuch of time, producing nothing,
nothing but waste and garbage
and then asking You to be my garbage-man to clean up
and listen to my mutterings about life not being fair.

There are days that I sigh like David that You are far away,
and sometimes, I rejoice like David that You are near.
I ask to take shelter with You against the lurking dangers of life.
I pray that You will always embrace me like the Prodigal Son,
that You will talk to me softly as with the eldest son,
and that the celebration will always begin, the celebration of life.
Thank You for being my Father.
Thank You for Your beautiful wood pigeon strolling past.
This is my psalm of life and love, sorrow and joy.

This is for You, my God.

Amen.

WE ARE LIKE CHILDREN OF HEAVEN

When I consider Your heavens, the work of Your fingers, the moon and the stars, which You have set in place, what is man that You are mindful of him? (Psalm 8:3-4).

When one thinks of the Psalms, one thinks of David the poet. Scholars sometimes argue about this, but numerous Psalms are attributed to him and this one, about the miracle of God's Creation and humanity, he probably wrote and set to music as a young shepherd in the field. It was as though virtually inexpressible awe about God flowed through David in the most beautiful language. It is like the music of Mozart; as if David was merely a conductor of heavenly melodies and words that touch our hearts.

David looked up at the starry skies, "the work of Your fingers": to the Northern Star, the Polar Star, the constellations, Orion, Job's bear with her young cubs – each one in its orbit and in exact patterns. And he felt small, insignificant, transitory, like Tennyson in *Crossing the Bar* "Sunset and evening star / And one clear call for me! / And may there be no moaning of the bar / When I put out to sea".

But David's wonderment increases: the far-off, mysterious stars and the entire cosmos are in God's hand, but he also knows that he, like every man, is in God's hand. He finds it glorious and a mystery, a miracle and an exaltation that the Lord so honors him, a "man". That He thinks about each of us at all. More: that we are "a little lower than the heavenly beings" whom God has "made ruler over the works of His hands".

One day, while John Quincy Adams was traveling in his carriage, the driver stopped during a so-called stellar rain and fearfully called out, "President, the stars are falling!" Adams looked out, pointed north to the heavens and said, "Do you see that big bright star? That is the Polar Star. It will not fall. Carry on driving!"

Jesus is the Polar Star, the bright Morning Star (cf. Rev. 22:16). We are His people, more than the stars, almost heavenly beings. God will preserve us.

You will preserve me and direct my path, just like You do with the host of angels.

THOSE WHO SEEK YOU

Those who know Your name will trust in You, for You, LORD, have never forsaken those who seek You (Psalm 9:10).

A visiting Dutch professor of Theology once said something during a lecture that has stayed with me over the years, "The Bible is the revelation of God to man. It is the Lord who mostly reveals His will to us everywhere. But in the Book of Psalms, we, man, address God – man in his love and misery, man in faith and in doubt, man who loves God, but who finds Him so incomprehensible most of the time. *And yet, man who deep in his heart, rests assured about God. And all of that together is God's Word!"*

It is good: God and man co-operate in the Holy Scriptures. A major discussion is taking place, depicting centuries and an eternity in truths that will never perish. David says with conviction, "You, LORD, have never forsaken those who seek You". God remains the awesome Presence, millennia ago for David, today for us and tomorrow and the day thereafter for new generations yet to come, for our children and their children.

Sometimes we think that God is far away, distant, difficult, reserved, on higher ground, uninvolved in our daily problems and anxieties, too busy to hear us, too high to bend down to us, too inexplicable to love. Browning wrote, "God forgot me, and I fell." But it does not work like that. We ourselves are the ones who go astray and, deep in our hearts we realize this, because even the biggest of strayers calls His name in times of need.

And God is ever merciful. He does not play games with us in order to amuse Himself with His Creation. Neither does He block His ears when we call. He hears us, but His answer is not always what we want to hear. Sometimes we inadvertently push Him back into the shadows of our lives, too busy with our own affairs. But He is there close by, "for You, LORD, have never forsaken those who seek You".

I know Your name. I know Your presence. Do not forsake me, O Lord!

A WICKED PROBLEM

He [the wicked man] boasts of the cravings of his heart; and reviles the LORD (Psalm 10:3).

It is an age-old complaint of believers that the psalmist is expressing here. Even today it is a familiar complaint and a familiar problem. Why is the "wicked man" allowed to go his arrogant way and to trample on all that is right? Why are the "cravings of his heart" always allowed to run riot? Why can he allege that he is man enough to take care of himself, and get away with it (cf. v. 6)? Why does God not "break the arm of the wicked man" (cf. v. 15)?

Some of the faithful even wonder whether God is not punishing them by helping the Evil One. Or they complain that the "wicked" are taking control of all that is human, from the state to the media, from the arts to the everyday world where the poor are miserable and the rich flourish.

Most often this would seem to be the case, but appearances can be deceptive. Philosophers have written volumes about all that is evil, and about the prosperity of the wicked. The eighteenth-century philosopher Leibniz even alleged that God was using the evilness of the wicked and their evil deeds as the dark background against which His radiant goodness could stand out. Therefore, we appreciate God more when we experience the vileness of the Evil One. This is a fair argument, but one that is not always firmly founded. Thomas Aquinas argued that God should permit the wicked to once again allow man to make a meaningful choice between good and evil.

Justifiably, the psalmist does not reach any conclusion because the problem is intertwined like the millions of wires at a power station, of which the layman does not have the faintest notion. Only the experts know which wire fits where. In this only God knows, not even the angels. However, what the psalmist does know, and what we know, is that the Lord hears "the desire of the afflicted" (cf. v. 17). If we trust in Him, He will help us, regardless of how small or big our problem is. And the wicked and the Evil One? Those we can leave to Him.

Lord, You can deal with the Evil One. Please, just abide with me.

A DANGER TO FOUNDATIONS

When the foundations are being destroyed, what can the righteous do? (Psalm 11:3).

Sometimes it seems as though everything that we once believed in is beginning to crumble, as if the main pillars are collapsing like when Samson destroyed the temple of Dagon. And right now it would seem as if chaos is attacking the very foundations of the kingdom of God! David knew the feeling, because long before his time chaos had threatened the ways of God. The patterns of life change, often so fast that we do not know where everything is rushing to at such speed. Small wonder then that a local pastor already sounded a warning during the nineteenth century against the dangers that "fast steam communication" had in store. One cannot help but wonder what he would have said today about cell phones and jet planes and the influence of television.

Our faith and our values are being undermined by numerous stimuli as was the case in almost every previous century. God's Word is being questioned, and His church seems to be unstable at times. What can "the righteous" do?

Well, they can persevere in their faith in God. God has never yet "resigned" from being God. He remains God and is in control. We do indeed live in a world where few things are lasting but, at the same time, we live within God's protection, in His all-encompassing world. And the righteous can continue to be "righteous" by living an honest life, by acting with integrity, and by upholding qualities such as loyalty, hard work, charitableness, courtesy, civilized behavior and common decency, as best they can.

The righteous can also bank on the friendship and merciful help of a righteous God. A man who ran a family business once had to witness his business empire crumble. "Now I have nothing left!" he cried. And then a small voice sounded behind him, "No, Dad, you still have us." His children were standing behind him. Later on, they rebuilt the family business.

The righteous still has God behind him. He knows that he is tested (cf. v. 5), but he also knows that he will see God's face (cf. v. 7).

There is much to do, Lord. Please help me.

BOUNDARY LINES

LORD, You have assigned me my portion and my cup; You have made my lot secure. The boundary lines have fallen for me in pleasant places; surely I have a delightful inheritance (Psalm 16:5-6).

At times I have the habit of – especially in strange places – writing down the name of a specific place in my Bible where I read a passage that struck me. At this particular text I wrote, Nashville, Tennessee, September 30, 1998. And what makes it even more special to me is that I remember that day so well. I was sitting on the balcony of a new apartment block. In the near distance I could see the city center … and next to the building cattle and sheep were grazing peacefully. I thanked the Lord who has granted me the privilege to visit so many places and to enjoy His world, also the way in which it is developing.

I thought about my parental home, thousands of miles away, years ago when I was still a child, safe and secure. And I thanked the Lord that He had "assigned me my portion and my cup". I "inherited" Him from my parents: their most precious knowledge, their greatest eternal possession, their helper in faith. Indeed, like David I can say He has "made my lot secure" and He has drawn my boundary lines to include laughter and tears, health and sickness, gain and loss, sheep that safely graze, as well as the bustle of the city. I sing the praises of His name.

David knew that when he was assigned the Lord as an inheritance, he was also assigned certain responsibilities. Every inheritance must be handled with care, especially if the "boundary lines have fallen in pleasant places". This fact often escaped David – like it escapes me. But when he took out his harp to praise God; when he praised the name of his God, the "boundary lines" fell back in place once again.

When we praise the name of the Lord, it does not mean that we are manipulating Him in order to receive favors. We praise Him because we realize that it is the only way in which we can cling to Him.

Lord, You are my inheritance. Thank You. Thank You so much.

GOD IS LOVE

I love You, O LORD, my strength (Psalm 18:1).

It is not romantic love of which David speaks here. In romantic love there is a physical attraction, the feeling of slight intoxication in the presence of the loved one. The poets say, "To have stars in your eyes," and Burns says, "O my luve's like a red, red rose." Neither is it the sincere love between friends that David praises in his lament for Jonathan.

To love God obviously entails a surrender as well as an acceptance and a contentedness, a joy and an incentive, peace and the will to take action in His name. Our love for God gives meaning to our existence. In fact, giving meaning is central to all kinds of love. Therefore, there is also a hint of a romantic idealism in our love for God (some Christians even become somewhat sentimental and overly romantic about it), but David is not syrupy sweet. David grabs hold of God with commitment and respect, with reverence and in worship as the Custodian and Judge of his life.

To love God is also a commitment, but above all it is a conscious decision that in everything I do, I want to exalt God. This does not mean that we are going to embrace every stranger and kiss lepers like Saint Francis did. It does not even mean that you have to like all people. Christ's command to love your neighbor doesn't imply that you necessarily have to like your neighbor, but rather that you treat people with respect and compassion.

To love God is to be aware of the fact that He is the source of everything in our lives, to constantly acknowledge this, and to live wholeheartedly according to the principles that He lays down in His Holy Scriptures. It is also gratitude because He grants us life out of good favor, and very often abundance, like He granted David. And as He did with David, He also at times gives us a quick wallop. It is all part of the discipline of God's love, as one would expect of a heavenly Parent.

You are my strength. I do love You.

GOD BESTOWS BLESSINGS

May the LORD answer you when you are in distress; may the name of the God of Jacob protect you. May He send you help from the sanctuary and grant you support from Zion. May He give you the desire of your heart and make all your plans succeed (Psalm 20:1-2; 4).

This verse is a wonderful benediction because, if the Lord were to bestow everything that is wished for here, what would remain that one could still wish for? It is a jubilation about the strength and the kindness of God.

A younger colleague at the newspaper that I worked for, a complete loner who battled with his health, walked with difficulty, had difficulty breathing and yet, always succeeded in retaining the faith in his own way, died peacefully in his sleep one night. They found him the next morning on his bed in his lodgings, lying serenely with his hands folded over his chest on top of his Bible that was opened at Psalm 20. What a wonderful departure from this life that must have been! In all probability it was precisely his wish to go to his God in Zion in this way. A privilege. The priest and poet, George Herbert, refers justifiably to God as, "Having a glass of blessings standing by" (from *The Pulley*).

But it is also the greatest of blessings for an individual or a family that the Lord will grant all these blessings. That He will "give you the desires of your heart", that He will support you and send you help, that His name will protect you in difficult times, that He will mercifully accept your offerings, and that He will advance with you in the battle of life.

This is a blessing and a prayer for all occasions, a blessing for today and every day. But there are also reservations and responsibilities for all prosperity and intentions must pass the test of what you will be doing with this blessing once you have received it. Should you want to squander it in your own interest, like the rich fool, you will lose the blessing and everything that goes with it. If you experience and employ all of it in the name of the Lord, you will continue to be blessed and you will be able to share your blessings with everyone. They will not run dry; they will actually increase. May the Lord grant you support from Zion today!

Thank You for Your blessing. It preserves me, Lord.

My god!

My God, my God, why have You forsaken me? (Psalm 22:1).

This is the so-called "Psalm of the Cross", because it contains some of the last words that Jesus spoke on the cross. Further on in David's complaint, we read, "They divide my garments among them and cast lots for my clothing" (cf. v. 18), as indeed happened during Jesus' last hours.

Loathed and rejected by people, a feeling of desolation descended on David, and also on Jesus in His humanness. It is the great fear of children who become afraid in the dark that Father and Mother have abandoned them. It is the great fear of the faithful in times of distress that God, our Father, has forsaken them. It is the great fear of the dying that God will not be waiting on the other side. There are times when we look around us and become fearful, for we no longer see any trace of God in His world.

It is a deeply human cry for help, but also a deeply religious cry. It is a cry for "my God", but a cry in the acceptance that God hears. Sometimes our walk of faith requires a crying out to God, to seize His name, to cry out in pain, to complain about helplessness.

As a child, I sustained a foot injury that throbbed painfully right through the night. My parents sat with me the entire night, listening to my wailing, while putting bread poultices on the infected foot. The next day the doctor drained it in a painful procedure, but it healed. To this day, I still remember how Mother and Father sat by my side.

God was always with David and He would deliver him – countless times. And God was with His Son the whole time, even when darkness fell upon Golgotha. From the cross, Jesus cried out these words, the words of His ancestor, ancient words in the language of the people for whom He had come to die. Words depicting the depth of suffering and the depth of consolation, and of eventual victory, when God will make everything new again in an uplifting morning of resurrection and a celebration of life. As He did for Jesus. As He did for David.

My God, You remain my God!

SHEEP AND GUEST OF HONOR

The LORD is my shepherd, I shall not be in want (Psalm 23:1).

These words probably constitute the best-known fragment of "religion" on all the earth. The faithful have known it since childhood, unbelievers remember it and use it when the world becomes too much for them, others ridicule it, and some regard it as nonsense because man has to take care of himself.

It was like that in David's time as well. But while tending his sheep David, with his artistic spirit and tremendous feeling for God (what astonishing emotional insight did this man have into the heart of the Lord!), noticed a lot of things and stood in awe about many things.

This psalm is a hymn of praise for God's care and God's abundance. The Lord is a shepherd who leads softly, and a host who entertains with generosity. And He does not merely entertain you for a day and then send you home again. You are allowed to stay with Him. His house is your house, as Moses said to Israel, "The eternal God is your refuge ... " (Deut. 33:27).

Sometimes you wander far in the world. Sometimes you stray from the principles according to which you have been raised. Sometimes you end up tending pigs, like the lost son. We are often like mindless sheep. But there is always a house in which we are the guests of honor. It even surpasses Robert Frost's observation: "Home is a place where ... they have to take you in."

We always have sufficient faith to kneel, with our eyes lifted up or cast down. You can always raise your two hands and say, "Lord, hear! Lord, forgive! Lord, take notice! Lord, take me in!" Perhaps you'll have to wait like Abraham had to wait with the sacrificial offerings. Perhaps the Lord is surreptitiously accompanying you like He accompanied the two people on their way to Emmaus. But most often, He has prepared a table for you, and you are constantly in His heart, in His Presence. Even though He might feel distant to you at times.

Guard us, guide us, keep us, feed us for we have no help but Thee.
(Old English hymn)

STANDING ON HOLY GROUND

Who may ascend the hill of the LORD? (Psalm 24:3).

Well, it is definitely not us who may ascend the hill of the Lord, because we have dirty hands and an impure heart. Sometimes we devote our souls to an "insignificant matter", and merely by abusing His name (regardless of our intentions), we swear by what is "false".

Psalm 24 is probably two psalms that had been integrated, with the second part – from verse 7 – written for two choirs: one that calls and one that answers. In all probability the first temple choir was outside, with the second inside the sanctum. It is a celebratory song, but the poet feels himself unworthy to approach the sanctum. One can identify with that: who indeed may ascend the hill of the Lord? Moses? And even he was allowed there only a few times by the grace of God. John of the Cross, that beloved pastor of the sixteenth century prayed, "O God, holy above all that is holy, holy above all that we call visions, holy above all perceptions of You, too holy in Your very nature: How could I ever stand in Your presence, in heaven or on earth? How, and in what way can I think of You at all? But could You perhaps come and stand next to me here where I am?"

And that is indeed what Jesus did: He came and stood next to us and identified with us. Where the high priest could only ceremoniously venture into the Most Holy Sanctum on behalf of the worshiping people but once a year, Jesus stood before the religious and legal authorities of His time on our behalf. He ascended the "holy hill" on our behalf, bearing a cross. And He, the Holy One, was struck down there on the hill of the Lord. In order to live anew.

Now we cling to Him, God's Son, who has clean hands and a pure heart. He carries us up the hill, over the rocky face of the holy hill. He is the King of glory in our lives, God's Son and our Savior, strong and mighty.

Indeed, Lord, You come and stand next to me. You Yourself come and stand next to me.

EYES ON GOD

My eyes are ever on the LORD, for only He will release my feet from the snare (Psalm 25:15).

We had a little dog that always used to watch us intently with her eyes that didn't miss a thing; every movement of our hands, every movement of our heads, especially at the dinner table when she was expecting a tidbit. When she sensed we were about to leave, she watched us extra carefully, with a touch of reproach in her eyes. One does not know whether David had a sheepdog – the Jews regarded dogs as scavengers, unclean – but his beautiful image of "my eyes are ever on the Lord" invokes something of loyalty and expectation. Something like our little dog.

As children we learned:

God be in my head, and in my understanding;
God be in my eyes, and in my looking;
God be in my mouth, and in my speaking;
God be at my end, and at my departing.
                              (Walford Davies, *God Be in My Head*)

A very simple prayer but, as with all things simple, it overflows with holy meaning: like the eyes of the psalmist that are fixed on God, like the eyes of a little dog, like the eyes of a trusting child.

Sometimes our eyes see the glory of the Lord. Sometimes our eyes see the justice of the Lord where the "grapes of wrath are stored". But always in that vision, there is the love of the Lord. David says, "He will release my feet from the snare."

Wordsworth remarked that a poet like Virgil always wrote his poems "with his eyes fixed on whatever he might be describing, the object of his verse. In this way, the poem actually writes itself. However, other poets write poetry with their eyes fixed on their own style, instead of on that which they are describing. Then the poetry falls flat and most often they have nothing lasting to say." In the entire "poem", which is our life, this is David's major rule: that we keep our eyes fixed on the Object of our lives, on our God. Then "life itself" will follow. Style and all.

My eyes are on You. Not as a little dog, but as a trusting child.

IN GOD'S HANDS

My times are in Your hands (Psalm 31:15).

There is a lot that one can say about time. Time heals wounds and allows one to forget. Time flies and as you grow older, it would seem as if it passes even quicker. You cannot retrieve time, because what is past, is past. You can trifle your time away, or become so interested in something that you do not notice that time is passing. Lovers seldom notice the passing of time.

In the Book of Ecclesiastes, half a chapter is devoted to the fact that there is a time for everything: to weep and to laugh, to plant and to uproot, to be born and to die, to embrace and to refrain (cf. Eccles. 3). Yes, and the author of Ecclesiastes was not a very cheerful man. One prefers the optimism of Longfellow: "Lives of great men all remind us / We can make our lives sublime, / And, departing leave behind us / Footprints on the sands of time" (from *A Psalm of Life*).

We hope to leave behind us a footprint in the sands of time, perhaps for someone to follow. A poet once said that when he crossed the bar into eternity, he would see the little footprints of his late children in front of him to guide him home. These are all beautiful images, but that of David is the most beautiful, "My times are in Your hands."

It is as if you see a large hand in your mind's eye, or rather two hands placed together forming a cup, containing everything, including my entire program here on earth. Those hands are protective, supportive, cherishing, eternal, strong and secure. Whatever happens to me, will happen within the protective sphere of those divine hands. It is obviously a very human image that David applies to God, but it expresses the feeling of God and His total supremacy and love. After all, that is what David said: Even for my punishment, I would rather fall into the hands of the Lord than into the hands of people ... With that, I, a human being, can identify – with surrender and acceptance.

It is good that my times are in Your hands. I shudder to think if this were not so ...

DIVINELY FAVORED

Blessed is he whose transgressions are forgiven, whose sins are covered (Psalm 32:1).

This was one of the first Sunday school lessons that the skinny little Sunday school mistress with her long dress and skew little hat, drummed into our heads. She said that "blessed" meant to be divinely or supremely favored. And, even after all these years, it still has the same impact on me as it did when I was a child. "Blessed" is the one who knows that God forgives, that his sins are covered. Divinely favored, indeed.

David discovered that the best way to be "favored" by God, is to put your cards on the table and not to try and hide anything. He "did not cover up his iniquity" (cf. v. 5). Not that he, quite often, just like the rest of us, did not try to cover things up. But that caused him sleepless nights, severe torment and even censure by the prophets. Yet, again and again, he poured out his heart in his songs and prayers about all that had gone wrong and in which he, more often than not, had been the cause of his own downfall. Then God heard him and surrounded him "with songs of deliverance" (cf. v. 7).

Paul Tournier, the famous psychiatrist, once told a patient, "There are two ways to treat you: I could listen to you and help you temporarily, then you can consult another psychiatrist and carry on like this, from one temporary crutch to the next. In this way you will barely survive. The other way is for you to constantly pour out your heart to the Lord, to hold nothing back and to try following in His footsteps. I advise you to choose the latter option. When you have truly done this, you might still need my help as a medical practitioner at times, but the cause of the problem, your disturbed relationship with God, would have disappeared."

That is what Jesus meant with the parable of the lost son. That is what David experienced. But he also experienced the joy of someone who may once again enter the presence of the Lord, one who is indeed "divinely favored".

You alone can make us feel divinely favored. You forgive us all our sins and You calm down our pounding hearts.

GOD'S LAAGER

The angel of the LORD encamps around those who fear Him, and He delivers them (Psalm 34:7).

Children in South Africa are taught how the first white settlers formed laagers with their wagons. It forms part of their history, like the American pioneers who moved westward and formed a circle with their wagons in which they could take cover for the sake of safety and as a protective measure against possible attacks. They were easily attacked when the wagons were not together. Even today reference is mockingly made to some people's "laager mentality", in so far as they "isolate" themselves. However, sometimes isolation is necessary before you move on, even though it may only be to reflect on your direction.

This holds true for every person, family, community and nation. After 11 September 2001, the entire world experienced how the American nation mourned their loss in an unprecedented act of unity, of "forming a laager".

This is also God's method, says David. Those who "fear" the Lord (that is, who acknowledge and worship Him), sometimes fear severely (that is, they are in anguish, literally in danger). Then the Angel of the Lord comes and encamps around them and "delivers them". Jesus Christ, our Lord, draws a protective circle around us with His blood. God defends us with a blazing sword. Yes, at times, arrows do penetrate the laager and strike you. And yes, you have to take refuge in the Lord constantly. The fact that you live within the protective enclosure does not mean that you can relax your vigilance. After all, our ancestors always posted sentries to see whether there was any danger lurking.

God is the great Sentry, the great Protector, but "a righteous man" still has "many troubles" (cf. v. 19). We are, after all, God's pioneers on our way to a new city. We are all God's "frontmen", who extend the frontiers of His kingdom, like the pioneers did. This action brings danger, but we can count on the Angel of the Lord to form an invisible encampment of strength around us every day.

We are Your pioneers and therefore find ourselves vulnerable on the unprotected plains of life. Form Your laager around me today.

THE RIGHTEOUS FORSAKEN?

I was young and now I am old, yet I have never seen the righteous forsaken or their children begging bread (Psalm 37:25).

This is a major truth that the majority of believers who are more advanced in years can endorse wholeheartedly. According to this psalm, David is no longer the young shepherd who walked in front of his sheep, singing and playing the harp. He had already taken on Goliath, fought as a guerrilla against his king, waged wars against the enemies of his people, fled before his own son, sinned and confessed, suffered personal punishment and disappointment … the entire spectrum. I have seen many things, he says, but never have I seen the righteous "forsaken" or their children not cared for by God.

This is one of life's most powerful truths. It is such a tried and tested confession, a declaration of experience in faith. No man is "righteous" – David knew that all too well. Your righteousness is based on your respect of, and love for, the Lord alone. Nobody can guarantee what His "children" will do with this love and respect. Sometimes they go horribly astray, like David found out. But the prayers of the righteous also surround them. Help is always near at hand for them.

And here you must please grant me a personal confession: I loved my parents, but I also regarded them in a smart-alecky kind of way at times. Yet I always knew that they were respected, righteous people, despite their many failings. For them, the jar of flour was never used up and the jug of oil never ran dry. After my mother's death I found an amount of cash in an old knitting bag in her cupboard. It was marked: My tithe to the Dear Lord. Out of that money she helped everybody. I have never begged for bread in my entire life, even though at times, the Lord drove me into tight corners. There were times of overwhelming darkness, but always the realization that I was not totally forsaken. I would like to pray with David that this heritage will last unto eternity.

Lord, David's inheritance will truly last unto eternity. Please help me when I doubt mine.

SHREWD

"Use worldly wealth to gain friends for yourselves, so that when it is gone, you will be welcomed into eternal dwellings" (Luke 16:9).

It is a highly complicated parable that Jesus is telling about the shrewd manager who was confronted by his master, and who promptly devised a plan. He called in each of his master's debtors and canceled large parts of their debt because, he reasoned, should his master dismiss him, he would at least be able to count on the favorable disposition of the debtors!

It is definitely not a lesson in economic morality. A member of my congregation, the chairman of a large insurance company, once asked me about it after a sermon. "It does not matter what Jesus says," he stated, "that man cooked the books."

The member of the congregation could never be convinced otherwise. It was indeed a piece of dishonesty. And yet, Jesus commended the manager because he had acted "shrewdly" as a "man of this world" (cf. v. 8). Jesus did not say that what he had done was good. Moreover, he had used worldly wealth to gain friends. But, for that matter, he could have called in the debtors, told them to pay up immediately, taken the money and made off with it before the master's inspection could take place. He reasoned rather "shrewdly" that if he were to cancel their debt, he would have friends who would welcome him and, at the same time, he would have witnesses to testify to the master that he was a good man. Highly dubious, but definitely not unintelligent. Jesus says, take note of how "shrewd" rogues operate, but the "children of the light" often work against one another – which is a tragic fact to this day.

Take note that "you will be welcomed into eternal dwellings". Could it be that God weaves everything into His ultimate Plan, which culminates in the "eternal dwellings" – including this type of "shrewdness"? It remains an enigma. Jesus actually made it quite clear that money is merely a means to an end, never the end in itself. And that, also in today's world, where we are sometimes involved in crooked and skew dealings, we must act in such a way that our final destination, the eternal dwellings, will remain open to us.

Lord, make me a child of the light who uses my common sense.

TWO MASTERS

"No servant can serve two masters. You cannot serve both God and Money" (Luke 16:13).

There was a gardener who worked for a certain woman, as well as for her physician. One day she found out from the doctor that he paid the gardener less than she did. She then confronted the gardener about this. To which the gardener replied, "When I work for you, I work. When I work for the miserly Doctor C, I do miserly work and I leave early."

Jesus was right: no servant serves one master exactly the same as another. The one whom he likes will always receive a little extra attention. When we thank God for what we have, it is like the famous painting by Nicholas Maes of an old woman, folding her hands in prayer and bowing her gray head to thank God for a very simple meal. At the side of the table is a little kitten that has dug its nails into the tablecloth. A serene picture of God first, and gratitude for His care.

Many people think that they can serve God, as well as their possessions. As a young man, William Booth, the founder of the Salvation Army, worked in a pawnshop. The owner was an esteemed elder in a reformed church. But the young Booth observed him and remarked, "My master knows everything about the divinity of Christ, but he knows nothing about the basic compassion of Christ." Booth resigned and shortly afterwards he took the Gospel to the poor and the outcasts and cared for them. Remarkable: a poor example resulted in a miracle of faith!

It is often an issue with us: greater concern about how much we have or do not have than concern about our love for God. It is human, because we are scared of landing ourselves in a financial quagmire of deficits. But God provides if we honor Him. He will also provide insight and wisdom with regard to our possessions. No, he does not promise wealth, but He does promise His presence and enough for every day for those who put Him first.

Lord, we know that we sin when it comes to our cares. Please help us to keep our eyes fixed on You.

OUR WEALTH

"If they do not listen to Moses and the Prophets, they will not be convinced even if someone rises from the dead" (Luke 16:31).

This many-faceted parable is often exploited to explain numerous personal points of view, inter alia that God is the God of the poor and not the rich and that the poor – because they are poor – will inherit the earth. It is true that wealth could become a trap, but this holds true for poverty as well. One person could say that he is rich and has no need of God, while the poor person could say that God does not care.

The last sentence contains a vital truth: the rich man asks Father Abraham as the Patriarch to send Lazarus to his five brothers on earth to warn them. Abraham says no, they have Moses and the Prophets, the entire Old Testament. They had better listen to them because all the instructions and warnings can be found in there.

Moreover, says Abraham, if they did not listen to the Word, they would not listen should someone rise from the dead either. But was Abraham right? Today our entire faith is based on the fact that Someone has risen from the dead: Jesus, who is narrating this parable. After all, God is not a God of voices from the realm of the dead, but a God of the living (cf. Matt. 22:32). We believe because our Lord has risen from the dead. What else distinguishes Him from Moses and the other great prophets? The cross is the distinguishing factor, and His resurrection and the joy in that He lives and is renewing our lives through His indwelling, living Spirit.

And yet, Abraham is right: today there are even (for the umpteenth time) theologians who want to teach "Christianity", but do not want to hear that Jesus has risen from the grave and that He is alive. While they refuse to accept this, they also reject the unutterable wisdom and the revelation of Moses and the prophets at the same time. They are indeed poor if they fail to recognize the wealth of eternal life in Christ. And we are rich if we do believe it and take it to heart.

Resurrected Lord, You are our only wealth, the only way.

ASKING INCESSANTLY

Then Jesus told His disciples a parable to show them that they should always pray and not give up (Luke 18:1).

This parable is about the widow who persisted with her case even though the callous judge refused to listen to her. The judge did not fear God or care about men, but eventually decided it would be wise to help the widow, "so that she won't eventually wear me out with her coming!" This little snippet of humor amidst all the realism brings a smile to one's face, also about today's bureaucracy.

But, says Jesus, will God not bring about justice for His children? Yet He adds, "However, when the Son of Man comes, will He find faith on the earth?" (cf. v. 8). Sometimes we ask the same question. Sometimes we despair about the world. Sometimes we despair about God. And sometimes we want to give up praying.

In this parable Jesus says, keep on asking like the widow did. If the small-minded judge saw to it that she got justice in the end, how much more will God not see to it that you get justice! Sometimes we ask incessantly in our prayers, and we often come prepared with a whole list. We may ask a lot, but our attitude should first and foremost be that we would like to be in the company of our Father. God first and our requests second. That is the difference between God and the cantankerous old judge.

Augustine said that the will of God has to dwell in our hearts together with our own will. Sometimes it seems as if these two oppose each other: what I want, God does not want, and what God wants, I do not want. But in God's love, should we place it first in our prayers, God's will and ours merge. He cleanses our will and purges our insight through His Spirit. And in the process of interaction between what God seeks and what we seek, we find diamonds of inestimable value crystallizing. God listens, but the process has to be completed. And what we eventually get will satisfy us.

Let me persevere so that Your will and my will may reside together and become one.

THE CHRIST PRAYER

"God, have mercy on me, a sinner" (Luke 18:13).

We sometimes hear the worldly reproach that church people are all Pharisees, like the one who went to the temple, and that the tax collectors are those people who are seldom seen inside the temple. However, tax collectors are not singled out because they are tax collectors. Jesus sought them out specifically because He wanted to help them, and because they sought Him out. Naturally, He touched the hearts of some, but there were still hundreds of them who did not go to the trouble of coming or listening to Him and who continued corruptly with the scandalous dirty work of the Romans.

This tax collector realized what he did and what he was. The Pharisee bluffed himself about what he was and, to top it all, he looked down on the tax collector in the process. We still find examples of both types in the "temple" today, in the church and outside the church. For that matter, the tax collector and the Pharisee are sometimes both present in our own hearts. On the one hand we are broken, but on the other we are judgmental.

The Lord expects of us a certain feeling of respect, holiness, love and the realization of an overwhelming Presence. Apparently the Pharisee lacked this, otherwise he would not have prayed the way he did. The tax collector sensed it and cried. The old Christian monks from the fourth and fifth centuries also sensed this and therefore sought solitude in order to concentrate on God alone. The "Christ prayer" had its origins during this time. They prayed over and over again, "Lord Jesus Christ, have mercy on me, a sinner."

One can safely use this one sentence over and over again, throughout the day, as a type of repetitive prayer. It puts the status of Christ as Lord in perspective, and it puts your dependence and your true state as a sinner into perspective. One can also pray it over and over again, out loud while driving, or whisper it while lying in bed. It creates a kind of attachment that is needed, as well as a tranquility that often increases the possibility of further conversation with God.

Lord Jesus Christ, have mercy on me, a sinner.

WHERE THE EVIL ONE WANTS TO RESIDE

The evil spirit says, "I will return to the house I left" (Matthew 12:44).

Many of us would have been good Pharisees: people who lived according to the law, kept to themselves and who liked tributes. They were most definitely not without "religion", but with this parable Jesus makes it clear that with all their interpretations and ceremonies, they actually created a vacuum for the Evil One to fill.

After the Jews returned from exile, they realized that their exile had been caused by idolatry and disobedience to the law. They removed all idols and strange objects from among them and the scholars examined the law to ensure that it would never be violated again. These people formed the core of the Pharisees who kept watch over customs and laws. They did a proper spring-cleaning among the people of Israel. The evil spirit moved away to find another shelter.

But the Pharisees and the teachers of the law gradually started worshiping the Law. The Lord was no longer in the clean "house". And then the evil spirit returned, bringing along seven others, "more wicked than itself": self-righteousness, pride, intolerance, vindictiveness, deafness to the truth, disregard for Jesus as the Christ, trampling on His love and miracles – to name but a few. Because nature abhors a vacuum. It is a principle according to which explosions work.

The problem with reform is that people often start throwing out stuff before they have something new, more useful, better and of greater vitality to replace it with. The Evil One is quick to fill the gaps. And when the Evil One is driven out and the house is renovated, he will not easily leave that house in peace.

We have been created to accommodate the Spirit of God. That was God's original intention. And where He is welcomed, He will offer His blessings, as well as His safe-keeping – alarm system and all. Just in case the Evil One and his friends come prying at the doors and windows, looking for a place of entry.

Lord, You reside in me. Please sound the alarm against the Evil One!

GERMINATION AND GROWTH

"A man scatters seed on the ground. Night and day, whether he sleeps or gets up, the seed sprouts and grows, though he does not know how" (Mark 4:26-27).

The gist of this short parable of the germinating seed is the method of the kingdom of God and how it works in us. It is also a parable about Jesus Himself. He is after all the Seed that God has planted in His cultivated field of the history of mankind.

Each one of us forms part of that cultivated field and sometimes we become impatient when we do not see growth soon enough. But between the sowing season and the seed sprouting, there is a long period of mysterious germination that does not have anything to do with us. It is programmed into the seed. And between the seed sprouting and the harvest, there are days and nights, and a period of growth and ripening.

We must remember that, as long as we live in this world, we are part of the cycle of sprouting and growth. We are mistaken when we simply want to see the harvest and, if things develop too slowly, we become anxious because there is no visible growth. We even do this with the things that we can see!

There is a very special type of cycad growing at the back of my garden. The person who gave it to me warned me that after being planted, the plant could shed all its leaves and only start sprouting new ones again later. It happened exactly like that. The plant shed its leaves and then just stood there. For two entire seasons, as dead as a rock. Disheartened, I decided to take out the dead stem. Then the gardener came and called me: beneath the surface of the soil, the stem had developed new, white, root-like offshoots. We put it back into the ground immediately, hoping that it would take again. We were lucky, the plant is now displaying its second fan of lovely leaves.

Jesus says that we must trust God and the mystery of His seed in our lives: with regard to our lives, our loved ones, our work, our hope. But it could take time, so we must just sleep peacefully!

Lord, teach us patience so that we do not become panic-stricken.

GOD WILL SEPARATE

"Let both grow together until the harvest. At that time I will tell the harvesters: 'First collect the weeds'" (Matthew 13:30).

We often wonder why the Lord is so slow to become angry with what we regard as evil weeds. Why doesn't He do something? The servants in this parable also felt like this when they discovered that an enemy had sown weeds among the good seed. They wanted to start weeding immediately. The master said no, let it be, because you may uproot the wheat as well. They would wait until harvest time to separate weeds and wheat.

Jesus looked at the crowds following Him and knew that many of them would only be there for a while, and others would actively oppose Him at a later stage. Where God is at work, the Evil One is also always busy in a negative sense; a tragic truth. God could destroy the Evil One, but as the Creator He also runs risks: He could destroy His good seed in the process. Therefore He uses His tried and tested method of waiting until the time is right and the harvest is ripe and then it will be easy to distinguish between wheat and weeds.

And once again the problem is also within ourselves, as the good seed, as well as weeds, grow within us. In a letter to a friend, Jane Austen complained, "Pictures of perfection make me sick and wicked." Understandable. And the Lord does not want to, and will not, destroy us. He will purify us on the day of the harvest. It is moreover not our task to separate the weeds from the wheat in God's world. It is God's work. Only He knows for sure. Because too often we are like Peter: sometimes bearing witness to the truth and sometimes to Satan.

Many people in the church have at times disappointed me. Many who profess Christ as well. I have at times disappointed God, other people and myself. But Jesus shows us that good and evil merge everywhere. And the activities of the Evil One will come to an end when the kingdom of God will stand holy and pure unto all eternity. In the meantime, we must beg for forgiveness from His Presence, cleansing through His Spirit, and for the courage to persevere.

You give us courage. You preserve us. You triumph over the Evil One.

SILENT LIKE YEAST

"The kingdom of heaven is like yeast that a woman took and mixed into a large amount of flour until it worked all through the dough" (Matthew 13:33).

When my mother baked bread she used salt-rising yeast. She was the only one who knew the recipe. To an onlooker, it looked like fermenting flour. Then she started kneading it early in the morning, while the air was still cool. The secret of getting the bread to rise well and evenly, she said, was to work the yeast through properly.

There is a secret to yeast. There is a secret to kneading and fermenting. There is a secret that only some bakers can apply with finesse, even if they clearly spell out the recipe. That is how God works as well. His great mystery is like the yeast that causes the flour to rise for the bread to be baked. That is how His kingdom grows.

Anyone who has worked as a member of a large staff knows that it takes only one person to change the atmosphere in the office: sometimes for the worse, and often for the better. Some noble people form the heart of a group: like yeast, they ensure the finest confectionery of success and joy. Others, however, only make things sour, nothing more.

The yeast of the kingdom of God has worked through everywhere from time immemorial. It works surreptitiously, like my mother's secret recipe. But it sure works and the baking will be successful. God's yeast also works in me, even if at times I feel like a loaf of bread that has fallen flat, or flour that is blown about in the wind. God's yeast works throughout His world, through His church, throughout a community.

On his eightieth birthday, John Wesley prayed, "I have this day lived fourscore years. God grant me that I may never live useless." He was one of the lucky ones. The majority of historians are unanimous that his preaching was like yeast that inspired masses of British workers to worship and to upliftment. May we be part of God's yeast, part of His silent but profound Plan, part of Himself, part of His "flour", part of His bread.

You are the baker. We are yeast in Your hands.

THE TREASURE

"The kingdom of heaven is like treasure hidden in a field" (Matthew 13:44).

There is something romantic about tales of hidden treasures. At the newspaper where I was editor, we dedicated a number of issues to the so-called Kruger millions: state gold that was supposedly buried somewhere when the British destroyed and burned down the historical old republics of South Africa. Someone bought land on which he believed the hidden gold would be found after a century. But there was nothing. Numerous readers wrote and told us where they thought the gold was hidden.

The laborer who ploughed the cultivated field did not search for anything. He ploughed the field and found the treasure. He did not run to the newspaper with his secret. He neatly covered the treasure, sold everything he owned, and bought the land, treasure and all. One could call him a clever man.

This parable is not so far-fetched either, because many people buried their coins and valuable possessions in the ground, especially when threatened by danger. We, the people, are the Lord's treasure who slipped away from Him with the Fall. In order to get us back, His Son would sell everything, His glory and majesty and even His life, so that He could get us back again and make His glory complete.

An old English rhyme by John Wilmot tells of "anxious cares, when past / prove our heart's treasure fixed and dear / and make us blessed at last" (from *The Mistress: A song*). Therefore, it is worth the anxiety and trouble. We receive the blessing. We are lucky.

One can only imagine how the man jumped for joy once the deed of sale had been written and the money paid. The land, as well as the treasure, belonged to him. Well, this world, the sun and the sky and the earth, are ours. And because all of it belongs to God, we also belong to God. And together with the earth, we received the blessing of living with Him unto eternity. And the blessing of the wind and the trees and the smoky-white clouds – and love as well as bread.

You give us the treasure of life. Forgive us our impatience and make us joyous.

FORGIVENESS DOES NOT COME EASY

"Shouldn't you have had mercy on your fellow servant just as I had on you?" (Matthew 18:33).

There are many similarities between Jesus' world and our world. When one listens to Jesus' narratives, it becomes clear that many people, as is the case today, were not really afraid of running up debts. The official in this parable borrowed a fortune and could not repay it when the king wanted to settle his accounts with his servants. He pleaded, and the king canceled his debt. However, immediately afterwards, he went and throttled a fellow official who owed him a very small amount! Then, after being tortured, he had to pay back his entire enormous debt to the king.

Good, one is inclined to say, that will teach him a lesson. But we do not behave much better at times. We expect God to cancel our entire debt; debt that we have built up over a lifetime and that we will never be able to settle. But we keep track of what others owe us, literally and figuratively, and we expect prompt payment. There is obviously also a flip-side: people, especially Christians, should rather not borrow right, left and center, if they know that they will not be able to repay their loan.

This parable concerns forgiveness and pity. It tells a story of two extremes. While debt may seem simpler, it often entails layers of emotions and meanings. I do you an injustice (sometimes unwittingly) and you refuse my apology. Or you break a promise to me and refuse to honor it. The possibilities are legion. The worst debt is hurt feelings, shock about hypocrisy, disappointment in motives. It is not always that easy to forgive.

And yet, the point that Jesus' parable is making, is that one must put these things behind one. It requires more than pity; it requires generosity of heart, a broad back to shake it off, and much mercy from God, wrestled out in prayer. It is easy to write off money, but wounds of the heart sometimes start to bleed again and leave scars. Only Christ can help us with that. And in that, we should remember that we, ourselves, have been forgiven.

Help us, Lord, because it is sometimes terribly difficult to forgive.

THE RELUCTANT SON

"'I will not,' he answered, but later he changed his mind and went"
(Matthew 21:29).

It is strange how many good things can happen in your life as a result of something that you did not feel like doing and yet did, simply out of a sense of duty or decency.

One evening, after a difficult day, I really did not want to go to a friend's dinner party and started thinking of possible excuses. In the end I went and that evening I met someone who would become one of my true life-long friends.

The man in this parable requested his two sons to go and work in the vineyard. The one did not want to, but in the end he went. The other one agreed, but stayed away. Jesus told this parable the week before His death. He rode into Jerusalem on the back of His donkey. He was asked by the high priests and the elders by what "authority" He was teaching, and His reply spoke of great wisdom and playful humor (cf. v. 27). He did however also drive the merchants from the temple. Here He is speaking about the will of God and those who do God's will.

Neither of the two sons are actually an example of good behavior towards a father. The one first growled "no" and then he went and did what the father had requested, but for the other it remained a mere unfulfilled promise. And yet the grumpy one received the approval. At least he took action. One wonders just what happened at table that night when the sons sat down to dinner and their father asked them about the day's work. No guessing who was thanked by the father. Would there have been a debate and apologies? That is the marvel of parables: they keep one wondering. One always creates new possibilities.

There is another possibility: the one son could have said yes, and could have done what he had promised. That is the ideal. One pursues an ideal. But let us resolve to obey our heavenly Father because we believe, and to believe is to be willing to obey. Then the blessing follows.

Lord, make Your will clear to us so that we may do it.

READY AND WAITING

"Here's the bridegroom! Come out to meet Him!" (Matthew 25:6).

There is a wealth of meaning and customs hidden in the parable of the ten virgins with their lamps who had to meet the bridegroom. In fact, it contains a warning that reminds me of a management conference held by my company years ago. It was held at a smart casino and holiday resort, boasting good conference and entertainment facilities. After our meeting one evening, a few colleagues and I enjoyed a light meal at a restaurant that had a view into one of the big gambling halls. We were curious. The antics and zeal of the people at the tables were something to behold. I asked my colleagues, all senior managers, "Guys, what would happen if Jesus were to come now?" (I must admit that I was somewhat mischievous.) One immediately said he was harboring exactly the same thoughts, and the others agreed. Not one of them was at ease! Which makes one realize that one can actually sense, for whatever reason, when something does not feel quite right. Because if you have to find excuses, you start to feel quite uncomfortable.

The bridesmaids waited with their lamps for the bridegroom because he had decided to come during the night (which, according to custom, was his right). A wedding in those days required a whole series of ceremonies of preparedness, welcoming, benevolence, celebration and strict etiquette, especially for the bride's family. The "welcoming committee", the bridesmaids, fell asleep. Five of them held their burning lamps up high. The other five had to go and buy some oil first.

We live in a world that is often dark, and we think that the Lord is taking His time. But we know that He is on His way. Sometimes the lamp of our faith burns low. But in our case the Bridegroom provides us with extra oil from His mystical Presence (also warning us at times!), even though we can only hold up a small flame to His glory. If only we could always, every day, succeed in holding a small flame of worship up high! He will not extinguish it.

Lord, once again You are gloriously on Your way, but You are already here. We pray for oil from Your Spirit.

SHUT!

"And the door was shut" (Matthew 25:10).

Jesus deviates here from accepted marriage etiquette in order to expand the point that the parable is making. In those days wedding ceremonies lasted for an entire week and everybody could come and go as they pleased. But even in those days parties came to an end. The people had probably already eaten and drunk a lot, and the bridegroom had waited until only the true family members and friends could enjoy the wedding feast, the actual celebration, with him.

Jesus makes it clear that there is a cut-off point somewhere, even an unexpected one. The five virgins, whose lamps had gone out, could indeed go and buy oil, but the master of ceremonies had already shut the door by the time they returned. When they called out, he stated very clearly that he "did not know" them. Bridesmaids who arrived late were an embarrassment.

It is a harsh word, that of the cut-off point. However, God is in the process of taking His kingdom to greater heights, even if it may seem as if He has left and there is no sign of the Bridegroom. He may come in our personal lives and He may come for the whole of Creation. He gives us enough time to buy oil, and keeps watch over us, even though we might not always be aware of it. All that He wants us to say is, "I believe, Lord, please keep my faith burning."

Years ago, the famous singer, Mary Lindsay, attended a series of services based on this parable in Chicago, led by that man of God, Moody. She accepted faith in Christ. A few days later, there was a major train disaster near Chicago and a dying Mary Lindsay was found in the wreckage. She managed to whisper a last message to rescue workers, "Go and tell Mr. Moody that Mary Lindsay went in just before the door was shut."

I believe that Jesus, with His heart so filled with love, eventually had mercy on the virgins waiting outside. The parable does not state this and there could be a difference of opinion about it, but they were, after all, waiting for Him ...

Lord, make me part of Your feast – disgraced and all – now and unto eternity.

OPPORTUNITIES

"To the one he gave five talents of money, to another two talents, and to another one talent, each according to his ability" (Matthew 25:15).

This man took an immense risk by entrusting his property to his servants. Many people who have invested a bit of their savings have a story to tell about such trust: how extremely poor the return on their policy was, or how they were, to their chagrin, led up the garden path by irresponsible or incompetent investment advisors. It is sometimes the same in a new relationship or a new company, because all emotion, like contracts, like faith itself, is dependent on inherent trust.

Neither was it an unfamiliar custom during the time of Jesus. Many businessmen and government officials went to Rome, the capital of the Empire, for long periods at a time, to expand or consolidate their interests there. During those times, they put their servants in charge of their possessions. In this parable, Jesus, in His Divinity, was the master who "went away". He meant physically, but He remained present in His Spirit, and what belonged to Him remained His property. In addition, His possessions had to be expanded because His kingdom was growing. The servants could not merely sit around and keep watch.

Each one received "talents according to his ability": five, two and one. Therefore, the "talents" do not refer to what we commonly regard as certain outstanding abilities (singing beautifully, being good at math). The servants were entrusted with property according to their existing abilities. But if the "talents" are not abilities, what are they then?

They are the opportunities offered to every person: the opportunity to raise a child, the opportunity to work, the opportunity to study, the opportunity to live for the Lord, the opportunity to love, the opportunity to turn away, the opportunity to catch a breather, the opportunity to start anew. They were not offered equal opportunities. But what they received, they had to utilize.

Lord, once again You are offering us the opportunity to live today. Let us seize it in Your name.

HAPPINESS

"You have been faithful with a few things. Come and share your master's happiness!" (Matthew 25:23).

The master returned from his journey (like the Lord will return one day) and the servants had to give account. The first two did well by doubling what was entrusted to them. The third one did not show any profit, but had buried his one coin. In addition, he was insolent, and told the master that he was in the habit of harvesting where he had not sown. The master was not impressed and he had him thrown out. The one who had received the most, now got his share as well.

This is an extremely realistic lesson of life – now, hereafter, and eternally. Those who utilize their opportunities, regardless of how slight or simple, will hear, "You have been faithful with a few things. Come and share your master's happiness!" Those who sat there muttering about a harsh master and difficult circumstances would be excluded from the celebration. It is a fact that in the business world there are many managers wandering around, who might have been better managers than those who are in charge. The question is whether they had the opportunity, and used it, and whether they would have been able to pull it off.

In my life I was afforded a few opportunities that I used, and a few good ones that I missed. The parable does not say anything about that. I trust in my God's merciful judgment, and that He would understand that I am embarrassed. Because opportunity creates opportunity. Once you have entered through one door, the next door is beckoning. That is why the buried talent – yet another opportunity – was given to the one with the ten talents.

We are afforded various opportunities to do something for the Lord, even though it may only be to take care of a friend or a child, or that your work could serve as an example of being a child of God. And we are all afforded the opportunity to believe in God. It is an opportunity, a leap into eternity and, sometimes a leap into darkness. But it is a leap into the arms of God: God who is always there to "catch" us and hold us.

———

We always get an opportunity, the one opportunity, with You. For that reason we want to celebrate.

SEPTEMBER

Lord, My God

Children passed me by in the street, holding hands;
I thought of my youth.
A beggar held out a sign: No food, no work;
I thought of all Your blessings.
A delivery boy passed me on a bicycle, whistling;
I thought of David, his psalms and his joy in Your love.
I passed a plot where they are building a new house;
I thought, "Unless the Lord builds the house,
the builders would have toiled in vain."

I watched an old woman crossing the street with a stick;
I thought of the wonder of being able to walk.
I heard someone playing the organ in a small church;
I sang, "Oh God, our help in ages past."
I saw the wild ducks on the zoo lake near my home;
I thought, "As the marsh hen builds on the slippery sod,
I will build myself a nest on the glory of God."

I thank You for my walk through the streets and through life.
I extol Your name for being a caring God, a God of renewal.
I pray for Your blessing every day of this month.
I hope angels will sing in the beauty of the book of Psalms,
and Jesus, our Lord, will teach me in the Sermon on the Mount.
I trust in You for Your nearness every day –
my heart being warmed by a strange but familiar warmth –
and that flowers will bloom along the roads and avenues of life.

Amen.

SONG OF JOY

But may all who seek You rejoice and be glad in You; may those who love Your salvation always say, "The LORD be exalted!" (Ps. 40:16).

Some Christians, especially those of us with spiritual roots in the Reformation, regard cheerfulness in serving God as less important. This dates way back. Already during the early eighteenth century, someone described the hymns sung during a church service as "a woeful bleating of sheep and a bellowing of cattle". The depressing singing did not impress him. (I also heard this kind of plaintive singing during a Russian church service in Sagorsk, just outside Moscow.)

David had a vision of God: a vision of joy, a vision of the grandeur of the Lord. He wanted everyone to sing or chant about it as in a choir. He was "drunk" with God, saturated with the Lord. Therefore he did not sing about anyone else but God. Cyprian, the patriarch, wrote that we have to pursue a "blessed vision": "just the experience of the eternal bright light, and the light that shines for us on our dark road, which once again results in the Presence, the Presence whom we can see and experience with God, His angels, His friends, His children, like a never-ending celebration, in an immense place of eternal fellowship."

David, like Cyprian, praises this state in song. At times we are not even aware of it and stumble forth "in our lamentations". Even that which we experience as joy here on earth is a mere foretaste of something totally different: the enjoyment of the imminence of God in Person. We will only become aware of heavenly joy if we succeed in escaping from time and space in our thoughts. Unfortunately it will remain a mere vision here on earth, and not an actual experience, because we are bound by space, regardless of where we travel. But we can all rejoice in the promise: Someone is waiting for us, something totally new is awaiting us.

Lord, grant me a joyous Song of David, singing Your praises.

HOPE SINGS

By day the LORD directs His love, at night His song is with me (Ps. 42:8).

There is something in these songs, like in David's, which sounds like Mozart's sonatas. The mood changes, but together they form a remarkable, complete, emotional entity. These psalms (from 37 to 43), remind one especially of Mozart's clarinet concerto with its quick, joyous first movement and its slow second movement, with the soul-stirring melody that brings a lump to one's throat. It is filled with longing and loneliness, and yet so familiar and consoling, with echoes from eternity. It is as though we once heard it light years ago, and will hear it again in future, but then perfect in its entirety and completeness.

Hope sings, "By day the LORD directs His love"; faith even sings "at night His song is with me"; and love sings of "a prayer to the God of my life". And the chorus continues in Psalm 43, "Why are you downcast, O my soul? Put your hope in God, for I will yet praise Him" (cf. v. 5).

A song in the night like one that I sometimes heard as a child when the Christmas choir walked through my hometown at night, from one house to the next, singing about a child in Bethlehem and a bright star. Something compelling and filled with longing resounded from their simple efforts to harmonize. Most of the people who came to sing were poor laborers who had every right to ask for a place in the sun.

The psalmist asks the Lord to direct His love again, saying that he "thirsts for God", that he is being ridiculed and longs for the days when he found himself "among the festive throng". Here it is dejection that sings, and the words mourn for all that is past, or that never even was. It resounds in our lives as well at times. But even at night God remains our Savior, and He is awake at night to hear our sorrowful song and prayer. And gradually, the light appears: first the morning star, and then the first rays of the sun of grace.

Lord, please hear my nocturnal song!

THE SILENT, CONSTANT GOD

Therefore we will not fear, though the earth give way and the mountains fall into the heart of the sea ... God is within her (Ps. 46:2, 5).

This verse is beautifully written in the Good News Bible, "God is in that city". The city of God will remain standing. Faith will last only until it is no longer necessary. The foundations may shake, but the wall of worship will not crumble. The earth may tremble, but trust in God will prevent fear from overcoming us like gushing streams that turn into devastating floods, because God is also present in the trembling and shaking. He Himself is the storm and the clouds of thunder. He is also tranquility and the dove of peace that soars from the ark over the foaming waters.

In the 1980s a devastating flood swept away a major part of the town of Laingsburg, South Africa in broad daylight – houses, institutions - everything. Dozens of loved ones could not be found that night and would never be found. Scores of people lost everything. In the middle of a storm, the president landed by helicopter on a wet field to come and offer consolation. A rain-soaked little group of people crowded around him, wrapped in blankets distributed by the army's emergency services. Then they started to sing, "Praise the Lord with joyous sound, Oh my soul, grace abounds." This to me remains one of the most poignant demonstrations of faith. Even though "the earth gave way", God did not give way.

At times we feel that we live in an era of great uncertainty, as if everything we believe in is being rocked; as if people are wantonly blocking our path with stumbling rocks, in the name of progress. Sometimes we feel like the devastated people of New York, after the Twin Towers were destroyed. Sometimes we feel that impossible demands are made of us. But God is in the city. Our heart is His city and His dwelling place. He stays there. We can let go of our anxieties "and know that He is God" (cf. v. 10). God is God. He will remain steadfast, standing firmly for us.

Let the earth give way and the mountains fall into the sea. You, Lord, keep us safe.

HOLY CITY, HOLY MOUNTAIN

Great is the LORD, and most worthy of praise, in the city of our God, His holy mountain (Ps. 48:1).

In the preface to his autobiography the well-known author Alan Paton wrote these soul-stirring words of the prophet Isaiah: "They will neither harm nor destroy on all My holy mountain, for the earth will be full of the knowledge of the LORD as the waters cover the sea" (11:9). What a beautiful truth to accept as motto for a life that has direction! The city of God. God's holy mountain. That is the direction to us all.

A poet put it into beautiful verse: "The Lord is great where Zion's peak / spirals up from the deep. / He is worthy of praise where, in their loftiness / the mountain and city shimmer in the splendor of the sun!" How this brings back memories of so many glorious things! Strength, holiness ... the essence of worship. It is difficult, even for the psalmist to describe the grandeur of God and His untouchable glory. Even the most inspired poet still has to use images, and images fall short because images are earthly. Therefore the statement is simple: "Great is the LORD, and most worthy of praise, in the city of our God, His holy mountain." How much further could it still go?

Thomas Aquinas, the great Medieval theologian, was right: whatever man writes about God, "feels like straw". Another poet goes further. Sheila Cussons describes Aquinas who remains sitting in the dark until late, in wonderment of God, "where the candle is long since snuffed, Aquinas blind with Majesty". He is like someone who has looked into the sun for too long, who experienced a magnificence and an insight, and yet afterwards said that his great work was of little worth.

One can understand that our best efforts remain earthly. And God is eternal. This means: Someone of a timeless moment of total perfection. And this is but one aspect of God, one of the eternal inexplicables. But His "holy mountain" speaks volumes and the name of His city "from that time on will be: The Lord is there" (cf. Ezek. 48:35).

Yes, Lord, You are there, in flawless white, where You have shown Yourself to be our fortress.

ALL THE CATTLE

For every animal of the forest is Mine, and the cattle on a thousand hills (Ps. 50:10).

An esteemed farmer owned a lot of land, forests and pastures that stretched all the way to the sea. He was well-known, respected and feared. He battled with his health, however, and died suddenly one day. It took a long time to settle his estate. The lawyer said that they had been gathering cattle from the forests for weeks on end, and yet they kept on finding more cattle – even though the man was dead.

It reminds one of God and of the fact that every animal is His, "the cattle on a thousand hills". The farmer with his large numbers of cattle could not determine his own fate. He also belonged to God, he and his cattle. This farmer had to report to God about what he had done with his "talents". Like in the parable of the talents, nothing was his property.

These words cause one to reflect deeply on the fact that God is rich in human and superhuman terms and does not need anything from us. He is, after all, the Origin of all things, of everything that is. A pastor once said during an argument, "This is my church and my pulpit!" If these things are "church" and "pulpit" indeed, they are God's, just like the cattle in the forests were the farmer's. But sometimes we want to confiscate these things. During a graduation ceremony, the vice-chancellor said that a degree was "your only inalienable possession". A good thought, but false, because one person who had received a degree that day became mentally disabled as a result of an accident shortly afterwards. And her degree … well, apparently she did not even know what the word meant.

But this is a psalm of thanks offerings. It asks of us to share with others and to "sacrifice" to God out of gratitude. It asks of us to acknowledge the Divinity and Majesty of God, also in our deeds. Because to sacrifice means that I am indebted. And if I am indebted, there is only one word that could free me from it: mercy. The mercy of God. Please note, the mercy of God.

Everything is mine, because everything is His, and I am my Father's child (Langenhoven).

Fear of rejection

Do not cast me from Your presence or take Your Holy Spirit from me (Ps. 51:11).

It is accepted that King David wrote this lament following the Bathsheba episode. He was terror-stricken with what is probably the greatest fear of all: that God would forsake him as He did Saul. "Do not cast me from Your presence," he prayed, nor "take Your Holy Spirit from me." He sat before God in sackcloth and ashes.

The fear of rejection is one of the major causes of emotional disorders. The child who is constantly seeking attention is secretly fearing rejection by parents, family or friends. Children who tell tales with themselves as the hero, often do so out of a fear of rejection. This fear flourishes among young people who would yield to peer pressure not to become outcasts. Elderly people fear that they would be sidelined and left alone.

David did not fear peer pressure, or seek admiration. He feared God and that he would, like Samson, be left powerless without the Presence of the Holy Spirit. That is why this song is one of the greatest examples of a heartbroken and pious confession of sins that has probably been recorded in human language. In addition, he prayed with the assurance, "a broken and contrite heart, O God, You will not despise" (cf. v. 17).

And he is right. God hears and forgives. David was not rejected. And whether we are young or old, God will not reject us either. People may ignore us. God never ignores us. As the late Queen Wilhelmina of the Netherlands wrote in her old age, "I am lonely, but not alone."

Because we sin and are forgiven. We stray, but are always accepted in Christ.

———

At times, Lord, I fear darkness and rejection. Abide with me.

THE GIFT OF TEARS ...

Enter my lament in Thy book, store every tear in Thy flask (Ps. 56:8, NEB).

This is a beautiful image of tears filling a flask. This image was unfortunately left out in the New International Version. It refers to the professional mourners of old who were hired to express grief at ceremonies of mourning and were then paid according to the amount of tears that they could catch.

David does not weep professionally. He weeps like an amateur, from the heart. And he asks God to remember this and to preserve him. Gregory of Nyssa wrote about the gift of tears shed in faith. He says that the human spirit is most often like a baby, vulnerable in a world still to be discovered. Or like a toddler, moving falteringly from one stumble to the next. Then he cries, out of fright, anxiety and his feeling of misery. Usually, the parent offers comfort and the child can laugh again. God is like that, says Gregory, "Should anyone be moved to tears by any issue, he must allow those tears to flow freely until there are no more tears left. This is an exercise in prayer and an exercise in catharsis, because anyone who wants to be freed of anxieties and troubles find relief in tears as a form of prayer. Everyone who is concerned about sinning or stumbling should cry their heart out and God's consoling hand will reach out towards them. This is what the fathers taught."

Swinburne confirms this, "Before the beginning of years / There came to the making of man / Time, with a gift of tears; / Grief, with a glass that ran" (from *Atlanta in Calydon*).

Are there any tears left? Yes, there are. They never really ran out in David's life. Time and again they become part of our lives. Should this not happen, it makes the path of prayer, the experience of greatness, and that of untold beauty and gratitude difficult.

Lord, keep my tears in Your flask, as David asks, and offer me Your comforting hand.

STILLNESS THAT "HAPPENS"

Nevertheless, my soul, wait thou still upon God: for my hope is in Him (Ps. 62:5, NEB).

When David says that his soul should "wait still upon God", he does not mean "silently", as my generation's mothers meant when they frowned at us when we were restless in church. He implies a creative silence, a silence harboring the "hope" that something will happen: God will come. God is there. God is always there (cf. Luke 17:20-21). In the Western world, in our civilization of noise, we abandoned the art of stillness and practising it as a religious encounter centuries ago. To our detriment.

It is for the sake of our inner peace and our sense of security in God that we should meditate on God in silence, and concentrate on Him in love. People who have a desire for God's tangible Presence will only find Him once He is no longer an "Object" (far above, far away or on the "other side"). They will discover that God lives in them, or that they are living through God, as if everything that they think and do is directed by a force from within, the power of the Spirit. As you start to concentrate less on the external, you experience God in your true inner being, and you move closer to moments of loving unification of your true self with your God in you.

The creative silence in which God can be found, can be learnt in prayer. One thinks about the grandeur of God, what He does in your life, how He preserves you … and you begin to realize that you are never without Him. You do not say anything. You do not ask anything. You do not think about anything but to free yourself from yourself, so that you can feel the strength of God flowing from within. You can harness your imagination for that as well and experience God as a beautiful fountain, welling up in your heart in splendor and refreshing coolness. Think of Jesus and how He laid His hands upon people and how they were cured. Think about the silence in the Most Holy Sanctum, with the ark of the covenant with you. In this stillness God manifests Himself as your "hope".

Lord, teach me to experience the silence where You dwell inside me.

LONGING FOR GLORY

I have seen You in the sanctuary and beheld Your power and Your glory (Ps. 63:2).

The person who has caught a glimpse of God but once, or sensed something, if only in the smile of a child, such a person will go in search of it again. David says he "seeks", he "thirsts" for God like a parched land. He "longs" to see God while "lifting up his hands". He wants to experience the "glory" once again. He wants to experience it forever.

The builders of cathedrals of old, painters who painted holy families with halos around their heads, poets, like Milton, who wanted to reflect a perception of God in words – how blessed they were. Michelangelo continued working passionately, but in pain with a "thirst" and accuracy, like someone who was divinely inspired. Very few builders of ancient cathedrals ever saw their work completed. But they knew, as David knew, that God is a God of beauty, of fine and eternal objects, of rapture and soul-stirring perfection.

Among the few builders who experienced the completion of their greatest works, was Sir Christopher Wren, designer and builder of Saint Paul's Cathedral in London. Materially, he received very little for his work, and even less praise. But criticism abounded, as well as grief and anxiety about all that could go wrong with the building operations, and he was eventually even dismissed. But he saw its completion and every year, for the rest of his life, he spent an entire day there in prayer, rejoicing in the beauty of brick and dome and window to the glory of a God of beautiful things. One can understand that.

But the glory lies in the vision and the heart is the true sanctuary. The poet Keats wrote, "'Beauty is truth, truth beauty' – that is all / Ye know on earth, and all ye need to know (from *Ode on a Grecian Urn*). Did he recognize God as the Principal Beauty? One will never know. But David searched for strength and beauty and truth in God and sang His praises "with singing lips" (cf. v. 5).

*L*ord, I want to sing the praises of Your beauty and glory with high hopes.

OUR GOD WILL GO INTO COMBAT

May God arise, may His enemies be scattered; may His foes flee before Him (Ps. 68:1).

Psalm 68 is the famous battle hymn of the Huguenots, the ancestors of many people in South Africa. They lost everything, yet gained everything because they kept their God. When the Duke of Burgundy came to capture Geneva, the city of Calvin's Reformation, on a Sunday morning early in 1603, the citizens of Geneva struck up this psalm and Psalm 124, while they were pushing the ladders of the Duke's invading army from the city walls with their bare hands. The Duke had to retreat. Cromwell's men sang this psalm during their battle against the troops of the absolute king. And soldiers of the old South African republics often sang it during camp devotions. Even though they lost, they retained their faith and self-respect.

"May God arise," David sings, "may His enemies be scattered; may His foes flee before Him." This indeed happens, but in reality it often seems anything but likely. Sometimes David had to take to his heels before his enemies. He found himself in tight corners and often in tears because he lost battles and was reviled by his mocking enemies. To lose the battle, however, does not mean that one has lost the war. In the name of God he was triumphant. Setbacks are there to be dealt with. The tide will turn.

For us the tide turns in the struggle of life as well. We lose battles, see the victory of God's enemies and fail to understand it. But God often allows the enemy to exhaust themselves before He intervenes. Besides, our greatest struggle is not against flesh and blood, says Paul, but against the Evil One (cf. Eph. 6:12). In that struggle there will be only one Victor, and it will not be the forces of darkness. Because the day will come when God will "arise", and then God's peace will follow, in the world and in our hearts.

The sound of cannons will no longer be heard, and the sword will be hung high against a wall in the museum of time. And God will be everything and in every one.

Lord, help me in my struggle today.

GOD RUNS THROUGH EVERYTHING

Though You have made me see troubles, many and bitter, You will restore my life again; from the depths of the earth You will again bring me up (Ps. 71:20).

A river flows through my town of birth. It meanders through the valley between vineyards and orchards and on an early winter morning, a mysterious haze hangs over the tranquil water, almost like a blessing, almost like a Presence. After torrential rains, it sometimes turns into a raging torrent, overflowing its banks, so that farmers have to stack sandbags against the flood. Once, a capsized canoeist was mercilessly swept away while onlookers stood watching helplessly from the banks. The river has moods. It offers tranquility and safe places for the children to play, but there is also the danger and the violence of David's "depths of the earth".

David had been in such raging waters many a time. That is life. He was swept away by events, by evil, by wanton people, by "troubles, many and bitter". Unlike the helpless onlookers on the banks of that river, God always rescued him. But how did he end up there in the first place? Obviously through his willfulness and foolishness, his brilliance notwithstanding. Most brilliant people are sometimes, momentarily, also the biggest fools. But God is also the God of flood and river.

There are many people who think that, after the Lord had created everything, He allowed His Creation to develop without His intervention. I increasingly feel that He is actively involved in everything, both in tranquility as well as in the raging flood. He is never neutral. He does not abolish His laws of nature, but He acts continuously in His Creation as the great Modulator, the Intercessor between powers and forces, the One who maintains the balance. Sometimes, actually, quite often, I fail to think of Him. But He always thinks of me and steers my course, like a river flowing calmly or raging over rapids. I do not know His thoughts, but He knows what is going on inside my head long before I am even aware of it myself. Like David, all of us see "troubles, many and bitter", but we remain sharply focused in God's thoughts, in His Plan. And He constantly casts a haze over us, a haze of protection and holiness.

You save my life and deliver my soul from the waters.

"DIFFICULT" GOD

When my heart was grieved and my spirit embittered, I was senseless and ignorant. Yet I am always with You; You hold me by my right hand (Ps. 73:21-23).

Here the psalmist struggles with the major problem of God's "injustice": the wicked prosper, but he who serves Him is tormented and punished. Where is the sense in this?

The psalm explains that it is not always easy to live with God, who is involved in everything, and that it is even more difficult to try and comprehend Him. His existence is so far beyond our understanding that the things that happen in our lives sometimes seem disorderly, so that what is supposed to be white suddenly seems black. The poet says he is "senseless" and "embittered". Who of us have not felt like that at times? Who has not yet doubted God's motives? Who of us have not tried to know better than God?

The psalmist does not only want to know better, but he also does not want to be left in the dark. He finds it difficult to accept the prosperity of the haughty. It upsets him. His "spirit is embittered". And he fails to find a solution. But something dawns on him: that "justice" enjoys high priority with God, but that the key is actually love. And God's love – His unfathomable, celestial love for all – is even more incomprehensible than the prosperity of the wicked. Einstein had a point, "God is mostly subtle, but never malevolent."

And the poet returns to the refrain time and again: "Yet I am always with You; You hold me by my right hand." Regardless of what happened, and his lamentation notwithstanding, in the darkness he felt a hand: a hand searching for his hand, a hand whose fingers intertwined with his in a gesture of protective love. That he can understand, although he does not grasp much beyond that. He can live with that, and says that he in fact desires nothing besides God (cf. v. 25).

Lord, it is all a mystery to us as well, but simply allow us to feel Your hand.

A THUNDERING ANSWER

"In your distress you called and I answered you out of a thundercloud" (Ps. 81:7).

God usually speaks in the silence, like He did with Elijah. But in this psalm the poet lets God speak. When Israel was in distress, He "answered out of a thundercloud". How many awesome facets the Lord displays! In how many ways does He show Himself! In how many ways does He reveal Himself! Nothing about Him is one-dimensional: no method, no intervention, no form of help ever follows the same pattern. God is a God of immeasurable diversity.

We have already seen that God is (mostly) not to be found in noise. And the issue here does not concern the thunder but a profound mystery. God is in the storm, "a thundercloud".

Behind the house where I grew up lies a mountain with massive granite rocks. Sometimes lightning struck those granite rocks and peals of thunder caused the windows to rattle. Then suddenly, we were all very quiet, and the old people said, "God has spoken." Although this was only said in a manner of speaking, there was majesty in that thunder.

The poet is probably referring to the dark cloud and thunder at Sinai in the desert, but he goes further: God answers from "a thundercloud". When lightning struck the granite in the mountain, that was the point of impact. The charge, however, originated far beyond that when powerful forces were unleashed by particles colliding with one another. That is where God is and even further and totally different. And sometimes He answers in such a way that the earth trembles. When God forcefully intervenes, everything will submit to Him: kings, empires, everything.

This reminds me of the old hymn, "Hark the songs of peaceful Zion / Thunder like a mighty flood."

Sometimes God answers us in a display of power. We know that He is majesty and strength, but we are scared of the thunder. Rather speak softly to us, Lord, and quietly take our hand.

Yes, Lord, rather whisper to us through Your Spirit.

You are our sun

For the LORD God is a sun and a shield; the LORD bestows favor and honor (Ps. 84:11).

E rnest Hemingway told the story of an old sailor who was sitting in a bar in Key West, when someone asked him "whether he had religion". Yes, he said, he "had" religion. In the morning, when the sun rose, he said "Good to see you, dear old sun". And in the evening, when the sun set, he said "Hope to see you again tomorrow morning". "And that," he said, "constitutes my entire religion." A humorous picture, even meaningful, when one thinks about the wonderful sunrise and sunset over the Caribbean Sea, but still a meager "religion", in fact, no religion at all.

But fill that picture with God. Imagine that the old sailor had said that, in the morning and evening, when the sun rose and set, he thought about eternity and the temporary nature of things, and saluted the God who had placed the sun and millions of other suns in the universe. The warmth and light, the endless expanses ... That moved the psalmist to jubilate, "For the LORD God is a sun and a shield." It also moved the Knight of the Cross, Richard the Lionheart, because there was a large sun engraved on his shield, accompanied by the first words of the Lord's Prayer. It moved the poet, Charles Causley, to write a poignant verse about God, "I am the great Sun, but you do not see me."

God is a shield indeed, according to this psalm. Not only does He provide light, strength and warmth, but He also provides protection. In the days when this psalm was written, shields were of vital importance against the arrows and swords of the enemy. But regardless of how modern we have become, in essence we are just as emotionally and spiritually vulnerable as during those times. We can still be attacked by the Evil One, exactly like in the days of old. We must seek shelter at the altar of God and rejoice in His light. Without God, without Christ, we are vulnerable and alone in the dark. With Him we can face a mighty host.

You are our sun and shield, our warmth, light and protection for this day and beyond.

DARKNESS

O LORD, the God who saves me, day and night I cry out before You (Ps. 88:1).

One clear Saturday afternoon in Jerusalem, I walked from the Mount of Olives to the so-called San Pietro in Gallicantu, the place where Jesus is thought to have appeared before the high priest and where He was held in a jail cell underneath the house. This jail cell is a piteous place, with primitive steps going down into oppressive darkness. A dim electric bulb burns in the cell, worsening the darkness in that confined space. Against the wall, someone had pasted Psalm 88 in large lettering, as though it was Jesus' prayer.

> *O LORD, the God who saves me, day and night I cry out before You. May my prayer come before You; turn Your ear to my cry. For my soul is full of trouble and my life draws near the grave. I am counted among those who go down to the pit; I am like a man without strength. I am set apart with the dead ... You have put me in the lowest pit, in the darkest depths. Your wrath lies heavily upon me; You have overwhelmed me with all Your waves. You have taken from me my closest friends and have made me repulsive to them. I am confined and cannot escape.*
>
> (Ps. 88:1-8).

Few things have touched me like this psalm did on that afternoon. The smell of decay and the realization of complete isolation were oppressive. Such a time came for the psalmist. It came for Jesus Christ. Sometimes it comes for you and me. One shudders to think that in all probability Jesus was here in this dark, dismal place.

But once I was outside, the sun was sparkling on the walls of the city and on the Mount of Olives. It was like living anew, a symbol of Jesus who rose from the dead and came out to be Light and Salvation, the Light of the world.

And He also ushers us from the darkness to where the sun sparkles in Zion ...

Lord Jesus, thank You for being there for me, and for ushering me from the dark.

A REALIZATION OF DEPENDENCE

"Blessed are the poor in spirit" (Matt. 5:3).

An old woman and her middle-aged daughter enjoyed a meal in a restaurant. After the meal, the daughter went to buy something from the bookshop across the street. The frail old lady sat there, waiting patiently. The daughter returned and helped her mother from the chair. She helped her to first put her left arm into the sleeve of her coat, and then her right arm. She took her mother's arm and, step by step they walked towards the escalator. A picture of total dependence, in fact a picture of ourselves before God, dependent like a small child or a frail old person.

If we realize that the Lord has to take us by the arm, like a frail old person, or press us to His heart like a bewildered infant, we are beginning to grasp something of a life in God. Then Jesus calls us "blessed". Sometimes one hears evangelists preaching dramatically about "surrendering to Christ", but perhaps we hear too little about a quiet, undramatic need for God, about seeking fulfillment in asceticism or "poverty" or a soul stripped bare. As you grow older, you realize that many things that you used to regard as indispensable have actually decreased in value. If you grow spiritually, you also become aware of this, and God provides what is needed. The fourth-century Hesychast monks from the desert prescribed a spiritual exercise for one another: examine every thought taking root in you, whether it is for or against God. Ask the Spirit to help you screen them and, in so doing, prevent anything that could impact negatively on your dependence on God. It is difficult, but worthwhile in our world which is trying to escape from God with so many "possessions" and "knowledge".

The Sinner's Prayer is a great help in this quiet, but powerful exercise: "Lord Jesus Christ, have mercy on me, a sinner." This prayer creates the need, and then the strong arm of God helps us put our spiritual arms into our sleeves, and to walk like the old woman in the restaurant. More: that we will eventually reach spiritual heights with God's help.

Lord, help me to practice the realization of my dependence on You.

MOURNING AS A PRINCIPLE OF LIFE

"Blessed are those who mourn" (Matt. 5:4).

The Beatitudes form part of Jesus' great Sermon on the Mount. It is possible that Matthew only wrote down the gists or "verses" from a series of sermons over the period of a few days because, unlike numerous parables, little explanation accompanies these powerful statements. Each one is a jewel, but virtually each one is difficult to deal with immediately. People who talk easily about the "simplicity" of Jesus and "it is enough to just stick to the Sermon on the Mount", have no idea of all that is being said here. It is a major reversal of the values of that time, the difficult ABC of the Christian faith.

For example, that those who mourn are "blessed". And their reward? Consolation. The realistic truth that it embraces, among other things, is that nothing can really be obtained without pain. Love is pain. Study is pain. Education is pain. Beauty is pain. Healing is pain. Struggling and striving involve exertion, pain and tears. Goethe sings with conviction, "He who does not eat his bread amidst tears / And has never sat weeping on his bed / In nights filled with distress / He does not know anything yet and knows no heavenly powers" (from *Wilhelm Meisters Lehrjahre,* my translation).

Never to mourn, never to be sad or dismayed, means living like a pot plant in a protective greenhouse atmosphere. It means missing the reality of life – and perhaps experiencing a devastating disappointment at a later stage. Christ does not promise the Christian a life in a greenhouse: we follow Him out into His world. One of John Bunyan's characters in *Pilgrim's Progress* is Valiant for Truth. When he crossed the final river on his way home, "all the trumpets sounded for him on the other side". We are sent into life to live as warriors, crusaders and scouts. We will sustain injury, but consolation will not be lacking. God is Present in our joy, but also Present in our sorrow. He blesses us and dries our tears. And we will be able to go home, filled with an immense gratitude: we have truly lived. We have the scars to prove it, exactly like Jesus.

A Young Man hangs from the cross, His eyes are more mournful than the rain. He will understand ... (Uys Krige).

THE QUALITY OF MERCY

"Blessed are the merciful" (Matt. 5:7).

Mercy epitomizes a core truth of Jesus' teachings. He especially expands on it in the parable of the Good Samaritan. But it always remains a problem: When, how and where does mercy hold good? One major issue to remember is that it must come naturally for the believer and that it must be without an agenda, ulterior motive or coercion. Shakespeare got it right in the biblical sense, "The quality of mercy is not strain'd; it droppeth as the gentle rain from heaven" (from *The Merchant of Venice*).

In other words, mercy in itself is a blessing, like gentle rain from heaven itself upon the person showing mercy. The reward does not lie in a prize that you are going to receive because you will live amidst the blessings of God's generosity. And Jesus makes this profound promise. The quality of mercy is the mercy of One who was shown preciously little mercy on earth, not by His judges and not by the incited crowds. He received no "reward", except to be crucified, and no one intervened to help Him. He walked His troubled course, carrying the cross, with only one objective in mind: mercy towards you and me.

People have many theories about mercy: from the unbiblical "God helps those who help themselves" to "God rewards the good deeds I do for poor children". It actually shows very little insight into Jesus' teachings because mercy implies a constant openness towards, and concern about the fate of others, and an understanding of transgressions. When we pray, we must ask the Lord to teach us mercy and concern, rather than the pious (and rather meaningless): "Think, Lord, of those who are less fortunate." It is an implicit instruction from Jesus that we should truly be thinking of them.

It does not help if we go out and scatter coins in the marketplace. That is pretence and that is wrong. We must pray for generous insight into human weakness and need, and for wisdom to show compassion and offer help. These feelings must rain down on us from God in an openness of heaven and heart. Then the Spirit will guide us.

Lord, teach me the true quality of mercy.

MULTI-PURPOSE SALT

"You are the salt of the earth" (Matt. 5:13).

There are many kinds of salt, but few would argue that Jesus meant sodium chloride, or table salt. In biblical times, salt was of major importance for the preservation and preparation of food, as well as for disinfecting wounds; a multi-purpose household article and a form of medication. Hippocrates, the "father of medicine", already recommended during the fourth century before Christ that the mouth and nose be rinsed with salt water. This remedy still works for some people today. Through the ages, salt has been regarded as an important part of our lives. Just observe how people in restaurants taste the food and then reach for the salt-cellar (and actually the tomato sauce as well, but Jesus did not say anything about that). For a long time, salt was used as a form of currency in the Roman Empire because it could be resold at a very high price. Our word, "salary", is derived from the Latin word for salt. Just like the saying that "someone is worth his salt". The poet Shelley spoke of salt-of-the-earth people as those "without whom / This world would smell like what it is – a tomb" (from *Letter to Maria Gisborne*).

Salt lends taste, it prevents decay, it sterilizes, it helps to preserve. And salt must be worked into food and kneaded into flour. It must be useful; it can't be kept in the container. And this, says Jesus, is how His followers should be: people who quietly lend taste, combat decay and heal wounds. In a letter to a newspaper, a prestigious Professor addressed people doubting the divinity of Christ as follows, "How could the followers of this Jesus exercise such influence in fields like education, medical services, the arts and physical science? ... They would furthermore do well to read about the elimination of slavery ..." That is the salt of Christ.

This metaphor speaks so clearly that no one can fail to understand it. It is a concise summary of our Christian calling, including the drops of sweat on our foreheads that taste salty in the service of God.

Use us as salt, Lord. We are Your salt.

FULFILLMENT

"I have not come to abolish the Law or the Prophets but to fulfill them" (Matt. 5:17).

The question is often asked whether the Old Testament still has any meaning in light of the New Testament. It is, after all, ancient history, which often concerns obsolete customs and laws, bloody wars and long and, at times, obscure prophecies. But the "Law and the Prophets" constituted Jesus' Bible, and forms the powerful first act to the coming of Christ. Without the Old Testament (or "the Law and the Prophets"), numerous Christian concepts would have been inexplicable: reconciliation, redemption, justice, holiness, the covenant, the paschal lamb, Passover, God's remarkable love for people. Already in the Old Testament the Father comes to the fore with overwhelming power and love; a love which He would expand immeasurably in His Son.

Jesus constantly quoted from the Old Testament because He knew how the one flows into the other. The world and customs of the Old Testament served as preparation for His arrival. Therefore, He justifiably stated that He did not come to abolish the Law or the Prophets, "but to fulfill them". It does, after all, offer a profound view of the nature of God and His realistic but divinely idealistic Plan. This still holds true today for we can still call on God with the psalmist, journey with Moses under the cloud, sing and cry with David, and console with Isaiah. However, the main purpose of it all was the coming of Christ. He Himself is the fulfillment of the Law and the Prophets.

Yes, we no longer sacrifice animals and neither do we kill people for stealing. But the principle of respect for the possessions of others remains the same in Christ, and "sacrifice" has taken on a new meaning: to bring Christ and His principles into your life, and to have the Most Holy Sanctum of the temple now dwell in your heart, saturated with His Spirit. Christ indeed brought it all to fulfillment. Just as He will bring to fulfillment and full significance all that He promises, in each of our lives.

Thank You for Your Word that was fulfilled in Jesus and that became flesh.

SETTLEMENT

"Settle matters quickly with your adversary who is taking you to court" (Matt. 5:25).

When Jesus says, "Settle matters quickly", there are numerous principles at play which He mentions here: reconciliation, punishment, anger, sacrifice and making peace. Jesus observed the scholars and jurists of His time and came to the following conclusion: Avoid a court of law as far as possible. A lawsuit has implications that people often do not expect. Unfortunately, judges are not angels with the wisdom of Solomon. Judges are often severely criticized for being prejudiced and biased.

Therefore you should rather try to reach a settlement with your persecutor, says Jesus, otherwise you could misjudge the situation should the process continue. There comes a time in our lives when we have to apologize or try to compensate for alleged damage. Once someone took the newspaper on for publishing a photograph of a painting without obtaining permission. I wanted to pay a fee and settle the matter. The legal advisors felt we should contest the issue. We lost with expenses. That was a lesson to remember.

To try and outwit one another or to seek revenge or to refuse to budge an inch, also in personal matters, is not the path of Christ. It is simply not the best of tactics. Because everything – forgiveness, peace, improved understanding, unencumbered worship – depends on whether a person is willing to yield a little. It could bear fruit in future. But should the other party be unyielding and refuse to listen to reason, one has to pray that the Lord will help, whatever the consequences. Jesus does not expect you to lie down and get trampled on. Later on, He makes it clear to His disciples that there are times when one has to shake the dust from one's feet.

But first and foremost comes the Christian way of forgiveness and settlement, because therein lies the birth of a new disposition and a spirit of understanding.

Grant us wisdom, Lord, to put Your principles above all things.

YES MEANS YES

"Simply let your 'Yes' be 'Yes', and your 'No', No' " (Matt. 5:37).

Like numerous of Jesus' teachings in this great sermon, this instruction seems rather simple, obvious, and without many problems or complications. After all, who cannot understand a yes? And who does not know what no means? But to prevent any doubt, people swear by that which is holy. This was accepted during Old Testament times. People swore allegiance with "as sure as my soul lives", and even God swore by Himself. But Jesus says it is dangerous for people to do so. It is also no longer necessary to "swear by your head" (cf. v. 36) when taking an oath. A new dispensation had dawned. What is important, Jesus says, is that God and man can count on you honoring your word and adhering to the truth.

To adhere to the truth may sound simple, but human inclination is to view it from your own perspective. Furthermore, everything depends on your supposition. Moreover, the truth often contains complicated facets that cannot be answered with only a yes or a no. And who of us has not yet succumbed to two little eyes, looking up at us to change a no into a yes? Surely that could not come "from the Evil One" (cf. v. 37).

What Jesus lays down is the commonly accepted rule of honoring your word as the truth and the practical principle that the man who is not sure about his word is going to end up in crooked places in his uncertainty. There are times when one has to reconsider one's solemn yes or no; but then it has to be done with much deliberation and prayer – but this does not fall into the same league as spoiling someone just a little bit.

Speak the truth and honor your decision is Jesus' rule. And strangely enough, most of us can describe an incident or two where we changed our initial decision – to our detriment.

Teach me, Lord, to adhere to the truth and to honor my word.

HOLY IMPRINT

"This, then, is how you should pray: 'Our Father in heaven, hallowed be Your name'" (Matt. 6:9).

In the Heidelberg Catechism, the Protestant fathers asked why Jesus instructed us to call God "Father" and to pray for His name to be hallowed. The answer to Question 120 states, *inter alia*, that God became our Father in Christ, and that He would refuse us far less of what we pray for in true faith, than our earthly fathers would deny us. And regarding the hallowing of God's name, the answer states (Question 122), "It means: grant us, first rightly to know You, and to sanctify, glorify and praise You in all Your works, in which Your power, wisdom, goodness, justice, mercy, and truth are clearly displayed; and further, that we order and direct our whole lives, our thoughts, words and actions, that Your name may never be blasphemed, but rather be praised on our account."

This is quite a mouthful and reminds us that perhaps we are neglecting our confessions of faith. It is written in somewhat old-fashioned language, but it clarifies numerous facets of biblical truths. Therefore, humanly speaking, God could be compared to a caring parent; in fact, infinitely better than the best of them. Therefore He may be called "Father" in sincerity and gratitude, while the intimacy of the title brings us closer to Him who dwells in the infinite light. It gives Him a "human" face, like Jesus. And since there are sometimes human parents who do not care very much, God, as eternal Father, is always there for us.

What the Catechism emphasizes clearly, is that His name is also at stake in our lives. He must be hallowed in us for all His works and kindness. But we must especially pray that people will not look at us, shaking their heads and wondering, and even blaspheme our religion (with or without quotation marks). We must live in such a way that they will be able to sense something of Him in us and praise Him for it.

It is difficult, but an honorable objective to pursue.

Let the faltering falter. You, Lord, keep us safe.

Our Father, we are Your children. Leave Your legible imprint on us clearly.

LILIES = BEAUTY AND CARE

"See how the lilies of the field grow. They do not labor or spin. Yet not even Solomon in all his splendor was dressed like one of these" (Matt. 6:28-29).

Most poets, painters and authors are fascinated by the simple beauty of lilies. I picked bunches of them for my mother, never considering that each lily was a miracle of beauty, earthiness, care and divine Creation.

Jesus saw the lilies in the field and recognized His heavenly Father in them, the God of beautiful things, the God who cares. There is a story about the author, Henry Thoreau, who during the nineteenth century, wandered through the forests in Concord, Massachusetts, filled with anxiety and torment. Among the trees, he came across a few lilies. Enraptured, he promptly decided: These flowers grow in simplicity and beauty, and I am concerned about all sorts of trifling matters. I must simplify everything in my life; become removed from everything artificial clinging to me; removed from the questions that divert my attention from the delicate heavenly beauty; removed from concerns about things that do not justify any concern.

Jesus says that God prepares glory for Himself from the simplici-ty of the lilies of the field. They are the result of His outward creative beauty. His kindness and care form His inward creativity. He calms our hearts in the same way as He allows a flower to grow peacefully next to a thundering stream.

The glory of God is what style is to an artist: every line is drawn with love and care. We only have human eyes and we cannot see God. But we can look at His wild flowers and stand in awe of so much care and beauty. And then we must also ask the penetrating question: Are those things that keep us awake at night really worth worrying about? And why would the Lord, who created exquisite lilies, neglect us?

You take good care of us, like You take care of the lilies. Let us radi-ate Your glory.

CHRIST IS THE GATE

"Enter through the narrow gate" (Matt. 7:13).

Somewhere I heard a song that makes sense in an odd way: "God is so high, you can't get over Him. God is so wide, you can't get around Him. So you'd better come in through the gate!"

Jesus makes it clear that it is not all that easy to get through the narrow gate or to even find it. In Jerusalem, they show you an extremely small gate in the wall, which is referred to as the Needle. This is apparently the Gate of the Needle that Jesus referred to when He said that it would be easier for a camel to go through the eye of a needle than for a rich man to enter the kingdom of God. Apparently the camel first had to be unloaded before they could guide him through that tiny gate. That is the story.

Our Puritan ancestors all knew the famous old painting of the Wide and the Narrow Road. On the sober, narrow road, there are people clothed in black and churches and halls of prayer, but on the wide road we find the dance halls, the gambling halls and the banks offering loans. This kind of faith fills the soul with steel, but it is rather dismal and morbid.

Christ is the Gate, the narrow Gate. Yes, we can adhere to the letter of the commandments. Yes, we can count our prayers every day and fast for weeks on end. But if we fail to find Christ, there will be no entrance through the wall of the eternal city. He is the way and the gate without which we cannot go over God or around Him. He is the key, the "program" of God that has to be printed in our hearts. Recently, friends wanted to go and visit an old aunt in Buffalo, New York. They were unfamiliar with the region, but they searched for and found Buffalo on the Internet, street map and all – the directions to the neighborhood of the aunt in the finest detail. They drove straight to her house.

Such a "gate" is Jesus. If we have Him, we have the way, the gate and the key: the entire divine Program.

Thank You, Lord Jesus, take us by the hand; we need not search any further.

BAD TREES, FALSE TEACHERS

"By their fruit you will recognize the false prophets" (Matt. 7:16).

What we refer to as Christian teaching, that is to say the dogma or doctrine of the church, did not originate with someone who sat down and philosophically devised something. It originated with a far-reaching experience. Centuries ago, people came across something that they could not handle, could never really understand or fathom, but neither could they stop talking about it. They had met God. They had Jesus in the boat with them and saw Him transfigured. After this encounter, they were willing to die for it. Throughout the generations, their spiritual experiences were repeated by those who received it from them.

People who truly serve God will, like in a love relationship, always put Him first, and not their own cleverness. People who put their shrewdness first have sat down somewhere and meditated about God, yet never really experienced anything. All the senses of deeper attunement never motivated them to "hunger". Eventually, they turn out to be false prophets. They were not unknown during the times of Jesus. Neither were they unknown through the ages, and subsequently not these days either. They are dressed in beautiful sheep's clothing and pretend that delicious grapes are growing on their own thistles.

The true fruit of faith is a lump-in-the-throat realization of an inconceivably loving Father and a redeeming Christ, filled with mystery and a Present Spirit; the three dimensions of the one true God whom we cannot describe in words, but whom we know is indeed there. Often we want to say with Peter: Go away, Lord, I am a sinner! But He stays. And everything is determined by what we believe: whether we bear edible fruit or sow weeds. Yes, we will also suffer despair, and sometimes we will have to climb the mountain, like David, while crying our hearts out. But that will also bear fruit again, fruit that we can share with others. And then we will state with conviction and a warm heart: You may debate, but I want to experience. You may doubt, but I have long since accepted, and I live in accordance with this Presence and in constant hope.

Lord, preserve us from false prophets and allow us to experience You constantly.

A MERE TITLE IS NOT ENOUGH

"Not everyone who says to Me, 'Lord, Lord,' will enter the kingdom of heaven" (Matt. 7:21).

During the time of Jesus, people liked titles and they liked using them – and abusing them. Titles were used with the utmost respect and abused with false intentions. Fawning people used them with emphasis, in order to get closer to the titled person. Sincere people used them with deference to show respect. It is still the case today. But something else has surfaced: the use (often without permission) of people's first names, even though they are total strangers. When this is done by people with good manners towards one another, it is acceptable. But when it is used to create a false sense of familiarity, it becomes irritating.

Jesus says not every person who calls out to Him at the top of his voice, as though He were an old acquaintance, will enter His kingdom. One can understand something of how Jesus must have felt when a beggar approaches with all sorts of praises about one's supposed kindness, saying "my master" and sometimes even "my king". He goes and does exactly the same at the next house. Bestowing titles and singing praises in this way are meaningless. Exaggerated use of titles is just as much of an irritation as exaggerated (and therefore false) respect.

Jesus says: Do not try to impress Me with "Lord, Lord". Rather show Me that I am indeed your Lord by doing the things that I care about: give to others; follow Me; seek My counsel. In other words, seek My help in everything; pray in My name; and do the will of My Father.

Because, says Jesus, there will be a cut-off point where pretence will be separated from reality. Jesus asks a lot, but in fact not all that much. He merely asks us to love Him, He asks for our often bemused earthly love. He already asks us here to accompany Him every day. "Tis the Father's pleasure, / We should call Him Lord / Who from the beginning / Was the mighty Word" (old English hymn).

Lord, we call You Lord and we mean it, because who else could You be, Lord?

SOLID FOUNDATION

"The rain came down, the streams rose, and the winds blew and beat against that house; yet it did not fall, because it had its foundation on the rock" (Matt. 7:25).

This is one of the most moving comparisons that Jesus used. In the 1950s, a devastating storm struck the Cape Peninsula. Torrential rain poured down incessantly and violent waves broke over the harbor wall, so much so that the water swept away pieces of the tarred road. Boats were torn loose from their anchors and boathouses collapsed. A fairly large ship got stranded on the rocks during the storm. Roofs were blown off and walls cracked. Where we were, fifty kilometers away, it felt as though the raging rain on the galvanized iron roof would never stop.

Jesus must have witnessed such a storm somewhere because the description is so realistic and the application so apt that one can never forget it. In the Children's Bible of old, there was a black-and-white drawing of the violent storm and the house that remained standing, almost like photographs of that great storm with the waves breaking high in crests of foam. Jesus says the foundation of the house was on the rock and it remained standing in all its glory.

Faith in God and in the words of Jesus constitute the rock.

Like the anchor of our lives, the foundation of the house is on rock. It is cast and entrenched there. Nothing can move it, just like no one can displace the truth of Jesus' teachings and love. People try and storms rage, but the house of faith remains standing because God will remain standing. And we will remain standing because we stand upon, and in nearness to Christ.

We remain standing because You remain standing unto eternity.

UNSTABLE FOUNDATION

"The winds blew and beat against that house, and it fell with a great crash" (Matt. 7:27).

Some builders maintain that one can actually dig foundations into the sand on the beach and build a solid house there, and that it is even advisable. Apparently it has something to do with the sand giving way and adapting to storms, exactly like a reed in the wind. But I would prefer a house high on a rock, where I have an unobstructed view, sitting high above the waves.

The house of which Jesus speaks was in all probability not well planned. It probably stood in a place where the sea was at its most violent, and had only shallow foundations. Such a house will not remain standing on sand, regardless of what builders say. The unstable house represents a life and faith built on your own perceptions, your reasoning, your own denial, your own assumptions, your own philosophy, your own way of life. Such a house may remain standing for a long time, but when the true test comes, it will collapse. During the French Revolution, they built an altar to the "Goddess of Reason" in Notre Dame in Paris, instead of seeking God's counsel. And when they started worshiping earthly "reason", the ghastly reign of terror broke loose and the revolution eventually also swallowed its own children. Paris became demented.

Build on the truth of God, says Jesus, and you and your house will remain standing. If not, your fall will be spectacular. Somewhere in the North Sea, a great lighthouse was erected in a very stormy place by a well-known builder. Upon its completion, he had the following inscribed on the foundations, "Come sea! Come storm! And test my work!" As he challenged fate, it happened: the storms came and destroyed the lighthouse. Another builder rebuilt it, but with the foundations sunk deep into the rock. He had the following inscribed on the foundations, "Unless the LORD builds the house, its builders labor in vain" (Ps. 127:1). The storms came ... and the lighthouse remained standing solidly.

Lord, build our house, our lives, our minds, our faith, our all.

INHERENT AUTHORITY

He taught as one who had authority, and not as their teachers of the law (Matt. 7:29).

There is a (mostly inadvertent) way of conduct, a stamp of truth, an attitude and a use of words, a kind of nobility, that causes one to listen attentively to some people, or that frequently moves people so deeply that they look up to them. Such people are true teachers of others, heaven-favored and true role models. There are others however, in positions of authority, who are as out of place as wine with morning tea. The latter are sometimes puffed up with their own importance, like the teachers of the law during the time of Jesus. Or they are unsure of themselves and force their impractical wishes onto others. Some of the Pharisees and teachers of the law – and even their modern counterparts – are like that. Some even mean well, like a recent leader of an opposition party: a decent man, but nobody took him seriously, and he was voted out.

The people who listened to Jesus, probably for days on end, were not only moved by His teachings, but also by the complete authority and authenticity of His Person. He was "not like the teachers of the law". After all, His authority was infinite and spoke directly to the hearts of people.

Charles de Gaulle once said that authority did not function well without prestige, and prestige did not function well without distance. This is worth a thought: there must be some "distance" between the person in authority and others. But Jesus did not call on any "prestige", only on what He did and taught. Authority radiated from Him. He was a man among fishermen and tax collectors, but everywhere they sensed that He was a prince, a "different kind" of Prince, One with Divine Power. What a privilege it must have been to hear Him preach! What a privilege for us to know Him from His Word and to know: We can entrust ourselves completely to the authority of His Word and Person. He knows. He will lead the way.

Lord Jesus, You are the One to speak the last word with authority. Let us listen.

Lord, My God

It is so commonplace and yet so unusual:
to be able to live with a touch of joy when seasons change,
to see young leaves budding or colored leaves falling,
to enjoy the sun, whatever the season, and know that all the suns
are but candles in the night compared to Your brilliance and light.

I sometimes try to sing along with Vivaldi's *Four Seasons*,
dreaming of conducting the Chicago Symphony orchestra,
fully knowing that You are the Great Conductor.
You change the seasons, the tunes of our lives, the joy and sorrow …
The thought of You as Conductor is also centuries old,
and like all metaphors fall far short of saying who You really are,
our unthinkably wonderful God and Father.
You are the Father for all seasons: You never leave,
You never turn Your back, You never give up on us.
For that we owe You a hymn of praise,
A life of dedication, be it winter or summer.

We grow older but You keep our spirits young,
and I pray that You will bless me and all those I love,
as with bountiful rains, green pastures and the dew
falling on the ancient stone walls of the city of Jerusalem.
Lord, I pray for the peace of Jerusalem!

I pray for Your peace for this earth
and for the advent of Your kingdom.
I pray that my life will be built on the Rock,
and that I will truly call You Lord and hear the mystic tune
of Your Creation, Your season, Your love.
I pray this in the name of Jesus.

Amen.

"BEAUTY" – LIKE GOD

Let the beauty of the LORD our God be upon us (Ps. 90:17 NKJV).

This emotion-laden song on the fleeting existence of man is attributed to Moses, "the man of God". This beautiful poem perhaps contains a few of his thoughts regarding the "days of our lives" in which he urges us to "gain a heart of wisdom". The closing verse is exceptional with its prayer that the "beauty" of the Lord will rest upon us, and that He will "establish the work of our hands".

There are many things that are "beautiful": both calm and stormy seas, high mountains covered with the last snow of winter, blossoms, green pastures and grazing sheep, a major orchestra playing Haydn or Mozart, a poem of love and sorrow, a prayer sung by monks in an old, candle-lit monastery, the paintings of Rembrandt and Rubens, tears of gratitude and remembrance, the rays of the sun shining on a woman's hair, to be touched by the wisdom that this psalm is praying about, and by God's unfailing mercy that satisfies us every morning (cf. v. 14).

All of this is very specific and personal, but nevertheless a poor reflection of the "beauty" of the Lord. This "beauty" is as mysterious as the "splendor" of the Lord that filled the temple of Solomon, and is characteristic of the radiance of the "countenance of the Lord" that Moses, like all of us, so much wanted to see. It is the knowledge that God exists, and the expectation of an experience that is yet to happen. It is like looking at the reflection of the moon in a pool of clear water. The image is so close, and yet it remains a mere mirage of something far away.

God's beauty is near, and yet it shines from a thousand different dimensions. Unlike a mere reflection of the moon that we can never grasp, God is fully with us through Christ. The beauty of His Spirit covers us like the warm quilt and bonnet of a very small baby, sleeping under the watchful eye of his mother. It means protection. It means Presence.

Yes Lord, allow Your beauty to cover us like the blossoms and new leaves of a tree in spring.

THE DANGER OF THE FOWLER

Surely He will save you from the fowler's snare (Ps. 91:3).

Our family turns to this psalm during times of celebration and disappointment. It would be good for believers to pray this psalm every morning and to learn it off by heart as a kind of "personal psalm".

The story goes that a gray-haired, sobbing Pierre de Villiers read it to his three sons in the harbor of La Rochelle, France, on the eve of their flight from the persecution of the Huguenots in 1689. Remarkably, he read about shelter and protection at a time when his sons were getting ready to flee.

God is also with us when we are persecuted and when pestilence breaks out. He protects us from the arrow that flies by day, the terror of night and from the lion and serpent. According to this psalm, the Lord guides and protects us through all of this. These things cannot be avoided because life is to be lived with all its glory and blessings, but also with its snares and dangers. As children of God we suffer these things in order to learn. And sometimes we have to take flight. But, in our flight we are accompanied by angels who lift us up in their hands and by the Lord who protects us because we acknowledge His name (cf. v. 14).

The fowler, the Evil One, is forever threatening. On the streets of Hong Kong, I saw many birds for sale in little bamboo cages. One Chinese man even sold snares that you could use to catch your own bird, but when you asked him where to find wild birds, he merely shook his head.

The Lord must preserve our souls from the same fate as the birds of Hong Kong. And He does it because we belong to Him and not to the Evil One. However, we do not always see the threatening snare of Satan. Therefore, God must deliver us and His angels must carry us over stony paths. These are truths presented in poetic language, and are wonderful. They speak of a God who is true and wonderful.

Lord, preserve me from the fowler's snare and carry me in Your arms today.

FRUITFUL OLD AGE

They will still bear fruit in old age, they will stay fresh and green (Ps. 92:14).

This is a beautiful image of old age, but is old age "beautiful"? Prince Talleyrand-Périgord, the crafty French statesman during the French Revolution, once rapped a young diplomat over the knuckles for his rudeness by saying, "What a dismal old age awaits you!" Do your faith and your behavior influence your age in any way?

I visited a man in a home for the elderly. A good man, pious throughout his life, but now gaunt, with hands trembling incessantly. As I look at myself in the mirror I see that the boy in the school photo is barely recognizable. I find that physical tasks I could perform with ease before, are now becoming more difficult, even if done in the spirit of Shakespeare, "So all my best is dressing old words new" (from *Sonnet 76*).

This psalm is not simply wishful thinking nor does it mean that the "righteous" will never become physically old and weak. It actually means that there will still be a fruitfulness of spirit and, last but not least, as an elderly clergyman said before his death, "Old age opens a window to God that is enchanting." My infirm friend drank his tea through a straw, but enquired about everything with great interest.

By "fresh and fruitful" the psalm does not necessarily mean energetic. Granny Rohlandt from my childhood comes to mind here. She was past ninety years of age and lived four houses away from us. Her sister had to help her out of her wheelchair. But many people came to her for advice and to ask for intercession. She radiated the tranquility, peace and "freshness" of God. I often played on her porch and something of her unquenchable spirit remained with me.

This is not granted to everyone. Like Ronald Reagan, we might even forget who we are. But, regardless of how ailing we may become, God will not forget who we are and He will always anoint us with "fine oils" (cf. v. 10). After all, our growth is eternal.

Lord, let my spirit grow, regardless of whether I am young or old.

Rejoice

R E B O T C O

Worship the Lord with gladness; come before Him with joyful songs (Ps. 100:2).

In the New English Bible, the words of this psalm of praise are beautiful, "Worship the Lord in gladness; enter His presence with songs of exultation." Psalm 100 is referred to as the Jubilate and some people are of the opinion that it is the most frequently used hymn of praise for liturgies, in synagogues as well as in the Christian Church.

When the new synod hall was opened in 1965, hundreds of delegates sang these words upon entering, repeating them until everyone was seated. For someone who had just become a pastor, this sea of voices rejoicing in God was a moving experience. Since then the hall has been sold, but the song continues, just as it did in Israel's time when they sang it with their praise offering.

Martin Luther, after receiving bad news, called Philip Melanchthon with, "Come, Philip, let us join in song and carry on singing until the devil flees!" What has happened to the spirit of praise to God which exists in the greatest timeless songs, like this psalm?

Psalm 100 was written after Israel's return from sixty years of exile. Those were bitter years of suffering and sacrifice. The cultivated fields had virtually ceased to exist and Jerusalem, the city of David, had been turned into a pile of rubble where the jackals skulked. They had to start working and rebuilding. They had to suffer hardships and terrible drought.

But the people came together and their poets received the great words of this psalm from the Lord. This is not superficial sentiment, it is jubilation, born from loss and suffering; two elements that usually bring out the best in God's people. Israel believed that the walls and the temple would be rebuilt, and that God would once again come and reside with them. But He was already there, an echo of a Presence in a song of rejoicing that resounded while they laid bricks and ploughed the lands. His people, the "sheep of His pasture", sensed it as we can sense it and sing a song of rejoicing today.

Lord, we live this day, rejoicing in Your name.

GOD WILL NOT ALWAYS ACCUSE

He will not always accuse, nor will He harbor His anger forever (Ps. 103:9).

This psalm is sometimes read as a prayer of thanksgiving at the end of Communion. This is fitting because Communion is the great meal of reconciliation, the toast to the King who will come and reign unto all eternity. And, through the bread and wine, we have the assurance that our sins have been forgiven. Indeed, God will not and does not want to "always accuse and harbor His anger forever".

Imagine a family quarrel: "My boy, you must get up and get going!" "Yes, Mom." And then again later, "Son, you are still in bed and look at the time!", followed by muttering from the bedroom.

This also happens in the Lord's household. As our heavenly Parent, God expects us to co-operate in His program and adhere to the basic rules of punctuality, love and diligence. But we occupy ourselves with other things or with nothing at all. Ongoing stubbornness can lead to tense relationships. But, after reading this psalm, it is as if the air is completely cleared in God's "family". It is as if God is saying, "Never mind, my boy, I do not want to quarrel with you, and you know full well that I cannot remain angry with you."

The example of the child wasting time is also fitting for another reason. The same psalm says that we do not have much time here on earth and that we should therefore do what is expected of us. Verses fifteen and sixteen say, "As for man, his days are like grass, he flourishes like a flower of the field; the wind blows over it and it is gone." With such a short time to live and learn, God does not want to quarrel with us and to accuse us. He wants His Creation to live in harmony. God is Love, after all.

God reprimands us or "quarrels" with us out of love: the love of a Father who cares for His children's maturity.

Lord, thank You for not wanting to accuse us or remain angry with us. Thank You for not "treating us as our sins deserve".

IN GRANDEUR AND DETAIL

How many are Your works, O LORD! In wisdom You made them all; the earth is full of Your creatures (Ps. 104:24).

The psalmist stands in awe of the immensity and beauty of God's Creation as he thinks of the heavens, the winds, the mountains and valleys. As he thinks of the sea which teems with life, the fountains and birds, the young lions and the crags for the coneys. Amazing is the leviathan that frolics in the sea, the sunlight and the moon, the beasts that prowl in the forest, and the wine and bread that sustain man. Magnificent indeed, is God's Creation!

One is inclined to agree with the priest and paleontologist, Teilhardt de Chardin who said that the entire structure of Creation; its development from protons and atoms, molecules and cells, which are minuscule worlds in themselves, cannot be counted by any man. Minerals, plants, animals and man, everything has a central point and everything moves towards a major climax when Creation will be made new and will reach full maturity. Teilhardt refers to this point as the Omega point. And the Omega point is Christ in whom all has been created and recreated. This Christ Point, the Omega Point, is the First Mover in the process of Creation and development (De Chardin, *The Future of Man*). This links up with Thomas Aquinas who saw Creation as one enormous wave, moving towards the eternal beach. Because everything in Creation moves, Aquinas teaches that it is logical that there should be a Mover who does not move Himself; the perfect beginning, the Perfect Being. And that First Mover, Aquinas says, is God.

As with all human theories about God and Creation, the arguments of Teilhardt and Aquinas are greatly lacking. But perhaps they inspire us to think about the Lord and His works in love. That we will appreciate it all with awe, seizing it like the poet who wrote this psalm.

The psalm states that Creation is great, that God is infinitely greater, and that we are small in the great Scheme. And yet God knows us by name and we are His chosen children. What an incomprehensible miracle! What a God of grandeur – even in the finest detail!

Lord, thank You for the privilege of being Your child in this great Creation.

WANDERING IN DESERT WASTELANDS

Some wandered in desert wastelands, finding no way to a city where they could settle. Then they cried out to the LORD (Ps. 107:4, 6).

This psalm expresses the joy of pilgrims who were delivered from desperate times. They had experienced great difficulties on land, at sea and within themselves. They praised the Lord who "breaks down gates of bronze and cut through bars of iron" (v. 16). They had started off in the desert, in the wasteland between the endless dunes and they had gotten lost. They could find "no way to a city where they could settle."

A man once said that the most beautiful sound is that of a wind-mill in a desert. He spoke of the enchantment and moods of the dunes, the small animals in the heat and cold, and the remarkable, sudden change when the rains come. These days there are people who travel all over the desert with their four-by-four vehicles just for the fun of it. But these exiles were not on a safari, and they wandered like Israel of old, finding nowhere to settle. They knew that to be lost in this wasteland could mean death.

Sometimes it happens that we, both emotionally and spiritually, find ourselves suspended in a situation between somewhere and no-where. We do not know what to do or where to turn. Robert Frost aptly wrote, "They cannot scare me with their empty spaces / be-tween the stars – on stars where no human race is. / I have it in me so much nearer home / to scare myself with my own desert places" (from *Desert Places*). One can understand this because many of us have found ourselves in that barren world of the mind, with no relief and no direction.

The Lord hears us when we call, rejoice the redeemed. He delivers us from our distress (cf. v. 6). How often does it not happen that God intervenes, pacifies us and shows us direction, as though He were guiding us Himself. He knows that we are children and strangers to this world and that we are looking for a "country of our own" (cf. Heb. 11:14). He brings us to our "city" if we keep on calling Him.

Yes, Lord, take us there.

Payback time?

How can I repay the LORD for all His goodness to me? (Ps. 116:12).

It is a very human trait to want to "pay back" a favor or a good deed, in order to achieve a "balance" in our minds again. Most of us gladly give to others and become confused when they want to return the favor. However, one must also learn to accept gracefully, otherwise the exercise of love, favor or friendship is in vain. This could be a bit of a problem.

Sudden favors offered out of the blue could be dangerous as one is quick to discover in the business world, where there is no such thing as a free lunch because ulterior motives are often involved. But the love and favor of God is no business transaction or secret agreement. And neither is a favor from someone you love. It could be insulting, should it not be received with a hearty thank you and a hug.

The psalmist is very grateful for the immense help that the Lord gave him when he found himself in need. He seized God's help and was freed from his chains (cf. v. 16). He knew it came from the Lord; that God had smiled on him. And then He wanted to return the favor. Well, to gratefully accept God's favor is, in His eyes, the greatest repayment. God expects heartfelt gratitude from us, but He also knows that we are unable to ever truly repay Him. All is pure grace, flowing from the greatest favor and payment of all and for everyone: Christ on the cross.

I once wanted to buy someone something in a souvenir shop. The person, a family member, claimed to be "too shy" to accept it and put it back on the shelf. It spoilt my entire day. Because, even though the psalmist solemnly promises to fulfill his vows to the Lord, most important is that he "lifted up the cup of salvation" (cf. v. 13) in grateful homage to the God who saves and provides so abundantly for us.

Lord, I drink the cup of salvation and call on Your name as King. Essentially, this is all I have to offer.

THE HILLS CANNOT HELP

My help comes from the LORD, the Maker of heaven and earth (Ps. 121:2).

Psalm 121 is the start of a small volume of "Songs of Ascent", or "Pilgrim Psalms", amazing in their simplicity and yet abundant in their splendor of prayer and poetry. These psalms were sung by the pilgrims on their way to the temple to celebrate the holy feasts in Jerusalem. In addition, a pilgrimage also signifies embarking on something special, which requires sacrifice as part of one's spiritual exercise, a training of the mind and a time of special focus on God.

The journey these religious Jews set out on was not easy. Along the road and between the hills robbers lay in wait to attack and rob the pilgrims. God was their only protection, and they realized this. "My help comes from the Lord."

There is an old children's rhyme by Ann Taylor that says, "Who ran to help me when I fell, / and kiss the place to make it well? / My mother." Well, respectfully, God is the Father who acts exactly like this. He has the strength of mothers and more, as well as their love and more. And it is to this God whom the pilgrims pray and sing out loud. Because, in the days when this psalm originated, virtually all prayers were said out loud and in public.

There were also silent, solitary prayers, but this only became common practice much later. People in those days did not regard privacy as highly as we do today and whatever they wanted to say to each other or to God, they said in public. Even private prayers were virtually always said out loud. Praying out loud has its merits, even when you are alone. You then hear what you are saying to God and also what you are neglecting to say.

These people heard in their prayers of confession that their help came from the Lord, and from no one else. They acknowledged their vulnerability and called out to their God. And as they called, we can still call today. God hears, even though we may only whisper.

Lord, please hear! I lift up my eyes to the hills … but the hills cannot help me, only You can.

PILGRIMS

May the LORD … bless you from Zion (Ps. 134:3).

This is the well-known psalm of blessing, which the pilgrims sang to the Levites as they ascended the hill to the temple. This short psalm is the last of the "Songs of Ascent" or "Pilgrim Psalms".

The pilgrims sang that the Lord was their help and their protector. They prayed for Jerusalem, a city surrounded by mountains, as it was surrounded by the Presence of God. They called "out of the depths" and sowed in tears. They remembered David and his house in their songs and, in doing so, unknowingly predicted the birth of Jesus Christ. They prayed for their fortunes to be restored "like streams in the Negev" (cf. Ps. 126:4) and praised brotherly unity "like precious oil poured on the head, running down on Aaron's beard" (cf. Ps. 133:2). They traveled together as a group and grew in faith. In all probability, they helped carry one another and supported one another in difficulties. And they rejoiced and wept before their God.

What an experience it must have been. Upon returning home, the pilgrims would have had many a tale to tell and, moreover, they would have come to know themselves better. There are still pilgrims' routes that Christians travel today for a spiritual experience. One such Pilgrimage is the route to Santiago de Compostela in Spain which, long ago, was thought to be the place where the world ended.

We are all pilgrims, all on our way to Zion, all with our tears and prayers, all with our hopes and faith, all with the burden of our troubles and the oil of God's blessing. We travel over hills and through valleys and we know that our God is with us. And sometimes, if it pleases God, in a clear moment of prayer and encouragement, we see the splendor of the city of God in the distance …

We are pilgrims, Lord, bless us from Zion on our path.

THE PLAN COMES TOGETHER

The LORD will fulfill His purpose for me (Ps. 138:8).

David realized more than once that life is not an ongoing feast that lasts for all time. Not yet. David realized that life included "walking in the midst of trouble" and experiencing "the anger of my foes" (cf. v. 7). But David said that the Lord would complete his purpose and his task for him. It is even more clearly written in the NEB: "The LORD will accomplish His purpose for me."

This is a psalm of trust, a poem of unwavering faith and inextinguishable hope. David knew what God would do. He knew that God would tie the loose ends of his life together. He also knew that, at times, he had his own purpose and followed his own direction. And he knew that God allowed him to do that, because he was a thinking, striving, investigative and explorative being, definitely not a stick or a stone.

He also knew that dangers, troubles and anxiety sometimes gathered around him like heavy thunderclouds. He was, after all, a poet and a singer, but also a fighter and a realist. Like W. H. Auden, he knew that, "To ask the hard question is simple." But the answer is sometimes a jigsaw puzzle of undiscovered stars.

But David knew that in a delicate and intimate way, God was in the process of working out a pattern in his life. And that pattern even provided for mistakes and blunders when he was focusing only on his own agenda. That is the great mystery of every life, the great question about the purpose of it all, the question about significance and meaning, "What does God want with me?"

In dark times we look back and only see our mistakes. In brighter times we see our countless blessings, all pointing in a direction that makes us realize that God will fulfill His purpose for us. And in times of spiritual balance – and there are times like that – we see how light and darkness alternate and recognize a pattern – God's design in our lives. The Designer is also the One who will fulfill it. We can count on that.

Lord, You will fulfill what You began. I trust in You as my God.

GOD KNOWS THE SECRET

My frame was not hidden from You when I was made in the secret place.
When I was woven together in the depths of the earth (Ps. 139:15).

David stood in awe of God's intimate knowledge and omnipresence. Regardless of where David went or what he thought, God was there. There was nothing at all that God did not know about him, right from the beginning. Indeed, God was his beginning, even before his earthly beginning. God already knew his "frame" when he was woven together in his mother's womb in the "depths of the earth".

This is reminiscent of Dostoevsky's internal/external vision. In *The Brothers Karamazov*, Alyosha gazes at the miracles of the autumn evening surrounding him:

> *The silence of the earth seemed to melt into the silence of the heavens. The mystery of the earth was one with the mystery of the stars ... Alyosha stood, gazed, and suddenly threw himself down on the earth. He did not know why he embraced it. He could not have told you why he longed so irresistibly to kiss it, to kiss it all. But he kissed it weeping ... and vowed to passionately love it forever. Oh! in his rapture he was weeping even over those stars, which were shining to him from the abyss of space, and "he was not ashamed of that ecstasy". There seemed to be threads from all those innumerable worlds of God, linking his soul to them, and it was trembling all over "in contact with other worlds".*

This quote reflects something of the kind of rapture so characteristic of David in his awe about God, Creation and self.

Would he have known that his body comprised billions of worlds? Would David have surmised something of cells and atoms? Perhaps not in these terms, but he was nevertheless ecstatic, aware of the miracles and secrets in and around him, many of which would only be partially understood thousands of years later. Perhaps we, the "scientific" era, could learn something from this. Maybe it makes us aware that God knows, but we know nothing yet.

It is good to know that You know.

THE FRAGRANCE OF GOD

May my prayer be set before You like incense; may the lifting up of my hands be like the evening sacrifice (Ps. 141:2).

It is remarkable that the Lord clearly stated to the Israelites that the temple had to be fragrant. The temple was consecrated with incense and the evening prayers were said (cf. Ex. 30:8). David asked that his prayer be set like incense before God, the haze of fragrant glory that ascended, filling the space of worship.

The "fragrance" of God is different from what we experience with our nose. When we are asked to "taste and see that the Lord is good" we must remember that taste and smell go hand in hand. But the "fragrance" of God is like an aroma that lingers after a woman has left a room, or is still nearby, but cannot be seen: the fragrance whispers the sensing of a Presence. Paul said that the gifts he received from the faithful constituted a "fragrant offering" (Phil. 4:18).

But the true characteristic smell of something or someone is inherent because it comes from inside. One cannot sprinkle fragrance on a rose, or change the characteristic smell of an old building with aerosol spray containing imitation fragrances. God's "fragrance" is His Person, and it penetrates people who live close to Him.

David asked for his prayer to come from within him, his deepest feelings of worship, his deepest, eternal "fragrance", invisible and melodious, delicately discernible and intimately personal, but there.

This is when worship becomes like a spring garden where the fragrances of the flowers ascend in the soft evening breeze, as though in invisible circles from the herbaceous borders and the soil. This is how David lifted up his hands and how he wanted God to "smell" his prayers, accepting them in love, and that he would not be given over to death (cf. v. 8), but that there would be oil for his head (cf. v. 5).

We also want to pray like that, we also want to be a fragrance like that before God. And when we pray, lifting up our hands entreatingly to God, He will surround us with His fragrance of solace.

Grant us, O Lord, that others will smell Your fragrance on us.

FULFILLED DESIRES

He fulfills the desires of those who fear Him; He hears their cry and saves them (Ps. 145:19).

One can wish for many things. There are the simple desires that express our heartfelt needs, like the Lord's preservation of you and your loved ones. Or you could wish for some realistic changes, such as job satisfaction, or that your children would excel, or that your labor would bear fruit, or that the dark feelings that have settled on your heart would disappear. Or you could unrealistically desire to win the lottery, enabling you to extravagantly resign from your job, to live in the supposed bliss of worldly riches. It is not difficult to guess how seriously the Lord will regard this kind of desire.

One can also wish negatively, like David, who wished he could fly away from trouble (cf. Ps. 55:6). Sir Walter Raleigh said he wished he could love the human race, but was still thankful that it was God's responsibility and not his. But to wish for a prayer to be answered is already a prayer. And to wish for that which we modestly hope for, is also a prayer.

This has got nothing to do with elves who can spin straw into gold. With "desires" the psalmist meant the yearning of the believer to be near God and to live life to the full from there. Because the person who has gained this insight, that God and the Presence of God in fact constitute everything we can desire … for that person, other, lesser desires will also be fulfilled.

The fundamental things are important to God. Should people "fear" Him, in other words, regard Him with respect and love, He will "hear their cry and save them". This rule holds unto eternity.

The sincere wishes of God's people, and their faith, cause God, so to speak, to listen twice, a third, fourth and a hundredth time. And when He feels that it is right and the time is right, He will fulfill their desires.

We have many desires, Lord, consider them in Your mercy.

BROKENHEARTED

He heals the brokenhearted and binds up their wounds (Ps. 147:3).

Healing and the dressing of our wounds are what many of us desire, because old wounds sometimes open up again and we are never guaranteed that new ones won't appear. Following my father's final sickbed, I wrote "about how your eyes are ashamed / of the ever-increasing stain on the pillow / the old wound, inside, has opened up again …". And the poet, J. W. F. Werumeus Buning, mourns for his wife, "Such tender injury as the flowers fear / of soft rain in the month of May / So cool and tender was your death to me. / Injuries sustained, that will never heal" (from *In Memoriam*).

There are physical wounds and emotional wounds and, more often, both; the one a reflection of the other. The psalmist rejoices in God, but also remembers his sorrow and heartbreak. And yet, he sings that the Lord "determines" everything. The Lord "sustains", "covers", "provides food", "strengthens", "grants peace", "sends His Word", and "reveals" it. This is how God dresses wounds and heals the brokenhearted. This is what we must seek because at some time or another, we all yearn, like the wounded King Arthur, for an Avilion, a quiet island of healing, "with orchard-lawns and bowery hollows crowned with summer sea / Where I will heal me of my grievous wound" (Tennyson, *Morte d'Arthur*).

Obviously, there is no mystical Avilion, and we cannot heal ourselves. And, as the poet Totius said, the scars of the wounds remain. We often hide our wounds from others. Sorrow is in essence a solitary experience, but the psalmist says God is aware of this. He understands, He heals and He "binds up their wounds".

Some people are of the opinion that this psalm was written shortly after the period of exile, when the construction work on the walls had already started. This means that Christ was coming, the great Physician, from whom strength flowed, and from whom strength still flows … to dress our wounds and heal us.

Lord, lay Your hands on all my raw spots and anoint the scars of my wounds with heavenly oil.

SINCERELY UNASHAMED

I am not ashamed of the gospel, because it is the power of God for the salvation of everyone who believes (Rom. 1:16).

Many of us have something we are ashamed of. It could be something that happened long ago, or a need, or a blunder, or sin, or the antics of family or (most often) imagined or real mistakes. However, when someone states quite frankly that he is not ashamed, he is either deceiving himself, or he knows that he is on solid ground. If it is the latter, one has to listen.

Paul wrote an ordinary letter in the proper style of his time to people whom he did not know and would have liked to visit: the Christians in Rome, the capital of the Empire. He introduced himself and wished them peace in the introduction, as the etiquette of the first century required. And then his words hit like blows against a heavy oak front door, "I am not ashamed ..." Like Shakespeare, he had no time for "The expense of spirit in a waste of shame" (from *Sonnet 129*).

He did not beg for their attention, nor was he a half-hearted salesman. He had an urgent, definite message that he wanted to deliver before he visited them: that the Gospel is the power of God's salvation. The mystery of God Himself is power, trust is power, certainty is power, truth is power, love is power, knowledge and attunement constitute power, moral courage is power, creative thought is power, light is power, persuasion is power, pain and endurance constitute power, faith is power, authority is power, the name of Jesus is power.

All of these are to be found in the heavenly electricity that flowed through Paul while he wrote this inspired letter. And God is the origin of it all. God alone has the power to deliver and sustain His people unto eternity.

This is the Gospel, says Paul: the glad tidings that God can change the shame of sin in every man into the sparkling power of a thousand suns. Therefore, we exult in God and look the world squarely in the eye in the name of Jesus Christ our Lord.

I am not ashamed of my God and rejoice in being Your child.

BELONGING THROUGH FAITH

For in the gospel a righteousness from God is revealed, a righteousness that is by faith from first to last, just as it is written: "The righteous will live by faith" (Rom. 1:17).

Voluminous theological works have been written about this verse because it constitutes the foundation of the Reformation. Paul personally came to realize that he had earned no points at all as a super-Pharisee who wanted to enforce the law and destroy "transgressors".

In his encounter with Christ on the Damascus Road, Paul learnt the lasting truth that it is not important who you are or what you have done, God wants you for Himself, on His side, on the side of love and forgiveness. And the only "passport" is that you must believe in the name of Jesus Christ. That is "justification by faith".

The first printers used the term *justificatio* to typeset the letters neatly onto a page, so that they would line up, with clean margins on the left and right. This is applicable here because, in Christ, God issues the invitation to justification, *justificatio*, to all. By accepting this invitation, our lives are cleansed and put in the right perspective on God's page. One need not travel to Damascus for that or be able to see visions either. You merely raise your hand to God and you say wholeheartedly: I accept in the name of Jesus. And then the letters of your life shift into line.

Paul further explains that you do not immediately acquire a halo, or turn into an angel, or are able to perform all the gifts of faith like a master pianist. A practice period is waiting, of progress and setbacks, of struggle, resistance and victory. Neither is your personality going to change so that you can swing like an innocent Pollyanna through a wonder-world.

You are *simul justus et peccator*: simultaneously righteous and sinful. But, thank God, an exonerated sinner, even though you often stumble. For all of this you must accept wholeheartedly that God is your Father and Jesus Christ your Savior. Then you have been accepted, correctly "typeset", and belong to God. Forever.

Thank You Lord, I raise my hand yet again. I accept.

A PATIENT, TOLERANT GOD

Or do you show contempt for the riches of His kindness, tolerance and patience? (Rom. 2:4).

The one major theme in the Psalms is the infinite kindness of God. Every religious Jew was familiar with this, but somewhere the idea of a God who condemned found a foothold in the synagogues, and also in the early church. This misrepresentation is not unfamiliar today either, and therefore Paul hammers in this strong peg of faith.

God is rich in kindness, Paul rejoices. And not only kindness, but also tolerance and patience. What a consolation! Recently, at the seaside, I watched a man teach his little daughter how to balance herself on a small surfboard on the waves. The child kept falling off and started becoming agitated. The father patiently supported her on the surfboard and did everything with her, placated her and cherished her. By late afternoon, she could progress a few yards on her own, with the father offering protection. This required patience, as well as tolerance!

God is also like that. We struggle to stay on top of the waves, but He is present and teaches us with infinite patience to brave the waves of life. Sometimes we set about things in a very confused manner, and then He helps us as the divine personification of tolerance and tranquillity. If we need help ourselves, Paul asks, what right do we have to judge others?

God's tolerance is to persevere to the end with impossible people, even though they may test His patience to the extreme. The British historian Trevelyan said of former Premier Stanley Baldwin, "In a world filled with hate, Baldwin made an attempt for people to at least tolerate one another." Difficult, but that is what God does. And patience: Job is always regarded as synonymous with patience, but Job was not all that patient. God was the patient One. God listened without interference.

God was Present, God answered and granted Job more than he ever had before. Surely, that must tell us something? And get us to follow suit?

Yes, Lord, it tells us that You are a true Father, filled with patient, tolerant love.

POINTING TO GOD

You, then, who teach others, do you not teach yourself? (Rom. 2:21).

This is a verse for everyone who offers tuition to others: pastors, educators, psychologists, "experts", fathers, and especially mothers. It includes everyone who sets an example. And that is difficult. Often a pastor wishes that he could do something more for someone in distress than offer a mere prayer and comforting words that can become so predictable. The soul-searching question should always be: How would I have experienced this distress, setback, issue, problem or discipline myself?

Here, Paul lashes out at the Jews and at those who over-emphasized Old Testament laws, who mercilessly preached and enforced these laws and who offered circumcision as the greatest sign of the Covenant, while God sought the "circumcision of the heart" (cf. v. 29). And, in Romans 3:10, Paul came to the conclusion, "There is no one righteous, not even one … " Just as well, because all of those who "teach others" struggle with this verse at some time, or constantly, like Jacob at the Jabbok. How many marks would "learners" award us, should they, on occasion, be privy to our "uncircumcised" thoughts?

There are many viewpoints on what people in the ministry should be like: they must be agreeable and get on well with everyone; they must be in constant contact with God and also listen with interest to all and sundry. Or people say that their time has passed and that they have lost touch. Actually, they can't, because then they would have to be angels, who can carry out everything with ease. But God specifically did not use angels and became man Himself. Those first disciples were also the first pastors, albeit bungling and foolish.

And yet, imperfect as they were, they spread the Gospel far and wide. Their only qualification was that they were willing to follow Jesus when He so instructed them. Indeed, God chose the foolish of this world to shame the wise (cf. 1 Cor. 1:27).

Fortunately, the kingdom of God is not dependent on the views, and even the moral excellence of pastors and worshipers. But to try and follow Jesus and to point to God is the major task of all those who call themselves "disciples".

Make me a disciple of experience, a follower who points to God.

TO SACRIFICE IS TO GIVE AWAY

God presented Him as a sacrifice of atonement, through faith in His blood (Rom. 3:25).

To make an offering or sacrifice is to sanctify something by giving it away out of compelling love and heartfelt respect. The Israelites of old took their sacrificial offerings to the temple as a gesture of worship, a holy act to the glory and love of the Lord, as something that they gave away, as something that filled them with astonishing respect and, in the process, lifted their spirits. What has been sacrificed cannot be claimed back. God realized this from the beginning and the primitive acts of the sacrificial offerings of animals and incense were accepted and ordered from that conviction. The people sacrificed to His glory, but by accepting their sacrificial offerings, He also paid homage to them.

The greatest expression of sanctified love was when the Father gave His Son to mankind, who subjected Him to a primitive ritual of death and punishment and, in so doing, consciously sanctified Him as the Atoner, an expression of the Father's deepest feelings.

God laid down the laws and, since the beginning, generation upon generation, has transgressed these laws. God could not repeal His own laws to reinstate His people, His Creation in His image, on His wavelength, because then He would not have been true to Himself. Therefore, He who laid down the laws would carry the consequences Himself. Right from the beginning, Jesus was God's insurance in His grand Plan. His creatures would have choices, choices that they would make a mess of.

But God would still have the sublime choice, out of love, in atonement: to surrender His Son to the cross and the blood of Golgotha. This is why that scene is etched and sanctified into the mind of everyone who believes. That was the final and absolute sacrifice, to be seized by all who believed. As a street preacher once called out "Take it or leave it. Jesus is God's last Word." It is to give away in love, a clemency, a sanctification. Ours. God's.

Lord Jesus, I believe this: You are mine.

HOPE CLIMBS THE MOUNTAIN ... OR JUMPS!

Against all hope, Abraham in hope believed (Rom. 4:18).

To hope is mainly to wish audibly or inwardly, but it is more: it is to wish as if something is already happening. When David wanted to build a house for God, the temple was already erected in his heart on the Temple Mount. When Abraham went up the mountain with Isaac, he was willing to sacrifice, but he was also attuned to a possible, probable, real intervention from God in an impossible situation. And this is how it was with every divine intervention. This is how it was with Jesus and the cross that brought victory. This is how it still is today.

To hope is not to simply dream. Hope constitutes dreams, prayers, expectations. Hope sometimes runs the risk of becoming wishful thinking but, in faith, the Spirit acts to prevent us from crossing the boundaries of hope. He who hopes in prayer can always count on this, even when one, like Abraham, hopes when there is no hope left. Such hope looks past the circumstances; it looks towards God.

Actually, it is an enormous risk, but the kind of risk that is also a leap of faith: a leap into the darkness, but into the secure arms of God. And should your hope be realized, you rejoice after the leap into the arms of God. If your hope is not realized, you are consoled in the arms of God. Therefore, risk it with God, says Paul. Risk it with God, says Abraham.

Every new day brings new hope. Hope is the wings of truth and faith is the direction. God is the one we put our hope in and who brings every new day. As every new morning dawns, hope is renewed. And remember, every new day is unique. In all eternity there has not been such a day before and, until the end of time, there will not be one like it again. God makes His Creation new every day. He makes us new, He renews our hope. He renews our hearts. We may gladly climb the mountain. We may gladly jump into His arms.

Yes, Lord, You are always there. Present, and with arms outstretched to catch us.

DEAD TO SIN

In the same way, count yourselves dead to sin but alive to God in Christ Jesus (Rom. 6:11).

Here Paul explains baptism as being united in the death and resurrection of Jesus Christ. Baptism is a simple, holy act with water, but a symbol charged with the power of Christ: power of forgiveness, of renewal and of a mystical processing of a grand, unbreakable unity unto eternity. Therefore, as Christ "died" to sin (cf. v. 10), so believers also "die" to sin.

But in the meantime we tell lies, commit fraud, covet and become sidetracked by our own idols. How can we then be "dead" to sin? Men who play in major rugby matches say that they are not even aware of the crowds, only of the ball and the game. They are dead to everything else. Lance Armstrong, the famous cyclist, says that during the Tour de France nothing counts but the finishing line in Paris. The celebrations along the road are all "dead" to him. He, his bicycle, the road and the ultimate objective become one. He has won this race seven times already. Yes, problems do surface at times, but the objective is of overriding importance.

It is the same for Christians: they become one with the objective in Christ; one with the Spirit of Christ; one with a life in Christ. It is often a process of falling off and hurting oneself, but nothing sticks that is not of Christ. It simply falls away because, in principle, the Christian is dead to it.

Obviously, when Christians fall, they, like Armstrong, can be badly injured and lose valuable time. But sin is no longer their major interest. A Christian is a person in Christ, and nothing unclean adheres to Christ. The man who braves the road with Christ starts breathing in the clean air of God and moving in the light of His Presence. The smell and smog of the world still surround the faithful, but they are of ever-decreasing importance.

You allow us to live in unity with You, Lord. Let us move forward in this unity.

TWO PAULS

For what I do is not the good I want to do; no, the evil I do not want
to do – this I keep on doing (Rom. 7:19).

At first glance it would seem as if Paul is contradicting himself
here after saying in the previous chapter that the faithful are
dead to sin. Now he says that he has been delivered, but inside him
there rages a spiritual battle between good and evil. Therefore, long
before psychoanalysis, Paul already knew that there were two Pauls:
one bound in the Spirit to Christ and the other bound to the law,
which he transgressed by doing that which he hated!

But this is the mystical battle of becoming one with Christ; the
battle to cleanse the residue of the carnal law and sin that are still
lurking in the conscious and subconscious. This battle forms part of
a cleansing from inside a "body of death". And this cleansing is the
work of God in "Jesus Christ our Lord" (cf. vv. 24-25).

As Jesus Christ moves into the heart of the believer through His
Spirit, as the process of unification begins, we become increasingly
aware of elements in our own existence that are not in line with
Christ. Christ is perfect. In principle, we become like Him, but we
will remain imperfect until the new dispensation. And it is this dis-
cord that irritates Paul.

What Iago said of Cassio in Shakespeare's *Othello*, Paul says about
Jesus and his own inner self, "He hath a daily beauty in his life that
makes me ugly." And it is precisely this "ugliness" that Paul wants
to rid himself of. But, like a therapist forces a patient to confront
unpleasant fragments in his mind, so must Paul and each of us go
through this process in order to be cleansed.

And he succeeded! We can succeed! Thanks be to God, says Paul.
In Jesus Christ, God takes over and the sinful Paul and the sinful I
are gradually confronted and cleansed. That is the ideal, the hope,
the faith, the purpose, the method of a mystical growth in Christ.

*L*ord, gradually cleanse me as I grow in You.

THE SPIRIT AND FEAR

For you did not receive a spirit that makes you a slave again to fear (Rom. 8:15).

A confused, emotional patient once sighed that fear was "probably the result of unforgivable sin". One would like to retort that it is probably not because God does not want to forgive fear, but because the patient despairs about the possibility of putting an end to fear. One can understand this because fear becomes an evil spiralling circle.

Fear is always specific, in contrast to anxiety which senses a threat but is not always aware of the reason behind it. The fear of which Paul speaks, turns people into slaves of the law of a vengeful God, slaves of ghastly thoughts of judgment and failure, unwilling slaves of the suggestions of Satan. Because, if the Evil One did not even leave Jesus in peace in the desert, he will definitely not pass us by in our times of emotional drought.

According to Paul, this is where the Spirit of God intervenes with tranquility and strength and the assurance that we are children of God, even though we sometimes harbor thoughts of "unforgivable sins". The Spirit is like a life-giving breath (after all, Spirit means breath in Hebrew, Greek and Latin) in our bodies, the true life-giving essence of God Himself.

And where God "breathes", everything becomes alive: our bodies, as well as our souls. Because this "spirit" (and "Spirit"), crops up in many places: the spirit of a team, the spirit of a community, the spirit of a place and the Spirit of hope and faith. The latter places us in the domain of God's deepest Self: the Spirit that resides in a church; the Spirit that sometimes leaves us intoxicated from worshiping, like the disciples at Pentecost; the Spirit that pervades our every fiber with "spiritual oxygen" for healing, also from fear.

This Spirit, says Paul, causes us to call on God as our Father. And the Father knows what to do, especially with fear.

Let Your Spirit stay attuned to my spirit and prevent me from starting to look around me in fear.

SIGHS AND PRAYERS

We do not know what we ought to pray for, but the Spirit Himself intercedes for us with groans that words cannot express (Rom. 8:26).

The metaphysical poet, William Blake, wrote with profound emotion: "For a tear is an intellectual thing; / And a sigh is the sword of an Angel King, / And the bitter groan of the martyr's woe / Is an arrow from the Almighty's bow!" (from *The Gray Month*).

One doubts whether a tear is indeed "intellectual", but the whimpers and sighs of a martyr, the prayer of pain, are truly like arrows from the bow of the Almighty. Somewhere, where it matters, it will strike with the truth. The dying and the suffering have sighed prayers out loud with me, or groaned in assent; some of those prayers were barely audible, and I could hardly make out anything but a few fragments from Psalms.

These prayers were little more than utterances, in times when one did not know what to pray. Then the Spirit sighs with us in our sighs, and the heart of God groans in unison with our pain, in an understanding based on experience that cannot be put into words.

But we do not fully know our own needs and very often our prayers do not correspond with what we really need. Then God must, like a mother to her infant, dictate what we must ask of Him. And the infant repeats the words, sometimes without understanding anything.

But the mother understands it and the heavenly Father understands it, because God knows and expects the sighs from that heart. Sometimes this sighing is merely consecrated silence, sometimes it is a moment of silent praise. Sometimes it is a painful petition, as with Blake's martyrs, but in all of it there is the sound of the Spirit's groans on our behalf.

It constitutes a mystery, but also an intimate strength flowing from our heart to the heart of God through the "breath" of God. Merely look up, or down, or to a fixed point, or close your eyes and sigh before God, and cry if you must, and laugh if you wish and, in so doing, celebrate God's Presence.

Let us repeat what Your Spirit dictates.

PATTERN FOR THE GOOD

We know that in all things God works for the good of those who love Him (Rom. 8:28).

This statement can only be made by someone who has walked a long road with the Lord. But it is there for all to believe, and it shines like a beacon in the Christian faith. You can relate all your experiences to this belief and, eventually, it forms a pattern – often a difficult pattern – and from it a Grand Thought shines forth. God is in the pattern.

The great poet, John Milton, became blind, but wrote, "God doth not need / Either man's work or his own gifts: Who best / Bear His mild yoke, they serve Him best ... / They also serve who only stand and wait" (from *Sonnet 16: On his blindness*). There are heroic people, like this, who overcome major setbacks. There are also others who, in disaster upon disaster – often beyond their control – are defeated. Thomas Carlyle, who never managed to come to terms with the death of his wife wrote, "Adversity is sometimes hard upon a man; but for one man who can stand prosperity, there are a hundred that will stand adversity." Not everyone can handle prosperity, but many more can handle adversity.

However, Paul does not philosophize about whether prosperity or adversity is better for man. He merely says: wait and observe at the full picture of prosperity and adversity. The greater balance sheet of God's Plan will work out, including the major wars and natural disasters. If we want to understand God's Plan, we will have to think like God. And that is impossible.

However, He assures us, time and again in His Word that He will let everything work out for the better. I once listened as my son, a computer engineer, tried to help a colleague sort out a problem. I did not understand anything of their strange terminology, but they solved the problem. We often do not understand anything about God's secret handwriting in the Plan of our lives, but Paul says, "Bear up. If you love God, everything will work out for the good of you and yours. I know it."

I experience it like this, Lord. Thank You, even though I understand very little of it.

AN UNSTOPPABLE GOD

If God is for us, who can be against us? (Rom. 8:31).

Marshal Bernadotte, founder of the modern-day Swedish royal family, warned his allies 200 years ago: "The mere presence of Napoleon on the battlefield is worth 100,000 men." But in the wars of the Old Testament, the mere Presence of God or that of His angel in battle caused the enemy to flee hastily.

No one can fight against God, not millions of soldiers and not thousands of "experts". They can try – and they do! – to wipe God from His Creation, but in the end, they get carried down the river of time and over the waterfall of eternity and God shines on, like the sun, in His power.

God has many enemies, but He also has many followers. God knows many people who want to dictate to Him, but there are also many who seek shelter with Him, and with Him alone. God has many detractors, but God also has many who bear testimony to Him. With this slogan – "If God is for us, who can be against us?" – Paul traversed the known world of that time, like a one-man army, with "Christ is Lord!"

They threw him in jail and stoned him, they ridiculed him and flogged him. He stood before courts and courtiers and high priests and enemies, without a sign of fear. God was with him and he was unstoppable, even while in jail. His highs were higher than those of a "normal" person; his lows lower, with his "thorn in the flesh" (perhaps endogenous depression?); his initial persecution complex and his pride worse and his humility greater than those of all the apostles.

But through all of this God was present and Paul was assured that nothing could stop God and that we would be wise to live according to this truth.

He was not an "easy" man to live with, but if God could perform His wonders through such a man, then God is indeed miraculous above all timeless miracles. This unstoppable God makes us unstoppable, safe, filled with courage, indestructible.

If You, Lord, are for us, who can be against us?

LOVE IMPULSE OF A CROSS

Who shall separate us from the love of Christ? (Rom. 8:35).

The famous theologian Karl Barth's first major publication on doctrine dealt with Paul's letter to the Romans because, he said, that constituted the focal point of Paul's thoughts, the focal point of his confidence in his faith.

The axis around which the entire Gospel revolves can be found in these immortal words. One can even argue that the pivotal point on which everything revolves is to be found in Romans chapter eight. He who senses the depth of Romans eight in particular – because it is too vast to debate – goes through a mystical experience of assurance and comfort; of peaceful and jubilant moods; through the mystery of the Spirit; the power of God and the love of Christ.

Paul says that nothing can separate us from the love of Christ. We may suffer pain, sorrow and death, we may be attacked by evil forces or by "height or depth, or anything else in all Creation" (cf. v. 39). But God will keep the unbreakable cord of atonement through His blood safely in place. He is attuned to us as our eternal and always-concerned-about-us Savior. Sometimes we feel as if we are being treated like "sheep to be slaughtered": threatened, vulnerable and alone. The forces of "the present and the future" events sometimes leave us feeling like the exiled Israelites in a strange land with a longing for happiness and peace that escape us.

But God is now present in the love of Christ, and this love forms a mystical wall of protection that even Moses and the prophets could not achieve. Love is the golden thread spanning time and eternity, charged directly to our hearts with a divine impulse. And nothing temporary or permanent, can break it. It is a great impulse of love aimed at us. It has accepted a cross, and in that act of acceptance, God embraces us – we who long to be close to Him in faith.

Paul suggested that, in this knowledge, we should gradually become more and more like Christ, "more than victors", exonerated by God, children of the King.

Lord, make me worthy of it all, completely dependent on You.

THE WORD IS "WILL"

Everyone who calls on the name of the Lord will be saved (Rom. 10:13).

Pastor, the word is 'will!'", a young woman once said to me after my sermon about this text. "Will, will, will!" She was not hyper-critical or dismayed, only determined to hammer it home to me. She was more than successful. There is nothing hesitant, fuzzy or enig-matic about this statement. The word is "will": "For everyone who calls on the name of the Lord *will* be saved."

One can, of course, with one's limited understanding, debate it until it becomes fuzzy, and many people do just that. They want to know whether "a sinner", who is whimpering with his last breath that Jesus must help him, "will go to heaven", and whether it is "fair" towards "others who have always believed". They also want to know whether "call on" is not a convenient way of living like you choose and then, at the end, seeking salvation. All these things are of lesser importance: the one who calls on the Lord at the last moment has, in any case, missed out on a great adventure and on abundant grace received by living according to the hand of God. What is more, God knows the heart, like Jesus did when He welcomed the criminal on the cross into the kingdom.

And to "call on" does not mean to play "I spy". People who feel that they are lost, mean it when they call for help. So does a child cry-ing in the night. And so does someone who no longer knows what to do. It is an existential cry, with your entire being. And it means that you face problems that are causing you to doubt the reason for your existence. It means that you are looking for a hand to hold on to in your existential fear.

A presence to comfort you, a wisdom that transcends all reason, a peace that calms your pounding heart, and contact with eternity which you sense is possible in Christ. And you will receive help here, tomorrow, the day after, light-years on and unto eternity.

The word is "will". Everyone who truly calls will be saved. The deed is done by God and the detail is provided by Him.

You will save! Amen, yes, amen.

GLORY!

Oh, the depth of the riches of the wisdom and knowledge of God! (Rom. 11:33).

Most of us would agree with the priest and poet, Gerard Manley Hopkins's statement that, "To lift up the hands in prayer gives God glory, but a man with a dung fork in his hand, and a woman with a slop pail, give Him glory too. He is so great that all things give Him glory if you mean they should" (from *Selected Prose*).

In our verse today Paul bursts forth in lyrical praise about the glory of God. He lifts up his hands. He stands, spiritual pitch fork in his hand and his slop pail … all for the Gospel, all for Christ, all for the kingdom that will come. And, at this moment, all of this fades, because he delights in the glory, the knowledge, riches and wisdom of God. He says that he does not understand the ways of the Lord (cf. v. 34).

God must flow through him and reveal everything. Because everything is from Him and through Him and to Him. He is like the major ocean currents, flowing still and deep and invisible beneath the surface. But that invisible, still and "mysterious" movement and force determine the temperature of the water, the weather patterns, the vegetation on land and the kind of life that people can lead on that land. Indeed, a "depth of riches", a wisdom and knowledge transcending all reason.

In this chapter, Paul talks about the Jews who had rejected the Anointed One, but he says God used this rejection precisely to afford the Gentiles the opportunity to be saved as well. But God will not completely sacrifice His former people; a remnant will be saved as "they are loved on account of the patriarchs" (cf. v. 28). He leaves that in God's hands while he, like David, sings the praises of God's wisdom and power.

This is a pointer to living in faith: while we fail to understand everything, we say to God, "Proceed, Lord, because You know." And then we proceed with our praises ourselves, the uplifted hands, and our pail and our fork.

For Yours is the glory for ever and ever.

IT IS DIFFICULT

Do not be overcome by evil, but overcome evil with good (Rom. 12:21).

In *Germanicus*, the masterpiece by the poet N. P. van Wyk Louw, the revered general, Germanicus, pays a visit to Emperor Tiberius in Rome. Tiberius, drunk and cynical, asks Germanicus, "Do you want to drink wine, or do you want to remain sober? Listen to me: Where everyone is drunk, to want to stay sober yourself ... that turns into madness. And, being chaste, my Germanicus – that turns into night ..." In other words, accept and become part of the evil as evil, as unavoidable, otherwise everything turns into a madness of resistance against evil that cannot be tamed.

Germanicus does not accept this. Neither does Paul. He knows what is going on in the world and in Rome, and that "man wants to be dark, reticent in his blood", as Tiberius puts it. Paul knows the argument that there is nothing one can do about evil and that you either become part of it, or you are excluded. He knows about hostility, revenge, persecution and unbridled lust (cf. Rom. 1:29). He is no stranger to the ways of the world, a charge that Tiberius levels at Germanicus. But he has some advice: "Do not be overcome by evil," he says, "but overcome evil with good." Feed your hungry enemy, leave room for God's wrath, do not take revenge or be conceited (cf. 12:16-20).

All of this sounds very idealistic, but it is the ideal in Christ. Paul does not maintain that he can do this by himself, but the Spirit will come to his assistance in this weakness as well, in the midst of all the surrounding weaknesses and filth. Paul visited some brutal cities of the world and everywhere he lit up the lamp of Christ. It is, after all, better to light one little candle than to hurl abuse at the darkness.

Moreover, this is about the glory of God in our lives. It is difficult to feed an enemy. It is difficult to let go of thoughts of revenge. But somewhere in all of this, there is a level-headedness, a wisdom that makes sense and brings balance to a contentious situation. The Spirit helps us in this.

It is difficult to learn, Lord, but let the Spirit of Christ teach us.

NOVEMBER

Lord, My God

Friends came to celebrate the birthday of a neighbor,
happily chatting in languages I do not speak.
But I could savor the festive atmosphere.
Friends brought gifts and I knew November was at the gate,
the month before Christmas.
Perhaps in their heart of hearts my neighbors were longing
for their home somewhere in Europe,
as we sometimes long for our eternal home,
from where we came. Perhaps this life is an exam.

This month is an intermezzo, before the festivities of the Advent.
This month serves notice that years may pass
but You, our God, are eternal "as it was in the beginning,
is now, and ever shall be, world without end."

This is the glory of Father, Son and Holy Spirit
of which the psalmist sings.
Accept my prayer like a gift, like an offering of incense.
You who know all my secrets.
For years on end You have been typesetting
the letters on the page of my life,
and You vindicate me, from season to season … You lead me on
while I, at times, live as if I know nothing of You.

The neighbors started singing ancient songs of their country.
I would love to sing a song of the new world to come.
Let Your angels sing to Your people this month
and every day, about Your works,
and, eternal Father, grant us hope, teach us faith,
embrace us and grant us peace.

Amen.

EVERYTHING IN PERSPECTIVE

The fear of the LORD is the beginning of knowledge (Prov. 1:7).

Once Anselm of Canterbury suddenly stopped in the middle of a lecture and told his students to go home until he sent for them again. "Because," he said, "if I want to teach you, I first have to go and learn from God." He returned to lecturing after more than a year. His students wanted to know if and how he had learnt from God. He replied in one short sentence, "I assisted a poor priest with altar duty."

To learn from God is simply to busy yourself with the things of God: His Word, your thoughts about Him, your honest labor, your gratitude for every ordinary day, your prayers, your service to others. Anselm produced great theological work, but it all started when he "wanted to learn from God". Because knowledge begins with serving the Lord. All other knowledge eventually proves to be futile. The philosopher, Leibniz, wrote during the seventeenth century: *Nihil est sine ratione* – there is nothing without a reason. And he agrees with the poet of Proverbs,: "It is God who is the absolute reason for everything, and knowledge of God is no less the origin of science, as His essence and will are the origin of existence" (Leibniz, *Philosophical Papers and Letters*).

Leibniz, Anselm and Proverbs tell us that we first have to "force" our intellect into our hearts, because the heart and mind sense the awareness and Presence of God. That is where all pure thought originate: with the yearning to serve God. The knowledge of good and evil flows from there, knowledge combined with wisdom, knowledge of the All and the Nothing, knowledge of God's mountain and the precipice, knowledge of others, knowledge of God's Creation – and knowledge of the sinister ways of the Evil One. And therefore we must return time and again to ordinary altar duty, of folding our hands devoutly in prayer saying, "Lord Jesus Christ, have mercy on me, a sinner." This puts everything into perspective.

---

*L*ord Jesus Christ, have mercy on me, a sinner.

LOYALTY IS MY HONOR

Let love and faithfulness never leave you (Prov. 3:3).

There is an old German proverb that says: Loyalty is my honor. It was the motto of a few Medieval German princely families and it was mostly interpreted in a military fashion: I fight for my prince, my people, my home – we fight out of faithfulness to our comrades. That is our honor, until death. During the American Civil War, General Robert E. Lee invoked this motto: "Loyalty is my honor" and went to fight for his Southern state, Virginia. This was also the secret of the Boer soldiers who fought a losing but heroic battle for three years against the British Empire. Abraham Lincoln said it was his honor to end that which he had started, to bandage what he had wounded.

Steadfast faithfulness and loyalty have everything to do with true honor and love. It is difficult to be faithful to something or someone or to a cause if it does not touch your heart. We sense that we "belong": to the region, the cause, the people with whom we identify, because there is no other place, cause or people where we would feel that way. There is a devotion, a love, a spirit of being there until the very end. Let this way of thinking never leave you, Proverbs states, bind it around your neck like a jewel.

This faithfulness, like knowledge and wisdom, resides in its purest form in God. Paul wrote to Timothy, "If we are faithless, He will remain faithful, for He cannot disown Himself" (2 Tim. 2:13). This motivated the early Christian martyrs to die in Roman arenas in combat with the lions and later on to die at the stake. But the message, the testimony that originated from that love and faithfulness rocked the world. The blood of the martyrs was the seed of the church, said Augustine. That is the big secret of any unstoppable cause. And the kingdom of God is unstoppable. It will remain until Christ sets His feet on the Mount of Olives again. Christ, the King lives! That is our honor.

You are our honor, Christ, our King.

THE KNIGHT AND THE BEGGAR

Do not withhold good from those who deserve it, when it is in your power to act (Prov. 3:27).

Tennyson wrote a beautiful poem about the young knight, Sir Galahad, who went in search of the Holy Grail, the Holy Grail being the silver cup in which Joseph of Arimathea was said to have caught a few drops of Jesus' blood. All of this is legendary hearsay, also that the Grail had disappeared without a trace. But, the legend goes that the one who finds the Grail will see Jesus Christ in it. In Tennyson's poem, a shining Sir Galahad leaves on his war horse with its golden harness to look for the Grail. Surging with optimism, he says, "My strength is as the strength of ten, because my heart is pure …" Years later he returns, without the Grail, without his horse, without money, on foot. Outside the walls of his home city, a beggar approaches him for alms. Sir Galahad only has half a loaf of bread which he shares with the beggar. When the beggar takes the bread from him, Galahad suddenly sees the silver Grail of Christ shining in the eyes of the beggar.

This is an illustration of the unattainable, and yet a glimpse of perfection and how it comes about. To do good to someone "who deserves it", in other words who really needs it, you must not "withhold", because in it lies the secret of partaking in the love of God and perhaps experiencing something of Him. One must also not send away the person seeking help. Help immediately "when you now have it with you" (cf. v. 28). There is wisdom in this advice because, sometimes, you get the feeling afterwards that you should have helped – when the opportunity is gone, and your soul is poorer for it.

After praying, the Greek patriarch, Basileus, started to build Christian hospitals and orphanages everywhere, to such an extent that a hospital in Greece is still known to today as "Basilios". May God use us to do good to others, to His glory and to our spiritual enrichment.

Do not withhold Your good deeds from me, and let me not withhold them either, from those who are truly in need.

DAY OF THE RIGHTEOUS

The path of the righteous is like the first gleam of dawn, shining ever brighter till the full light of day (Prov. 4:18).

This is a beautiful image and a remarkable statement. All of us have experienced the early morning hour and how the light is a lesser darkness at first, as if the quality of the darkness is changing. Then with increased pace it becomes lighter and lighter, until one can see the thin edges of the mountains and the horizon, tinted with soft sunlight. And then the splendor of the sun on the horizon becomes brighter while the sky above takes on a silvery appearance, like a big, dimly lit dome of an enormous theater. Shortly afterwards, a fragment of the sun appears. Then the sun lifts itself from behind the ridge. The day has dawned, we say, with an open azure sky above us. But the day grows steadily and the light becomes brighter and the blue deeper towards the afternoon, and the cool morning air becomes warmer and more intense ... This is the path of the righteous, according to Proverbs.

This is the complete picture of the progress of the man who serves God in Christ. However, Proverbs does not say that every day will have clear blue skies and joyous, lovely sunshine for the righteous. I, who can barely call myself "righteous", experienced this when I had to go to a police mortuary and identify the body of a dear young colleague, who had died in a car accident one night. When I walked out into the street, crates of milk were being unloaded from trucks and the newspapers were being delivered. The day had dawned, exactly like this. And I was shattered.

God does not promise us a perfect day every day: it is a path of growth in the greater unity of God's Plan that is important. And there sometimes lie incomprehensible paradoxes. But, also through the major paradoxes of joy and pain, everything becomes brighter as our lives continue and the sun still rises and sets.

But are we "righteous"? Yes, if we call upon the name of the Lord in true realization of our vulnerability and a heartfelt desire to serve Him.

Lord, grant me the opportunity to serve You while the full light of day remains.

THE JOY OF WISDOM

I was there when He set the heavens in place, when He marked out the horizon on the face of the deep, when He established the clouds above. I was filled with delight ... rejoicing in His whole world and delighting in mankind (Prov. 8:27-28; 30-31).

It is a formidable experience of joy in Creation and a delight in creative activities that is painted here. These are also the Scripture verses that the Christian author Eugenia Price read in desperation from a Gideon Bible in a hotel room one night, and which resulted in her decision to follow Christ. She saw Jesus in this Scripture.

Textualists could argue that it is wisdom, and nothing other than wisdom, that is speaking here. But, like Eugenia Price, one clearly senses Christ in it. The poet of Proverbs was at his lyrical best here, but one can't help wondering whether he realized what great future truths in Christ flowed through him at that moment. Right up to the "delight" in "mankind".

And once again, this contains a paradox. The Man of Sorrows, the Wisdom of God, also experienced "delight in mankind". There were good experiences – Him sleeping in the boat while the disciples rowed; how the women anointed Him; Him giving a dead son back to his mother and seeing a cripple walk again. There were the wedding celebrations where the wine ran out; and the presumptuous Peter who wanted to die for Him. For these people, He was prepared to die from the beginning. In fact, for *all* people.

The Wisdom of God was there "from the beginning, before the world began" (v. 23). Everything was created in this Wisdom, the Word of which we read in John 1:1. In this Wisdom, this Word, this Son of God, everything was once again reinstated in principle. The Great Architect put His plans on the table and laid His foundation in Christ. He now builds on this in the splendor of creating anew, also in your life and mine.

And Christ? He who has been with us "from eternity", He will also be there until the fullness of time. He *is* the Fullness of Time.

Lord, You are man's Wisdom, strength, beginning and new beginning.

How everything works out

Commit to the LORD whatever you do, and your plans will succeed (Prov. 16:3).

The truth of Proverbs 16 suddenly hits home like a sledge-hammer after strings of copy-book maxims in this book. The majority of us live our lives according to the principle of "business as usual". We get up, take a shower, we get dressed and have a quick breakfast … and so carry on with our daily routine. Sometimes we feel as if we are ensnared by life and nothing makes much sense, but we buckle down and get on with it.

However, there are moments when we do things that we love, moments of great joy and passion, moments in which we see or hear something soul-stirring, and also moments of tears. To experience this is to experience something higher than yourself and your daily routine: you "lose" yourself but at the same time, you "find" yourself. You can also only find your purpose if it were aimed at you from God via His Spirit, like an impulse or a signal saying: the light is green, proceed. Then you may dream your dreams and set your goals high … and do your duty. God will bestow His blessing on you.

There is much talk in Proverbs about the "righteous" and of "righteousness" (cf. v. 8). And "righteous" means exactly that: to "get it right" – to live, to do what is "right". God alone is the touchstone here. When I was a child, I complained to my piano teacher that there was this piece by Liszt that I could not "get right", while I could play Mozart, Chopin and Beethoven with relative ease. I said that Liszt was "difficult". She replied, "No, Liszt is no more difficult than the others. His music is simply not in your heart." She was right. It still isn't. It is a question of personal taste, but he is not my favorite.

We can get every piece of life "right" with our own God-given abilities, but then the Composer, the Lord, must be in our hearts. Otherwise, we merely play the notes as they are arranged on the page. And then the chances of our getting it wrong are multiplied a hundred times.

With You in my heart, my plans will succeed.

THE DICE FALLS IN VAIN

The lot is cast into the lap, but its every decision is from the LORD (Prov. 16:33).

Casting lots or hoping to win the lottery is a rather risky exercise. People sometimes draw lots if there is a tie in a vote. Perhaps there is some merit in this. The ancient disciples cast lots after Jesus' ascension, but God did not exactly use their choice. He determines who receives and who does what. But people "cast lots" with their lives, often by chasing shadows along the lines of: If that girl can go to Hollywood and become a star, then so can I. Well, perhaps, but that is a slippery road.

Some people think there are easy solutions to a difficult life, that it is a case of how the dice falls. Because they think life is like vegetable stew, containing a little bit of everything: few choices, too little "meat", too little salt, too tasteless, too much of an unappetizing blob of watery, gravy-like hotchpotch on your plate. They hope that their luck will turn and change the meal into caviar and champagne. Some blame God for their fate, like the poet Adam Small puts it, "The Lord rolled and the dice fell in the wrong places for us, that's all." This sounds familiar, but it is nonsense.

We have two major cards that we can play with complete confidence: the cards of faith and hope that, I feel, are closely related. Use these cards in prayer and humility and get the biggest prize of all: get God! Because He hears when He is being called upon in truth. And then you have everything and will be able to learn to master life in His name, even though you might not like everything on your plate. To be in God and with God, to live in His decision is, after all, peace and comfort. Angels will help you, like they helped Elijah in the desert.

"God does not play dice with the universe," Einstein said. He does not allow Himself to be ridiculed by little games. Neither does He ridicule you, and especially not your honest prayers, labor and ideals. He helps you with them.

Lord, teach me to handle everything in Your Presence.

SHIFTING BOUNDARIES

Do not move an ancient boundary stone (Prov. 23:10).

This is a difficult proverb that should be applied with great care, because major progress has been made in all spheres through shifting boundaries – geographical boundaries, boundaries of thought, boundaries of worship, social boundaries and scientific boundaries. That day in the Groote Schuur Hospital, when Dr. Chris Barnard transplanted the heart of a deceased girl into the chest of a man, David would probably have taken up his harp in wonder and even Solomon would have been amazed.

However, this verse is more of a warning: think carefully before you fiddle with boundaries that have been laid down years before. This holds true for anything, from territory to new ways of thinking. At the turn of the century a bloody war raged in Kosovo about boundaries dating back to the thirteenth century that had been gradually moved. Peace has not been fully restored. And with regard to ways of thinking: people talk easily about the pre-modern, modern and post-modern spirit of the times, usually with the implication that we must adapt urgently. But he who marries the "spirit of the times" often ends up a widower, or a deserted individual. In my lifetime, the "spirit of the times" has changed from imperialistic to nihilistic (following the bombing on Hiroshima), to optimistic during the sixties with "swinging London", to the extreme pessimism of the cold war, to optimism about "freedom", followed by fear of terrorism. He who adjusts his thought patterns according to this will have to think again.

This verse merely states what Paul said to Timothy, "But as for you, continue in what you have learned" (2 Tim. 3:14). While I worked at the newspaper we constantly reminded one another of the saying: Do not try to fix something that is not broken. If, after due consideration and deliberation accompanied by prayer, you are not sure that the time has come for something new, rather stick to the "old boundaries" until you are sure that the cloud is moving ahead and God is Present ... and that you have looked past the "spirit of the times" and can sense the eternal Plan somewhere.

Lord, we continue in what we have learned, but at Your clear Word we will lower the nets.

TOMORROW

Do not boast about tomorrow (Prov. 27:1).

Prof. J. C. G. Kotzé, who was probably one of the most inspired men of God of the previous century, sometimes quoted R. L. Stevenson somewhat cynically, "The world is so full of a number of things, I'm sure we should all be as happy as kings." He wondered if "kings" were truly "happy"? And what evil could there be lurking in "a number of things"? For example, electricity is wonderful, but it can kill and can leave even a city like New York in total darkness.

Our origin is eternal, but at this moment we are residents of time. And time can be just as fickle as electricity. While I was writing this devotion, fitting it in to my detailed schedule, there was suddenly a power failure and my writing, which I could not "save" in time, was lost. I had to redo almost everything and my planning for the next morning was a thing of the past. One of the greatest lessons that a believer should learn is that time is a precious commodity that must be utilized today. Tomorrow circumstances could change completely.

We know that there are times when we find ourselves as bystanders on the periphery of great events which we fail to understand. All of this determines our "tomorrow" and whether there will be a "tomorrow". Isaiah says God lives in a "high and holy place" (cf. Isa. 57:15) forever, but we know that He also moves in time. In Christ, God planted His flag firmly on earth and in Christ we get an indication of what eternity is all about, and what God is all about, and what we are all about. But it is impossible to pin down time in advance as belonging to us, just as it is impossible for our intellect to capture eternity. And yet, we form part of it and the warning is very clear: deal with time praying, believing and carefully regard it in the light of a Presence.

Instead of counting on "tomorrow", *use* today, rest at night and then sing a prayer to God in the morning for His protection and care.

"*To Thee our morning hymns ascend*" (old English hymn).

TOO AMAZING

There are three things that are too amazing for me, four that I do not understand: the way of an eagle in the sky, the way of a snake on a rock, the way of a ship on the high seas, and the way of a man with a maiden (Prov. 30:18-19).

Today, one would easily explain these "things of nature" scientifically, with theories of atmospheric pressure, air currents and human hormones and testosterone. Perhaps the poet of Proverbs already understood a fair amount of the "technique" of these things, but he nevertheless continued to experience it all as miraculous mysteries. We can, after all, logically state that water is H_2O, two atoms of hydrogen and one atom of oxygen, but does that explain the beauty of a river flowing quietly through a thick forest? ("Oh, it is merely H_2O flowing through vegetative material with too much chlorophyll"!?)

Much of what we observe and try to understand still has dozens of other wonderful mystical dimensions. When one has finished speaking about hormones and testosterone, how does one explain love, the emotional "chemistry" that is at work between two specific people, but not between others? We merely presume and guess, says Robert Frost, "We dance around in a ring and suppose, but the secret sits in the middle and knows." And we cannot get to that "secret in the middle of it all". The poet of Proverbs knew this.

One wonders if the Pharisees ever looked at the lilies of the field and saw God in them? Or did Jesus first have to point it out to them and did they then understand? One can stand amazed, looking at the famous stained glass windows of the cathedral at Chartres. You have an idea how they were created, but do you have any idea of the inspiration behind them? The Inspiration. God.

When Jesus looked at the lilies and the birds and the grass, He took a mystical delight in them. We will move closer to God if we stand in grateful awe of everything in us and around us.

Lord, the miracles of the snake, the eagle and the ship, as well as the ardor of love are all just faint silhouettes of the "Miracle" of Your Being.

ETERNITY

Whatever is has already been, and what will be has been before; and God will call the past to account (Eccles. 3:15).

Many of the biblical writers were fascinated by the concepts of "time" and "eternity". The theme still comes to the fore, with the emphasis on eternity, and it even points to a kind of cyclical repetition in the present of what has happened in the past, either in principle or in reality, and what will happen again in future. We often use the term "transcends": Christ "transcends" time. But – in reality – He does not transcend anything. He is time-in-eternity, or eternity-in-time. He does not need to tune into any wavelength. We often speak of eternal life as something that will reach a kind of fullness at the end of time. It will simplify matters if we think of eternal life as a fullness from the start, which carries on in fullness and that item which we refer to as "time", is constantly repeated in it.

The Teacher devotes a large part of this chapter in Ecclesiastes to the famous "destined time" theme. He says God will call the past to account, also in what will be. Theories exist that the things formed in one's mind – for example an image of a situation or place or idea – has already existed before and that by imagining it, you are merely recreating it. This forms part of the eternal bank of total understanding and therefore "there is nothing new under the sun". Perhaps this is the key. Perhaps this is what artists work with, who knows? And will we not maybe when our "destined time" on earth is past, wake up in our real life, saying, "I just had an interesting dream ... but I am glad to be awake now?"

All of this is speculation. A preacher once used a significant image of eternity being like an immense circle of infinite light, tranquil like a quiet summer night. In this infinite circle of light, little circles of time and days are moving around, and they shine and darken and shine and darken ... Be that as it may, to be eternal is to be in Christ and to be in God, like Christ is in God.

Lord, how wonderful is everything that is repeated, and has been and is and will be forever – in Christ!

DREAMS AND WORDS

Much dreaming and many words are meaningless. Therefore stand in awe of God (Eccles. 5:7).

The Teacher of Ecclesiastes is someone with a healthy dose of morbid realism, even toward the cynical and the negative. After all, he has seen much and experienced much, highs and lows, and enjoyed everything and mourned over everything. He confronts the reader with the harsh facts of life in a repetitive theme of "Everything is meaningless". However, the Teacher is looking for a realistic perspective. At times, he sounds like a modern-day newspaper editor who does not flinch from any photograph or disaster or news event, as long as it will sell newspapers. The Teacher also does not hate anything about life or himself, the way a person suffering from depression does. But neither does he overestimate anything that is temporary, and he shares that which he has learnt.

He says that there are many dreams, ideals and expectations. Dreams are light like shadows, building castles in the air. The same applies to lofty ideals like peace on earth, if only people would stop making war. Sometimes dreams are the wrecks of failed plans, or the megalomania of tortured souls. Often dreams are visions, or the creative spirit at work with lovely results. Dreams are also longings, the glory of a little bit of perfect individual happiness. Dreams are love and perfection. But dreams are also fragile and ethereal, the Teacher says, they disappear like the morning mist.

The same with words. Oscar Wilde said billions of words are spoken and written in London in one day, mostly rubbish. All writers run this risk. On the other hand, words can also bring comfort, like those of Milton and Shakespeare. In addition, words can teach, often harshly, like the Teacher's dark themes. However, the word to which all must say yes, the great dream to make a reality is: "Stand in awe of God." He makes dreams come true and He hears our words of joy and prayer. Stand in awe of Him – serve Him.

Lord, we cannot mend broken deeds by dreaming, but we can learn to serve You in sincerity.

WINE AND WHITE CLOTHING

Go, eat your food with gladness, and drink your wine with a joyful heart. Always be clothed in white, and always anoint your head with oil (Eccles. 9:7-8).

In addition to the Teacher's realism, here and there one finds a touch of humor and even joy. He says that he likes beautiful clothing, white clothing, festive clothing and clean clothing. He also likes perfumes and oil on his head, which probably has a pleasant smell. He would probably also have liked oil in his bath water and, even rose petals, like those that were added to the baths of Eastern kings for fragrance.

He furthermore likes good food, bread eaten with gladness, and good wine drunk with a "joyful heart". He also wants to "enjoy" love with his wife and "do whatever his hand finds to do with all his might". Because he knows that the time for all these things is passing. He has learnt the lesson that life is indeed filled with simple pleasures, provided you use them in the right way. Dale Carnegie tells the story of a rich industrialist who visited a new factory that manufactured technical marvels. During his sightseeing tour, the lunchtime whistle blew and they took him to a reception room where he asked for a small glass of milk and a soft biscuit because he suffered from stomach problems. One of his managers wanted to know what had impressed him most in the factory. He answered, "At lunchtime, a worker sat down against the wall, opened his lunchbox and feasted on his sandwiches and eggs. I wish I were him because I cannot eat properly!"

The Teacher might have said, "This is what I mean." Or he would have agreed with Samuel Pepys, who complained in his diary that a good dinner party cost him twelve pounds (a lot for the seventeenth century), but he said it was still worth it "to have such a merry day now and then".

The Lord grants us joy. The Lord grants us everything. Yes, we will not taste joy every day or see fairies dancing. Fairies are a fantasy. But God is Present in everything. And that is inner joy.

Thank You, Lord, for days of joyous wine and white clothing.

CAST YOUR BREAD …

Cast your bread upon the waters, for after many days you will find it again (Eccles. 11:1).

Perhaps this image refers to the Egyptian rice farmer, who walked knee-deep in the water of his small rice fields, or even sailed with a small boat to sow rice seed in the water. Perhaps it refers to bread crumbs scattered on the dam for the ducks, ducks that would later become a tasty roast. Perhaps it refers to bait for fish that can be caught with a net. Perhaps it is just an imaginative way of saying that you must be willing to share the things that are important to you, like your food and possessions. And what it also does say is that it will be to your advantage – you will find your bread again.

"Bread" represents a wide spectrum of association. We speak about the bread of sorrow, the bitter bread of resistance, the bread of affliction, the bread of strength, the bread of joy, and the bread of sincerity and truth (cf. 1 Cor. 5:8). But what is meant here is actually "sharing". We receive our "daily bread" from God. In fact, everything we have has been bestowed upon us through grace, sometimes via others upon whom God has bestowed His gifts.

"After many days you will find it again". This is also sound economics. One must be willing to risk capital in the business world before you can expect good returns on your investments. To accumulate everything in cash is very poor business acumen and inflation will decimate it. The same applies to the risk of helping someone, the willingness to take another person's hand, the comforting hand on the shoulder, the willingness to listen to both sides of a story and withholding judgment. Bread must be cast "upon the waters" where it will disappear beneath the surface. But in this process of "sharing", a specific balance is maintained. The patriarch Saint Ambrose even said that if you helped someone in distress, you might be settling an old debt dating back generations.

Or the bread comes back on its own accord and, come a day, you will receive an unexpected blessing, even though it might only be the lovely smile of a small child.

Lord, teach us to sow bread, teach us the economics of caring.

KNOW YOUR CREATOR

Remember your Creator in the days of your youth, before the days of trouble come (Eccles. 12:1).

The idea to "remember your Creator" actually means that you must get to know Him. This does not happen overnight and knowledge of Him increases over many years, like a friendship deepens or becomes shallow. The Teacher insinuates that there is a good chance of you becoming shallow or embittered, or cynical and negative. Quite often, as people grow older, their interests begin to diminish. Therefore, it is good to know the Lord when your knowledge may still develop. Because to know means to take the trouble to find out.

In addition, thoughts should occur spontaneously to you and be shaped in you. In my life, I took the trouble of finding out who Napoleon really was, but over the years it occurred to me that, as a heroic figure, he was both a genius and a fool in many ways. I found out for the first time from my parents that there was Someone called God. Gradually it occurred to me that, if God is God, then I should serve Him. And it was indeed true: many crises would have been impossible to handle without Him. The "finding out" was with the intellect. But what happened to me was an awareness in my spirit as a result of the work of God's Spirit.

But Christianity was not "found out" or invented: it is an entire process, first of a few fathers, followed by a people, followed by a series of prophets, followed by a life and a death, as well as a resurrection of a Savior, followed by the spreading of this "life" – and through all this, a "kingdom" is being built. Everything "happens" in God and continues in Him. We form part of it all. And, if we remain truly curious about God and focus our thoughts on Him, and reflect on that which spontaneously originates in our thoughts, we will not age as tragically as the Teacher describes. The knowledge must grow in us, in attunement with the fact that we live in a Presence, and that that Presence is everything.

Lord, we are always young enough to get to know more about You.

FULFILLMENT

Love does no harm to its neighbor. Therefore love is the fulfillment of the law (Rom. 13:10).

One would not have been surprised if the Christians of Rome, many being Jews, listened to these words of Paul with some surprise. They were, after all, not unfamiliar with the Legislator who appeared to Moses at Sinai in smoke and thunderclouds, issuing the one "You may not!" after another. They would also have known about Moses' radiant face. They were probably also aware of the *Sjema Jisjrael* of "Hear, O Israel: The Lord our God, the Lord is one. Love the Lord your God with all your heart and with all your soul and with all your strength" (Deut. 6:4-5).

God's law has been traditionally conveyed in terms of do's and don'ts. It lays down the rules for social order, respect and worship in a wasteland. But God's law – as Jesus said – is based on love for Him and your neighbor. That is where the center of gravity lies for how everything, God's Creation, fits together. And, in human terms, how God's heart works. God is love. It is His Being. And from this great truth, love runs like a silent gravitational force through everything that He undertakes. And we are the conveyors of this "gravity".

Do your neighbor no harm, says God, otherwise you fiddle with the intrinsic multi-dimensional "law of gravity" of the Creation. Withhold your love and substitute it with hate and you could as well try walking out of the top story of a very high building. If you do not come to your senses, the same gravity will cost you your life. But practice love *through* your neighbor to God, and you will be able to move around on the highest planes of the human spirit without fear.

Therefore love is "the fulfillment of the law", says Paul. And John agrees, but adds a warning: "Anyone who does not love remains in death" (1 John. 3:14). We live in God, we live in Christ and then we pray for the love of God to continually saturate us. This love is a necessity of life. Of everything.

Help us in love, Lord!

THE HONOR OF LIFE AND DEATH

If we live, we live to the Lord; and if we die, we die to the Lord. So, whether we live or die, we belong to the Lord (Rom. 14:8).

People sometimes refer to life in negative terms: it is a humdrum existence, a battle, a daily boredom, an empty dream and, sometimes, an elegiac transience, like Hopkins's sad question to a young girl, "Margaret, are you grieving / over Golden Grove unleaving?" (from *Spring and Fall: To a young child*). At other times, people regard life as a small jewel, precious moments, the joy of love, or Tolstoy's "positive meaning of goodness, which I have the power to put into it" (from *Anna Karenina*).

Paul sees everything, life and death, in the light of the Lord. We live to honor the Lord, we die to honor the Lord and we belong to the Lord. This, more or less summarizes everything, the elegiac sadness, as well as the precious moments of golden days. It puts the right of ownership, even the patent rights to the secret of "life" in perspective: it is the Lord's. We are His.

This is one of the most comforting verses in the entire Bible. It is the consolation of the love of God and specifically the honor of belonging somewhere. Even more, to belong in the company of God, to belong to God. It is the consolation that Someone cares. It resembles an invitation to a house where you immediately feel welcome and at home, feeling like you could stay there forever. It is a joy and a promise that everything has meaning, often wrapped in mystery, yes, but a mystery filled with expectation and protection.

Actually, Paul implies that what we do, sometimes good, sometimes less good and sometimes evil, is woven into a pattern to honor God. And that our departure, our death, sometimes filled with pain, sometimes sad like the trees of Golden Grove losing their leaves – is also to the honor of God. Because He receives us as He received David at His festive table – with heads anointed.

It is our honor, Lord, that our life and our death honor You.

JOY AND PEACE

May the God of hope fill you with all joy and peace as you trust in Him (Rom. 15:13).

The letter to the Romans is a systematic account of the framework of Paul's faith. But, as the letter draws to a close, it is as if Paul is becoming more cheerful, and his spirit lifts. His lengthy greetings actually already start here. He once again points out that God is the God of hope and that He works and "fulfills" through faith. He wishes them joy and peace, as he did at the beginning of the letter. Not only is he familiar with the rules of respectability of his time – he is, after all, just as abundantly grateful as he is serious in his admonitions – but he also makes it clear that, alongside all the facets of the seasoned man of God, there is a grateful and appreciative person behind his complicated but committed personality.

He wishes the Romans joy. But joy, as William Barclay justifiably remarked, is not only dependent on external things, upon banquets and beautiful days, sometimes joy also causes us to shed a tear about what we feel inside. It is also not only the joy of labor and the fruits of labor or the joy of the spring ball. It is closer to what Tennyson said, "There is no joy but calm!" (from *The Lotos-Eaters*). This means that, regardless of what may happen, man is able to handle things with inner calm. I once saw a mother doing this in a parking lot with a fretful child. She firmly pacified the child without yelling or shaking the child because her face radiated an inner calm. Christ is like that: our joy is the awareness of the inner Presence of the Savior through the tranquility of His Spirit.

And peace – that also comes from inside. It is not merely ending hostilities, but it is an inner dignity and balance, a gracious and gratifying feeling of quiet waters, an atmosphere of whispers with worship. It is the work of the Holy Spirit and it strengthens the hope. That's Paul's wish for his dear friends in Rome. It is his prayer for us.

That joy and peace, grant us that, Lord.

A VISIT WITH A DIFFERENCE

I know that when I come to you, I will come in the full measure of the blessing of Christ (Rom. 15:29).

There is something tragically realistic, but also true and remarkable in this: Paul desperately wanted to go to Rome, but he had a feeling that he should go to Jerusalem first, to help the struggling church there. For him, Jerusalem and Judaea were lion territory, and he knew that (cf. v. 31). The high priests of the temple and the city had placed him high on their list of enemies. He asked the Romans to pray for his safety, for hope against all hope.

And yet, his great wish would be fulfilled: he would meet the Romans in person, but as a prisoner in chains. He would come with the blessing of Christ, because God had assured him that He would keep Him safe to stand before the emperor of Rome. He could have avoided it. In Caesarea King Agrippa listened to him intently and remarked that he could have been set free if he had not, as a Roman citizen, appealed to Caesar (cf. Acts 26:32).

All of this was "in the full measure of the blessing of Christ". But for us it sounds counter-productive, even cruel and, at times, futile. Could he not have traveled to Rome as a free man to "be refreshed" there, before traveling to Spain? Why, on his last journey, did he have to suffer the humiliation of chains and, in addition, be shipwrecked as well? That is part of God's mystery. But, in the mystery, and in captivity, God was Present. That is why Paul could act with dignity in any situation, chains and all. That dignity in adversity must have made an impression on hundreds of people, to the glory of God.

Paul could stay in Rome for a considerable length of time in relative freedom, and perhaps he even continued his travels. But eventually, in Rome, he left on the journey of his great longing: his journey from this life to meet his beloved Christ. In all of that, the Plan turned out for the good: for Paul, for the Romans, for us as their Western heirs in faith … and for God.

Regardless of how strange Your method might seem, thank You that it always turns out well.

GREETINGS TO ROME

Greet one another with a holy kiss (Rom. 16:16).

Paul's list of greetings is impressive and significant. And he says that they should greet one another with a "holy kiss". From the list it could be gathered that there were already Christian members of Caesar's household, numerous leading women, important officials, and a number of other believers whom Paul had become acquainted with during his travels. And his secretary, Tertius, also came in the spirit of friendship and added his own greeting (cf. v. 22).

This says something about Paul – that either through personal encounters, or via correspondence, or even through other disciples, he had a large circle of friends. Priscilla and Aquila, for example, had lived all over the world after being exiled as Jews, but they returned again later. All roads lead to Rome. Andronicus and Junias were previously in jail with him somewhere. The mother of Rufus was, at some time or another, like his own mother. In this spirit, he greeted them all with expectation and he kissed them on both cheeks. It reminds us of Lord Byron, "If I should meet thee / after long years, / How should I greet thee? / With silence and tears" (from *When We Two Parted*).

How many of them would still have been in Rome when he landed there as a prisoner? One guesses at least a few of them and that they would welcome him with tears and a kiss and embrace him. And yet, Paul says that, at his first defense (a year or two later?), "no one" came to his support (cf. 2 Tim. 4:16). People are not always that trustworthy when a major crisis strikes.

But the Lord stood at his side (cf. 2 Tim 4:17) and, for the time being, he was acquitted. All of that was still awaiting him. In the meantime, he was traveling with his message and his God. Because, in friendship and in adversity, all that mattered to Paul was to convey the message of the love of God in Christ. For that he deserves a holy kiss in spirit from all of us. As well as from his beloved Christ, although he would have said that he did not deserve it.

Thank You for Paul, and for everything, Lord.

THE GREAT UNSEEN

Now faith is being certain of what we do not see (Heb. 11:1).

The author of Hebrews made his voice heard toward the end of the first century after Christ. They were already second-generation Christians, but the bonds with the first generation were still strong. We hear, for example, that Timothy, Paul's beloved child, had been released from prison somewhere (cf. Heb. 13:23). These were difficult and discouraging times of persecution and confusion. Jerusalem had already been destroyed by the Romans in 70 AD, as Jesus had predicted, and Peter and Paul were dead. The apostle John was still alive, although he was very old. He wrote Revelation somewhat later as a prisoner on Patmos, so the legend goes, after he sat for weeks on end with his long white beard in the wind, gazing across the sea. The author of Hebrews, a man who fathomed the wisdom of God, once again put the facts of faith into perspective for the Jewish believers, using strong arguments from the Old Testament. Chapter 11 provides a brief overview of where everything is anchored in Christ.

He says that faith is "being certain of what we do not see". That, says the unbeliever, is too much to ask. That which is unseen simply does not exist, and neither does God. But someone who says this and cares for the world around him, alleging that he is "acting for the good of mankind", faces the same difficulties that believers sometimes have to deal with. After all, atheists take it upon themselves to try and save the world and, up to now, all their experiments in this regard seem to be floundering.

The believer says: I have long since accepted that I cannot save myself, and definitely not the world either. It is also difficult, but I accept that I do not see more than 10 percent of everything that exists. But I try and attune myself to an awareness and sometimes, if I am willing to become still and listen, I become aware of voices speaking to me from eternity, and that through everything, the Plan continues.

Lord, bring a stillness over us and attune our hearts to the Unseen.

OUR ETERNAL GOD

By faith we understand that the universe was formed at God's command, so that what is seen was not made out of what was visible (Heb.
11:3).

This is a very powerful argument. Only God is eternal, and His
Word, His invisible Idea, was embodied in everything that had
been created. Therefore, the visible originates from the Invisible and
the reality of the Invisible could by no means be tangible or "visibly"
explained. Faith must lend a hand and take over.

The scientist Sir Julian Huxley argued that God was not necessary –
the universe managed itself. The universe, he said, had been there
forever. And with that, he came very close to turning the universe
into God. Apparently, when asked about this he merely shrugged.
To say this is to argue that a house builds and manages itself.
The believer says God has no beginning, but then he elevates his
inadequate thought processes through faith to an infinite dimension
where the Creation was an event in time. Huxley denies eternity, but
argues that nothing was the architect and the ultimate objective is
also nothing.

Who wants to live for nothing? What sense is there in the absurdi-
ties that everything is incidental, a sick joke, like Sartre sporadically
alleged? The author of Hebrews gave this a lot of thought. At times,
his arguments were founded on rather thin ice, but he realized this.
How can one, with questions during sometimes distressing times,
both then and now, do much more than indicate a direction using
the compass of faith?

All that we see, says the author of Hebrews, was invisible once.
So were we. We simply became visible. Our true being, our true existence, our anchor and source, our God and our origin, cannot be
touched, tasted, seen or imagined. At most we can sense something
of it in holy moments, or hear something of it in a word from the
Bible or in the silence of a church, in the beauty of a song, or we can
sense something of it in the perfect imperfection of the blossoms of
spring. God attunes us to it, to see God in everything. A Presence.

I believe, Lord, please help my unbelief.

In this faith …

All these people were still living by faith when they died. They did not receive the things promised; they only saw them and welcomed them from a distance (Heb. 11:13).

This verse follows the brief histories of great believers from the Old Testament, people who moved at God's command without knowing where they were heading, like Abraham did (cf. v. 8). However, as they followed the Lord's instruction, they saw something of the promise in the distance, like the splendor of a city, an angel going before them. They welcomed it. They knew – we are on track.

It reminds me of my first airplane trip when I was a young student; the wonderful feeling of something new, but also the slightly familiar fear about where I was going to land during the night. When the plane circled over the lights of the big city and descended, the anxiety and the joy increased. Where to go in a city that I didn't know? But when the plane landed and came to a standstill, I saw my close friend, John, standing at the gate. I would never forget the excitement of that entire trip – not repeated on any of my many later flights across the world.

I still see the lights in my mind's eye, and my friend at the gate of the (to our eyes now) primitive airport. Would it be something along these lines that the Hebrews were referring to? Would it be what Christian in Bunyan's pilgrimage experienced toward the end when he saw the lights of the city of God twinkling in the distance?

If so, what excitement this journey brings! What existential joy is there to be found in the familiar unfamiliar! God travels with *and* God waits. Jesus came and He is waiting to come again. Every day of our lives is yet another part of this exciting journey toward Him. I do not know whether the French poet Villon meant it like this, but I seize his words in this context *En cette foi je veux vivre et mourir* (from *Ballade*): "In this faith I want to live and die."

*A*men, Lord, let it be so.

STRANGERS ON EARTH

And they admitted that they were aliens and strangers on earth (Heb. 11:13).

Some two or three generations ago, many South Africans, due to setbacks – especially after the Anglo Boer War – had to find a livelihood on other people's farms. They were allowed to keep a few head of cattle and sow a few crops, but the land they lived on was never theirs. Furthermore, they could be told to leave at any time. This is true of us here on earth too. The Hebrews knew that we arrive with nothing and we leave with nothing. In truth, we are all strangers like the poet Totius said, "The earth is not our dwelling." There is no permanence in our worldly existence. We come to "farm" for a while on God's land – and then we leave again, like the believers of old who set us an example. This thought fills one with the sadness of Paul Verlaine, "The long sobs of autumn's violins wound my heart with a monotonous languor" (from *Chanson d'automne*).

But it also sings a subdued song of joy: Our home is elsewhere! We actually want to go to our real home, the "country of our own" that we are looking for (cf. v. 14), where we belong and which awaits us. We do not want to be "strangers" forever. We do not always want to be lonely and on the outside like a robin redbreast in the rain. God is with us as He was with Abraham, Noah and Enoch, but they did not stay either. And yet, their faith remained, something of their unquenchable spirit. Without them we would have been poor share-croppers on earth. Then Jesus, like us, became a "share-cropper", and He came to live with us and give us the rich passport of faith, so to find our home in Him again. This passport we still carry in our hearts: the assurance of God in Christ that we belong to Him. Because someone carrying a passport has citizenship, regardless of where he may roam. An eternal citizenship – and eternal joy.

You are traveling with us, and we are traveling with You, to a Fatherland of our own.

FAITH CLIMBS MOUNTAINS

[They] who through faith conquered kingdoms, administered justice, and gained what was promised; who shut the mouths of lions (Heb. 11:33).

This verse mentions all the heroes of faith: Moses, Samuel, David, Gideon and prophets like Daniel who continued fearlessly in their faith and gained victory. It also mentions the martyrs of the time who endured brutal suffering, but never faltered. They were the building blocks of God's kingdom, with Christ as the cornerstone of the New Testament. The cement is faith, which faces every challenge, every resistance, every query, mockery and every disappointment, and charges at it with a cry of victory. Or deals with it in sweat and tears, or with the holy laughter of certainty.

Faith looks the Evil One straight in the eye. Faith stumbles through deserts and climbs mountains, driven by the Spirit on authority of the Word of a Holy God. And, should the thought occur to you that action taken in faith and adhered to is sometimes a little foolish, then you find yourself in good company. Paul and others also thought so, "We are fools for Christ" (cf. 1 Cor. 4:10). And if someone thinks that he is wise by the standards of this age, "he should become a 'fool' so that he may become wise" (cf. 1 Cor. 3:18). Because the "wise" of this world also climb mountains and see nothing, except the other side of the mountain. And when they see God's splendor beckoning, they explain it as a bunch of fireflies or a mirage. And when they read the Word, charged with holy meaning, they would rather start analyzing the sentences than trying to sense something of the truth in them.

As with Moses, David, and others, faith is trying to pick up God's signals. Sometimes, as is frequently the case with us, they did not hear anything. Sometimes they heard wrong, and sobbingly confessed their mistakes, picked themselves up and listened once again. And they always knew that God was Present to shut the mouths of lions. Because faith is to say: God will do something!

Yes, Lord, You will. You will!

BEHIND THE CLOUD

Therefore, since we are surrounded by such a great cloud of witnesses, let us throw off everything that hinders (Heb. 12:1).

The mystic Evelyn Underhill wrote a classic book, *The Cloud of Unknowing*. It alludes to this "cloud of witnesses" that is to say, "witnesses to faith around us like a cloud" (NEB). It makes the grand statement that the cloud of witnesses is wonderful, but that it remains just that: witnesses. The truth is still above the clear cloud, like the sun, and that is God. However, the truth also lies beneath the cloud, under the surface of our skin, beneath the clouds of our own thought for the Truth. God, is *in* us.

We must also become part of that cloud, part of the cloud of witnesses, part of the great melody of Creation and recreation that resounds through the ages and eons with powerful choruses. But for that, we must "throw off everything that hinders" us. This does not mean that we should leave our work and family to go and live in a cave, in seclusion from "the world". All honor to people who did this, but the "cloud of witnesses" must go out into the world: into factories, offices, courtrooms, hospitals, conversations, documents, and thoughts. They must comfort, assist, show compassion, and charity ... you name it. However there are things that can become "hindrances" to us: our willfulness, our sinful thoughts, our crooked nature, our jealousy, our spiritual pendantry ... It causes the cloud to disappear in a haze of: "Where to now?" and "What?"

We often have numerous objections and grievances, and our own portrayals of how the things of God should be. But Christ must pour the knowledge of Him, His Presence, for us wherever we find ourselves, without the burden of our own objections, without the burden of our judgment, only with the destitution, the need for Him.

Pour, Lord. Cover us with Your Presence.

THE UNSTABLE AND THE STEADFAST

The words "once more" indicate the removing of what can be shaken – that is, created things – so that what cannot be shaken may remain (Heb. 12:27).

In the entire ordination of God, there are things that can be shaken and then disappear, unstable things, replaceable things, as personal as cells in our bodies, and as impersonal and distant as the stars that die in the universe. And in the entire ordination of God, there exist diverse, unshakable things, like God's kingdom in us, and God's "heaven", which are beyond our understanding. The created things are time-bound. To the unshakable things, time is only the moment when a little bird comes to rest on the branch of eternity.

The entire Plan is one of great paradoxes and contrasts, of which some sometimes seem to be contradictions and irreconcilable conciliations. Christ is as simple as a man walking next to the lake, and as incomprehensible as One sitting at the right hand of God. The lake and the man are transient, but God's right hand remains unto eternity.

The devil asked immutable things from Jesus, "Make bread out of stones." Jesus looked past the bread to the unshakable, "Make peace with God." Man is constantly enticed by transient things: a house, food and clothes. All necessary but, as Jesus answered the devil, "Man does not live by bread only." We exist to love and be loved. The more we receive of God's love, the better we are able to live and give pure love fully in all its forms. We receive God's kindness, the church father, Irenaeus, wrote during the second century – shortly after the Hebrews letter – because He will never change from being "He who gives Himself". Therefore God is also "immutable" in His glorious and loving emotions.

Everything that we see, except through the eyes of our faith, will eventually disappear and change. But everything that we are – being in and bound with God – will "remain".

Lord, I know that everything will be shaken and fall down, but we will remain in You.

THE SAME CHRIST

Jesus Christ is the same yesterday and today and forever (Heb. 13:8).

As I look out the window of my study at this moment, I see traces of raindrops and streaks of dirt on the windowpane because it rained non-stop last night. When I look past the dirty patches, I see my hydrangeas, and further away, big green trees and bright blue skies, with two small, white clouds drifting slowly south on the invisible winds far above. If I look only at the traces of dust and mope about it, I should rather stop looking.

However, this is how our thoughts about God often work: we are blinded by our muddy perceptions and in doing so, we miss the enchanting view of the horizon. Sometimes we look back on the past and hear questions and confusing debates about who and what Christ really was. These are dusty panes that obstruct the mystic vision. Christ was what the Word says He was. We look at the present and ask where Christ is in all of the violence and power politics and fraud, sometimes even in His church. Actually, it hasn't changed since His time. He saw it all in His time and pointed it out as traces of dust, but then He rejoiced in the vision of the kingdom. It would also pay off to see it like this.

Eventually, these traces of dust will also be wiped away. And the future? It stretches further than the little drifting clouds on the invisible winds. All of this is in Christ. What He once was and is today and will be forever, falls outside space and time where *nothing* changes .... And all of this is in God who is so far beyond our understanding, that we cannot even see Him through a clean window of the mind (should this be possible).

However, what we can do is to accept this major fact: that we are transient and not Christ. That the love which He bestowed at the lake, upon lepers and sinners, He still bestows upon you and me today, and will bestow on us forever. What comes between us are traces of dust, but these also disappear when we look beyond it all in faith.

---

*f*aith *moves us, Lord, and we look towards You.*

TO MOVE HOUSE

For here we do not have an enduring city (Heb. 13:14).

It is good to sometimes read the Bible in another translation. Certain phrases, which you regard as obvious, might come alive in another translation or language. In the NEB, this verse reads, "For here we have no permanent home ..." This statement is shorter and perhaps somewhat stronger. People who moved house often in their lives will be quick to understand it. One day, the big removal van comes and stops in front of your door and your possessions are loaded and your neighborhood and address change. Sometimes so radically. You might have hoped that you would be living there "permanently", but the van might come again. In my career, I became attached to one particular house, but I was unable to settle there because it was a rented house and not for sale.

There are no residential rights for sale on earth. The author of Hebrews realized this so clearly that he repeated it in almost all the final chapters of his letter. And there is nothing morbid about it, he simply had one direction in mind. As a pilgrim, he was experiencing wonderful adventures and he was blessed as well as rejected. Sometimes he even lingered for a while. But, like the poets of the songs of pilgrimage, he knew that he was moving on and he sang the praises of the beauty of the New Jerusalem, of the salvation of Christ and of the forgiveness and love of God. Tennyson sings, "Our little systems have their day; / They have their day and cease to be: / They are but broken lights of Thee, / and Thou, O Lord, art more than they" (from *In Memoriam A. H. H.*).

Many of us can testify that moving house made us richer in experience. Our journey through life is an adventure, with God as our companion. He will take us over mountains and across stormy waters like He did with Noah. He will make us realize just how little our "minute systems" are really worth. Until we reach Ararat one day, where we will no longer need an ark.

Lord, we reside here in tents and arks. Please make today's journey an adventure.

SUFFICIENT SUPPLIES

May the God of peace … equip you with everything good (Heb. 13:20-21).

Some time ago, there was a debate about British troops being sent to the war front without sufficient equipment, or even with the wrong equipment. Some apparently received outdated weapons and there was a shortage of bulletproof vests. The widows of slain soldiers threatened to take the army to court. This, of course, is nothing new. A century ago, the British came to fight on South African battlefields, wearing red-coated uniforms, very swanky, but excellent targets for the sharpshooters of the Boer forces. They had to replace these very quickly with less flashy and less visible khaki uniforms.

Sometimes we also expect God to "equip" us with lots of privileges, some that can make us more vulnerable to the sharpshooters of the Evil One. Or they could just fit us as badly as Saul's heavy suit of armor fitted the slender David. The Lord will grant us the necessary, and He will not abandon us without shield or shelter, to the savage mercy of the elements. He did not do it with His people of Israel, even though they complained so much at times. He did not do it with His prophets, even though they sometimes wept like Jeremiah. He did not do it with Christ, and accompanied Him through death. He did not do it with Paul, even when he landed in jail. He has not done it with any of His children on their journey through life, even though they sometimes have to venture on painful roads. He remains Present and ensures that we are equipped with "everything good", everything that is within our ability to handle, "for doing His will" (cf. v. 21).

And to "do the will of God"? In that He will lead us unwaveringly, if we accept the mystery of a call to go on a pilgrimage with Him. He will see to it that we have sufficient supplies. And we will become increasingly aware that, underneath the realities of each day, there is a Reality to be found that we will not fully understand before we are in it. And that we entrust fully to God.

Lord, supply me with the necessary provisions today. I am going with You.

Lord, My God

In the shops we see green wreaths and strings of lights
and special offers and even promises of peace on earth.
(Later on, almost everything will be for sale at discount prices.)
This sometimes annoys me and sometimes it amuses me,
and yet, it also creates a feeling of joy and excitement,
an expectation of something special in the offing:
a festival more profound than gift-wrapping and shiny ribbons;
the restrained joy of people who stand at an airport,
waiting for the late arrival of a plane, bringing home a loved one.

This time of year sings to us that You have come, Lord Jesus,
that You are coming, this time with Your holy angels.
All of us will see You as we see each other.
But the Advent also sings in a minor key of Your humiliation,
of Your suffering, which already started in a stable in Bethlehem,
where the invisible shadow of a cross already fell
over the manger and the virgin mother.
Everything is so delicately, but so permanently intertwined:
Advent, humiliation, angels, victory, Second Coming.

Oh, we are also waiting with the lights and the green wreaths,
until the day when our last tears have been wiped away
and when we will laugh together
because all of us will know and understand everything:
that You came and came again and will never again
be out of our sight, not even for a single second,
because seconds and seasons will no longer exist.
Come, Lord Jesus!

Amen.

LOOK OUT FOR HIM

His own did not receive Him (John. 1:11).

It is rather strange, the birth of Christ. It was the major theme of the prophets, but Israel looked the other way. They were like employees in a big business who were waiting for the boss at the front door while he slipped in by the back door, unnoticed, to become one of them. Not to spy on them, but to feel what they feel, to do what they do, to suffer what they suffer, and to teach them a better way of working and living.

The people of Israel were aware of the prophets' warning that they were going to be caught unawares. Not that the prophets were fortune-tellers; they were merely God's spokespeople and their visions were also not always that clear. Isaiah received a cryptic message: "… Go and tell this people: 'Be ever hearing, but never understanding; be ever seeing, but never perceiving'" (Isa. 6:9).

However, the prophets warned of a heavenly visit and almost every prophet, like in the Psalms, sketched a recognizable profile of the Savior who would come. Devoted teachers of the law studied these. They were like people hearing the rumble of thunder in the distance, but saying that it might only be a low-flying airplane. Or like me, when I went to watch an international golf tournament, and, because of the crowds, could not see a thing – apart from the balls whizzing past every now and then. I left and took a nap in the clubhouse. Perhaps the people of Israel were also like that. They still do not recognize anything and certain Christian exegetes keep on arguing about it, as is happening at the moment.

The danger is real that Christ may come in glory while the world is looking elsewhere. No one knows the hour, but hours are mostly irrelevant to God. And yet, in the history of the world, events are slowly unfolding before us that, at least, should make us more attentive. Besides, God will enter your life somewhere today, for a visit of love. Be on the lookout for Him everywhere.

Yes, come and visit us, Lord, and walk with us, like with the men of Emmaus.

ANOTHER NETWORK

He made known to us the mystery of His will according to His good pleasure, which He purposed in Christ, to be put into effect when the times will have reached their fulfillment (Eph. 1:9-10).

This is one of those Scripture verses that is like a deep well. You drop a pebble into a well and then you have to listen for a while before you hear it drop into the water far below. There is talk here of "the mystery of His will", which God "made known to us according to His good pleasure", and which He "purposed in Christ". All of this pertains to the Advent of Christ and it did indeed happen like this. But it also whispers of a million other possibilities that are locked up in that "will", and still have to be played out like an extensive "computer program", although the latter is an inadequate image.

To listen to this verse is to pick up signals from another wavelength; news from another network. Our own news gets dominated by "world events". This verse broadcasts grand, eternal, cosmic events. Why, for example, does Jerusalem remain controversial in the news rather than Cairo, Warsaw, Amsterdam and even New York? Just as we are today, the Christians in Ephesus were also exposed to the events of the day, the world politics of the Romans, while they unknowingly formed part of the establishment of a worldwide church. We may argue that they were much closer to the events surrounding Christ than we are 2,000 years later, but we are closer to things that were mere dreams to them. Across the world people are once again looking for comfort outside themselves. Following the September 11, 2001 disaster, the Americans' prayers and hymns to God were televised across the entire world. And in this, God is moving toward the major highlight: Chardin's Omega point where everything is subjected to Christ.

We can only hear this news on the Other Network while meditating on the Word in prayer, in the breaking of the Communion bread, the crystal clear baptismal water and the "small" miracles that take place in our lives everyday – so "ordinary" that we sometimes miss them, so profound as a pebble splashing into the invisible water of the well far below.

Tune us in, O God!

REALISM AND LIGHTS

They will say, "Where is this 'coming' he promised? Ever since our fathers died, everything goes on as it has since the beginning of creation" (2 Pet. 3:4).

The Bible is never and nowhere found lacking in realism. Every human sigh, every human lament, the despair and hesitation, all the anguish and disappointment that one can think of, every loss of faith and failure, every rejection and derision – all of these are recorded without the cover of a fig leaf. God can handle criticism.

The age-old rhetorical question is spelt out here: "Where is God? What about all His promises? Ever since our fathers died, nothing has changed ..." The Dutch poet Van Schagen laments, "The great trees stand dreaming. / God has once again not come tonight. / Perhaps He was not ready yet, / Perhaps He did not know the way ..." (from *Nocturne*).

Peter probably had to listen to this question many times. We also ask it often because, at times, everything seems so transient, so uncertain and so fleeting, so bleak. But God does not concern Himself with superficial thoughts and easy answers. After all, He has to reveal Himself to us in perpetuity in human terms, and we battle with the letters and punctuation.

Then again, how many apples had to fall on Sir Isaac Newton's head before he got the message of the law of gravitation? How many thunderstorms had Benjamin Franklin experienced before he risked sending up his kite during a thunderstorm to conduct electrical power, and realized the immense charge of a bolt of lightning? How often do we hear the thunder and shrug our shoulders, saying, "Nothing out of the ordinary ..."

It fell upon the shoulders of a Benjamin Franklin to risk going outside with his kite. It falls upon our shoulders to risk going outside in faith and look up. It falls upon the shoulders of the faithful to stand up and say, "But Christ did not forsake the world. He is coming again! In fact, He comes every day. God is Present in all that happens." And so we may joyfully hang our festive lights.

Lord, we know, we hear, we believe.

JUDGMENT AND PRIORITIES

He is patient with you, not wanting anyone to perish (2 Pet. 3:9).

When we were children we spoke negatively about "when the world would end". After the Second World War there were frequent reports of seers, who dramatically predicted the end of the world, accompanied by terrible anguish and sorrow.

For an only child of ten, this was on the one hand oppressive and on the other hand it held a cynical charm, some kind of entertainment-in-fear, like the "ghost cave" at the fun-fair. And then, one day, our beloved Reverend Loots, said quietly, "Never see the end of the world only as the 'world being destroyed.' It is actually a beautiful cleansing and renewal that awaits us. And where God is already with us now, we will be able to see Christ, and He will rule over us and protect us as He is doing now in an 'invisible' way. But then He will be in and over all of us." That was more or less what he said. And I still experience it like that, with all the nuances that surpass human understanding.

Peter provided a glorious reason for the waiting for renewal and that is also a great comfort. I vaguely remember Reverend Loots mentioning it as well: God is not bound by time and He first wants to grant everyone the opportunity to be saved. He does not want anyone to perish. He is extremely patient and busy. He constantly builds and renews. His concern with us does not imply guessing games, but He makes things happen, delicately planned, and immensely complicated.

Yet He enables us to understand something of it (often only in retrospect): Newton's "apples" fall on our heads! As an English priest once said, "God gentles us." But this "gentling" does not mean that He always strokes us approvingly. He quietly asks us – like a Father who cares – about our priorities. He does not want us in hot water. He does not want anybody to perish.

I do not understand exactly how this works. But something of His glorious intention with everyone and everything in His Plan is shining through.

I leave these judgments and perceptions up to You while You guide me in my priorities.

OPEN THE DOOR!

"Here I am! I stand at the door and knock. If anyone hears My voice and opens the door, I will go in and eat with him, and he with Me" (Rev. 3:20).

Toward the end of the nineteenth century, a small yacht was stranded near Bristol one evening. The two-man crew narrowly escaped death on the rather inhospitable coastline. They were wet, cold and hungry and started walking toward a tiny light they spotted in the dark. A farmer opened the window and saw the two young men shivering in the cold. They asked if they could please come in to dry themselves next to the fire. The farmer refused, because he did not allow strangers into his house. He did, however, explain where they could stay overnight in a small hamlet ten miles down the road.

Later on, the farmer and the community discovered that the two young men were the then Prince of Wales who was a naval officer at the time, and one of his cousins. This Prince of Wales would later become King George V, the so-called "sailor king", a brave seaman and a beloved king. But the evening of the storm he was looking for a place next to the farmer's fire. I'm sure the farmer felt ashamed of his shabby treatment of his future king.

Through the word of John, Jesus told the church in Laodicea that He is standing at their door in the same way. He comes to us like that too. He does not force the door open. He does not hit His fist against the wood, rattling the door frame. He knocks as it becomes the Gentleman that He is. And if He is not invited to come in, He passes by.

In Holman Hunt's famous painting in St. Paul's Cathedral of Jesus with His small lantern in front of a dark, closed door, the painter himself wrote a prayer at the bottom of the painting: "Don't pass me by, O Savior."

It is a plea, but also an assurance. It is a warning, and the promise of a feast. Jesus comes knocking at the life of each of us. Today and every day. Open the door!

Do not pass me by, O Savior!

REJOICING TEARS

Rejoice greatly, O Daughter of Zion! Shout, Daughter of Jerusalem! See, your King comes to you, righteous and having salvation, gentle and riding on a donkey (Zech. 9:9).

This prophecy of Zechariah regarding the coming of the Messiah reminds one of the song of ascents in Psalm 126: "When the LORD brought back the captives to Zion, we were like men who dreamed. Our mouths were filled with laughter, our tongues with songs of joy" (vv. 1-2). However, the key soon changes: "Those who sow in tears will reap with songs of joy" (v. 5).

Rejoicing and tears, salvation and humility, a crown and a donkey. These things form such an integral part of the fiber of the reality of everyday life, the pattern of our faith ... everything is a mystery. Keats sings, "Ay, in the very temple of Delight / Veil'd Melancholy has her sovran shrine" (from *Ode on Melancholy*).

It is therefore not strange that, when Jesus was riding into Jerusalem on a donkey on that wonderful morning, with hosannas resounding, He was weeping for the city. There were the mountains in the distance and the walls. He knew that destruction by the Romans was coming. He knew that the rejoicing around Him would soon die down. He knew that He would die Himself. But He also knew that He would rise from the dead and would come again; not on a donkey, but on the clouds, as the Ruler who administers justice.

Jesus' joy as well as His tears indicated something of the transitory nature of the present. It also demonstrates just how precious we are to God: that Jesus was on His way to bloody suffering in order to open the road to eternity for us.

As Zechariah said, Zion had to rejoice, Zion the city of the great kings David, Solomon, Uzziah, Hezekiah ... and the city of the prophets Isaiah, Jeremiah and Zechariah. How they would have rejoiced about this day, swallowing their tears!

"And, conquering down the centuries, / Came Christ, the Swordless, on an ass ..." (Harry Kemp, *The Conquerors Riding By*). He is still coming, closer to you and me, every day.

Lord, we rejoice with a lump of gratitude and hope in our throats.

ANSWER, OR STOP THE FESTIVITIES!

"Tell us if You are the Christ, the Son of God." "Yes, it is as you say," Jesus replied. Then the high priest tore His clothes and said, "He has spoken blasphemy!" (Matt. 26:63-65).

That was the big question that the King had to answer: "Tell us if You are the Christ." The entire Gospel centers around this major question regarding the humble birth, Jesus' teaching the crowds, the miracles, the redemption, the Resurrection.

Virtually everything stands or falls by this question. If Jesus is not what He said He was, we may as well switch off the festive lights and throw the keys of every church into the sea. Then He was at most, a good, confused man who cannot promise anything on God's behalf; neither eternal life nor shelter, not His reign, and even less His Second Coming. Then we might as well hang out wreathes for "festive greetings" or else, like Dickens' Scrooge, cynically remark, "Bah! Humbug!"

But Jesus answers, "Yes, it is as you say. I am the Son of God. And later, He says to Pilate in the same non-triumphant way, composed and in control: Yes, but My Kingdom is not of this world.

Pilate remained calm. Could it be that something had dawned on him, something of Roman justice, a feeling that he was dealing with someone special? That seemed to have been the case. But the high priest tore his clothes and shouted, "He has spoken blasphemy!" and the Jews spat on Him.

This has not come to an end yet. The criticism against Him. The questions from human reasoning are not quite as heated as those of the high priest and his minions, but the modern arguments against Jesus have become temperate and civilized, and one wonders if this is not actually worse than the vehemence of the high priest.

But Jesus answered and we have a choice: we reject Him and embrace the transient world as the beginning and the end, or we accept Jesus' word and embrace God and eternity. Should we do the latter, we may celebrate with lights and gifts.

Lord, in my acceptance of You as King lies my only hope and joy.

THE RIGHTEOUS MAN

Don't have anything to do with that innocent man (Matt. 27:19).

That was the warning from Pilate's wife when the trial was in its final stages. Rather leave this man alone; in Greek, *dikaioo ekeinoo*: literally translated as "righteous person". The King James Version of the Bible also refers to "this righteous man", a translation that creates the impression that Pilate's wife might have been familiar with the Jewish faith, that she could even have been "a proselyte of the portal" who had been "catechized" in the Jewish faith.

It could perhaps mean that she was familiar with an ancient Jewish tradition along the lines of the King Arthur legends: the so-called *Tsaddiks* in Hebrew or "righteous people" who succeed one another through Jewish history until the coming of the Messiah. It could be that she referred to Jesus as a *tsaddik* (in Greek, *dikaios*), one in the holy line of exceptional prophets.

According to Jewish legend thirty-six *tsaddiks* or righteous people would appear in Israel. A *tsaddik* is sent by God to take the sins of the world onto his shoulders. All these sins cause the soul of the *tsaddik* to "freeze", so that God has to warm him in His hands for all eternity. This could be a "parable", perhaps just a tale. But it indicates something about Jesus. Mrs. Pilate perhaps dreamt that He was one of the select righteous. Of course Jesus qualified as the righteous one, much more so than Moses and Elijah. This tradition indicates that the "Lamb who takes away the sins of the world" – as John the Baptist referred to Jesus – was perhaps not an entirely foreign concept. In all probability, even Isaiah and the others joined in with this.

But Pilate had already committed himself through his own compromise by offering the crowds a choice: Barabbas or Jesus. This choice had to be carried out. This is always the problem with an ill-considered compromise – it could compromise *you*. We cannot afford compromises in our faith. Either we acknowledge the King, or we free Barabbas. Either we light the candles to celebrate Jesus, or we celebrate the debauchery of chaos.

Lord Jesus, we want to celebrate You in our festivities and every day.

SHAME AND SALVATION

He saved others ... but He can't save Himself! (Matt. 27:42).

Some of the most awful moments in a person's life happen when you publicly make a fool of yourself. Perhaps you tried to do something in the presence of others (perhaps to help, perhaps to impress), and failed dismally. You told a joke and nobody laughed. You, who are usually a good batsman, went out to bat and blocked one difficult ball after the other while the fielders mocked you. Or you spontaneously expressed an opinion, just to realize you did not know what you were talking about and the people laughed at you. All of this could actually get much worse.

In Jesus' case it was much worse, but also very different. There He was hanging, stretched out between heaven and earth, and above His head His "crime" was written: This is Jesus, the King of the Jews. That caused the Jewish high priests to complain, but it did not stop them from mocking Him. Neither did it stop the other passersby: "He is the king, but cannot save Himself!" No wonder the American poet Claude McKay prayed wryly, "If we must die, let it not be like hogs / Hunted and penned in an inglorious spot, / while round us bark the mad and hungry dogs, / Making their mock at our accursed lot" (from *If We Must Die*).

Jesus described His own suffering in poetic terms in the fate of Jerusalem, the city of the great king: "... you who kill the prophets and stone those sent to you, how often I have longed to gather your children together, as a hen gathers her chicks under her wings" (Matt. 23:37). But now they were mocking Him. And when He rose from the dead, the majority did not believe it. He knew that many would not believe and asked His disciples if, at His Second Coming, He would still find faith on earth. He will, yes. That He knows. We will persevere in holding on to Him and His cross because we are very aware, especially during this time of lights, of a mysterious Presence and a restrained joy.

*L*et the world go on mocking, Majesty, King unto eternity!

A Christmas visit

Suddenly Jesus met the women. They came to Him, clasped His feet and worshiped Him (Matt. 28:9).

Imagine if someone wrote a drama where Jesus pays a visit to a major city at Christmas – for example Johannesburg. Would there be major traffic jams? Respectfully, would the city fathers receive Him at the Hilton Hotel with cameras flashing? Would they take Him on a guided tour of the major shopping centers? A modern "lamb to the slaughter", with people milling around Him for favors as it happened at that time at the lake? Or, what if He, unannounced, walked among the stacked counters, looking at electronic toys, cooked hams and Christmas puddings?

But what about David's city? There is one gate in the old wall of Jerusalem which is closed off with rocks. According to legend, the rocks will crumble when the Messiah comes. Upon my inquiry, a Jewish friend from Tel Aviv wrote to me: "The gate you are asking about is the Mercy Gate, and when the Messiah comes, He will go into the city through this gate. It is between the Herod and the Garbage gates." This reply suddenly developed a realistic immediacy for me. They are expecting the Messiah through that selfsame gate!

But, here, with Jesus unannounced in the shops at Christmas: Would someone notice Him in the hustle and bustle? Yes, it works like that, because the women who went looking for Him in Jerusalem on the day of the Resurrection, recognized Him, clasped His feet and worshiped Him. They were sensitive to His appearance. And Jesus is sensitive to people who are sensitive to Him and who seek Him. He reveals Himself to them in various ways, even between the shelves of a shop, in their homes and offices, on the street and especially in the silence.

He might come and sit next to you in the car. Would you, like the women, be "afraid but overjoyed" if He becomes visible, and embrace His feet, crying with joy? I believe we will, just like the women of Jerusalem did.

Let the gates crumble before You, Lord, as long as You come, regardless of how You wish to come to me, to all of us.

A MESSAGE IN STONE

"Look, Teacher! What massive stones! What magnificent buildings!"
Jesus replied, "Not one stone here will be left on another" (Mark
13:1-2).

If Jesus were to visit a big city like New York at Christmas, "one of
His disciples" would be absolutely right to say, "Look, Teacher!
What magnificent buildings!" But there is something sinister, something sad, and even something forgivably naive in this conversation
between Jesus and the disciple.

Something naive, because people are impressed by what other
people can do, and the temple complex was indeed impressive. It
is also typical of busy city dwellers staring in awe at major building
constructions. It is also sad, because it forms part of the earth, and
buildings and cities are transitory. It is a process in which everything
dies and everything is renewed, or totally collapses into ashes. Until
someone comes and completely rebuilds it from scratch.

This is an image of what is happening in this dispensation,
with Christ as the Architect, who will clean up all the "dilapidated
premises" and build them anew, forever. It is also sinister, because
woe the people who believe, like the ancient Jews, that their holy
and impressive buildings will remain standing forever, together
with civilization and knowledge. Everything changes. The Romans
completely destroyed Jerusalem shortly after Jesus. Only a small
fraction of wall remained standing from what was once the temple
and the impressive buildings, the so-called Wailing Wall where the
Jews pray for salvation unto this day. And the Savior was actually
there when the wall was still intact, in times that were just as
uncertain as today.

And He is about to come again at a given moment in time,
which the Father will "sense" (it is impossible to talk about God's
"thoughts") as the keystone of His Plan. We can speculate about it,
but it may not cause us to be unobservant. Not in the cities with
their major buildings, and neither in places "where nothing ever
happens". God is everywhere. Everywhere is His earth. Everywhere
is His Presence. Everywhere is His feast.

Lord, we thank You that You are making everything new.

FALSE DOCTRINE

"Many will come in My name, claiming, 'I am He,' and will deceive many" (Mark 13:6).

Once, just before Christmas, a quaint little report appeared in a New York newspaper. People were warned against dishonest Father Christmases, especially in front of the major department stores on Fifth Avenue. They quoted beautiful Scripture verses and sang "Peace on earth and mercy mild, God and sinners reconciled!" while their criminal colleagues watched from around the corner to see where people put there purses, in order to steal them almost immediately.

This also portrays what Jesus warned the people against. The Gospel has been abused throughout the ages by villains, false "christs" and Christians with false doctrines, many of whom also take money. It started way back in Acts where someone offered money for the gift of the Holy Spirit, like Simon the Magician, or the seven sons of Sceva who wanted to drive out an evil spirit in the name of Jesus and Paul. The reaction was devastating. The "man who had the evil spirit" shouted, "Jesus I know, and I know about Paul, but who are you?" Then he attacked them so that they "ran out of the house naked and bleeding" (cf. Acts 19:15-16). It is a realistic warning.

As has been the case throughout the ages, false "saviors", people or ideologies, are not unfamiliar today. They pretend to "interpret" things anew, but miss the point of the mystery of the eternal God and Christ His Son, who came in time and simplicity to fulfill a mystical deed of love that transcends all human understanding. In addition, evil takes on false appearances, often attractive, but never trustworthy. Milton says of "Belial", the Evil One, as of false preachers, "But all was false and hollow; though his tongue dropped manna" (from *Paradise Lost*).

Most often, truth whispers urgently and influences with true conviction and dignity. Falsity often presents chaos. Let us pray at Christmas time for a Spirit of truth and pureness, which can often be sensed in prayer and silent reflection ... and a feeling of joy in God, even though we cannot really explain it.

Lord, please teach me the truth every day.

GARDEN AND SPRING

The LORD will guide you always; He will satisfy your needs in a sun-scorched land and will strengthen your frame. You will be like a well-watered garden, like a spring whose waters never fail (Isa. 58:11).

Think of a green garden with lots of water: trees and ferns, chrysanthemums and dahlias, roses and thick lawns edged with violets. Through Isaiah God promises that His people, including you and I, will be a garden. Isaac Watts, the famous poet of hymns (*When I survey the wondrous cross* and *Jesus shall reign wherever the sun*) sang, "We are a garden walled around ... a little spot enclosed by grace, out of the world's wide wilderness" (from *Hymns and Spiritual Songs*).

Think of a spring with water that never dries: it is surrounded by greenness, there are palm trees and a resting place, there is shade and relief. God promises all of this to His people, therefore to you and me as well, and this is how it will be. Life and strength stem from the spring, joy and glory, healing and wisdom, love and abundance – all the good things that have been associated with a spring throughout the ages in our thoughts.

I think of "a sun-scorched land", endless desolate dunes without landmarks, a blazing sun by day, without water, and icy cold nights with dust storms that come up and last for days. This is how our spirits feel, at times. But here, at this point, the great proclaimer of the coming of the Savior, Isaiah says, "the Lord will guide you always", "satisfy your needs" and "strengthen your frame".

A garden and a spring in a sun-scorched land are soul-stirring images of a tranquil and cherished existence. This is a prophecy about the coming of the Messiah and the comfort of God. It is an assurance of the secure life. It is a reality, experienced by everyone who follows the Lord, that there are indeed gardens and springs in sun-scorched lands, and that we are always equipped with the necessary strength to face new dunes.

The Spirit of Christ has become our spring and turns us into gardens of beautiful festive flowers, despite all our weeds.

Come to my festive garden, Lord, my Beloved.

FIG TREE EXPECTATIONS

"Now learn this lesson from the fig tree: As soon as its twigs get tender and its leaves come out, you know that summer is near" (Mark 13:28).

A child experiences Christmas in a unique way , with a growing excitement. When the last school bell for the year has sounded, it signifies that Christmas is just around the corner. When my mother's ginger beer bottles stood clean and shining, drying out on the sink, it exclaimed Christmas. When we drove to the city for an entire day's shopping, it meant: Christmas is near. Heaven to a child, because, sings the Dutch poet, Nijhof, "A child's heart is so warm and free, *Domino infantium libera nos!*". Lord of children, set us free.

But there are even more signs, says Jesus, simple natural signs, that resemble a Plan that is unfolding and is slowly brought to completion. The fig tree announces the season of growth, the prelude to great cosmic events, the splendor of the city of God. While a budding fig tree is still bare, green buds start to grow everywhere on the ashen branches. For the people of the Middle East, it was a joyful promise of the coming of sweet fruit as food and delicacies, of abundance and life. Jesus says it means the cold has come to an end, the summer is near. On the one hand, He will look for fruit on the fig tree. And he adds: Be attentive to what God is doing everywhere, how delicately everything fits together, how one season flows into another, and how God ensures that fallen leaves are replaced again. As it happens in nature, it happens in God's grand, all-embracing transformation plan.

But what does the fig tree signify? Many people take guesses, like my father who firmly believed it referred to the Jews who would return to Israel in preparation for the day when Jesus would stand on the Mount of Olives. But Jesus does not say, and nobody really knows. It is probably indicative of the comprehensive sum total of the cryptography of prophetic predictions and historical and natural events. But in reality it is a reminder to be attentive and see God and His work in everything, and to stand in awe of how it all develops. Because, as the festivities approach, so does the height of the season.

Let us expect You like children expect Christmas, Lord.

HE SAVES, AMEN!

"For God did not send His Son into the world to condemn the world, but to save the world through Him" (John 3:17).

These words of Jesus to Nicodemus confirm John 3:16: For God so loved the world ... And immediately Jesus adds that His coming had nothing to do with condemnation – the people who refuse to accept this in fact condemn themselves – but with saving "the world".

A philosopher once said that, in principle, Jesus also sanctified the world and the Creation with His death. I still do not know exactly what he meant, but I do have a vague idea of what he tried to say. It is as if the graph of God's "world" found a base and started to rise again. Like Marconi heard the first telegraph signals over the Atlantic Ocean, God once again "got through" to us fully through His Son. And the message is clear: Believe, and I will accept you.

Recently, a businessman referred to religion as "an escape mechanism", an imagined way of escaping a testing reality. It is ironic that, in a sense, he is right, but not as cynically as he regarded fiction: Jesus is the escape from the chaos of futility, from a vacuum of nothingness, from being condemned to a miserable existence without meaning. The famous diarist, Samuel Pepys, noted how the city precinct's night-watchman called out at the top of his voice when he walked past the jail, "Here lie the condemned. Pray for the souls of the condemned." Pepys was not a particularly compassionate man, but on Christmas Eve this call touched him deeply.

"Condemned" ... not condemned. Not lost. The best moments that we as human beings can experience, that "the world" can experience, are when we escape from ourselves and to truly become ourselves in God. Simply to cling to facts of faith, without necessarily looking for explanations. Such an acceptance is the first step in experiencing the true Reality that lies behind it: Jesus came. Jesus lives. God forgives. Amen.

You save, Amen.

TRADITIONS AND VOWS

For you have heard my vows, O God; you have given me the heritage of those who fear Your name (Ps. 61:5).

In the South African tradition this day is referred to as the Day of the Covenant, the commemoration of a vow that was made to God, before the Battle of Blood River. A group of pioneers were surrounded and at their wits' end. They promised that if the Lord led them to victory, they and their descendants would celebrate the day in His honor.

They achieved a remarkable victory. But how the "descendants" dealt with this vow is debatable. And yet, tradition and commemoration are important, like the English discovered after Oliver Cromwell abolished Christmas as a holiday during the seventeenth century. Cromwell was a staunch Calvinist, a skillful ruler and a brilliant soldier, but he regarded Christmas as a Roman Catholic/pagan, unbiblical festival. After Cromwell's death, Christmas was quickly reinstated in England.

Obviously the Bible does not mention anything about celebrating Christmas. It was indeed the "festival of the immortal light", which was given a Christian content by the early missionaries in Europe. They "converted" the day, as it were. There is nothing wrong with christianizing a festival for the Lord, adding a new Christian tradition. And when one has made a solemn treaty with God, you must adhere to it. We often abuse the name of the Lord in difficult situations, with solemn intentions in prayer and supplication, only to casually forget about it afterwards.

One must be careful when making promises, and even more careful when making a vow to God. We can give Him nothing that He does not have, but we can adhere to our faithfulness to Him. Moreover, the experience of the mystery of a covenant or the tradition of such covenant is a spiritual foothold. As T. S. Eliot said, "Humankind cannot bear very much reality."

The Lord gives shape to those things that we mould in our hearts with sincere and honorable intentions and thoughts. We must never forget: not Christmas Day as His Advent, and neither on the days we have asked Him for deliverance.

Lord, remind us of our personal traditions and vows, and especially of Your love. We are inclined to forget about them.

THE GREAT MERCY

Yet He was merciful; He forgave their iniquities. He remembered that they were but flesh, a passing breeze that does not return (Ps. 78:38-39).

One Christmas in Geneva, I marked this passage in my Bible. The mist was hanging so densely over the city that one could see nothing of the beautiful mountain peaks or the lake. I struggled through stacks of snow to reach the Reformation Monument. There, the statues of the great reformers stood in a row, wearing their snow caps: Calvin, Luther, Farel, Zwingli and others. All of them people who had helped to form what I believe in; all of them people with shortcomings. They were blown past in the breeze of time because "they were but flesh" and God was merciful, like He was towards His people. But their great testimony lives on powerfully: God alone delivers through mercy.

Because the Lord is merciful, the psalm says. He knows people, His people. He knows that they are merely people, yet heaven-favored. They are on this planet for only a short while, but God is with them and leads them, as He led His people, as an awesome Presence, through the desert (cf. v. 52).

Mercy is the great Gospel. It means that you are guilty or embarrassed or in disgrace and you have no case, no leg to stand on. Then you or your legal representative plead for mercy, or someone "puts in a good word" for you to ease your predicament. But God exonerates because Jesus bears the scars of suffering that qualify Him to speak on our behalf.

Mercy, said Matthew Arnold, is a word charged with poetic beauty and the understanding of God, and not a theological term to anchor somewhere in human reasoning. Mercy is God's kind assistance and our acceptance of it. The fathers of the Reformation discovered this anew in the Scriptures, and they immediately and jubilantly grasped it.

When I left Geneva after Christmas, the airplane suddenly broke through the mist and clouds and I could see the sun shining beautifully on the peaks of the Alps. An image of deliverance. Mercy.

You deliver us in mercy.

God's thoughts about the future

"For I know the plans I have for you," declares the LORD, "plans to prosper you and not to harm you, plans to give you hope and a future" (Jer. 29:11).

This verse dates from the last days of Jerusalem, six centuries before Christ, before the Babylonians finally conquered the kingdom of Judah and took virtually all the people into exile. Zedekiah was in Jerusalem playing king, a helpless vassal of Nebuchadnezzar who was making plans to offer resistance.

Confusion and rumors and conspiracies abounded. A number of Jews had already been taken into exile to Babylon. Jeremiah wrote a letter of great consolation to this group, "The Lord has not forsaken you." Almost like the American poet, J. R. Lowell, who wrote during the nineteenth century, "… behind the dim unknown, standeth God within the shadow, keeping watch above His own" (from *The Present Crisis*).

These were very brave words, especially for a prophet who often ate his bread in tears. He gave the exiles a glimpse into God's "thoughts": that the Lord still kept watch over them through all the hardships away from their fatherland. They had "hope and a future". As if to confirm this with a deed, Jeremiah concluded a transaction that a speculator would have avoided: he went and bought a field at Anathoth, which was family land (cf. Jer. 32:9) and put the deed of purchase in a clay jar for someone, someday – because Jeremiah had no children. He did this on the Lord's instruction.

People would once again live and farm on this land. In the darkness, the darkness was not that dark everywhere. In a crisis, God remains a God of hope who at times stands guard in the shadows "behind the dim unknown".

Sometimes Christmas is celebrated with misty eyes, about times that were, or plans that failed, or unrequited love. Jesus proves that God's love never returns unrequited. He always has an answer. There is always a future and, even though we sometimes stand in the shadows, we are never out from underneath His watchful eye. Go and mark this text.

We know that this is indeed so. Thank You, Lord.

AN ETERNAL VISIT

He came to a village where a woman named Martha opened her home to Him (Luke 10:38).

There have been thousands of sermons about Jesus' visit to Martha, who was so busy and concerned, trying to be a good hostess, and her sister, Mary, who merely sat listening to Jesus: Why Jesus accosted Martha and why Mary did the right thing by simply sitting there listening, not caring about the preparations for the meal.

In all probability Jesus would not have said anything if Martha had not complained to Him because He was a civilized guest. But regardless of what has been said, Jesus visited these people. They were His friends. Few people received Jesus Christ from Galilee in their homes, gave Him a plate of food and listened to His golden words. Actually, few people from the entire world of that time had the privilege of experiencing a sermon of His, or even witnessed a miracle.

Amen to this mystic view which is an almost unimaginable experience of God longing for us in Christ! We, who are so broken and full of cracks. We, who are so human that we keep complaining that no one is helping. We, who listen and yet forget about Him so shamefully. We, who carry on asking favors of Him. We, who are nothing without Him. He comes to us.

He comes to us during Christmas, on the wings of His Spirit and is received in our thoughts and in our hearts. And He makes Himself at home in our thoughts and starts to talk. A momentary and eternal visit, that cannot be described in any language, or in a thousand sermons, because we can only experience it.

Welcome, Lord.

THE LORD REIGNS

Praise the LORD, O my soul. I will praise the LORD all my life (Ps. 146:1-2).

A pastor once asked his congregation at which major occasion in the life of Jesus they would have liked to have been present, and to give reasons for their choice. Some wanted to be present at the manger in Bethlehem, others when the wise men arrived, others at the Sermon on the Mount, still others at the Last Supper. A few brave ones said at Golgotha, others said, the garden after the Resurrection.

I have always loved any kind of procession, from marching soldiers to cheerful floats through the streets. Therefore, I would have chosen to stand next to the road with a palm branch when Jesus rode into Jerusalem. I would have liked to start singing Totius's rhymed version of Psalm 146: "Praise the Lord with joyful sound, oh my soul there is much to rejoice about ..." This hymn always formed an integral part of the religious and cultural fiber of my generation. It was sung in prosperity and in adversity, in jubilation and in sadness. Yes, I would have waved my palm branch. I would have laughed and cried, and shouted "Hallelujah!" and "Hosanna!" Perhaps with a premonition of disaster, that everything would end in tears but, with hindsight, also with awe about the King who would challenge death and triumph.

The Bible is a book of triumphant faith, like Psalm 146 sings, but not a blind or comfortable faith. It accepts the fact that there are "the oppressed", "prisoners" and "the blind" (cf. vv. 7-8), but also that the Lord reigns forever (cf. v. 10). He would come in Bethlehem as a small baby. He would be riding with poignant glory on a donkey, with palm branches on a road and one would have wanted to shout that He should rather turn around.

At His manger they would pay homage to Him and, after His triumphant procession they would betray Him. But He rides on. He is on His way again.

Praise the Lord, O my soul.

MAGNIFICAT

And Mary said: "My soul glorifies the Lord and my spirit rejoices in God my Savior, for He has been mindful of the humble state of His servant" (Luke 1:46-48).

One Palm Sunday afternoon – the last Sunday before Good Friday – I attended a wonderful church service in Paris where we all waved palm branches and sang old songs, among them "When I survey the wondrous cross" and Psalm 146, in French and English. At the end of the service, the priest struck up Mary's song of praise in Latin: *Magnificat anima mea Dominum; et exultavit spiritus meus in Deo salutari meo* – My soul glorifies the Lord and my spirit rejoices in God, my Savior.

It was overwhelming and filled with majesty: the Passion songs and the palm branches, as well as the song of praise to God by the young girl from Galilee who would become the mother of Jesus, the Christ. With the last robust and magnificent sounds of the great organ, I left in a spiritual ecstasy that still moves me when I think about it.

Milton sings, "And hell itself will pass away / and leave her dolorous mansions to the peering day" (from *The Hymn*). The pendulum was swinging against the prince of darkness. The greatest cosmic event since the Creation was taking place in the womb of a teenage girl from Nazareth.

Often this is God's method: He starts microscopically small, with a little seed that becomes a dense forest covering the earth. Everyone who only expects great things of God, like stars and comets, or great and dramatic interventions to help with personal problems, must remember that His great Plan of Salvation started with a vulnerable baby.

His Son, God's little "computer disc", with the entire divine pattern stored in Him, would become human, the way we all become human: in a mother's womb. Often God starts small and insignificant in everything He does with us, but afterwards we see His firm hand that knew exactly what He was doing. And then we say in awe with Mary: God is miraculous!

My soul glorifies the Lord!

WARMTH OF WONDER

His mother Mary was pledged to be married to Joseph, but before they came together, she was found to be with child through the Holy Spirit (Matt. 1:18).

Through the ages, and still today, long debates have raged about the so-called "virgin birth". Matthew simply said, "She was found to be with child through the Holy Spirit", and Joseph was not very happy when he discovered this. He was within his right to quietly end the engagement, which was stringently binding at the time.

As a civilized man, he did not want to cause problems for Mary. All credit to him. And all credit to Mary who had to tell him about her pregnancy, an embarrassment for her where he was concerned. He thought exactly what people have thought through the centuries and still think today: that she tried to deceive him with an improbable yarn.

Once again it is the strange way God works: that even the intimate news of His Son's forthcoming birth creates suspicion and possible disgrace for those concerned. It is as though, time and again, the Lord puts a piece of mystery into the jigsaw puzzle, which emphasizes that He works with perceptions that differ from ours. In fact, that He (with all due respect) likes to cross out what we expect to see as "acceptable behavior". He overturns all values. He even prepares glory for Himself out of a situation of disbelief and possible disgrace. And even today, many of us do not understand a thing about it.

After a dream, Joseph accepted that God was miraculously at work. Nothing is explained any further. Why do people want to use their "level-headed" reasoning as a smokescreen for an unwillingness to replenish themselves in their faith in God's immense and overwhelming eternal mystery?

Even the little thistle is a mystic miracle of "little wings and a system", writes Sheila Cussons. After all, every visible and invisible reality is surrounded by billions of eternal possibilities. To deny this is to completely miss the excitement of the eternal here and now. To acknowledge this is to surround yourself with God.

Enfold me, Lord, in the warm blanket of Your mystery.

BETHLEHEM AND BUREAUCRACY

So Joseph also went ... there to register with Mary, who was pledged to be married to him and was expecting a child (Luke 2:4-5).

The Dutch preacher Okke Jager made an interesting point in his *Daglicht*: that the "census" was probably a register and poll tax for land tax (the cadastre). The Romans were competent administrators and commissions went from place to place, covering the entire Empire, to update tax registers of landowners.

Everyone had to go and personally identify his land to the commission. That, in all probability, explains why Joseph had to go to Bethlehem. He probably laid claim to land there and, in the determination of land tax, the owner could also object to an assessment that was too high. Therefore, Joseph was probably not the poor man we learnt of as children. With such a registration, the owners of every piece of land also had to indicate their heirs: a possible reason why Mary had to go with him to Bethlehem when the commission was there.

It is a remarkable turn of events: God uses imperialistic, bureaucratic directives to have His Son breathe His first breath as a human being as "heir" to King David who, as a young boy, tended sheep in that neighborhood. Therefore, ordinary times for ordinary people, times of financial worries and tax, times of "filling in forms" (perhaps in triplicate!), times of traveling, times of robberies on the roads and times of no place to stay overnight because of the crowds. All of this still sounds so familiar today.

The Son of God does not come in times of splendor and greatness. God also does not see to it that Christ's mother is exempted from the fatiguing, expensive journey of 150 kilometers. Right from His birth, He would experience everything, from bureaucratic red tape and the fears of a king, to the "diplomatic" to-and-fro between Pilate and Herod during His last hours here on earth.

Jesus was truly man, subject to human, fickle legalities. And truly God was Jesus, to put up with all of this in divine love, in order to come and mark out His property, the world, as well as you and I, anew for His Father.

Lord, in our ordinariness we stand in wonder of Your wisdom.

SILENT WITH WONDER

When Zechariah came [out of the temple], he could not speak to them
(Luke 1:22).

Shortly before Jesus' coming was announced, an overwhelming
encounter took place in the temple. The angel Gabriel appeared
to the elderly priest on duty at the incense altar and brought him
the message that he and his elderly wife would have a child (one of
God's favorite methods!). The child would be John the Baptist, the
forerunner of Jesus: "And he will go on before the Lord, in the spirit
and power of Elijah" (Luke 1:17). Zechariah was overwhelmed, but
he still tried to argue, and as a result was unable to speak until after
the baby was born.

Would the angel, apart from the slight reprimand, have allowed
him to see things that rendered him speechless? Flashes of who
his son would be, the great eccentric, innovative preacher from the
desert, announcing the coming of Christ, with all the struggles and
supernatural perceptions of an Elijah? It would have rendered any
sensitive soul speechless.

The poet Keats said that if a poem did not come like a vision, then
"I shall be dumb". But here it worked differently: in the holy moments of the encounter, Zechariah received so many heavenly signs
that his tongue got stuck until after the birth of his child. Would he
have known that the dispensation of sacrificial offerings was passing
with the coming of the Christ, for whom his Son would be an Elijah?
Would he, during his silent days, have seen what price would have
to be paid by the Christ, as well as by his son, John? Because, when
the child had to be circumcised, he suddenly burst forth in a glori-
fication of God and a prophecy of "light in the darkness" (cf. Luke
1:79).

Tonight is Christmas Eve. A multitude of people are praying, like
they did in those days, both outside and inside the temple. May each
of us, deep down inside, hear the voices of angels and get a glimpse
of God's splendor. May that render us "silent" in love and prophetic
in our joy. May the Holy One enter us through our prayers, like the
angel came to Zechariah when the sharp, sweet smell of incense rose
from the altar.

*Let our Christmas prayers rise like clouds of incense offerings in
Your Presence.*

CHRISTMAS

She gave birth to her firstborn, a Son. She wrapped Him in cloths and placed Him in a manger (Luke 2:7).

The romanticism of the birth in the stable is actually not as sadly sentimental as it is in our imagination or in paintings: depictions of sheaves of wheat piled high, a donkey and a cow. During busy times, clean stables were often rented out as places to stay overnight and it was in such a place that Mary had placed her Son. Milton sings in exultation, "This is the Month, and this the happy morn / Wherein the Son of Heaven's Eternal King … Our great redemption from above did bring; For so the holy sages once did sing …" It is a beautiful poem in which his jubilation, imagination and vision reach dizzy heights, up to the significant: "But see the Virgin blest, / Hath laid her Babe to rest. / Time is our tedious Song should here have ending (from *On the Morning of Christ's Nativity*).

It is no sin if one's imagination runs away with you over such a simple, profound, but heaven-shattering event. Parents sing songs of praise at the birth of their children, in itself a miracle surrounded by God. Therefore, let the candles burn and the songs resound. The Son of God came from the House of the poet king, David, in the neighborhood of his "green pastures". God came to reclaim His people who had been estranged from Him.

In front of me, against the wall, hangs a copy of a centuries-old Austrian altarpiece with a regal Mary, staring resolutely into the distance, and a little Boy on her arm who turns His eyes towards the two angels watching over them. It is pure artistic imagination, but it touches me in an inexplicable way. It is as if Mary is looking far into the future, past the cross, into eternity. It is as if the little Boy already knows everything.

Sometimes artists succeed in capturing mystic truths that escape us in reality. Milton exults about thousands of worlds in God's Creation. Hopkins sees visions of the virgin, the stable and the Child in the soft flowers of March and in the starry skies.

Christmas is jubilation, gratitude and remembrance. Christmas is Christ. Christmas is a star that started to twinkle in Bethlehem and keeps on twinkling until the Bright Morning Star comes again.

Magnificat!

BUT MARY ...

This Child is destined to cause the falling and rising of many in Israel. And a sword will pierce your own soul too (Luke 2:34-35).

According to Jewish custom, Jesus was circumcised on the eighth day after His birth. In the temple there were two elderly servants of the Lord, who had both been looking forward to the coming of the Savior. When they saw the small Child, they praised God in delight. With the Child in his arms, Simeon spoke prophetically and ecstatically about the salvation that he had witnessed (cf. v. 30).

But he added that choices would have to be made about this Child, choices that could mean falling or rising. And for Mary he predicted a sword through her soul. Anna simply sensed God in the Child and prayed in gratitude.

But Mary ... What would have gone through her mind? During the preceding months and days she had experienced so many things: the bureaucracy of the state and the adoration of simple people and important people, strange predictions and events in her body, heavenly joy ... and now a piercing warning. Right from the start she therefore already had a title, woman of sorrows, mater dolorosa. She must have possessed joy and discipline because this combination opens the path to true compassion. Would she have possessed insight and the acceptance that joy is never joy without a touch of sadness? That, in the fiber of faith, there are also dark patches of despair? That major paradoxes are built into God's plan, contradictions that run parallel to one another, but also cross one another, often in friction and lack of understanding?

Her child would be a salvation, a falling, a rising ... and a sword for the truth that would also hit her in the heart. Here she was standing with her child in the temple in prophetic glory. One day she would follow His trail of blood to Golgotha, and once again experience the joy of His resurrection! Paradox, paradox!

She and Joseph would leave from there with her "strange" Child and a heart overflowing with prophesies and encounters. But nothing would ever be the same for her again. Where Christ enters, nothing and nobody is ever the same again. Amen.

Lord, enter into me, and transform and renew.

ONCE AGAIN, ABRAHAM

By faith Abraham, when God tested him, offered Isaac as a sacrifice.
He who had received the promises (Heb. 11:17).

Where Mary is standing in the temple with her child, filled with awe, and yet inwardly in a kind of daze about everything she has experienced and heard, it takes one back to the man with whom, the Great Plan began: Abraham, the father of the faithful. He also stood there with a child, his son, facing a mountain. He had received a strange instruction from God: He had to go and offer his son, God's great promise, as a sacrifice.

He had a choice, like he had a choice when God called on him to leave his native city. At the beginning of Thomas Mann's famous novel, *Joseph and his Brothers*, Lot wanted to know from him what would happen, should he discover in the wilderness that he had merely heard imagined voices. Abram replied that he would then be totally lost, but he nevertheless loaded his wagons and started to move on. And at Moriah he went up the mountain with his son, with his sacrificial wood and his knife.

Would he have thought that God was a fickle God? Would he have regarded it as an "examination", confused about what impossible things God would ask next? Nothing of this is mentioned. He kept on walking up the mountain in the hope and firm belief that God will do what is right.

The people that the Lord uses in His plan, sometimes find themselves in extreme circumstances of confusion, faced by virtually impossible instructions. Under extreme pressure diamonds are formed out of black carbon. God forms His great people in exactly the same way. In a poem about a mystic union with Christ, Gerard Manley Hopkins writes: "I am at once what Christ is, since He was what I am ... immortal diamond, is immortal diamond." Abraham was a diamond. Christ is an eternal diamond star. That is where our light comes from, and from where we are formed ... "And the dark will not overwhelm it."

Lord, we are not Abraham, and not Mary. Rather form us in the soft light of Christ, in the lovely warmth of Your Presence. If that is Your will.

"ENCORE" FOR MOSES

What does the LORD your God ask of you but to fear the LORD your God, to walk in all His ways, to love Him, to serve the LORD your God with all your heart and with all your soul, and to observe the LORD's commands and decrees that I am giving you today for your own good? (Deut. 10:12-13)

Moses, one of God's diamonds, received God's commandments in stone, a kind of "encore" of the divine right. He conveyed it to Israel and said they had to love and serve the Lord "with all their heart and with all their soul", "walk in His ways", "observe His commands and decrees". And that it would be for Israel's "own good". That is "all" that the Lord asks, as well as that He be feared in everything. The people accepted this with enthusiasm and gradually forgot about it again.

But even for Moses, this message could not have been easy. There is no doubt about the fact that he feared God. Whether he always walked in God's ways is doubtful. That he loved God in an exceptional way and respected Him is true, but would he have scored ten out of ten? God spoke to him in the way a man speaks to a friend, but friends also disappoint at times. Did he adhere to every detail of the commandments and decrees, or did he sometimes also invent escape routes for himself, a typical human trait? In all probability, yes. Centuries later, yet another of God's diamonds, and an expert of the law, Paul, would write, "There is no one righteous, not even one" (Rom. 3:10). It is only Christ, and "mercy" is the word.

It is nevertheless clear that Moses followed God in extremely difficult circumstances. Respect and love for God constituted his directive. There was a passion for God in him, and passion turns into respect, and respect turns into obedience, and sincere obedience again turns into a passion of love. This was something of the great driving force of Jesus Christ.

Naturally, this directive would be for our own good. Moses can teach us, but Christ must hold us by the hand, the Father must have mercy on us and the Spirit must inspire us. God does this ... for our own good.

Once again, write Your law of love in our hearts, Lord, and forgive us when we forget.

YET ANOTHER BOW FROM DAVID

Yours, O LORD, is the greatness and the power and the glory and the majesty and the splendor, for everything in heaven and earth is Yours. Yours, O LORD, is the kingdom; You are exalted and head over all (1 Chron. 29:11).

This is one of David's greatest doxologies or eulogies to the glory of God. His exultation in the Lord is, after all, the major theme of his psalms, as well as of his life. The Lord has everything, is everything, is above everything and, in His splendor, all things created fade into ethereal mistiness.

David has come a long way from tending sheep, and shone highly as an extremely heaven-favored man, a diamond of God, but also containing black flaws – flaws that brought him many tears and defeats. But, in all of this, he was precious to God, so much so that God spared His people "for the sake of David My servant" (cf. 1 Kings 11:13). What a relationship between a man and his God!

Throughout his entire life, David praised the Lord in minor and major keys on his harp, in his songs and poems, in his wars, in his disappointments and in his tears, in his wisdom, as well as in his haste. Here he greeted the people with a powerful doxology and reminded them of the fact that God is eternal and that "our days on earth are like a shadow" (cf. 1 Chron. 29:15). That which Wordsworth wrote, is also true of David, "But trailing clouds of glory do we come / From God, who is our home" (from *Ode: Intimations of Immortality*).

Generations of prophets and poets would sing about David, up to this very day. Because, all his complex emotions and deeds notwithstanding, he possessed one sincerity: he loved the Lord with emotional passion, perhaps more so than any other human being ever. In that he was the great forerunner of the Son of Man.

The passion of the heart asks no explanations and provides no solutions. It is more than a feeling, it is a celebration of each other, a celebration of God. And David was a master of this since his younger days. Let us celebrate God with a thought of gratitude every day: His Presence, as well as the Christ who is coming again.

Now, our God, we give You thanks, and praise Your glorious name (David in 1 Chronicles 29:13).

A SALUTE FROM PAUL

Now to the King eternal, immortal, invisible, the only God, be honor and glory for ever and ever. Amen (1 Tim. 1:17).

This is yet another great doxology or laudation, a rapturous salute to the eternal King, from yet another of the great splendid ones of faith: Paul, who was first called Saul. He exulted in the "immortal, invisible, the only God", in Jesus Christ. Where Abraham was the man of faith and hope, Moses the man of God's commandments, David was the man with the lion-heart, filled with a passion of love for God, and Paul the man of mercy alone. Mercy through the cross and the resurrection of Jesus Christ.

Yes, there was Elijah and Peter and the other heaven-favored, but the first-mentioned four are like enormous pillars in the old classical Greek architecture, chiseled in beauty with enchanting decorations, and yet not one without finer or broader cracks. They were human beings, but with an appetite and a taste for the miracle of experiencing God.

Their personalities differ like those of the four points of a compass, but they all possessed an unbiased intuition and acceptance. When I was a very small child, we often had to sing English hymns in school. A popular one was: "Glory be to God the Father, Glory be to God the Son ..." Our English was poor, but we sang at the top of our voices: "Glory be to *guard* the Father, Glory be to *guard* the Son ...!" I still remember the image that I had formed of the song in my mind: of us little ones who rigorously stood guard around God's throne, like angels with spears and shields. Perhaps God found pleasure in this gap-toothed children's song of imagined courage ...

But Paul, the scholar that he was, had no illusions about himself or in whom he believed and how the great mercy was engineered: in Christ alone, in His cross and in the power of His resurrection. In this lies the "sublime and heavenly greatness" of which the mystic, Thomas Traherne, spoke. God keeps vigil over us and only in His greatness are we safe and free.

Let me also live in the splendor of Your honor and glory.

THE MORNING STAR

"I am the bright Morning Star" (Rev. 22:16).

The morning star is the symbol of a new dispensation, a halcyon, a radiant announcement that the new day is coming before the sun has risen. It sometimes shines so brightly in the still skies – which are already, on a clear night, a vast, open field of diamonds – so that a man like Keats wishes he was such a star: "Bright star, would I were as steadfast as thou art … and watching." Jesus Christ says He is the bright Morning Star, the Offspring of David (cf. 22:16), the Alpha and the Omega, the First and the Last, the Beginning and the End (cf. 22:13).

He is from the heavens, we are still from the earth. But He keeps vigil and, in Him, everything will be brought to masterly fulfillment. Like God shields everything with His hand and ensures that everything in His Creation will once be speechless in the silence of understanding: understanding the vast Plan that God has woven into the stars and in the hearts of people.

When I was a student, one night we drove through a barren semi-desert. At 3:15 in the morning we became aware that the landscape was bathed in a soft light. Naively I asked whether dawn came that early in the morning in those parts. My companions laughed and showed me the brightest morning star I have ever seen in my life. It shone like a brilliant diamond in the sky. It would have been possible, but risky, to drive without our headlights on. The darkness was still there, but so was the light. This is true of the earthly journey of the believer: through the desert, on sometimes risky roads, with darkness all around, but also enough light. We live under the guidance of the Morning Star. As we traveled on that day, we were aware of a certain mystic peace.

God grants peace in Christ, peace that mostly does not mean lack of strife, but a Presence of love. God takes care of us, as He did by providing quail and manna in the desert. God provides sufficient light and sufficient *viaticum*, necessities of life, for the journey that lies ahead. The angels will preserve and even the crows will bring food. The Morning Star moves through the night towards the day. In Christ God keeps vigil, and He goes along.

*A*men.